# Cairo

# Cairo

ANDRÉ RAYMOND

*Translated by Willard Wood*

HARVARD UNIVERSITY PRESS
CAMBRIDGE, MASSACHUSETTS
LONDON, ENGLAND
2000

Library of Congress Cataloging-in-Publication Data

Raymond, André.
[Caire. English]
Cairo / André Raymond ; translated by Willard Wood.
p.   cm.
Includes bibliographical references and index.
ISBN 0-674-00316-0 (alk. paper)
1. Cairo (Egypt)—History.  I. Title.
DT148.R3913 2000
962'.16–dc21    00-056747

*To the memory of Jeannie and Jérôme*

# CONTENTS

PART FOUR
# CONTEMPORARY CAIRO (1798–1992)

# ILLUSTRATIONS

Photographs accompanying the text are © André Raymond except where specified otherwise. The three photographs taken from Doris Behrens-Abouseif, *Islamic Architecture in Cairo: An Introduction* (Leiden: E. J. Brill, 1989), are by Martin Huth; © Koninklijke Brill N.V., Leiden, The Netherlands. The maps were produced by Etudes et Cartographie, Lille; the sources on which many are based are cited in the Select Bibliography.

# EDITORIAL NOTE

In the spelling of Arabic words and names no diacriticals have been used, though hamza and ayn have been retained when they appear within a word. *Jim* has generally been transliterated as *j*.

# Cairo

# Preview

Fifty years ago, one still traveled to Egypt by ship, landing first at Alexandria, from which the last visible traces of antiquity had all but disappeared. The Mediterranean port, rebuilt in the nineteenth century, would lose its Levantine character after the 1952 revolution, and the subsequent departure of the British brought to an end a society that Lawrence Durrell transformed into a literary myth. But under the cosmopolitan veneer, impressed on it by the dominant Western social model and long colonial rule, Alexandria was already the Egyptian and Arab city that, on a July evening in 1956, heard Nasser's announcement of the nationalization of the Suez Canal—and the close of an era—with astonishment and jubilation.

One proceeded to Cairo by the desert road. Halfway to the capital, the four monasteries of Wadi Natrun, the last remnant of about fifty founded on this site starting in the fourth century, stood as a reminder that Egypt had been Christian, and more specifically Coptic Christian, for several centuries before the Arab conquest. "Copt" is a term laden with history and symbolism; it is the Western form of the Arabic word *qibt,* itself derived from the Greek *aigyptos* ("Egyptian"), which is in turn a corruption of the ancient Egyptian *Hikuptah* ("castle of the [ka] of Ptah," the name of Memphis, capital of Egypt), the Greeks having applied the name of the principal port to the country as a whole. The monasteries testify to the vitality of a local form of Christianity that defined itself in opposition to the orthodoxy of the Byzantine rulers. The victory of Monophysitism in Egypt, despite its condemnation as a heresy at the Council of Chalcedon in 451 and its persecution by the Greeks, and the survival of the Egyptian language, despite the use of Greek by the ruling class, represent two facets of an Egyptian nationalism that flourished in provincial Egypt.

Arriving in the Giza region, one beheld the great pyramids that, a century and a half earlier, had prompted Bonaparte's famous exhortation "Soldiers, from the heights of yonder pyramids forty centuries gaze down on you." Starting down into the valley from the plateau, on which there had as yet been no construction, and after rounding Mena House, a British-built caravanserai of Victorian tourism, one took in at a glance five millennia of Egypt's history and all its successive capitals.

Twenty kilometers due south of Giza, at the edge of the cliff where the pharaonic tombs are scattered, one could almost make out the pyramids of Saqqara, which looked down on the ruins of Memphis, the capital of the Ancient Kingdom, its site marked by two colossal statues of Ramses II in the middle of a vast field of palm trees and rubble. The emergence of other centers such as Thebes in Upper Egypt did not diminish the importance of Memphis: the city's nodal position at the head of the Nile delta and at the juncture of Upper and Lower Egypt ensured its continued viability. The commercial mission of the port of Memphis was reinforced rather late (probably in the reign of Necho, 610–595 B.C.), when a canal was excavated between the Nile Valley and the Red Sea, using a former channel of the Nile. A remarkable feat, the canal proved difficult to maintain. Restorations were undertaken first by Darius during the Persian occupation, around 518 B.C., again by the Roman emperor Trajan, and finally by the Muslim conqueror of Egypt, Amr. It was only with the founding of Alexandria in 332 B.C. that Memphis declined for good.

Farther east, the Nile Valley was still a green corridor into which construction was making only its first inroads. For many millennia, time had been marked in Egypt by the life-giving floods of the Nile. Until the Aswan dams were built in 1902, the river water regularly lapped against the western cliff at the foot of the Sphinx and the pyramids during flood season, creating the landscape described by the philosopher Seneca and still visible in postcards from the beginning of the century: "The moment when the Nile invades the countryside is a magnificent sight: the floor of the plain disappears . . . The villages rise like islands."[1] The flood, which occurred around 15 June, was measured on the Nilometer *(miqyas)* installed on the southern tip of Rawdah Island. When it reached a height of sixteen cubits (dhiras), indicating a flood of normal size, the Egyptians' anxiety would subside, but if it failed to reach that mark, worries mounted in anticipation of a bad harvest. The traditional ceremonies of breaching the dams, and in particular the dike across the Cairo Canal in July (the Coptic month of *mesori*), carried over into Christian and Islamic Egypt rituals that had originated in the time of the pharaohs.

The Nile, though apparently eternal, was not immobile. Over many millennia silting continued to displace the head of the Nile delta north, moving it some twenty kilometers between the time of the Ancient Kingdom and the Arab conquest. Meanwhile the Nile's course moved slowly westward after the Arab conquest, leaving exposed the ground that would be occupied by the growing settlements of Fustat and Qahira, until the eastern bank and the islands of Cairo stabilized in their present positions in about the sixteenth century.

Almost directly across from the pyramids, an outcrop of the eastern cliffs formed a spur of the Muqattam Hills, seeming to keep watch over the Nile Valley. It was a sacred place during pharaonic times, the kings traditionally passing there on their way from Heliopolis in the north to Memphis in the south. This processional way overlooked the lower areas closer to the Nile where Fustat would be built in 642 at the time of the Arab conquest and Qahira in 969 by the Fatimid conquerors from the Maghrib. The road joined two regions, both of which preserved marks of antiquity and Christianity.

To the north lay Heliopolis, the "City of the Sun," once one of Egypt's spiritual centers dedicated to the cult of Ra—an obelisk still perpetuates the memory of the rites performed there. Nearby, at Matariyya, was the garden ritually sought out by European visitors because of a sycamore (replanted in 1670) under which the Holy Family was said to have taken shelter during the flight into Egypt. To the south, in Old Cairo, a tradition claims, Christ made his longest stay. Traces of antiquity persisted more obviously in the small fortress of Babylon, rebuilt during the Roman era under Trajan and linked according to tradition to a settlement of prisoners established there during the Persian era. Its two massive towers (still extant) perhaps governed the entrance to the canal to the Red Sea. Farther south is Hilwan, on a site that served Heliopolis as a cemetery during the early dynasties.

For forty kilometers along the valley on either side of the Nile, the history of several thousand years was written in summary form in the space where Arabic Cairo would evolve. From a projection of the Muqattam Hills where the Ayyubids built the Citadel (in 1176), one could contemplate this space and, as it were, pass the stages of its history in review: the pyramids rising against the horizon; Old Cairo, visible in the distance; at the foot of the Citadel, the grandiose mass of the Mosque of Sultan Hasan, a Mamluk masterwork and celebrated forerunner of the city of the *Thousand and One Nights;* and all around, no matter where one looked, the ancient city's landscape of minarets and cupolas being gradually transformed into a modern city, whose boundary at the Nile could only be guessed at in the distance.

# I
# Foundations
# (642–1250)

*The history of Cairo starts with the Arab conquest of Egypt in 640, three centuries before the founding of the town of al-Qahira by the Fatimids. The process that gave birth to Cairo extended over nearly six centuries and involved a series of foundations: Fustat, established by the Arab conquerors (642); al-Askar (750) and al-Qata'i (868), royal cities of the Abbasids and Tulunids; al-Qahira, founded by the Fatimid conquerors from the Maghrib (969); and the construction of the Citadel by Saladin in 1176, all of which influenced the city's shape for centuries afterward.*

# 1

# Fustat, the First Capital

*The God of vengeance, who alone is all-powerful, who can alter the dominion of men as he sees fit, giving it to whom he pleases and raising up the most humble, having observed the malice of the Greeks, who cruelly pillaged our churches and monasteries wherever they had dominion and condemned us mercilessly, brought the sons of Ishmael from the south to deliver us from the hands of the Greeks. It was no small advantage to us to be freed from the cruelty of the Romans, their malice, their anger, their cruel zeal toward us, and to be left in peace.*[1]

THUS DID MICHAEL THE SYRIAN, writing in the twelfth century, describe the Arab conquest of Egypt. The vituperative tone of this Monophysite Christian despite five centuries of intervening Islamic rule says a great deal about conditions at the time of the conquest.

Only four years after the death of the prophet Muhammad, the Arabs won a shattering victory over the Byzantines on the Yarmuk River in Palestine (20 August 636), following a victory over the Sasanids at Qadisiyya (February–March 636). These victories gave the Muslims dominion over Iraq and Syria. The caliph Umar, thus released from any worry about the two greatest empires of the day, was free to contemplate the conquest of Egypt.

Circumstances were propitious to the undertaking. Egypt was a

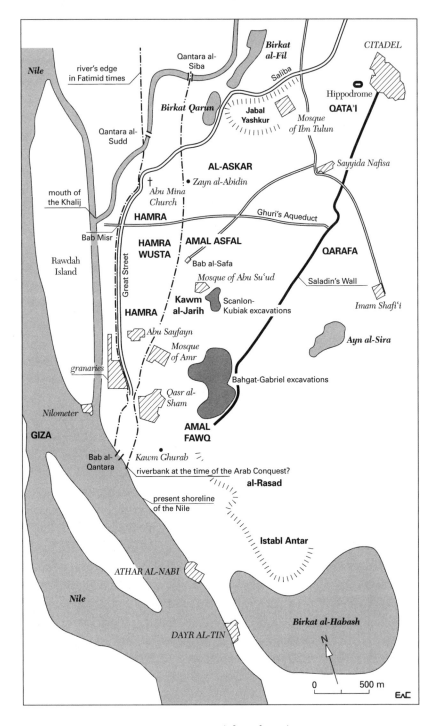

Map 1. Fustat (after Clerget)

Byzantine province, but its Coptic population largely adhered to the Monophysite doctrine, which the Orthodox Church had condemned as heretical. And Egypt had just gone through turbulent times: in 609 the country had sided with Nicetas, a lieutenant of Heraclius, in the rebellion against the emperor Phocas. Hardly had Heraclius overthrown Phocas than the Byzantines were attacked by the Persians. The armies of the Sasanid king Khosrau II invaded Egypt, inflicting cruel suffering on the inhabitants. The Persian occupation lasted six years. The conquerors treated the Orthodox Christians harshly but dealt more gently with the Monophysites, who welcomed deliverance from Byzantine rule. The Coptic patriarch (first Andronic, then Benjamin) was even able to resume his seat in Alexandria. When the emperor Heraclius regained control of Egypt in 629, the Orthodox Church again faced difficulties as its patriarch, Cyrus, was held responsible for persecuting the Copts. Menas, brother of Benjamin, preferred to be thrown into the sea tied in a sack rather than recognize the Council of Chalcedon (451), which condemned Monophysitism. One of the martyrs brought before Cyrus cried out: "We have no other archbishop than Benjamin; accursed be the blasphemous edict of the Roman emperor; accursed be the Council of Chalcedon and all who accept it." Egypt's long crisis revealed the weakness of the empire and its army, fanned religious dissension, and diluted Egyptians' loyalty to a political and religious power whose removal, as they had just seen from experience, could prove an advantage to them.[2]

A national problem pitted the majority of Egyptians against the Byzantine power structure. The Monophysite Copts fiercely opposed the "Chalcedonians" (later known as Melchites), whom they considered heretics, and suffered persecution at the hands of the Byzantines. There was also a sharp linguistic division within the Egyptian population: Greek was the language of the urban ruling elite, while the majority spoke Coptic, the language into which the sacred texts had been translated as early as the third century. Finally, the Byzantines had imposed burdensome taxation that was all the harder to accept when civil and religious administration was entrusted to the Orthodox patriarch Cyrus in 631.

The rapid success of the Arab invaders can be explained in part by the deep hostility of most of the local population toward the Byzantine power structure, which was foreign and oppressed them in fiscal and religious matters, and in part by the exhaustion of the Byzantines, which was visible in their conflict with the Sasanids. Then, too, the Arab invaders brought a religious message that was in some aspects familiar to Christians and advocated tolerance toward "People of the Book," that is, Christians and Jews. The arrival of the Arabs might augur an era of religious freedom such as the Copts had not known for centuries. The immediate result of the Arab victory was the triumph of the Jacobite Copts over the Chalcedonian Melchites, who lost all their churches. Paradoxically, the Copts' nonresistance to the Arabs probably contributed to their survival as a community.[3]

It was apparently the caliph Umar himself who decided to attack Egypt with an army drawn from troops in Syria under the command of Amr ibn al-As. The Egyptian campaign proceeded without undue difficulty. Having reached al-Arish on 12 December 639, Amr overcame the Byzantine defenses at Farama, then at Bilbays, reaching Heliopolis in July 640. The Byzantine fortress of Babylon was besieged in September. On 9 April 641 the city fell after a spirited resistance. The Arab army had by this time received reinforcements that brought its number to about 15,000.

This event drew significant comment from the bishop of Nikiu: "God punished the Greeks thus for not having respected the vivifying passion of Our Lord. That is why God rejected them . . . Their religion was debased . . . They believed themselves to be servants of Christ but in reality were not." Elsewhere he wrote: "Everyone knows that the defeat of the Greeks and the conquest of Egypt by the Muslims was in punishment for the tyranny of Emperor Heraclius and the wrongs he inflicted on [Egyptians] through the patriarch Cyrus."[4]

Amr built a semipermanent camp for his troops behind a protective trench, then turned to Alexandria, Egypt's capital, laying siege to it in June 641. Although the surrender of the city was signed on 8 November 641, the Arabs did not take possession until 29 September 642, after the Greek forces had sailed away. By that date Amr had already established the new capital of Egypt at Fustat.

## THE FOUNDING OF FUSTAT (642)

Fustat was founded at the beginning of the year 642. As to the name of the town, one tradition traces its origin to the moment when Amr chose not to strike his tent (*fustat*) as he left to besiege Alexandria because a pigeon had landed on its ridge, built a nest, and laid its eggs there. Others claim that it derives from the Byzantine Greek word *phossaton*, meaning "entrenchment," or from its Latin cognate *fossatum*, which may refer to a place-name antedating the Arabs' arrival. But from the beginning, the city was referred to as Misr, a name that also denoted Egypt as a whole and would later take the form Fustat-Misr.

The foundation of what was to become one of the largest capitals of the Arab world is shrouded in uncertainty. The oldest historical source to mention Fustat's origins is the *Kitab futuh misr wal-maghrib,* by Ibn Abd al-Hakam, written almost two centuries after the fact. Not until the early fifteenth century did two historians provide a detailed and accurate description of the city, blending ancient and contemporary elements. These accounts are the *Kitab al-intisar,* by Ibn Duqmaq, written after 1394 and before 1401; and the *Khitat* of Maqrizi (1364–1442), written between 1415 and 1424. There also exist numerous documents (many of them on papyrus) written in Arabic and Judeo-Arabic from the Jewish archives of the Geniza, but they belong to a period generally much subsequent to the founding of Fustat and provide limited information about the city. Archaeological excavations at the site of Fustat—primarily those of Ali Bahgat and Albert Gabriel (1912–1914) and those of George Scanlon and Wladyslaw Kubiak (begun in 1964)—have concentrated on an area east of the city's ancient center; the center itself remains inaccessible because of its continuous dense habitation. Complicating the archaeological picture are long periods of destruction, during which Fustat was covered with rubble, then used as a source of building materials and fertilizer, and, most recently, as a dumping ground for the garbage of Cairo and an attractive site to treasure hunters. Most of the digs have uncovered evidence from the later, Fatimid period; only recent excavations by Roland-Pierre Gayraud at Istabl Antar, at the very southern limits of the original settlement, have yielded information on the earliest period of Fustat.[5]

Choosing a capital for the newly conquered country was naturally of great importance. The Arabs could have placed it in Alexandria. Militating against this were Alexandria's cosmopolitan character, its powerful population, its location, as it were, outside Egypt, and the fact that the Egyptians associated it with a hated rule. Caliph Umar may have given Amr explicit instructions: "Put no water between yourselves and me," he is said to have told his lieutenants. "When I travel to you from Medina, my horse must take me directly to the place where I join you." It was clearly logical to put the new capital near the Roman and Byzantine stronghold of Babylon, at a site that allowed control of the agricultural production of the delta and at the most convenient point for crossing Egypt. And that is where the Arabs, as they set off to conquer Alexandria, left their first settlement.

The site chosen on the east bank of the Nile for the encampment probably included no population center of any size other than the fortress of Babylon. This stronghold was also known as Qasr al-Sham, meaning "Fortress of the Candle" in Arabic, although the second word is a corruption of the Coptic *khemi,* "Egyptian." It was a quasi-town some five hectares (twelve acres) in extent with a population of Copts and a few Jews. It included churches (among them the Mu'allaqa, which is still extant), markets, a port on the Nile, and fortifications. The encircling brick wall was 12 meters high. It incorporated towers, two of which flanked the opening on the west side for the canal that traversed the town. The canal had been built by Trajan, who also rebuilt the city's defenses. A moat surrounded Qasr al-Sham. Impressive remains of the structure survive. Somewhat to the south, on the summit of what was later called the Observatory (al-Rasad), stood a fortification. Qasr al-Sham in all likelihood resembled traditional Egyptian towns, and in the new city it was to remain an area where the native population resided.

The site of the original Muslim settlement is difficult to recognize today because the Nile's course has shifted westward. The river's bank, at first just west of the Mosque of Amr, had moved 300 meters farther west by the Fatimid period, more than 400 meters by the

12

time of the Ayyubids and Mamluks, and more than 500 meters by our own time. The shift was greater toward the north, with the river gradually receding from the lands on which Fustat would expand in succeeding centuries. Working back from the river at the time of Fustat's founding, one would have encountered first the relatively narrow alluvial plain along the Nile, a low area (*amal asfal*) with a few higher spots where Qasr al-Sham and the Mosque of Amr were built; farther east were a rocky plateau (*amal fawq*, high area) comprising elevations (Kawm al-Jarih) and a depression containing the brackish waters of a pond (Ayn al-Sira), with the Yashkur hill (Jabal Yashkur) overlooking it to the north and the Muqattam Hills on the east. To the south, beyond the rise of Qasr Babiliyun (today's Istabl Antar), was a water-filled hollow known as the Abyssinian Pond (Birkat al-Habash), which flooded during the annual high water and whose fertile lands supported the village of Ma'adi and, somewhat farther on, those of Tura and Hilwan, which are today suburbs of Cairo. To the north were agricultural lands and villages, among them Tendunyas (Umm Dunayn in Arabic), where Amr defeated the Byzantines, and farther still Heliopolis (Ayn Shams).

Opposite Qasr al-Sham was an island. The branches of the Nile were approximately equal, each measuring some 350 meters across, while today the eastern branch measures 80 meters and the western 600 meters. The island (Jazira) must have stood more or less where Rawdah is today, judging from the position of the Nilometer (*miqyas*), which was used to measure the height of the water. Rebuilt in 861, the Nilometer had already been for some time on the southern tip of the island. On the river's left bank, reached by a bridge of boats, was the floodplain with the settlement of Giza and, some 15 kilometers to the south, the ancient city of Memphis.[6]

According to Arab tradition, Fustat was organized as a kind of camp-city, divided into sections for the different tribal units of the army: "After the conquest of Babylon by Amr ibn al-As," wrote Ya'qubi in 891, "the Arab tribes took their quarters around Amr's tent [*fustat*] . . . Subsequently they extended outward from it as far as the edge of the Nile."[7] The land was staked out into separate areas or cantonments (*khitta;* pl. *khitat*) for the fifty or so tribal groups that composed the army, along the lines of what had already been done at

Basra and al-Kufa (in Iraq) and at Jabiya (in Syria). Some disagreements arose over the size and location of the cantonments, and Amr formed a commission to arbitrate them.[8] The extreme boundaries of the territory occupied in this uneven fashion were, to the north, a line extending past Jabal Yashkur from the Bridge of Lions (Qanatir al-Siba) to the future site of the Citadel; to the east, a line joining the Citadel to the Kawm al-Jarih and the Birkat al-Habash; to the west, the waters of the Nile, which ran right by the Mosque of Amr and Qasr al-Sham. The total area measured some 600–800 hectares, but it was a loose conglomerate of tribal concessions rather than a truly organized urban settlement.

Yet a few organizing elements were already apparent. One of the main groups was composed of the "people of the standard" (ahl al-raya), some 400–500 people including members of the Quraysh tribe (the tribe of the Prophet), the "companions" (ansar), who were quartered in the central area near the Mosque of Amr and Qasr al-Sham. Non-Arabs, among them "Greek" Rumis—perhaps remnants of the Byzantine army—were quartered near the northern border of the settlement. In the low area to the west were two north–south roads (one bordering the Nile) and a number of roads running toward the river, which gave the settlement a relatively regular aspect. On the higher ground to the east (the amal fawq), where the terrain was more uneven, the early network of roads was more irregular.

Although each tribe undoubtedly established a place of prayer in its own khitta, Amr built a small mosque of unbaked brick measuring 17 by 29 meters. Its prayer hall used palm trunks in the place of pillars, and it had no courtyard, no minaret, and no mihrab, or niche indicating the direction of prayer. Because of its central location in the midst of the ahl al-raya, who were its primary users, this soon became the city's main mosque. Amr is also credited with the construction of a small public bath. On the orders of the caliph Umar, a fortress was also built in 642–643 to protect Giza. There existed no "palace of government" (dar al-imara) at that time, as the governor lived in his own house. A port took shape on the unoccupied shore at the height of the Mosque of Amr and Qasr al-Sham, in an area where the main commercial districts would develop. Boats landed at the site of a pre-Islamic port, where there was a wharf.

It is entirely likely that the earliest inhabitants of the cantonments lived in temporary shelters that were gradually transformed into houses. While excavating Istabl Antar, situated at the southern limit of the newly founded Fustat, R.-P. Gayraud found on the rock itself what he believes to be archaeological evidence of the arrival of the Arabs: "The surface of the ground is pitted with many holes, none of them more than 4 to 5 centimeters in diameter. Some seem to reflect a highly specific organization, possibly indicating the pitching of an encampment . . . Other holes were for picketing livestock . . . This evidence is remarkable for providing insight into a very short span of time . . . perhaps as brief as a few days." This marginal settlement was replaced quite rapidly, almost immediately in most cases, by more sophisticated dwellings. It would be absurd to suggest that the native Egyptians provided their conquerors the model of a more advanced construction. Islam, after all, had developed in an urban environment (Mecca and Medina). Besides, the conquering armies, which drew largely on reserves of Arab nomads, included elements from such anciently urban countries as Yemen and the Hijaz. In the area of Istabl Antar, which was allocated to Yemeni tribes, Gayraud has found a first horizon that he dates to the half-century following the settlement in 642. These habitations "reflect an evident concern for quality." The structures, set on large carved stones, are "of mixed materials, using both baked and unbaked brick," and coated on the inside with clay and plaster. "The supports are regular, and the walls are at right angles." The general effect was of "large and rather airy houses, serviced by roads that are of course not orthogonal." These structures, which were built very soon after the conquest, are far from the primitive houses imagined by Marcel Clerget as "miserable, built of reeds, dried mud, and unbaked bricks" and more aptly called "huts or cabins." Whether the organization of these first Fustat houses imitated ancient Egyptian living quarters, with their unbaked brick and curving streets, or was an Arab model imported by the conquerors has not yet been adequately determined.[9]

Amr had still to provide for a quicker and more direct link between the newly founded city and the Hijaz than the land route. One of the Arabs' goals in conquering Egypt had been to make it easier to resupply Arabia with grain. According to tradition, the conqueror wrote to Caliph Umar: "I will send to Medina a camel train so long that the first camel will reach you before the last one has left me." This goal could be achieved by restoring the canal. It had linked the Nile and the Red Sea in pharaonic times, been restored under Trajan, and subsequently fallen into disuse. According to another tradition, Amr informed the caliph of the possibility: "If you want . . . the price of goods in Medina to be the same as in Egypt, I can have a canal excavated." The caliph is said to have answered: "Proceed at once."[10]

When the Egyptians protested, saying that "the project would be too burdensome and ruin the country," the caliph supposedly retorted, "Never mind, Allah will fully approve of ruining Egypt for the sake of Medina." Whether this correspondence actually took place is uncertain. But Amr did give the order to reexcavate the canal, which took the name Canal of the Leader of the Faithful (Khalij Amir al-Mu'minin). But whereas Trajan's canal had joined the Nile at Qasr al-Sham, entering the bastide between two western towers and traversing it entirely, Amr decided to have his canal start a bit farther north, near the future site of Sayyida Zaynab, perhaps because there were already Arabs in Fustat settled on the canal's former bed. This new iteration of an ancient public work was to be no more successful than its predecessors. By the next century, the Abbasid caliph al-Mansur (754–775) ordered the canal blocked, and its waters formed the Pond of the Pilgrimage (Birkat al-Hajj) northeast of Cairo, so named because it was the first station on the Muslim pilgrimage to Mecca.

In 644, when Amr was recalled from Egypt—Caliph Uthman summoned him abruptly on his accession—the conqueror left an organized capital behind him in which some 10,000 soldiers had settled and an Egypt that, though pacified, was still almost totally Christian. Its status was guaranteed by the treaty of surrender Amr had drawn up:

> In the Name of God, the Merciful, the Compassionate. Here is the guarantee given by Amr ibn al-As to the inhabitants of Egypt for the safety of their persons, their religion, their goods, their churches, their crosses . . . The inhabitants of Egypt are required to pay a tax . . . If by the end of the annual flood the river has not reached the appointed height, the tax will be proportionately reduced.[11]

## THE DEVELOPMENT OF THE CITY

Now a province of the Arab empire, Egypt was further organized during the Umayyad caliphate (661–750). Prefects sent out from Damascus administered the country, governing Egypt's political process, managing its finances, and maintaining law and order. A prefect of police, who was also governor of the capital, was responsible for public safety, while a judge (*qadi*) arbitrated civil and criminal cases. The Arabs retained the administrative and geographic divisions established by the Byzantines; during the first hundred years, all the provincial officials were Christians.

The uneven political fortunes of the caliphate were felt in Fustat. There was unrest in the army during the reign of Caliph Uthman and after his assassination (656). During the revolt of Abdallah ibn Zubayr against the caliph Yazid in 683, Kharidjite troops entered Egypt. The Zubayrid governor ordered a deep trench to be dug around Fustat. Its construction was completed in a single month (September 684), and the rebels were able to hold out for some time before the new caliph, Marwan, regained possession of the country. During a conflict in Syria between the southern Arabs (Yemenis) and the northern Arabs (Qaysis), who were aligned with the caliph Marwan II (744–750), the Yemeni troops in Egypt proclaimed the overthrow of the caliph. Marwan II was able to reestablish his authority in Egypt but was then threatened by the growing power of the Abbasids. After his defeat at the Great Zab River (January 750), he had only Egypt to fall back on. He took refuge there but was pursued by Abbasid troops and killed in Middle Egypt on 1 August 750.[12]

During Egypt's first century as a province of the caliphate, Fustat developed into a true city. Alexandria's significant decline contributed to Fustat's economic development. The new city also benefited from being at the meeting point of Upper and Lower Egypt, and on the route between the eastern and western lands of the empire. Gradually Fustat established itself as the political and administrative center of the new province. A provincial court grew up there. The prefect Abd al-Aziz ibn Marwan, appointed by the caliph in 685, surrounded himself with poets, built a handsome residence known as the House of Gold, and in 698 rebuilt the Mosque of Amr. Local

Mosque of Amr (photo J.-Ch. Depaule)

craftsmanship developed. A boatyard was established on Rawdah in 673.

The first occupants of Fustat (some 10,000 men) were followed by fresh arrivals of Arabs, sometimes as part of mass migrations. Thus, the intendant of finances Ubayd Allah (724–734) imported Qaysi Arabs to counter the influence of the Yemenis, and 5,000 men settled in the Bilbays region. Troops sent at various times to Egypt reinforced Fustat's core of initial settlers: an expeditionary corps was sent in 684 by the caliph Marwan; detachments arrived from Syria in 739 to quash a Coptic rebellion in Upper Egypt and, apparently preferring Fustat to their old cantonments, refused to leave until forced to do so by a military action in 743. The archaeologist R.-P. Gayraud judges from the city's size, population density, and Arabism (indicated by the abundance of Arabic inscriptions and the paucity of Coptic ones) that Fustat received a sizable influx of Arab populations, more than 200,000 individuals.

Finally, a large non-Arab population started to settle in the new city. From the start, the three areas to the settlement's north, called the Hamras, appear to have been inhabited by foreigners, many of them Christians who belonged to the army. The immigration of non-Arabs from the countryside followed, with the new arrivals performing subordinate functions (servants, water carriers, artisans). Churches were built in the northern areas: one beyond al-Qantara, outside the city limits; the Church of Saint Menas, rebuilt in 737 at Hamra al-Wusta for the Christian dignitaries who lived there, provoking a riot among the Muslims; and closer to the center, in the Hamra al-Duniya quarter, which was adjacent to the *ahl al-raya* quarter, a church dedicated to Mary. Its prominent siting near the Mosque of Amr caused it to be demolished in 786, though it was subsequently rebuilt. Fustat's population thus grew at a rapid rate during the city's first century. According to Wladyslaw Kubiak, the number of Arabs living in Fustat increased from around 30,000 in 670 to 50,000 in 750, indicating a total population of around 200,000, not counting slaves, clients, and Copts.[13]

As the original pattern of settlement was fairly sparse, the extent of the city probably changed little until the end of the Umayyad period. The increase in population was easily accommodated by settling the inhabited quarters more densely and occupying the spaces previously left vacant between the cantonments. In some of the outermost areas, urbanization even retreated. The northern portions of the original site are undoubtedly a case in point. At Istabl Antar, Gayraud has observed "more densely grouped dwellings" with "numerous partitions of space"; the natural demographic increase was augmented by the arrival of Egyptians in Fustat, marking "the end of the Arab city" and the transition to a "mixed city where the native population combined with the Arab conquerors." The boundaries of the city, as defined for that time by Kubiak, are, in the south, Birkat al-Habash; in the southeast, al-Sharaf hill. In the north, the boundary was probably defined by the trench *(khandaq)* dug in 684, which Kubiak places beyond Jabal Yashkur, although this hardly seems logical since the areas where the Abbasids would establish their camp at al-Askar in 750 and Ibn Tulun his city and palace in 868 were uninhabited. To the east, toward Ayn al-Sira, the city boundary extended beyond the area where the cemeteries of the Great Qarafa would later develop, north and south of the mausoleum of Imam Shafi'i.[14]

The blocks of land granted to tribal military groups probably turned gradually into neighborhoods. Many centuries later, the historian Maqrizi would observe that the *khitat* of the town of Fustat-Misr corresponded to the quarters *(harat)* that then existed in Qahira.

The development into neighborhoods must have taken different forms depending both on the character of the cantonments, with the smaller ones possibly being absorbed by the more powerful, and on the location, as settlement was denser in the central than in the outer areas, where the unused space between the cantonments gradually filled with buildings, no doubt leading to greater diversity in the populations. In consequence, the almost purely tribal character of the original divisions was dissipated, and the quarters lost their cohesion. In the three Hamra quarters to the north along the Nile, where the ethnic composition had been quite varied from the start and Copts had always been numerous, residential quarters undoubtedly developed very quickly.[15]

The *ahl al-raya* area continued to evolve until it formed a genuine urban center. Within this area of 25 to 30 hectares, bounded on the south by Qasr al-Sham, on the west by the Nile, and on the north by al-Hamra, were located the Mosque of Amr, which was the focus of religion in the city; the seat of government; and the largest markets, grouped around the port. The richest people lived there in handsome houses. The influx of new arrivals, most of whom were well-to-do, made this quarter a diverse community in which the old bonds of tribal loyalty gradually relaxed.

That the camp-city was gradually evolving into a metropolis is signaled by the fact that the Mosque of Amr was enlarged and restored (or rebuilt) several times during this period, until it became a monument worthy of a provincial capital. In 673 the governor Maslama ibn Mukhallad doubled its area and placed minarets at the building's four corners. A second extension, built by Abd al-Aziz, doubled the mosque's area again in 698. It was probably during the construction undertaken by the prefect Kurra in 711 that the mosque finally received a semicircular niche *(mihrab)* to indicate the direction of prayer, just after the caliph Walid (705–715) had one built in the mosque of Medina. The monument's size had increased tenfold in less than seventy years. In the midst of the Muslim city, Qasr al-Sham retained its individual nature and administrative autonomy. The quarter remained an island of minority peoples, inhabited largely by Copts, Orthodox Greeks, and Jews. From the ranks of its artisans and merchants, the conquerors also drew the bureaucrats they needed to administer the country.

Another indication of increasing urbanism can be seen in the development of a true network of streets. In the beginning, there were probably only areas for traffic between one *khitta* and another and the rudiments of streets along the Nile. Archaeological excavation has uncovered streets that appear to date from the Umayyad period. They are narrow, five to six meters at most, but often only two or three, or even one. They widen at crossroads, which are sometimes very complex: one intersection with seven streets or alleys was found near the Mosque of Abu al-Su'ud. Few streets were paved—the exception being one mentioned by the historian Ibn Abd al-Hakam that was known as Darb al-Balat, or Pavement Street—and rested directly on the rocky soil, which was simply leveled. An accretion of dirt, dust, and debris eventually formed a surface layer. The streets traced irregular courses, understandable given the origin of the street system, which included the paths within each *khitta* as well as those connecting one *khitta* to another. The connecting paths provided access between the outer quarters and the center. There also existed several main arteries. The main east–west street led to the boat bridge over the Nile, which was destroyed and rebuilt several times, and crossed the two north–south streets that were laid out at the city's founding: the Main Street (Khitt al-A'zam), which ran along the Nile; and the "Way" (al-Tariq), which followed a course somewhat farther east from Qasr al-Sham to the Mosque of Amr and the Khalij (Canal), which was crossed by a bridge built in 688. Al-Tariq may subsequently have become the Suq al-Kabir (Great Market Street). In the central part of the city, some streets took on names during the Umayyad period that reflected the commercial activities starting to take place there, or an important monument, or the characteristics of the street's inhabitants: Suq al-Hammam (of the Public Bath), west of the mosque; Zuqaq al-Ashraf (Nobles' Alley), between the mosque and Suq Barbar, a likely reference to the aristocratic houses found there.[16]

The adoption of the Arabic language by the local population and their conversion to Islam would determine Egypt's future.[17] As discussed earlier, the Copts' submission to the conquering Arabs no doubt contributed to the long-term preservation of their community. Yet many Christians converted to Islam at the time of the conquest because of their hostility toward the Greeks, according to the bishop of Nikiu. The risk that the Christian population would gradually shift more and more toward Islam was therefore very real. Islam's simplicity and its links with the Judeo-Christian tradition militated in its favor. Also, any mixed marriage between a Muslim and a Jewish or Christian "protected" *(dhimmi)* woman benefited Islam, since the children became Muslim. Finally, fiscal factors (the heavy tax on Copts) and social factors (the possibility of integrating into the dominant caste and escaping the burdensome *dhimmi* restrictions) tended to encourage conversion to Islam.

Nonetheless, there were countervailing factors. The strong solidarity of communities made it difficult for an individual to convert. And the fiscal disadvantage to the conquerors of having Copts convert often kept the Arabs from pressuring the Copts to do so. A policy of tolerance is evident during the early years of Arab rule. In light of the Copts' complaisant attitude toward their Muslim conquerors, they were even allowed to build new churches—a remarkable concession in the context of a Muslim city. Nothing indicates any large-scale movement toward Islam before the reign of Caliph Umar II (717–720). The adoption at that time of a more favorable policy toward converts (exempting them from the poll tax) and the stricter collection of taxes from Christians (including monks) can only have favored the progress of conversion. The recognition in 725 of the Melchites and the restoration of their churches, which had been ceded to the Copts at the time of the conquest, probably had a similar effect. Coptic unrest took the form of rebellion, first in the eastern delta in 725, then in Upper Egypt in 739, both harshly repressed. This set of circumstances may explain the 24,000 conversions obtained by the governor Hafs ibn Walid toward 740.

Arabization was naturally linked to Islamization, but this factor played only a small role during the first century. The growth of the Arabic language resulted more from the large-scale immigration of Arab groups, whether military detachments imported to Egypt in times of crisis and of whom a certain number stayed on (for instance the Syrian detachment that, imported to subdue the Coptic rebellion in 739, refused to leave afterward), or people who settled as a group (such as the Qaysis in 725) or individually. If we accept Gaston Wiet's estimate that 92 percent of the current Egyptian population is Coptic in origin, the importation of Arabs was on the whole rather limited.

But Arabization was aided considerably by the gradual adoption of Arabic as the language of local government, which made it incumbent on the people, and particularly on all who took part in the administration, to learn the conquerors' language.

The process was a slow one. It can be followed in the languages of the papyruses, which were at first almost all written in Greek. The first bilingual Greek-Arabic papyrus appeared in 643, and the last in 719. Meanwhile, in 706, the governor Abdallah ibn Abd al-Malik decreed that all government documents be written in Arabic. The earliest known papyrus to be written solely in Arabic dates from 709. Thereafter Arab papyruses grew more and more common while the use of Greek declined. The last papyrus written in Greek dates from 780. The earliest inscription in Arabic dates only from 735. It was as an official language that Arabic prevailed in the first half of the eighth century and replaced Greek, while the spoken language of the people continued to be Coptic. The patriarch Michael (728–752) did not know Arabic; he sent the governor Abd al-Malik a petition written in Coptic and Arabic. But Copts who spoke only Coptic would decline in number as a result of Islamization, the need for Arabic in dealing with the authorities in the course of daily life, and the interests of the people themselves. In the ninth century, even the clergy learned Arabic, and Bishop Ashmunayn observed: "I asked for help from Christians who translated the facts for me, which they had read in Coptic and Greek, into the Arabic language, which is now so widespread in Egypt that most of the population do not know Greek and Coptic." The situation had reversed since 750.

### THE DYNASTIC CITIES NORTH OF FUSTAT

The creation of palatine cities north of Fustat, first by the Abbasids at al-Askar in 750, then by the Tulunids in 868, should not be taken to mean that the city was gradually extending northward. The governor Abd al-Aziz had already taken steps to move the center of government to Hilwan in 689, perhaps to escape the plague that afflicted Fustat. The attempt did not succeed, doubtless because the distance from the capital was too great. In both cases in which the foundation of an adjacent settlement was successful, a new dynasty wanted to create a command center separate from the city. Building dynastic cities was a common phenomenon. Examples abound outside Egypt: Madinat al-Zahra, near Córdoba; Fez Jadid, near Fez; Raqqada, near Qayrawan; and so on. To a certain extent, the Fatimids' al-Qahira would also be a governmental and dynastic city, but one conceived on such a vast scale and at such a distance from the urban center whose political alter ego it was that it survived and turned into a true city.

As the reign of the last Umayyad, Marwan II, ended in Egypt and the Abbasids came to power, fire destroyed a portion of Fustat. Yet the decision by the Abbasid prefect Abu Aun in early 751 to found a palatine city should not be attributed to this event. It was more likely that he wanted to establish a command-and-control site—it significantly received the name al-Askar, "the Cantonment"—at some distance from the great and busy city that Fustat had become in order to mark in a spectacular way the accession of a new caliphate. The site chosen was an unbuilt area north of Fustat in the area below Jabal Yashkur, between Kawm al-Jarih to the south, the Bridge of the Dike (Qantara al-Sudd) over the Khalij to the west, and the Bridge of Lions (Qanatir al-Siba) to the north, along the Nile, which at that period flowed farther to the east. In the center of the newly founded city was the governor's residence (*dar al-imara*).

Somewhat later, in 786, the cantonment was completed by the building of a mosque (Jami al-Askar). Beautiful houses were built around the core, and, as often happened with settlements of this sort, markets sprang up in response to the substantial demand created by the presence of the court and the army. Later, in 810, governor Hatim set a pavilion on a spur of the Muqattam Hills, where the Citadel would later stand, but his Dome of Fresh Air (Qubbat al-Hawa) gave rise to no lasting structure, and the site would wait three and a half centuries to enter its period of glory. No trace of the princely city of al-Askar has been found, so presumably it had only limited success as a city. Perhaps it was built too close to Fustat to grow, whereas Fustat, once the crisis of 750 was past, resumed its forward progress. Al-Askar continued as a political and administrative center until the arrival of the Tulunids. Ahmad ibn Tulun took up residence in the *dar al-imara* there before building his own palace.

The appointment of Ahmad ibn Tulun as prefect of Egypt in 868 came at the end of a long period of political strife. The Bashmurite rebellion of 832 in the Nile delta between the river's Rosetta and

Mosque of Ibn Tulun, 879

Damietta branches was the last and most violent of the Christian uprisings in Egypt. Caliph Ma'mun spent forty-nine days in Egypt taking part in its suppression. "From then on," wrote Maqrizi, "the
Copts were obedient and their power was destroyed once and for all;
none were able to rebel or even oppose the government, and the
Muslims gained a majority in the villages."[18] In 853 the Byzantines
successfully attacked Damietta. From 866 to 868 an Arab-led revolt
smoldered in a vast region of the delta and Fayyum.

A military man of Turkish ancestry, Ahmad ibn Tulun had lived
in Mesopotamia, specifically in Samarra, where he served Caliph

Musta'in (862–866) brilliantly, thus earning his appointment to Egypt, succeeding a series of Turkish governors. With the Abbasid caliphate facing difficulties, Ibn Tulun was able to establish his authority in Egypt and even to conquer Syria in 878, inaugurating an Egyptian tradition that would be followed by the Fatimids, the Ayyubids, the Mamluks, and, much later, by Ali Bey (in 1771–72) and Muhammad Ali (in 1831–1840). For the first time since the Roman conquest, Egypt would constitute, in the reign of Ibn Tulun (868–884), his son Khumarawayh (884–896), and their successors (896–905), an autonomous state, albeit under Abbasid suzerainty. The political power of the Tulunids, the flowering of their arts, and the pomp of their court life were expressed in the capital they created for themselves.[19]

Like the Abbasid prefects before him, Ahmad ibn Tulun decided to build himself a palatine city commensurate with his ambitions. It was laid out a slight distance northeast of al-Askar on higher ground where there had been a Jewish and Christian cemetery, which was razed. Its boundaries were the Mosque of Ibn Tulun on the east, Birkat al-Fil (Pond of the Elephant) to the north, the sanctuary of Zayn al-Abidin to the south, while Jabal Yashkur rose at its center. The name given this settlement, al-Qata'i ("the Wards"), at once suggests Samarra, which was divided into quarters known as wards, and the conditions of its own creation. The site (whose area has been estimated by Kubiak at around 270 hectares) was divided as Fustat had been into "blocks" in which soldiers, servants, slaves, and a variety of ethnic groups—Nubians, Sudanese, Rumis/Greeks . . .—were settled.

As had occurred at al-Askar, markets evolved to supply the needs of the court and the military, with the various trades grouped in different areas. The Mosque of Ibn Tulun was erected between 876 and 879 at the center of the settlement on the lower slopes of Jabal Yashkur. The *dar al-imara* built by Ibn Tulun to replace the one at al-Askar was located to the south of the mosque and linked to it by a door that opened beside the pulpit *(minbar)*. The palace *(qasr)* of Ibn Tulun was built next to what would become the Citadel of Cairo, with its back to the mountain and a good view of the Nile and the port of Fustat. The castle overlooked a maydan, or field for equestrian games, perhaps on the future site of Rumayla Square. It was used as a parade ground where the ruler reviewed the troops. A road led from the palace and its maydan to the mosque and the "Main Avenue" (Shari al-Azam), which possibly coincided with what would become Saliba Street. The founder's son, Khumarawayh, a splendid and luxury-loving ruler, enlarged and embellished the palace. He converted the maydan into a park and installed "an artificial garden with plated and gilded trees in the Mesopotamian fashion." He had an enormous pool filled with mercury: "The light of the sun, the moon, and the stars reflected on this amazing lake to produce an extraordinary effect," and "a gigantic cushion full of air" was set out on its surface "on which the sensual ruler was rocked softly." He gathered around him "a prodigious number of young and beautiful women, celebrated songstresses whose statues he had carved in wood and placed in his appartments." The resplendence of his audience hall (the "House of Gold," Bayt al-Dhahab) has excited the imagination of historians and poets. Ahmad ibn Tulun also erected a hospital to the southwest of al-Askar, starting construction in 872 or 874. To supply this large aggregation with water at such a distance from the Nile, Ibn Tulun built an aqueduct of which several arches are still extant between Birkat al-Habash and the palace.[20]

Although the Tulunid palaces were systematically destroyed when the Abbasids ended that dynasty's rule in 905, one grandiose element of Ahmad ibn Tulun's palatine city survives, the mosque that occupied its center. It remains to this day one of the most impressive monuments of Muslim architecture. Construction on the building began in 876 and was completed in 879, as the foundation text inscribed on a slab in the sanctuary informs us.

On the whole, the monument followed the style of Samarran monuments. It was built entirely of brick except for its stone minaret. Four arcaded halls or porticoes extend around a square courtyard; the domed ablution fountain there was added by the Mamluk sultan Lajin (1296–1298), who once sought refuge in the mosque and made the vow to restore it. On three sides, the porticoes have a double row of arcades. The prayer hall on the *qibla* side (the direction of Mecca) has five arcades, supported by piers with engaged columns at the corners. The use of bricks rather than marble for the piers and columns is also a trait of Mesopotamian architecture, justified in this case because brick was a local product. On the north, south, and west the mosque is surrounded by an open space (ziyada) enclosed by high walls that isolate it from the outside world. The dar al-imara once stood on the east. The mosque has nineteen doors. The overall floor plan and the pointed arches betray further Mesopotamian influence. The walls are crowned with crenellations of open brickwork and their decorative motifs (a frieze of rosettes, bays) again suggest Samarra. The windows (128 in all) have stucco grills with geometric patterns, perhaps from a later restoration. The six prayer niches date from different periods, the most remarkable of which was commissioned by al-Afdal, the vizir of the Fatimid caliph Mustansir (1036–1094), and is richly decorated in stucco. The wall of the prayer room is decorated with a long inscription in Kufic characters carved in wood. The decorative elements of the Mosque of Ibn Tulun simultaneously show the last traces of Byzantine influence and the political hegemony of Samarra.

The minaret, located outside the mosque in the ziyada, is so original a structure, with its stone construction and helical exterior staircase, that it is the subject of a charming legend. Ibn Tulun, interrupted while distractedly rolling a piece of parchment around his finger, was asked about the meaning of his gesture. He is supposed to have answered that he was thinking about the design of the minaret of his mosque. In fact we know that the ruler commissioned a minaret whose ziggurat shape would evoke Samarra. The top of the minaret, which was in a style known as mabkhara (shaped like an incense burner), was probably built at the time of Lajin's restorations, and that sultan is doubtless also responsible for the bridge by which the minaret is reached and its restored square base. But there is little doubt that the overall structure with its exterior staircase and stone construction belongs to the monument built by Ibn Tulun and that subsequent restorations preserved the main traits of the original monument.[21]

A dynastic city, al-Qata'i did not long survive the Tulunids who built and inhabited it. The traveler Ibn Hawqal, who describes Fustat toward 969 (the date al-Qahira was founded by the Fatimids), mentions its disappearance. "Outside Fustat," he writes, "there used to be constructions built by Ahmad ibn Tulun over an area of a square mile where his troops were quartered, and it was called Qata'i. It was comparable to Raqqada, which the Aghlabids founded outside

Qayrawan. Both of these sites have today fallen into ruin. Of the two, Raqqada was the stronger and better appointed."[22] The decline of al-Qata'i can be sufficiently explained even without the hostility of the Abbasids, who were now restored to their place in Egypt and occupying a city founded by their defeated enemy, for the simple reason that al-Qata'i was no more a true city than al-Askar. Located a considerable distance from the Nile, it could not develop as an autonomous economic center. And being at a distance from Fustat with a large nonurban space between them, it could not become an extension of that city.

The expenditure of effort and the burdensome investment made to construct these dynastic cities no doubt slowed the growth of Fustat during this period. Arab sources, though unreliable with regard to numerical data, estimate the cost of Ibn Tulun's aqueduct at 40,000 dinars, his mosque at 120,000, and his hospital at 60,000. Construction of the palace and especially its interior appointments undoubtedly consumed considerable sums. Yet the descriptions of eastern travelers to Fustat in the second half of the tenth century show it to be active and prosperous to the point of being one of the great metropolises of the Muslim world. The Iraqi traveler Ibn Hawqal, whose notes combine information gathered in the course of two stays in Egypt, one toward 943–947 and the other slightly after 969 (the date of Cairo's founding), writes that the capital of Egypt

> named Fostat . . . is a very beautiful city . . . a large city one-third the size of Baghdad in area. It extends over approximately one parasang [4 kilometers], its site densely peopled and wonderfully fertile. The city has other eminent and agreeable qualities. Its various quarters possess vast open spaces, enormous markets, impressive commercial centers, spacious private lands, not counting its splendid exterior, a pleasant atmosphere, flowering gardens, and parks that are always green no matter the season.

The description left us by the Palestinian Muhammad ibn Ahma al-Muqaddasi, who traveled to Egypt between 969 and 985, expresses similar admiration: "The Egyptian Fustat is today what Baghdad was in times past. I know of no city in all of Islam that is more impressive." And: "Al-Fustat is a metropolis in every sense of the term

. . . It is the seat of government. It is at the intersection of the Maghrib and the Arab lands . . . Al-Fustat has eclipsed Baghdad. It is the glory of Islam and the commercial center of the universe. More magnificent than Baghdad, it is . . . the hub of the Orient." The traveler returns to the theme of the city's commercial importance: "Al-Fustat astonishes by the breadth of its commerce . . . No other river port has as many ships as Fustat's." He relates a significant anecdote:

> One day as I was walking along the banks [of Fustat] and marveling at the multitude of ships at anchor or just setting sail, a man said to me: "Know, sir, that the ships moored in this port added to those that have sailed from here to other cities and settlements are so numerous that if they traveled to your native town they could take on board all its population, all its machinery, all its stones, all its beams, so that, as one might say, they could carry off your entire city."[23]

# 2

# Cairo, Fatimid City

IN THE ARAB AND MUSLIM EGYPT whose evolution started with the establishing of Fustat, 969 was a decisive year. However great the prosperity and influence of Fustat, which was soon to reach its high point, the foundation of the Fatimid city al-Qahira opened a new chapter. Thereafter Cairo would evolve steadily until modernization began in the mid-nineteenth century. The Fatimid settlement was conceived as a dynastic city, and its development might have been arrested as in the case of al-Askar, the city of the Abbasids, or al-Qata'i, the city of the Tulunids. But the fate of Qahira was to be altogether different. During its transformation into a city, Qahira would absorb the first settlement, Fustat, and the two dynastic cities, which would become elements in a larger conurbation. All the seeds of Cairo's future evolution were sown in the two centuries between the time of the Fatimids' arrival in Egypt in 969 and their disappearance in 1171.

The Fatimid era opens a window, paradoxically, onto the older settlement of Fustat. Archaeology has provided little insight into Qahira itself. The city has become increasingly active, more densely populated, and always on the site of its original founding. Hence no direct knowledge of the Fatimid period has been forthcoming. What we know of it comes from historical sources, and from what passed down into such later chronicles as Maqrizi's *Khitat*, written in the early fifteenth century. By contrast, excavations conducted on the site

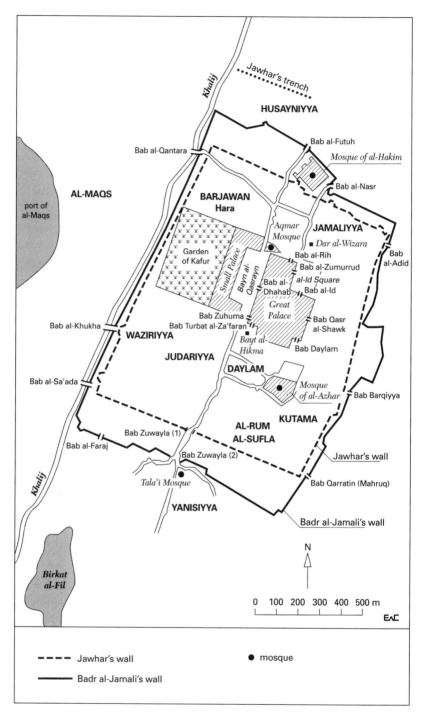

Map 2. Fatimid Cairo (after Ravaisse)

of Fustat have thrown vivid light onto the part of the city that was susceptible to archaeological probes—not in the most central (and therefore most public) zone along the Nile but in the peripheral quarters that were later abandoned (and which have again become inaccessible as a result of the city's recent expansion). Excavations conducted by Ali Bahgat and Albert Gabriel over an area of 12 hectares in eastern Fustat have brought to light a series of private homes that composed a residential quarter of the town probably dating to the eleventh or twelfth century. Excavations by George Scanlon and Wladyslaw Kubiak over another 3 hectares have provided additional information on residences in Fustat, as well as on the town's urbanization.[1]

Just as important is recent research based on the Geniza documents, which are contemporary with the events they record. Jewish communities believed that documents containing the name of God should not be destroyed. They therefore preserved them in a storeroom in the synagogue called the Geniza, eventually to be buried. The vast Geniza in Fustat was never filled in; this trove, rediscovered in the nineteenth century, consists of probably more than 250,000 documents, of which 7,000 are of historical interest. Scattered today among many libraries, they form a varied corpus: court documents (marriages, sales, leases), private and business correspondence, and public matters. The language of these documents is Hebrew, often written in Arabic script. Their subject matter naturally concerns mainly the Jewish community in Fustat, but given the active and ecumenical trade relations existing in the Mediterranean, the documents also provide quite a detailed picture of economic life around the Mediterranean basin.

Most of the documents date from between 1002 and 1266. The great fire of 1168 does not seem to have affected either the storeroom or the subsequent activity of the community, but the documents become scarcer toward the end of the Ayyubid period. They provide extraordinarily rich documentation on the Fatimid period and allow us to form an image of the social and economic life of the Muslim world from the eleventh to the thirteenth century. S. D. Goitein, who studied the Geniza documents, gave the book in which he synthesizes his findings the apt title *A Mediterranean Society.*[2]

## THE FATIMIDS AND THE FOUNDATION OF CAIRO (969)

Restored in 905 to the authority of the Abbasid caliphate after three decades of Tulunid autonomy, Egypt found itself again enjoying a de facto autonomy under the quasi-dynasty of the prefect Muhammad ibn Tughg, whose title, *ikhshid* (sovereign), borrowed from the Iranian rulers of Sogdiana and Ferghana, gave its name to the Ikhshidis (935–969). This dynasty consisted only of its founder, who died in 946, and his two sons (946–966), who were raised under the tutelage of the regent Kafur, a black eunuch from Nubia. Kafur, a wily politician who eventually received investiture from Baghdad, was able to maintain the autonomy of Egypt in the face of proliferating external pressures. Of the many constructions attributed to him, among them a sumptuous palace near the Birkat Qarun (said to have cost 100,000 dinars), no trace has been found. Yet his architectural projects, sited to the west of the Mosque of Ibn Tulun, may have helped orient the Fatimids toward the area where they eventually founded their settlement. This is particularly the case with the park and maydan along the Khalij, which were absorbed by the Fatimid foundation of Qahira.[3] During these several decades Egypt was already living under the shadow of the Fatimid threat.

The dynasty derives its name from Fatima, the daughter of the Prophet and the wife of Ali, from whom the Fatimid caliphs claimed descent. The genealogy by which the Fatimids traced their connection to Isma'il, son of the imam Ja'far, is shrouded in obscurity and has been contested both by their Abbasid rivals and by Sunni historians. At any rate the Fatimids were adherents of Ismailism. A branch of Shiism, it is a religious, philosophic, political, and social doctrine whose followers believe in the appearance of the Mahdi, a descendant of the Prophet through Ali and Fatima. In the ninth century, Ismailism appeared in the form of a secret revolutionary organization, proselytizing intensely and sending its *da'i* (propagandists) into every part of the Muslim world.

The Fatimids' history really starts in Syria, in the town of Salamiya, where the future caliph Ubayd Allah al-Mahdi became the leader of the Ismaili movement. Missionary efforts were successful in Ifriqiyya in North Africa, an area centered around modern-day Tunisia, where Fatimid propaganda was taken up by the Kutama Berbers.

Ubayd Allah was recognized as the imam, the Commander of the Believers, in Qayrawan in 910. In 915, presumably to escape the strong Sunni resistance in Qayrawan, Ubayd Allah founded a dynastic city at Mahdiyya, on the Tunisian coast. Several aspects of this city anticipate those of Qahira, in particular its two palaces (one for the caliph, with the entrance facing west, and one for the heir to the throne, facing east), its esplanade *(rahba)*, and its mosque, some traits of which would pass into the Fatimid monuments of the Middle East. The same applies to the settlement founded at al-Mansur in 947, southeast of Qayrawan: the names of Mansuriyya's two gates, Bab Zuwayla and Bab al-Futuh, would reappear in Cairo.[4] But the ambitions of the Fatimids were always directed eastward, perhaps out of nostalgia for their origins and perhaps also because the future of the dynasty seemed uncertain in the Maghrib, as the great revolt of Abu Yazid (945–947) was to show. Al-Mahdi sent three expeditions against Egypt (in 913, 914, and 918), and his son Qa'im made an equally unsuccessful attempt in 934.

After the accession of the fourth Fatimid caliph, al-Mu'izz (953–975), a cultivated and energetic ruler who found an able second in Jawhar, an ethnic Greek, conditions for the conquest of Egypt improved. Kafur could have no hope of outside help. In 968 the Byzantine emperor Nicephorus Phocas attacked northern Syria and incapacitated the Hamdanites. In Palestine and southern Syria, the Qaramita, a dissident branch of Ismailis, undertook an offensive that temporarily left them masters of Damascus (late 968). Fatimid diplomacy may have played a part in bringing about a conjunction of circumstances propitious to their plans in Egypt. Within the country prices rose abruptly, and famine spread as a result of an inadequate annual flood in 967, when high water never rose above twelve cubits and seventeen fingers, the lowest recorded level since the beginning of the Muslim era. The resultant turmoil was favorable to Fatimid designs. Kafur's death in 968 triggered a domestic crisis. Fatimid propaganda, which was very active in Egypt, prepared the ground for a military incursion. The Fatimid caliph received detailed information on all these matters through Ya'qub (Jacob) ibn Killis, an Iraqi Jew who had settled in Egypt and caught the attention of Kafur for his ability. The Egyptian leader reportedly said of him: "If he were Muslim, he would make a good vizir." Ibn Killis converted to Islam in

967, but after Kafur's death and his own arrest he fled to North Africa, where he entered the service of the caliph al-Mu'izz, whom he persuaded to launch a military expedition.

Al-Mu'izz had learned from his earlier failures and made careful preparations for his invasion of Egypt. "Already in 966, the state of the wells on the road to Egypt had been ascertained, and forts had been built from place to place." In 968 the caliph started to enlist soldiers: 100,000 men were assembled and equipped, at a cost of 24 million dinars. The army, led by Jawhar, set out on 5 February 969: "He carried with him a thousand caskets filled with silver, while numerous camels carried gold ingots in plain sight, cast in the shape of millstones, to impress the local peoples." The army arrived in Egypt in June. Jawhar issued a proclamation promising financial reforms and an end to injustice, and guaranteeing freedom of religion to all Egyptians, including Sunni Muslims and the minority Christians and Jews (dhimmi). The Ikhshidis offered only token resistance, and on 6 July 969, Jawhar, who had made camp at Giza, was able to cross the Nile, march through Fustat, and establish himself north of the city on the plain where he would found the new capital.[5]

In his marching orders to Jawhar's troops as he passed them in review before their departure, the caliph al-Mu'izz announced that the expedition's goals were to conquer Egypt and build a city that would rule the world. In selecting a site for the city, Jawhar had several choices: he could follow the Tulunid example and remain at a distance from the river; he could stay near the Nile because it provided water and a transportation route; or he could come south again to Fustat. He chose a sandy plain north of the Tulunid city, bounded on the east by the Muqattam Hills and on the west by the Khalij. There were no buildings on it except a Coptic monastery and a small castle where Kafur had already established gardens. The site had the advantage of being beyond the reach of the Nile's floods and course-shifting, and it was also at some distance from Fustat, where the native Christian and Sunni Muslim population lived. The new city was after all to be the political capital and the residence of the elite, in keeping with the earlier foundations of Mahdiyya and Qayrawan. This arrangement left an empty area between the new city and Fustat on which the army could camp while construction was under way and still keep an eye on Fustat. Finally, the city may have been intended to provide protection against the Qarmat menace that was soon to threaten Egypt.

On the very night Jawhar settled on the site he marked the perimeter of the city with wooden stakes strung together with belled ropes. It was decided to break ground for the perimeter wall when the astrologers determined that the time was most propitious. According to legend, a crow landed on the cord and set the bells jangling, which the workmen took as a signal to start work. The astrologers reckoned that the planet Mars (al-Qahir, "the Ruler," whence Qahira) was in the ascendant, which was considered an unfavorable sign. But according to another tradition, Mu'izz had given Jawhar instructions to build a city called Qahira that would rule the world. Yet another tradition has it that the city was first called al-Mansuriyya (the Victorious), like the city founded near Qayrawan, and that Mu'izz later renamed it Qahira (the Conqueror) when he arrived in Egypt four years later.[6]

The original outline of the city's ramparts, which were made of large sun-dried mud bricks (labin) and were wide enough for two horses to walk abreast on, was a nearly perfect rectangle oriented on a roughly north–south axis and enclosing an area of some 136 hectares. Maqrizi writes four centuries later about seeing remnants of this wall. It was a very fragile one, however, as it had already disappeared by 1050, when Nasir-i Khusraw traveled to Cairo. "The city is not enclosed by a fortified rampart," he observed.[7] The exterior wall was penetrated by eight gates: two on the north side, al-Futuh and al-Nasr; two on the east, al-Barqiyya and al-Qarratin; two on the south, Zuwayla and Faraj; and two on the west along the Khalij, Sa'ada and Qantara. All these gates subsequently disappeared. Maqrizi reports seeing the remaining arches of a number of them.[8]

When building started, Jawhar had an iron gate from the emir's palace at Fustat transported to the new city, presumably in emulation of Mahdiyya, which reportedly had two iron gates. Jawhar also had a trench dug in front of the north wall of Cairo to protect the city from Qarmat attacks. Inside the new dynastic city, a pendant to the real city of Fustat, a palace was erected according to Mu'izz's instructions and later enlarged. Because a second palace was subsequently built under the caliph Aziz (975–996), the first came to be known as the Great or Eastern Palace and was intended as a residence for the caliphs. It was again Jawhar who, in 972, built the Mosque of al-Azhar south of the palace, which was to become the center of Shiite propaganda in Egypt.[9]

As with all the earlier foundations, Qahira would provide quarters for the often tribal contingents of the Fatimid army. These were placed in cantonments (*khitat*), each of which came to be known as a "quarter" (*mahalla*, then *hara*) and very likely resembled the earliest divisions of Fustat: "relatively closed quarters that were entered through a gate and that may have been separated from one another by empty spaces, with a parade ground inside and streets." It is likely that only a part of the great area set aside by Jawhar was used for these twenty or so "quarters," which held the soldiers and their families and had meaningful names: Zuwayla contained soldiers from Qayrawan and Mahdiyya; Kutama housed the Berber contingents; Daylam was where the refugees from Iran near the Caspian Sea took up residence. Many of these names have survived in the toponymy of Cairo, though the location of the original quarters is often uncertain. A number of the army's contingents were, for lack of space, quartered outside the town limits defined by Jawhar: black troops (the Abids) were cantoned outside Bab Zuwayla. But despite Jawhar's orders forbidding troops to lodge in Fustat so as to minimize their contact with the native population and preserve their military character, many soldiers—Berbers in particular—settled in that city. During the civil unrest of 1020, the Berbers of Kutama and the Turks joined the native population in resisting the corps of black slaves sent by Hakim to plunder and burn Fustat: they lived there, had married local women and begotten children, and held property in that town.[10]

Muslim travelers who visited Cairo shortly after its founding by Jawhar have left us a fairly detailed record of its early aspect. Ibn Hawqal, writing not long after 973, described Cairo thus:

> The Maghribis have just founded a town outside Fustat called Cairo. Jawhar, the Maghribi general, staked it out on his arrival in Egypt for his army, stores, and retinue. It now has different quarters and markets, as well as places for breeding livestock, facilities such as baths and inns, and even well-built palaces and useful facilities. Jawhar has surrounded it with a strong, high wall, which encloses a space three times greater than the built-up area: these are parks

kept in reserve for the livestock in case of outside attack. Inside are offices for the administrators of Egypt, and a beautiful and elegant congregational mosque tended by an abundance of clerics and muezzins.[11]

Ibn Hawqal still considers Fustat the real city. He gives a good description of Qahira as the dwelling place of the royal family and the country's administrators, noting the appearance of the first elements of a city proper (markets, baths, and inns). Al-Muqaddasi, writing at the end of the tenth century, describes Fustat's considerable activity in detail. In contrast, he deals with Qahira summarily as nothing more than a fortified town:

> Al-Qahira is a town that was built by Jawhar "the Fatimid" when he conquered Misr and subjugated [*qahara*] its inhabitants . . . Qahira is where Jawhar's troops and his palace are. The town is a large one, counting forty baths and fine markets . . . [and] a superb main mosque. The government castle, fortified and equipped with iron-faced doors, occupies the center of town.[12]

Once Jawhar had established the capital, pacified the provinces, instituted financial reforms, introduced new religious observances in conformity with the Fatimid faith (a call to prayer that included the Shiite invitation to "come to the best prayer," a new prayer sequence, and the setting of the fast according to the calendar), and successfully fought off the Qarmat attack (December 971), there was nothing left to do but install the caliph Mu'izz in Qahira. On 10 June 973, the ruler, who had traveled from the Maghrib, crossed the Nile on the Rawdah bridge, bypassing Fustat, and proceeded to Cairo, where he took possession of the palace. It was Ramadan of A.H. 362. On the feast marking the end of the fast, al-Mu'izz "conducted prayers at the new mosque in Cairo with a piety so pronounced that some may have felt it to be an affectation." Then he ascended to the pulpit *(minbar)* to give the sermon *(khutba)* and "managed, by his eloquence, to draw sobs from the audience." Jawhar stood on the steps of the pulpit. Once outside, al-Mu'izz mounted his horse, "surrounded by his four armored and helmeted sons, while two elephants led the procession."[13] The caliph then ended Jawhar's able proconsulate. Egypt and

Cairo were entering a new era that would last almost two centuries and constitute one of the most brilliant periods in their history.

## FATIMID GRANDEUR

The splendor of the Fatimid dynasty, as S. D. Goitein has noted, is somewhat puzzling if one considers that aside from its first two caliphs, al-Mu'izz (969–975) and al-Aziz (975–996), it counted few exceptional personalities. Al-Hakim (996–1021) was one, although his excesses were considerable: some of his follies were relatively innocuous, such as outlawing the eating of mulukhia, a vegetable highly prized by the Egyptians, but others were serious, such as his persecution of Christian and Jewish subjects. His reign ended in a curious way: he disappeared during one of his nightly walks. Of eleven Fatimid rulers, seven came to the throne very young (four of them in childhood), so that power was generally in the hands of vizirs. Some were certainly remarkable statesmen, for instance Badr al-Jamali (1073–1094) and Tala'i ibn Ruzzik (1154–1161). But many were as mediocre as the titular rulers, and some were even disastrous, such as Shawar (1161–1169).

The dynasty's success can be attributed in the first place to the well-regulated administrative system instituted by Jawhar and perfected after his retirement by Ya'qub ibn Killis, a vizir to Aziz from 979 until his death in 991. Thanks to this masterly organizer of Fatimid finances, the state's revenues increased from 3.25 million dinars in 968 to 4 million, giving the Fatimids the wherewithal for an extensive political program and a level of splendor that has been the wonder of historians. It is reported that during Aziz's reign, 220,000 dinars (approximately a ton of refined gold) was raised in three days. Syria, which remained under Fatimid governance until 1076, contributed largely to Fatimid political and financial power.[14]

But the primary source of Egypt's power and prosperity was international economic activity. An indication of its scope comes to us from the Geniza documents. Although they document the Jewish communities, they show us the remarkably free movement of men, goods, and money in Egypt. Merchants could travel without restriction: Fatimid Egypt received traders from Sunni Tunisia at a time when the governments of the two countries were openly at war. The

Mediterranean region, in Goitein's words, formed "a free-trade community." But the free movement of men and merchandise extended well beyond the Mediterranean. A letter was found, written by the highest Jewish authority in Jerusalem, announcing that the bearer, a native of Khorasan (a province in northeast Iran), held a letter of recommendation from a merchant in Seville (at the extreme west of the Muslim world) and was traveling to Egypt. Another, sent in 1016–1017 from the Jewish community in Qayrawan to the Jews of Old Cairo, contains the following request: "A Jewish merchant from Baghdad died in Sijilmassa, in Morocco . . . The local Jewish authorities have informed the writer of the property left by the deceased in that town. In addition, the traveler left merchandise . . . in al-Qayrawan." The writer (in Qayrawan) asked Ibn Awkal (in Fustat) to ask the Jewish authorities (in Baghdad) to transmit the names and instructions of the deceased's heirs (in Baghdad) to the appropriate authorities in Qayrawan. This was the case of a man whose business covered an area from present-day Iraq to Morocco, regions then separated by months of travel and by countries that were often at war.

This Mediterranean community extended well beyond the Jewish communities whose detailed records have come down to us in the Geniza documents. Maqrizi reports that al-Mu'izz wanted the trunk of a rare tree for his coffin. Two months later, the trader who had been contacted in Mecca sent word that his correspondent in Aden had shipped the block of wood, which would arrive at any moment in Qulzum (present-day Suez). This is proof that there existed an efficient trade network between the Indian Ocean and Egypt.

There also existed close ties with European trade. The terms *Ifranj* (for Western Europeans) and *Rumi* (for Byzantines and Italians) are found in the Geniza documents. "Business has been quiet this year because no one from the West has come, only a few Rumis," we read in a letter sent from Fustat to Aden. And around 1085 an Alexandrian merchant wrote to his correspondent in Fustat: "The alum has not yet arrived [from Upper Egypt or Yemen]. The Rumis are here; we will offer it to them; and we hope that they will buy it." There was a Suq al-Rum in Fustat even before the foundation of Qahira. There existed regular ties, in 973, with Amalfi. In 996, some 200 natives of Amalfi lived in Fustat, 107 of whom were massacred after a fleet of warships on the Nile burned, for which they were held responsible. In 1143 a trade agreement was signed between Egypt and Roger II of Sicily. The Pisans had a caravanserai (*funduq*) put at their disposal by the Egyptian government before 1153. Genoese and Venetian traders among others had the right to conduct business in Egypt. The Fatimids made a valuable contribution to commercial prosperity by issuing gold coins whose value remained constant for almost two centuries.[15]

It is therefore no surprise to find Fustat described as an emporium of all the world's goods. Nasir-i Khusraw, writing in 1048, provides a description of the Market of the Lamps (Suq al-Qanadil) in Fustat that, while clearly impressionistic, must take the place of unobtainable trade statistics:

> It has no equal in any other country, and one finds there rare and precious objects from all parts of the world. I saw objects made of tortoise shell, such as caskets, combs, knife handles, etc. I also discovered rock crystal of great beauty, artistically worked by artisans of surpassing taste. It had been brought from the Maghrib, but some was said to have recently arrived from the Sea of Qulzum [Red Sea] that was even more lovely and transparent than the Maghribi crystal. I saw elephant tusks from Zanzibar, some of which weighed more than two hundred minas. There was also the hide of an ox from Abyssinia that resembles leopard skin and is used to make slippers. From this same country there also came a very large domestic bird . . . I saw copper vases from Damascus that can hold thirty minas of water each and that shine so brilliantly they look like gold.

Egypt was also a transit center for imported merchandise: "At Aidhab [on the Red Sea], import tax is collected on goods arriving by sea from Abyssinia, Zanzibar, and Yemen . . . They are then transported through the desert to Aswan. There they are loaded on boats that go down the Nile and land in Fustat."[16]

The generally tolerant attitude of the caliphs toward minorities also contributed to Egypt's prosperity and splendor. Yet the Fatimids propagandized energetically to spread their beliefs throughout their domain, which, at the height of Fatimid power, included North Af-

Courtyard of al-Azhar Mosque, 972
(the minarets date from the Mamluk period)

rica, Sicily, Palestine, Syria, and the region along the Red Sea (including the Hijaz).

The Fatimid caliph was not just an imperial ruler. He was also the Ismaili imam, the spiritual leader of the believers, "the incarnation of the plan and will of God on earth." He had an army of missionaries at his disposal, agents who were secretly organized under the general command of a head missionary *(da'i al-du'at)* in Cairo, where the al-Azhar Mosque (972) was built to disseminate Ismaili ideology. This effort received further impetus when the caliph Hakim created the Hall of Wisdom (Dar al-Hikma) in 1005. Set in the middle of Qahira behind the Khan Masrur and near the Western Palace, where the caliph resided, this institution had a very beautiful library, whose main holdings came from the caliph's own collection. When it opened, "people of all classes flocked to it because it was meant for everyone. They went there to read, to copy, and to transcribe. Work was facilitated for them . . . Paper, pens, and ink were provided." Scholars were appointed to it. Just as significant was the attention given to erecting shrines to members of the family of the Prophet and Ali. Guides were written for the use of pilgrims with, at first, a specifically Shiite orientation. And efforts were made to popularize Shiite festivals.[17]

This propaganda campaign on behalf of Shiite ideology seems to have met with little success outside Egypt or even within it. The Sunnis believed in a general way that "one should remain patient under the king's banner, whether he proves a tyrant or a just man," that one should attend public prayers "whether they are conducted by a pure man or a libertine," and that for other prayers a Muslim could choose "an imam more in keeping with his own piety." This amounted to an acceptance of "a two-tiered Islam, the state's version and the individual's." Passive resistance sometimes flared into open conflict when the imams tried to go too far, as they did in Fustat in 1019. The missionaries announced the divine nature of Caliph al-Hakim, causing riots that lasted three days, in retaliation for which the town was sacked and a third of it burned down. When the Fatimid caliphate started to weaken, Sunni resistance cropped up in a movement to build madrasas (schools) for the teaching of orthodox Islam. The first of these appeared in Alexandria in 1135 and 1151.[18]

The marginal position of Ismailism in the Muslim world probably accounts for its tolerant attitude toward the *dhimmi*. As a rule, when a minority group finds itself in power, it is generally accepting of other minorities. One symptom of Fatimid tolerance was the absence of any effort to convert Christians to Islam except during a brief period in Hakim's reign. Another was its extensive enrollment of minorities in government. The long domination of Fatimid administration by Ibn Killis, a converted Iraqi Jew, first as minister of finances and then as vizir from 977 to 991, and the brilliant military career of Fadl b. Salih, a converted Christian, from 979 to 1009, were part and parcel of the dominance of Christians and Jews within the central administration. As an epigram from the reign of Aziz (975–996) put it: "Become a Christian, for Christianity is the true religion, so much is patently clear today. Have faith in three persons and forsake all others as useless: the vizir Yakub is the Father, Aziz is the Son, and Fadl is the Holy Ghost."

The strong influence of Christianity probably explains Hakim's reaction against it and his persecution of Christians. At the beginning of Mustansir's caliphate (1035–1094), the regent's main counselor was a Jew, Abu Sa'd, and these verses were popular in Cairo:

> *These days the Jews have reached their dream*
> *They're rich; they reign supreme . . .*
> *O Egyptians, here's my advice to you*
> *Turn Jewish, since the heavens have turned Jew!*

Later in the same reign the Armenian Badr al-Jamali, vizir from 1073 to 1094 and restorer of Fatimid power, favored the promotion of his Christian compatriots. "Because of his nationality and religion," wrote the Armenian Christian chronicler Abuh Salih toward 1168, "Badr helped the Christians of Egypt . . . He was a friend to all Christians." A Coptic monk, Abu Najah, was the main adviser to Amir (1101–1130). And in the reign of Hafiz (1130–1149), the vizir was an Armenian Christian general named Bahram, who was known as the "Sword of Islam" (Sayf al-Islam) (1135–1137).[19]

By chance, we have detailed knowledge of how the tolerance and broad autonomy granted to non-Muslim communities benefited the Jews, whose Geniza documents amply show their activeness and prosperity. It is likely that Fatimid liberalism coincided with a period of domestic peace that benefited all elements of the population, Christians in particular. The progress of Arabization and Islamization had probably reduced the relative size of the Coptic community until it was by then a minority. In 1131 the patriarch Gabriel ordered the parish priests to explain the word of God in spoken Arabic, showing that Coptic was no longer much understood in Egypt. Yet though the majority of the Egyptian population had converted to Islam by the end of the ninth century, the trend must not have been rapid during the Fatimid era, when the attitude toward Christians was much more favorable. A decree issued by Hafiz in 1136 is characteristic in tone: "We believe that we should spread wide the mantle of justice and benevolence and embrace the different religious communities with mercy and compassion. Measures to improve conditions should include Muslims and non-Muslims alike, who should be provided everything they might hope for in the way of peace and security." The existence of a pluralist society (as pluralist as might be in those times) within a solidly built state and one long sheltered from foreign incursions undoubtedly constitutes one aspect of what has often been called the "Fatimid miracle."[20]

The Fatimid era was equally remarkable for its intellectual and artistic activity, perhaps because of the great area over which its trade relations extended and also because of the enriching contacts between its various coexisting communities. The great mathematician and physician Ibn al-Haytham (the Alhazen or Avenetan of medieval Latin texts) was summoned to Cairo from Basra by the caliph al-Hakim. Ibn Butlan, a Christian physician and theologian from Baghdad, who lived in Cairo from 1050 to 1054, had a famous controversy with Ibn Ridwan, Mustansir's chief physician. Ibn Maymun (Maimonides), the Jewish theologian and physician from Córdoba, settled in Cairo in 1165 and died in Fustat in 1204; his reputation was so great that the learned traveler Abd al-Latif wished to meet him in 1192 and judged him to be "a man of very superior merit."[21]

The Fatimid period was also renowned for its decorative arts (ceramics, glass, bronze, and textiles). Their originality, particularly in their representation of animate beings, both men and animals, owes a great deal to the ambient luxury of that era, to the circulation of artists and art objects. Though the splendor of Fatimid palaces is known to us only through texts, the monuments having disappeared, the structures that still stand in Cairo (mosques and sanctuaries) attest to a highly original art whose formulas spread as far as Western Europe: the decorative use of stalactites *(muqarnas)* is one instance; another is the house recently excavated in Murcia, whose organization is reminiscent of Fatimid houses in Fustat.[22]

Fatimid grandeur is best illustrated by two different but complementary manifestations: the luxury of its libraries and the splendor of its ceremonies. The initial elements of the caliphal library were perhaps established by Ibn Killis. By the year 1000 the palace library employed a head conservator and occupied forty rooms in the Great Palace. As Gaston Wiet has written:

> It contained eighteen thousand manuscripts on the sciences of antiquity alone. The books were arranged on shelves all around the rooms. The shelving was partitioned and enclosed behind shutters equipped with locks and bolts. In all there were more than one hundred thousand bound volumes. These included works on the laws of every religion, treatises on grammar and lexicography, collections of traditional lore, history books, royal biographies, essays on astronomy, works relating to the supernatural, alchemical research, all in various forms of writing.

The caliph Aziz took a personal interest in the library, having the works it contained presented to him (for example, twenty copies of Tabari's famous *History,* one of them autograph) and visiting it from time to time. The historian Ibn Abi Tayyi (1180–c. 1230) estimated that the library contained more than 1.6 million volumes and considered it one of the marvels of the world.[23]

Fatimid ceremonial centered on the divine nature of the caliph, in whom the imamate resided, and sought to highlight both the sovereign's power and his religious authority. The etiquette of the caliphal audience was recorded by William of Tyre, who came to Cairo in 1167, and by Maqrizi: the caliph settled on his throne in the audience hall behind a curtain that was raised once the ceremony began. "The caliph appeared seated on the royal throne, facing those in attendance . . . The vizier entered and, after kissing the caliph's hands and feet, drew back three cubits . . . upon which the caliph invited him to come sit on his right." The people present were assigned places according to strict etiquette. The Frankish envoys caused a small scandal when they proposed that the caliph, whose face and hands were swathed in silk, extend his bare hand to Hugh of Caesarea on concluding an agreement. The emirs who were present "said the insult was very grave, when the Christians spoke to their lord so boldly and as equal to equal." The caliph "was greatly offended, but smiled to cover his ire" and offered his hand.[24]

The ceremonies for which the caliph solemnly ventured forth from his palace were attended with the same shows of respect, whether the occasion was a civil one (new year's day, the anointing of the Nilometer, the opening of the Khalij) or religious (the first day of Ramadan, the lifting of the fast, the Feast of the Sacrifice). The historians of the Mamluk period, clearly fascinated by such great pomp, gave detailed descriptions of the ceremonies. When water was to be let into the Canal, a great tent was erected on its west bank near the dike. The caliph left the palace on horseback, bearing every emblem of royalty, shaded by a parasol, and escorted by a large retinue that included forty trumpeters (thirty silver trumpets and ten gold). The cortège passed in front of the Mosque of Ibn Tulun, then proceeded to the Canal. The caliph took up his place in the belvedere and waited for the workers to breach the dam, at which point boats were launched on the Khalij and advanced toward the belvedere. The sovereign, who had in the meantime assumed a new set of clothes, with a new parasol to match, now made his way back to the palace. The ceremony of anointing the Nilometer, which took place as the flood neared the optimal sixteen-cubit mark, employed a slightly different itinerary: the caliph crossed Cairo, exited by Bab Zuwayla, made his way to the Mosque of Ibn Tulun and the Great Bridge, passed through Misr, crossed the arm of the Nile to Rawdah Island in a special craft (al-harraqa), anointed the column of the Nilometer with saffron and musk, then returned to his palace, sometimes after going downriver by boat as far as Maqs. Both of these were popular festivals of native Egyptian origin, which the Muslims adopted and made official.[25]

The new year's procession, which took place entirely within Cairo, was typical. The dignitaries, who gathered in Between the Two Palaces Square (Bayn al-Qasrayn), proceeded to the Golden Hall, where the caliph mounted his horse in full ceremonial regalia. Several thousand men of different corps (one of which was a band corps) joined the cortège, which proceeded to the Gate of Victory (Bab al-Nasr) and came back by the Gate of Conquests (Bab al-Futuh) to the esplanade, where the caliph parted from his vizir, answering his salute with a faint signal, "which was the very greatest favor that the caliph could bestow." "The streets through which the procession passed were decorated by the shopkeepers . . . 'to obtain the blessing of the caliph's glance': shops, houses, squares, gates to the quarters [harat] were decked with brocade and fine linen."[26]

These ceremonies gave the people an occasion for rejoicing and allowed them a rare glimpse of their sovereign in the full display of his pomp and power. Nasir-i Khusraw, who witnessed the Festival of the Opening of the Canal around 1050, has described the popular high spirits. When the caliph gave the signal to open the dike, "The men of the people immediately rushed onto the dike and attacked it with picks, hoes, and shovels until it gave way under the pressure of the water . . . The entire population of Misr and Cairo was on hand to revel in the sight and took part in all manner of entertainments."[27]

## QAHIRA

Designed on the model of the caliphal residences of Mahdiyya and Qayrawan in Ifriqiyya as an imperial city, the seat of political power, and the base for Fatimid efforts to encourage the spread of Ismailism, Qahira was never intended to become a true city. Next to it was Fustat, where the masses lived and where the economic activities were pursued that supplied the financial means to maintain the ruling elite. The functional difference between Qahira and Fustat was not fated to persist. Even before the end of the Fatimid dynasty and the accession of the Ayyubids, whose policies and works would signally affect the history of the capital, Qahira started to change into a veritable city.

Jawhar had only sketched in the palaces that were to be at the center of his new city, following a plan that clearly emulated the one implemented by the Mahdi Ubayd Allah in Mahdiyya. The Eastern and Western Palaces lay on either side of the main thoroughfare, which was designed by Muʿizz to run in an almost straight line from north to south between Bab al-Futuh and Bab Zuwayla. The avenue widened in the middle to form a square known as Bayn al-Qasrayn.

The palaces were not compact structures, as at Versailles. Rather, they consisted of a scattered complex of buildings. The space designated by Paul Ravaisse as belonging to the Great Eastern Palace covers approximately nine hectares.[28] Begun in 970 by Jawhar, who built a mausoleum in the southwest corner to inhume the remains of the sovereigns he had carried with him from Ifriqiyya, it was completed by al-Aziz (975–996) with the construction of the Golden Palace (Qasr al-Dhahab) and the Great Iwan (open hall). But structures were added to it until the middle of the twelfth century: the vizir al-Maʾmun al-Bataʾihi (1122–1125) built three pavilions (manazir) there. The palace comprised three rectangular buildings, while the northeast quadrant formed an esplanade, Festival Square (Rahbat al-Id), measuring 157 by 105 meters, where the caliph's retinue assembled before processions.

The palace had nine main gates: three to the west, one to the north, three to the east, and two to the south. The largest and finest of these was the Golden Gate (Bab al-Dhahab), which opened in the middle of the western facade and whose uprights were made of the gold millstones brought by Jawhar from Ifriqiyya. Through the archway, some 30 meters high, one gained access to several of the palace's main halls. The western facade (345 meters long) apparently ran along a line some 25 meters back from the present course of Muʿizz li-din Allah Street, which occupies what was once Bayn al-Qasrayn. The north facade had only one gate, the Gate of the Wind (Bab al-Rih), which was used by the devout in coming to hear the chief propagandist (daʿi). This gate survived until 1408 and was seen by Maqrizi. The east facade is described by Maqrizi in less detail, probably because it fell into ruin soon after the palace was abandoned. The Emerald Gate (Bab al-Zumurrud) led into the Emerald Palace, the caliph's residence. On the south facade was the Daylam Gate, which opened onto a monument that was to become the shrine (mashhad) of al-Husayni. The head of Husayn (son of Ali, killed in 680 at the battle of Kerbela in Iraq) was deposited there after it was discovered at Askalon and a treaty concluded with the Franks to allow its transfer to Cairo in 1153. The Gate of the al-Za'faran Tomb *(turbat)* led to a mausoleum intended as a burial-place for the Fatimids. When the Khan al-Khalili was later built on this site (I 4–5; see the grid coordinates in Map 4), the skeletons buried there were loaded into baskets and thrown onto the mounds of rubble east of the city. When the man responsible for this desecration, Emir Jaharkas al-Khalili, died an ignoble death in Damascus in 1389, Maqrizi read it as a judgment from on high: "His body was left where it fell, naked, his genitals uncovered, his flesh swollen . . . His corpse rotted in place. Such was the punishment God dealt him for having handled disrespectfully the bones of the imams and their descendants."

The Eastern Palace contained several buildings surrounded by gardens where the daily life and ritual of the court took place. Their loveliness and luxury have been described by William of Tyre, who walked through them at the time of his audience with the last Fatimid caliph, Adid, in 1167. After passing through a number of long, narrow vaulted alleys "where you could not see a thing," the Franks emerged into a vast open courtyard paved in various colors of marble set off with gold and surrounded by magnificent columned porticos.

> It was so beautiful, so pleasant to the eye, that the most preoccupied man would have stopped to look at it. There was a fountain in the center, fed on all sides by gold and silver channels carrying water of admirable clarity . . . Flitting here and there were an infinite variety of birds of the rarest colors . . . brought from different parts of the Orient, which no one saw without marveling.

In another and still more luxurious garden, the knights saw a menagerie of quadrupeds so strange "that whoever gave a description of them would be accused of lies." Of the buildings, the most remarkable was the caliph's residence. William describes the sumptuousness of the great audience hall, where a large "hanging composed of gold thread and silk of every color, inset with animals, birds, and people, sparkling with rubies, emeralds, and a thousand rich stuffs" was whisked away to reveal the caliph "seated on a gold throne studded with gems and precious stones."

In addition to the Golden Hall, the palace had many pavilions surrounded by gardens for members of the ruling family and the court, as well as areas devoted to catering to the needs of this court, whose number Nasir-i Khusraw estimated at 30,000. East of the palace was the Storehouse of Standards (Khizanat al-Bunud), the arsenal where arms were manufactured. To the southwest were the kitchens, from which, writes Maqrizi, during the month of Ramadan, "one daily saw twelve hundred pots emerge laden with every kind of food for distribution among pensioners and the poor." The palace gate on that side was named "Bab Zuhuma . . . or Gate of the Kitchen Odors, because all the meats and other victuals passed through this gate" by means of an underground passage that joined the kitchens to the palace. The name remained in use into the modern era: the *Description de l'Egypte,* written six centuries after the fall of the Fatimids, mentions it in a scarcely altered form as "Bab el-Zoumeh." Awed by the court's magnificence, Nasir-i Khusraw records that fifty people worked full-time in the kitchens, and that fourteen camel loads of snow were delivered each day to the sultan's pantries. After visiting the banquet hall at the end of Ramadan 1049, the traveler added that 50,000 minas of sugar were used to decorate the sultan's table, on which he saw "a tree resembling an orange tree whose branches, leaves, and fruits were made of sugar; also decorating the table were a thousand statuettes and figurines equally made of sugar."

The small Western Palace, located on the other side of the Great Avenue (Shari al-Azam), consisted of a central structure with two wings at either end. This design allowed for the vast rectangular Between the Two Palaces esplanade, Bayn al-Qasrayn, measuring 105 by 255 meters and covering an area of 2.5 hectares. According to Nasir-i Khusraw, an underground passage allowed the sovereign to go from one palace to the other on horseback. Distinctly less expansive at 4.5 hectares, the Western Palace occupied land that had once formed the eastern end of Kafur's gardens. The caliph Aziz (975–996) built it for his daughter, Sitt al-Mulk, and it was completed in 1064 by al-Mustansir, who planned to install the caliph of Baghdad there. This palace is less well known to us than the Eastern Palace because its facade was replaced by a series of large religious edifices built between 1225 and 1384 by the Ayyubid and Mamluk sultans. Its southern portion was taken over by the large hospital *(maristan)* of Sultan Qalawun (1284), which seems to have preserved a part of the original layout, a set of four open rooms arranged to form a cross around a pool.

This central complex was surrounded by ancillary buildings, some of which were later additions. The stables occupied two buildings: one, the Rotunda, lay to the southeast, just north of the Mosque of al-Azhar; the other, the Sycamore Stable, was south of the Western Palace. Each could hold 500 horses and had a large complement of stableboys, grooms, keepers, and equerries. The palace storehouses, which were south of the Eastern Palace, contained books, beverages, harnesses, tents, rugs, and clothing. The Hall of Knowledge (Dar al-Ilm) was established by al-Amir in 1116 on a site just outside the southwest corner of the palace so as to lessen the scandal caused by freely voiced controversies on problems of politics and religion. The Palace of the Vizirate (Dar al-Wizara), the official residence of the vizirs until the end of the Fatimid caliphate, was built after 1094 by al-Afdal, the son and successor to the vizir Badr al-Jamali. The iron-work grill (*shubbak*) that separated the vizir from those in the audience hall still existed in Maqrizi's time.

As the center of political and court life, the palace area and the Bayn al-Qasrayn at its heart were the setting for an elaborate ceremonial. Maqrizi observes that movement was strictly regulated in Cairo, particularly near the palace, where "fifty horsemen kept watch at night near the palace gate." After the last prayer, an emir known as the Sinan al-Dawla would come out on the threshold of the palace gates:

> He would order the band leader to let the drums and trumpets sound, which they did, accompanied by other instruments, playing beautiful music for about an hour. Then an officer . . . came out of the palace and announced: "The Emir of the Believers sends greetings to Sinan al-Dawla." He would flourish a spear and strike it into the ground before the gate, then remove it and pull the gate shut, afterward going around the palace seven times . . . He posted the night watchmen and their pages . . . A chain [*silsila*] was stretched across the narrowest section of the Bayn al-Qasrayn. From that moment on, traffic ceased in the square until the sentry band [*nawha*] announced the dawn. The chain was then removed and traffic could resume.

The large square itself served as a setting for ceremonies and resplendent parades, whether civil, religious, or military. Ten thousand armed men, cavalry and infantry, could gather there, Maqrizi assures us.[29]

The general structure of the city was strictly organized by Jawhar from the start. The Shari al-Azam and the Qasaba (Boulevard) formed its north–south axis. Intersecting this broad, straight thoroughfare, secondary streets led to the areas where the various contingents of the Fatimid army were housed and that gradually developed into the city's "quarters," while the empty space between them gradually filled in as Qahira turned into a true city. East of the central artery was a parallel road, eventually to become the Jamaliyya, which ended at Bab al-Nasr. It was to play an important role in the caliph's official life, being used, for example, for processions beyond the city walls to the place of prayer at the *musalla*.

Qahira was first a city reserved for the caliph, his court, and his army corps. Writing around 1050, Nasir-i Khusraw notes that "no one may own a house or building [there] unless he has had it built himself." But the presence of a large population living at the court or in houses in the vacant areas between the quarters inevitably led to increased commercial activity on the part of artisans and shopkeepers, given Fustat's great distance. Nasir-i Khusraw notes the existence of some 20,000 shops in the caliphal city (an obvious exaggeration), "which are all the sultan's property" and were leased by the shopkeepers. The traveler reveals that he lodged in Qahira on one of the upper floors of a four-story house. Specialized markets began to appear very early on: the market of the roasters (*shawwa'in*) was established near Bab Zuwayla as early as 975.

Maqrizi mentions other markets as well: the market of the waxmakers (*shamma'in*) near the Mosque of Aqmar, and that of the moneychangers near Bab al-Zuhuma—both along the central artery of the Qasaba, which was destined for a great commercial future. He also mentions eight public baths founded during Fatimid times in different quarters of Qahira. Although most of the local economy remained grounded in Fustat, which impressed travelers for its vitality, some commercial activities began to take root in Qahira itself. Early concerns with city planning, as described by Maqrizi in a discussion of established usages on the Qasaba during the Fatimid period, are telling. A Byzantine ambassador arriving in Cairo, he notes, "would alight at Bab al-Futuh, where he kissed the ground, before continuing on foot toward the palace," suggesting the almost holy character of the royal city. Yet a few lines later, Maqrizi cites regulations that illustrate the direction in which the city was evolving: in 992 water carriers were ordered to cover their containers to avoid splashing passersby; in 993 the caliph Aziz ordered that a large jar full of water be placed in front of every shop as a precaution against fire; in 1001 Hakim ordered inhabitants to light the city by placing lanterns in front of shops and house entrances; in 1005 people were forbidden to enter Qahira riding an animal led by a mule-driver, and no passage was allowed along the palace wall between Bab Zuhuma and Bab al-Zumurrud. All these edicts indicate that the avenue and the city quickly showed a secular character, which became more pronounced with time.[30]

As Qahira became "citified" it began to extend beyond the limits fixed by Jawhar. Even at its foundation, or at least very soon afterward, certain parts of the army were quartered beyond the walls for lack of space: black troops, for instance, were quartered outside Bab Zuwayla; and Husayniyya, which became a suburb of Cairo, owes its name to a tribal contingent quartered there. Aziz, and Hakim after him, built the great Mosque of al-Hakim outside Mu'izz's north wall. A certain amount of development occurred in this area with the construction of belvederes around the *musalla* and the subsequent establishment of cemeteries. To the west, where parks and gardens extended to the Khalij, pavilions were built, and the area became a popular place for walks. To the south, probably because of the road leading toward Fustat, a few quarters developed. To the east, on the other hand, mounds of rubble thrown against the far side of the walls to protect the city from the water coming down the mountain effectively stopped the city's spread and fixed its limits. But Qahira's expansion during its first century was limited. When, between 1087 and 1092, the great vizir Badr al-Jamali decided to build a second wall around Qahira, he enclosed only a small amount of new territory, including the Mosque of al-Hakim in the north and an extra 200 meters in the south, for a total increase of 24 hectares. This brought Qahira's area to 160 hectares, which would remain constant for this part of Cairo until 1798. If this enlargement reflects the total progress of ur-

Bab al-Nasr (Gate of Victory), 1087
(*Description de l'Egypte,* Bibliothèque Nationale)

ban development in slightly more than a century, its modesty is apparent.[31]

Badr's public works were nonetheless of considerable importance in the history of Cairo. Jawhar's ramparts had consisted of nothing more than a very inadequate earthen wall that quickly disappeared. It was probably the establishment of the Seljuks in Syria that prompted the vizir's decision to install a wall of real military value around the capital. The new enclosure wall, as we have noted, was built outside Jawhar's original one, which explains why there are quarters to the east and west known as Between the Two Walls (Bayn al-Surayn), but the enclosed area was enlarged mainly to the north and south. Portions of this wall with its square or rectangular salients have survived in the northeast quadrant, its monumental stone gates in particular. The Bab al-Futuh (built in 1087) and Bab al-Nasr (1087) on the north wall, and the Bab Zuwayla (1092) on the south wall offer re-

Bab al-Futuh (Gate of Conquests), 1087
(*Description de l'Egypte*, Bibliothèque Nationale)

markable examples of Middle Eastern military art. They were the work of Armenian architects brought in from Edessa, in eastern Turkey, which explains their Byzantine-Syrian style. The two northern gates have offset entries, and all are protected by flanking towers, square ones in the case of Bab al-Nasr, rounded in the others. In terms of their size (8 meters in height), strength, and severity of decoration, they are among the grandest of Cairo's monuments and lasting models for Muslim architects.[32]

The Fatimids constructed their great religious edifices inside the royal city—the only exceptions being the mausoleums (*mashahid*) built to the south of Qahira particularly and the Mosque of al-Juyushi on top of the Muqattam Hills. The Fatimid predilection for this kind of building, dedicated to a member of the family of the Prophet or Ali, obviously reflects a political intent (to bolster the dynasty's prestige) or a religious one (to popularize Shiite concepts). The most remarkable products of Fatimid architecture and decoration, the palaces, are known to us only from descriptions and fragmentary elements. It is therefore from the few surviving mosques that we can understand the originality of Fatimid art and its persistent influence.

The art that developed in Egypt under the Fatimids was truly a national art. Originally from North Africa but linked by their religion to Persia, the Fatimids encouraged an art that brought together highly diverse influences and was characteristic for its freedom and its realism in representing animate beings.[33] The Fatimid mosques retained the hypostyle plan, with arcades supported on columns around a courtyard. The facades were aligned with the street, a trait that would persist in Cairene architecture, and were highly ornamented (as in the Mosques of Aqmar and Tala'i). The prayer niche was enhanced architecturally, either by a dome, a transept, or a widening of the aisle. The minarets took the *mabkhara,* or incense-burner, form, with an octagonal section supporting a ribbed helmet that would remain characteristic of Cairo's minarets for the next two centuries. The Fatimid period introduced such decorative elements as the keel-arched niche with a fluked radiating hood, a reworking of a theme widely used in Coptic art.

Except for the Mosque of al-Azhar, built on the edge of the city center next to the Great Palace, the main mosques in Qahira were built along the major axis of the Qasaba. The first two, al-Azhar (970) and al-Hakim (990–1003), which are also the largest, seem strongly influenced by the Mosque of Ibn Tulun: a central courtyard, surrounded by porticoes, with aisles parallel to the wall of the *qibla.* But there is also a marked resemblance to the mosque of Mahdiyya, with a stressing of the axis of the *mihrab* (domes and central transept) and, in the case of the Mosque of al-Hakim, a projecting entry.

The Mosque of al-Azhar, which has been thoroughly expanded and rebuilt (the last time at the end of the eighteenth century by Abd al-Rahman Katkhuda), formed a rectangle measuring 88 by 70 meters, with a large central court surrounded by three arcades (keel arches supported on pre-Islamic columns) and a sanctuary 85 by 25 meters with five aisles. The original minaret has disappeared. Most of the additions to the facade and the minarets date to the Mamluk period. The decorative elements reflect the influence of the Mosque of Ibn Tulun but derive from different periods of Fatimid art, as work continued on the mosque until the reign of Hafiz (1129–1149). The decoration includes stucco work with realistic designs (palm tree).

The Mosque of al-Hakim, situated outside Mu'izz's north gates, was begun under the caliph Aziz in 990 and completed in 1003. This enormous monument (123 by 115 meters) has features of the Mosques of Ibn Tulun (pointed arches resting on rectangular brick piers) and al-Azhar, but the facade, with its monumental portal and projecting minaret bases, shows the influence of the mosque in Mahdiyya. The two minarets on the facade are very original in shape and decoration: in 1010, for reasons unknown, the caliph Hakim decided to hide them partially in a kind of pyramidal stone casing. The tops that emerge from the stone casing were restored during the Mamluk period. The courtyard is lined on four sides by porticoes. The sanctuary, like those of Ibn Tulun and al-Azhar, has five aisles.

Built much later, the Mosques of Aqmar (1125) and Salih Tala'i (1160) are on a more modest scale, being the work of two viziers, Ma'mun al-Bata'ihi (Caliph Amir) and Tala'i ibn Ruzzik (Caliphs Fa'iz and Adid). The inside dimensions of the Mosque of Aqmar are 28 by 18 meters. Yet the architecture and decoration of these two structures are not without innovation. The facade of the Mosque of Aqmar, just north of the two palaces, is aligned with the street although the building itself is oriented toward Mecca—a formula that would often be repeated. The facade is heavily ornamented, and its elements—the keel arch, radiating shell motif, and stalactites (the first to appear on a Cairene facade)—would have a strong influence in Cairo. The Mosque of Salih Tala'i, south of Bab Zuwayla just on the way out of Qahira, was intended as a sanctuary for the head of Husayn (which would ultimately be housed in a shrine inside the city on the site of today's Husayni Mosque). It, too, is a strikingly original monument: the facade incorporates a columned portico, unique among Cairo's monuments, and arched recesses with grilled windows that would be used in most later mosques in Cairo.

Both mosques were "suspended," or built above a row of street-level shops. Because of the subsequent rising of the street level, the shops are now more than 2 meters below it. One of the characteristics of Cairene architecture of the twelfth century is the plethora of influences at work: Byzantine (and, in its provincial form, Coptic) in the decorative elements (shell pattern in the niches, capitals); Syrian (stone construction of the minarets and gates); Persian (arches, cupolas); Mesopotamian (recesses in the walls); North African (architectural elements). Drawing on so many traditions, Fatimid art began to offer a synthesis and an art that was truly Egyptian. The role played by Christian architects (the gates in Badr al-Jamali's wall are attributed to three Armenian brothers from Edessa who were probably Christian) is another example of the relative ecumenism of the Fatimids.

### FUSTAT AT ITS ZENITH

The two centuries of Fatimid rule following 969 saw Fustat reach its zenith. From the rich and varied documentation for this period (Geniza documents, archaeological excavations), we are able to measure the flowering that occurred in many areas of its economic, social, and domestic life. It is obviously paradoxical that the founding of Qahira should have encouraged the rise of its sister city, when it might as easily have competed with it and hampered its development—a trend that emerged only at the end of the caliphate. The vast potential for development resulting from the installation in Cairo of a powerful and autonomous state allowed both the gradual expansion of Qahira, which had been founded as a political center and as the seat of the ruling class, and which consumed important quantities of goods (luxury goods in particular), and the continued development of the market city, Fustat, which would provide for these needs by mobilizing the resources of a vast and prosperous empire and the capacities of a commercial market that extended well beyond the Mediterranean world.

We have noted the strong impression that Fustat made on the traveler Nasir-i Khusraw. Writing around 1050, he echoed and amplified the admiring comments made around 985 by Muqaddasi. Fustat was the main center of a nexus of trade extending the length and breadth of the Mediterranean and beyond—Fustat and not Alexandria, which was entirely dependent on the former in economic matters. When a load of cargo was shipped overseas, the customs duties had first to be paid in Fustat. To buy Mediterranean products imported through Alexandria, one had to go to Fustat. Besides, the ships that traveled between the ports of the Mediterranean could unload their cargoes in Fustat: "The ships that left Syrian ports in early spring often sailed from Tyre to Damietta, then took the eastern branch of the Nile to Fustat, afterwards descending the western branch to Rosetta and continuing their voyage on the Mediterranean to Alexandria, Tripoli, and Mahdiyya . . . In a letter written in September of around 1050, we read that a *harbi* ship, or warship, reached Alexandria with merchandise from Sicily and was traveling from Alexandria to Fustat." Hence the importance of the port of Fustat as a Mediterranean center: "The mobility of the people of that time was astonishing," writes S. D. Goitein. "The Geniza documents contain references to artisans who had come from Spain, Morocco, Byzantium, Palestine, Lebanon, Iraq, Iran, and even Tbilisi."

The products traded in Fustat form an impressive list: Nahray ben Nissim, a merchant from Qayrawan who is known to have been active in Egypt from 1045 to 1096, traded in at least 120 different articles. Egypt exported linen to Sicily and Tunisia, and received silk from Spain and Sicily, cloth from Tunisia, Iran, Sicily, and Greece; leather and hides came from Tunisia and Sicily. Goods from Asia also passed through Egypt: oriental spices, gums, perfumes, and aromatics, as well as products used in dyeing, tanning, and varnishing, and precious metals and stones. Metals were also traded, as were chemical and pharmaceutical products, comestibles, and agricultural products (olive oil, soap, wax, and sugar). That all these goods were traded helps us understand the migratory nature of many industries: the valuable cloth known as *susi* was undoubtedly connected to Susa, but a document from 1098 mentions a *susi rusi* made in Russia and sent to India. *Tabari* tapestry originally came from Tabaristan on the Caspian Sea, but it was also made in the Palestinian town of Ramleh. A felt known as *talaqan* after a town in northern Iran was exported from the Libyan town of Tripoli.[34]

This trade naturally encouraged the development of an artisan class, whose products swelled the flow of goods and helped satisfy local needs, particularly in Qahira, where demand for consumer products was high. Not surprisingly, the number of occupations was large, with extensive division of labor and high specialization. Some of the trades have fallen by the way: the "sawdusters" who collected and sold the sawdust used to dry ink on a freshly written page, or the makers of the small sticks (often of crystal, gold, or silver) used to apply kohl to one's eyes. But certain commercial activities reached an almost industrial scale. Such was the case with the manufacture of linen cloth, paper (the North African traveler Abu Sa'id tells us that the paper factories were located in Fustat), and especially sugar, which was manufactured in refineries, some of which were worth around 1,000 dinars. Nasir-i Khusraw describes faience "so fine and so diaphanous that one can look through the walls of a vase and see one's hand on the outside" and glass that was "transparent and of great purity." And Abd al-Latif affirms that in twelfth-century Fustat there were 900 looms for weaving mats. The profusion of commercial activity is evident in the many place-names relating to trades reported by Ibn Duqmaq and Maqrizi, though writing as they do some two and a half centuries after the end of the Fatimid period their information is often difficult to date.[35]

Estimating the area and population of Fustat under the Fatimids is no easy task. The few figures that we have from contemporary historians are unreliable: neither the 36,000 mosques and 1,170 baths reported by al-Quda'i, nor the more "modest" estimate by Ibn al-Mutawwaj ("only" 480 mosques) can be credited. Marcel Clerget's estimate (an eleventh-century population of 300,000 for both cities, with half in Fustat) is based on evidence that is not much solider. Thierry Bianquis's estimate (a population of 175,000 in Fustat and of 75,000 in Cairo around 1055) is based on grain consumption and takes better account of contemporary reports of Fustat's superiority. Any attempt to trace the boundaries of the city faces the problem of determining the exact extent of the Nile's gradual withdrawal to the west.[36] The city of Fustat must have had a surface area of approximately 300 hectares and a population of about 120,000. These figures assume their true meaning when we compare them to known values for other cities at that time: the walls built around Florence in 1172–1175 and completed on the left bank in 1250 enclosed an area of 97 hectares; in Bologna, the ramparts *dei torresotti* encompassed 120 hectares; in two years from 1158 to 1160 Genoa built a wall 2,500 meters long, increasing its area from 20 to 52 hectares. The population of Venice was probably less than 100,000 at the end of the twelfth century. Damascus covered an area of only 120 hectares at the time of the Crusades. The population of Córdoba around the year 1000 is estimated at 90,000, Seville's at 52,000 (over an area of 118 hectares). Fustat was certainly one of the largest cities in the Mediterranean basin at that time.[37]

Fustat's importance was due not only to its own commercial activity as a port trading throughout the Mediterranean world and as an active center of artisan manufacture but also to its linkage to the existence of Qahira, whose population it fed and supplied with everyday consumer products as well as objects destined for the ruling class (weapons, luxury goods). Consequently, Fustat's population ranged widely in socioeconomic terms. We know a fair amount about the merchants who dominated commercial activity in the city, the administrative personnel who worked in Qahira and lived in Fustat, and the minority populations. But a segment of the population in this industrious port was more modest and quite certainly rather mixed, as could only be expected in a large Mediterranean port. This explains the sometimes qualified appreciation travelers gave to Fustat. Muqaddasi for one did not hesitate to pass severe judgment on it: "The most respected men have no scruples about drinking wine, nor the women about fornicating: the women take two husbands, the men drink to inebriation . . . The native population is dark in color, their language horrible."[38]

Without accurate geographic landmarks, it is very difficult to give a detailed account of the city's structure. According to S. D. Goitein, a loose division of the city into zones of commercial, manufacturing, and residential use was occurring, though not according to any rigid plan. Commercial activity was most likely concentrated in the western part of the city along the port, on the low ground recently uncovered by the retreating Nile. The caravanserais, markets, and streets bearing the names of trades (at least those whose locations have so far been established) have indeed been situated in this zone, and we may suppose that this late configuration (Mamluk period) was prefigured in the Fatimid city. The residential districts were situated in higher regions to the east, where the excavations conducted by Bahgat and Scanlon have uncovered residential dwellings.[39]

The heart of Fustat was naturally the port, which, as we have seen, could be reached directly by maritime vessels, a fact explained by the small size of the ships used. S. D. Goitein has noted that the word for "sea" in Arabic and medieval Hebrew is *bahr*, a word also applied to the Nile, and that to convey the idea that a ship sailed beyond the Nile and into the Mediterranean, they would say "it has gone out into the salt sea." The port was actually nothing more than a crude wharf where boats could be tied up for passengers and goods to be offloaded. It also had facilities for building and refitting ships, however, and there were warehouses for storing goods. Payment of the various duties could be made at the arsenal (sina'a). A bridge of boats joined Fustat to the island and crossed the Nile to Giza on the western bank.

The city's economic activity was centered within a triangle formed by Bab al-Qantara to the south, Bab al-Safa to the north, and Bab Misr to the west. The centers of commerce and artisan manufacture, the markets (suqs or *suwaqqat*) and caravanserais (*qayasir* or *funadiq*), were situated in the main streets running parallel to the Nile. Travelers have often described the bustle and crowds there: "I saw a caravanserai in Misr called Dar al-Vezir where all the merchants of gold thread [*qasab*] were gathered," writes Nasir-i Khusraw. "On the ground floor were the tailors, while the menders were on the upper floor." The establishment had an annual income of 20,000 Maghribi dinars, although the renovations then under way reduced it to 12,000 dinars. "I was assured that there were two hundred caravanserais in the city" every bit as large. The al-Mahalli caravanserai was large enough to hold a mosque. Merchants lived and pursued business in these caravanserais alongside other, less reputable residents: women of doubtful virtue. One Muslim author would define a prostitute as "a woman who lives in a *funduq*."

For each trade, each product, to have its own area within the city seems to have been the general rule. In the Geniza documents as well as in the writings of travelers and historians, there are many mentions of markets, streets, and squares named after a group of artisans or shopkeepers—tailors, perfumers, tinsmiths. Of course, the practice was not universal or invariable. S. D. Goitein mentions, for instance, a grocer located at the Turners' Gate (1104) and a glassworks on Tinsmiths' Street (1125). One of the important centers in Fustat must have been the Exchange (Dar al-Sarf), mentioned in the Geniza documents of the eleventh and twelfth centuries, where (Jewish) bankers and moneychangers had their stalls. The markets were generally closed at night; contrarily, the caliph Hakim one day gave the order for markets to be kept open and remain lit all night.[40]

One of the most unusual characteristics of Fustat, and the one that invariably excited comment from travelers and historians, was its tall communal dwellings. This type of housing was found mostly in the central parts of the city and was traditional in Fustat, mention being made of it in the very earliest accounts. In Fustat, writes Ibn Hawqal around 950, "the houses have five, six, or even seven stories, and as many as 200 people may live in a building." This description is confirmed by Muqaddasi: "The houses, which have four or five floors, are like lighthouses, with light entering through the center, and each holding about 200 souls." Nasir-i Khusraw writes more lyrically still:

Looking at the town of Misr from a distance, one has the impression of a mountain. There are houses fourteen stories high, while others are limited to seven. A person I believe trustworthy has told me that a certain man laid out a garden on the terrace of a seven-story house . . . He installed a water wheel, powered by an ox, which raised water to the terrace where he had planted orange . . . banana, and other fruit trees . . . each [of these houses] can hold 350 people.[41]

Much has been written on the origins of these apartment dwellings. Their precursors include the tower houses of pharaonic Egypt, the multistory houses of Yemen, and even a local analogue, the buildings of Rosetta, but they are closest in concept to the Roman *insula*. They are multifamily dwellings, apparently intended for middle- and lower-class residents, not luxury buildings for one or several families as in Rosetta and Yemen. No remnants of Fustat's tall buildings have been discovered, presumably because their height predicated a relatively light construction, and because they were located in the most economically active section of town, the central district, which has totally disappeared today. The house found by Jamal Mehrez in 1964 seems to be a single-family house with an upper story. Given their characteristics, the tower houses of Fustat appear to be prototypes for the communal dwellings with rental apartments that would become common in Cairo during the Mamluk and Ottoman periods.[42]

The town of Fustat was governed by a *wali* (governor) who was effectively chief of police. A *muhtasib* supervised the activities of shopkeepers and artisans and saw to the observance of religious law. Some public services were provided. Trash was carted away for a fee that varied according to the size of the building and the frequency of collection. In the Geniza documents, a memorandum from the Jewish community discusses "the removal of dust from above the door of the Synagogue of the Palestinians, the building itself, and the square across from the synagogue." The digging, clearing, and maintenance of underground channels was also subject to official supervision. The costs of these clay channels for the removal of waste water and other trash toward the Nile are frequently mentioned in the documents of charitable institutions in the Jewish community. Excavations of houses in Fustat, particularly those uncovered by Scanlon, do in fact confirm that a complex and highly developed sewer system was in place. And finally, the upkeep costs of the streets themselves were borne by the streets' residents. Here again, the accounts of the Jewish community allow us to see how the system functioned: "For repairs to the road leading to the synagogue, four dirhems; for Sulayman, one dirhem for repairs to the road leading to al-Azraq House . . . For the mason, for work on the road of the Building of the Jerusalemites, three dirhems and a half." In these cases, the reference is clearly to compensation to various individuals whose work was perhaps conducted under the supervision of city authorities.[43]

The residential quarters no doubt extended outward from the central, public areas of the city. It is in the peripheral sector that Fustat has been excavated and houses found. The residential zones appear to have contained more or less closed neighborhoods or quarters. The Geniza documents mention neighborhood supervisors (*sahib al-rub* and *hami al-hara*), officials who apparently exercised authority over the quarter and saw to its security, particularly at night. The sentinels who walked the nightly rounds were paid for by a monthly tax (the guard duty, or *hirasa*), which figures in the accounts of the Jewish community. The *sahib al-rub* also directed communal activities: it was he who assembled the people of his quarter to greet the sovereign on his triumphal entry into the city. We also know of "porter-guards" who opened and closed the alleys through which one entered quarters, some of which had gates or posterns. Traces of a gate have been found in a street excavated by Bahgat and Gabriel. But there is nothing to prove that the quarters were generally closed. Nor do we know whether housing was segregated according to socioeconomic level. According to S. D. Goitein, people of different levels

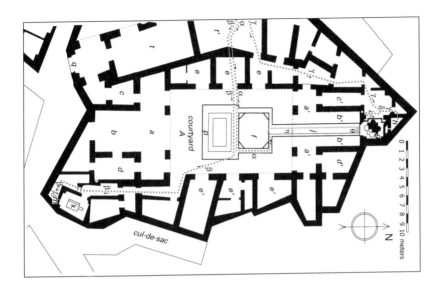

House in Fustat (after A. Bahgat and A. Gabriel)

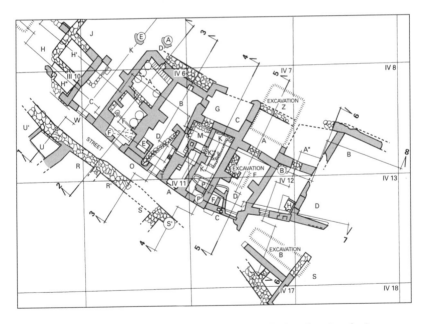

Dwellings of the poor in Fustat (after W. Kubiak and G. Scanlon)

of wealth lived side by side, but there were also concentrations of well-to-do houses—Bahgat's excavations have uncovered an entire set of them.[44]

At odds with a long-held belief, the houses of Fustat were as varied as the society that resided there. Fine houses from the eleventh century have been brought to light southeast of Fustat's central district by Bahgat and Gabriel and by Scanlon and Kubiak. All these houses were organized around a square or rectangular central court *(sahn)*, often featuring a pool of water. A group of three rooms opened onto it through a two-columned portico: a main room (called a *majlis* in the texts) flanked by two smaller rooms, that together with the portico formed a T-shaped floor plan. There was also often at least one room (iwan) on the opposite side of the courtyard. Texts confirm that there were rooms on the second floor (for instance, loggias anticipating the *maq'ad*). The quality of the decoration, often highly refined, and the presence of further amenities (additional iwans, a corridor around the rooms, air vents, kitchens, cool storerooms, a privy, a bath, a water distribution and waste-water removal system) varied according to the size of the house. Although these dwellings may reflect a Hellenistic or Roman source, it is well to remember the likely influence of Iraq, and of Samarra in particular.[45]

It would be wrong to consider these houses, which are at the very least "middle-class" and in some cases luxury dwellings, representative of the housing stock in Fustat generally. An excavation by Kubiak and Scanlon to the east of the area studied by Bahgat has proved that there were also houses for the truly poor. This finding confirms the rather vague information we have on this point, such as the mention of mud shacks in a description of Egypt from 1191 by Abd al-Latif. An area apparently abandoned in 1050, a century before the construction of Saladin's wall, has yielded six poorly constructed houses with an average footprint of 35 square meters that seem to date from the tenth to the eleventh century. Abutting directly on a narrow street only 2 meters wide and consisting of two or three communicating rooms with earthen floors, they have no courtyard and only the barest amenities (a primitive latrine and drain for waste water). The room farthest from the street was in some cases probably used as a stable. Some of these houses had a second floor. Most likely they were roofed with thatch. From the many lime kilns discovered in the area, Scanlon has proposed that this was a sector where mean and polluting activities took place, and was therefore allowed to be settled by an indigent class. The rustic character of these houses suggests that they were deeply rooted in local tradition. The pharaonic town of Deir al-Medineh, which housed the workers of the Theban necropolis, consisted of "working-class" houses with two or three rooms in a straight line, a second floor or a terrace, and measured 40 square meters in area, strongly resembles this underclass housing in Fustat.[46]

Fustat contained a large Christian community and a somewhat smaller Jewish one. We have already mentioned the generally tolerant attitude of the Fatimids toward non-Muslims (*dhimmi*), most notably seen in the relative autonomy they were granted in the running of their daily business. As we saw earlier, Jews were allowed to conduct business well beyond the boundaries of Egypt. Although the *dhimmi* experienced difficult times, particularly under the caliph Hakim—but he subjected his Muslim subjects to no less harassment—they were in general well treated. Certain discriminatory practices traditionally applied to them were probably not imposed continuously. Thus S. D. Goitein believes that the strictures on clothing (the wearing of certain colors—yellow—and the avoidance of others—white) were not strictly followed in Fustat: a Jewish physician whose possessions were itemized in a document dated 1172 owned a white turban, a large white shawl, a white coat, and a white scarf. It is not certain either that Jews and Christians were segregated in Fustat. Although the Geniza documents mention quarters in which the majority of the inhabitants were Jews and which were sometimes even called "Jewish quarter," there was no ghetto as such and the members of various ethnic and religious communities had ties through their neighborhoods that were seemingly more fluid than would be the case in later periods. The Muslims had no wish for daily contact with the *dhimmi*, whose religious practices would have disturbed them despite the ban against public worship. But for a number of reasons the minorities themselves had little inclination to mix with the Muslims. To forestall the disagreeable prospect of cohabitation, Jewish authorities from time to time issued rules against the sale or rental of a house to Muslims. In short, as Goitein observes, "the Christians and Jews [at this period] occupied a position that was both protected and precarious. Islamic law protected their life, property, and freedom, and gave them the right to exercise their religion with only a few restrictions. On the other hand, it imposed segregation and subjection on them, which under a weak government could and indeed did lead to situations that ended in civil disorder or outright persecution."[47]

After the ninth century, when social restrictions, fiscal pressure, and discriminatory practices had probably brought about a wave of conversions, Christians were doubtless no longer a majority in Egypt, but there were still many in Fustat in the districts where Christians had traditionally lived around the fortress of Qasr al-Sham and in the Hamra suburb. Fatimid toleration certainly benefited the Christian community—in 1086 a council was convoked in Fustat that drew the participation of forty-seven bishops. But Arabic made slow but steady progress and became the language of the clergy. In fact Gabriel ibn Turaik, the seventieth patriarch (1132–1146), copied books in Coptic and Arabic and "understood their contents."[48]

The Jewish traveler Benjamin of Tudela, who visited Egypt in 1170, estimated that there were then 7,000 Jews in "Mizraim." They were divided into two sects, each with its own synagogue: the Syrians (Shamiyyin) and the Iraqis. While not all the Jews of Fustat achieved the power of the Ibn Awkal family, whose archives extend over a long period (980–1076), it is reasonable to suppose that the community was on the whole prosperous. "The Jews who live there are very rich," says Benjamin. The community was governed by a ra'is al-Yahud, who became known as the najid (the title would appear in Egypt around 1065), and owned sufficient property to finance charitable foundations and aid the needy. Despite the discrimination they were subjected to and the ever-present threat of a return to less liberal policies, the Jews of Fustat unquestionably experienced their most prosperous period in Egypt under the Fatimids.[49]

### THE VICISSITUDES OF FATIMID HISTORY

The vicissitudes of the Fatimid period affected the development of the two capitals. Although a measure of caution is necessary in assigning causes and effects—attributing important urban changes to specific historical occurrences can lead at times to dangerous oversimplification—several events require mention.

What is known as the Mustansir Crisis, which occurred during the long reign of that caliph (in fact the longest in the Muslim history of Egypt: fifty-eight years, from 1036 to 1094) resulted from a combination of factors. The weakening of the dynasty, following the incoherent reign of Hakim and the insignificant one of Zahir, was exacerbated by the long regency necessitated by Mustansir's extreme youth (age seven) at his accession. That Egypt was going through troubled times can be seen in the rapid succession of viziers: five between October 1060 and October 1062, and twenty-two between 1062 and 1066. There were also grave domestic disorders in the form of armed struggles between black and Turkish troops. A period of economic disaster compounded these difficulties: a severe famine started in 1065 and prices rose exorbitantly. The hyperbolic figures reported by chroniclers are to some extent confirmed by the Geniza documents. The wife of Judah b. Moses ibn Sighmar wrote to him in 1069: "We face anarchy and hunger, with a tillis [of wheat] costing 25 dinars," or twenty-five times the normal price, while the chronicles report a hundredfold increase in the price (100 dinars). The crisis seems to have reached its peak in 1070. Gaston Wiet records: "People ate all their beasts of burden, and the caliph had only three horses left. Next they set on their dogs and cats. Finally . . . people began to eat human flesh . . . Men stood on their terraces and caught passersby using hooks on the end of ropes."

These economic and political cataclysms had devastating consequences. The Geniza documents mention that Jews emigrated, and the fact that no documents relating to religious foundations can be found for the years 1060–1090 is another likely index of the social disruption. The cities felt a measurable impact, confirmed by many signs. In their excavations of Area C in Fustat, Kubiak and Scanlon have observed that dwellings inhabited by the poor, in Fustat's eastern zone, were abandoned. At Istabl Antar, another marginal area, the destruction of the Fatimid necropolis can be read, according to R. Gayraud, as pointing to the unraveling of the caliphate and the decline of the city. The large area of ruins *(kharab)* on the east and southeast sides of Fustat probably developed at this time. It appears to extend from Kawm Ghurab and Kawm al-Jarih to the wall that Saladin would build and, toward the north, almost to Jabal Yashkur, which is to say a large part of the *amal fawq*. Maqrizi also describes the ruin of the al-Askar and al-Qata'i areas around the Mosque of Ibn Tulun, which were abandoned for more than a century.[50]

The spectacular recovery that began after Badr al-Jamali took control of Egypt's affairs in 1073 may have contributed to a permanent weakening of Fustat. The minister in point of fact devoted all his efforts to Qahira, building a massive encircling wall, as already noted. To accelerate the country's return to order, Badr al-Jamali authorized anyone wanting to build in Qahira to use materials from the abandoned sections of Fustat. According to Maqrizi, it was the first time that "the people" *(al-nas)* had been authorized to settle in the caliphal city. The areas between Qahira and Fustat were abandoned and converted into parks and gardens. But the Mustansir Crisis and its aftershocks in fact only accelerated a process that was already under way: the transformation of Qahira into a "normal" city and the shrinkage of Fustat from east to west. The easternmost areas of Fustat were beginning to be abandoned before the 1060s; the vizir al-Yazuri (1050–1058), noting the deterioration of these neighborhoods, built a wall to hide the ruined buildings from the caliph's sight on those occasions when the ruler ventured into Fustat. This development, perhaps related to a westward shift onto the land left uncovered by the Nile, therefore has every appearance of a natural phenomenon.

As to Qahira, its growth was apparent from the very beginning of the century if not before. The Mustansir Crisis dramatically accelerated what would otherwise have been a gradual trend. And historical sources, whose excess in deploring the irreparable damage due to great catastrophes is matched only by their fervor in celebrating the splendid new prosperity, all take note of a renaissance in the affected areas. In the same breath, Maqrizi describes the successive stages of a perhaps less strongly marked development, in the area south of Qahira after the reign of al-Hakim (996–1021).

> Houses multiplied without a break from the New Gate to an open space . . . outside the mausoleum of Nafisa . . . After the great famine of . . . Mustansir when the cities of Qata'i and Askar were abandoned, their sites remained in ruins until the accession of al-Amir [1101]. The people hastened to build there until no area of ruins re-

mained between Old Cairo and Cairo . . . Houses sprang up without a break from the New Gate to Bab al-Safa in Old Cairo, etc.[51]

The restoration of the Fatimid state under Badr and his successors proved only temporary, as disastrous external developments threatened its very foundations. Syria was lost for good in 1076, severely truncating Egypt's base of resources (the tax revenues from Syria totaled between 1.5 and 2.6 million dinars) and leaving its eastern flank exposed, a circumstance whose dramatic effects would be felt after the Crusaders took Palestine (1098–99). With their poor understanding of the new era announced by these changes and their poor national government, which was left in the hands of incompetent viziers who styled themselves *malik,* or prince, the Fatimids slid into decline. The downward trend slowed only briefly under the viziers Bahram, an Armenian Christian (1135–1137); and Tala'i ibn Ruzzik, "al-Malik al-Salih" (1154–1161). A single issue was henceforth to govern the fate of the dynasty: its relations with the Franks in Palestine and their main adversary, the great Muslim ruler Nur al-Din, who captured Damascus in 1154 and began to cast his eyes on Egypt in 1150. The viziers of the last Fatimid caliph, al-Adid (1160–1171), would invite one after the other of these two mortal enemies into Egypt, forming contradictory alliances with them until the country fell under their combined weight.

The vizir Shawar, ousted from power in 1163, sought help from Nur al-Din, promising him a third of Egypt's revenues in return. Nur al-Din sent an army commanded by his Kurdish lieutenant Shirkuh, the uncle of Salah al-Din ibn Ayyub, whom we know as Saladin. Once reinstated (August 1164), Shawar sought a way to avoid fulfilling his promises and asked Amalric I, king of Jerusalem, for help in fighting the Syrians (at the price of 1,000 dinars a day). Amalric, who had already campaigned in Egypt twice (1161 and 1162), accepted. Shirkuh drew back, and the Franks followed suit (1164). In 1167, at the request of the caliph al-Adid, Shirkuh returned to Egypt with his nephew. Shawar again obtained the support of the Franks, this time in exchange for 400,000 dinars, and the treaty was concluded by the caliph in person and Hugh of Caesarea. An account of this embassy by William of Tyre includes wonderful descriptions of the splendor of the Fatimid palace. After an inconclusive battle at Babayn in March 1167, Shirkuh retired to Alexandria, blocked by the Franks and Egyptians. In the wake of negotiations, both Shirkuh and Amalric quitted Egypt.

Yet the Franks established a protectorate in Cairo. They obtained the promise of an annual tribute of 100,000 dinars and, to ensure its payment, installed a high commissioner in the capital, with cavalry detachments to guard the gates and protect the royal functionaries who collected the tribute. A "Treasury of Debt" was thus established in a palace at the center of Cairo on the Bayn al-Qasrayn. Located near the caliph's palace, it would later become the residence of the emir Baysari (H 6). "The day Christian forces entered this large Muslim city was a glorious day," writes G. Schlumberger. "The entire length of the ramparts, all the towers and gates . . . the caliph's residence itself were ceded to the Christian knights who all . . . had free access to the sovereign at any time," to the great scandal of the faithful and the jubilation of the Frankish knights. "The riches and delights and other great secrets that had until this time remained under lock and key and hidden from view were much sought out and examined by our Christians and even by Turks, who saw things that astonished them."[52]

The situation was untenable for any length of time. Amalric, breaking his agreements with Shirkuh and the Egyptians, decided to conquer Egypt once and for all and launched a war "that would confer on him," wrote William of Tyre, "but little glory." Amalric's fourth invasion, which was to topple the Fatimids and bring Saladin to power, held disastrous consequences for Fustat. On 5 November 1168, Amalric seized Bilbays, and his troops treated the residents horrifically. "Our men entered the city with swords drawn and started to massacre all whom they found, men and women, old and young, sparing no one . . . When they found maidens or old people hidden in rooms, they ran them through with their swords, sparing only those who might provide a substantial ransom. The destruction was horrible, and the pillage no less so." Amalric sent an insulting message to Shawar, whose son he had captured: "Your son Tari wonders whether I thought Bilbais a piece of cheese that I might eat. Yes, in truth, Bilbais is my cheese, and Cairo is my butter."

The Franks' behavior was not only inhumane but also politically ill advised. When they learned of the capture of Bilbays and Amalric's further preparations, Shawar and the caliph decided to appeal to Nur al-Din. They knew they could expect no quarter from the Franks and readied themselves for a desperate defense. The Frankish troops arrived before Cairo on 13 November. According to Arab historical tradition, Shawar, unable to defend the unwalled city of Fustat, ordered its population to be evacuated. The residents responded with alacrity, having heard the terrible fate of the people of Bilbays. Then Shawar ordered Fustat to be torched so that it could not serve as a base of operations for the Franks in their attack on Qahira.

Arab historians, and Maqrizi in particular, have given detailed and highly colored accounts of this patriotic incident, which has overtones of Rostopchin's order to burn Moscow at Napoleon's approach in 1812. Shawar is said to have had 20,000 jars of naphtha and 10,000 torches set in Fustat. The conflagration lasted for fifty-four days, and looters ran riot. From that time on, writes Maqrizi, Fustat "became the ruin known today as the *kiman* [little mounds]." While Fustat burned, Amalric laid siege to Qahira from the east (the Barqiyya Gate). Both sides entered into negotiations to gain time. When the announcement came that Shirkuh and Saladin were approaching with the Syrian army, the situation resolved itself: on 2 January 1169, Amalric ordered the retreat. The Syrian troops reached the walls of Cairo six days later, after allowing the Franks to evacuate unopposed. On 18 January Shawar was drawn into an ambush by Saladin and killed. Shirkuh became vizir. When Shirkuh died unexpectedly on 23 March, Saladin assumed the vizirate himself.[53]

The putative destruction of Fustat in late 1168 poses a serious problem for the historian. That the fire took place is not in doubt, but its causes, size, probable course, and consequences are veiled in obscurity. Dates for its start range from 12 November (Schlumberger, Ehrenkreutz) to 2 December (Maqrizi), putting its end sometime between 4 and 24 January. There is also the question of how a fire that completely destroyed Fustat could have left no discernible traces in the archaeological record; the areas of rubble *(kharab)* can date no later than the Mustansir period (1036–1094), a century earlier. It is also surprising that this voluntary and systematic burning should have spared the Mosque of Amr and Qasr al-Sham entirely, lying as they do at the heart of Fustat, and that the Geniza documents contain no mention of Fustat's destruction. A single document (dated 1174) mentions a house destroyed by fire, but the documents relating to Jewish religious foundations show no lessening of activity after 1168, the community's assets are handled in a normal way, and account books show no unusual expenditure for repairs and rebuilding. Benjamin of Tudela, who visited Fustat in 1170, notes its ruin but describes the Jewish community's situation favorably: "The Jews who live there are very rich." William of Tyre recounts Amalric's Egyptian campaign in detail yet makes no mention of the Fustat fire, though the event should have captured his attention if only for the sizable Christian population that lived there. None of the other contemporary writers reports a systematic destruction of Fustat. The Armenian traveler Abu Salih, visiting Cairo in 1173, speaks on several occasions of the Fustat fire and of the damage done to several churches by fire and looting, but not in terms of a devastating cataclysm. Ibn Jubayr, who traveled to Fustat in 1182, took lodgings in a *funduq* on the Lane of the Lamps, in the very center of the city, near the Mosque of Amr. He records the damage to the city: "The town of Misr preserves traces of the ruin brought upon it by the fire . . . of 564 [1169]." But the damage was limited and had at any rate been repaired: "Buildings now adjoin each other without intermission. It is a large city." Admittedly, we know that Shirkuh took immediate steps to repair the damage done to Fustat, but it is difficult to imagine that the city could have been so completely restored had its destruction been total. Finally, we should note that when Saladin decided in 1172 to build a wall to protect Cairo, he included all of Fustat in it as well, which would make little sense if the city had been laid in ruins and deserted by its inhabitants.

The damage done to Fustat in 1168 was therefore probably limited, a likelihood that eliminates the possibility of a systematic fire, set for reasons of strategy. On this point, the Christian Abu Salih gives telling evidence. After recounting incidents that took place in March–April 1164, when Syrian troops and inhabitants of Cairo burned some churches in Fustat, the author describes the looting and burning of churches in *safar* 564 (4 November–2 December 1168). He explains that the embellishments made to a church had provoked the hostility of the Muslims: "And so, a great number gathered and gave free rein to their fury, setting fire to the Church of

Saint Mercury (Abu Sayfayn) at Hamra al-Duniya, with the result that only its walls were left and a small interior chapel, which was not burned." The burning of Fustat may then have been of limited extent and caused by anti-Christian riots, brought on by the approach of the Franks, which heightened tensions between diverse groups and fanned hostility against local Christians.

This version of the events of 1168 is confirmed by Ibn Jubayr, who speaks of the destruction caused by the fire of 564/1168 "during the troubles." Neither account mentions the Frankish invasion or a deliberate burning of Fustat by Shawar. Ibn Jubayr also mentions the speed with which the damage of 1168 was repaired: "The greater part [of Fustat] has now been rebuilt." The traditional version of the story, handed down by Maqrizi, should therefore be understood as a subsequent reconstruction of the event, upgrading the fallout from an interethnic dispute (admittedly made sharper by the approach of the Franks) into a deliberate decision, "a patriotic sacrifice as pitiless as it was necessary."[54]

### THE TWO CITIES

The end of the Fatimid period, marked by the deposition and death of the caliph Adid in 1171, heralded the great changes of the Ayyubid period. On the one hand, Qahira was in the process of becoming a city and no longer simply the seat of government and the residence of the caliph, his court, and his troops. We get some sense of this change in the writings of the traveler Ibn Jubayr, who admiringly describes Qahira's "four congregational mosques" and its "great many" ordinary mosques, whereas Misr could boast only the venerable Mosque of Amr. Just as significant was the development of economic activities, which attracted Egyptian settlement there. The Maqs area, then still bordering the Nile, already served as a port to Cairo and boasted a *funduq* for the merchants of Amalfi.

One particularly significant index of this change is the slow migration of Christians and Jews from Fustat to the caliphal city. It certainly began early on. In Hakim's time there already existed a quarter near Bab Zuwayla, where Jews lived, which the caliph shut down and ordered burned. In 1038 Qahira already had a "Wine Sellers' Street" in the small Vizir Market, though its name used the harmless term *nabbadhin,* or makers and sellers of *nabidh,* a drink based on honey or dates; the word could also refer to a less innocuous beverage, whose sale (though not its consumption) was limited to the *dhimmi.* There was already a synagogue in Qahira at this time and therefore also a Jewish community. The Zuwayla quarter, where the Jews congregated, also contained a Christian residential area, where the Jacobite patriarch lived. Two Christian quarters had formed in Cairo: at the time of its foundation, the Harat al-Rum al-juwaniyya ("inner"), south of Bab al-Nasr, and the Harat al-Rum al-sufla ("lower"), near Bab Zuwayla, for the Fatimids' Greek mercenaries. Coptic churches were later built there.

In return, Fustat was no longer the "native" city, occupied solely with commercial activities, following the traditional division of labor in a society split between a ruling caste and a subject population. During the troubles in Fustat provoked by the aggressive religious policies of the proponents of Hakim's "divinity," the residents who defended themselves against the black troops attempting to sack the town were supported by Turkish and Berber soldiers with families living in Fustat (1020). We also know that many "functionaries" who worked in Qahira dwelt in Fustat and returned there at night. Maqrizi describes this evening migration toward the "dormitory city": "The people who earned their living in Cairo and the functionaries, after performing the evening prayer in that city, returned to their homes in Old Cairo . . . from the New Gate, outside Bab Zuwayla, to Bab al-Safa . . . in the midst of a perpetual bustle, both night and day." As their functions and inhabitants grew gradually more similar, the two cities came into competition, and Fustat declined as Qahira asserted its preeminence. The events of 1168 further weakened Fustat's prosperity even if they did not cause its utter ruin.[55]

No serious estimates of the populations of the two cities can be formulated. Clerget's figures for the end of the twelfth century (100,000 inhabitants in Cairo, 50,000 in Fustat) are based on no solid foundations: Fustat probably remained more heavily populated than Qahira even after the crisis of 1168.[56] But Qahira's development would gradually tilt the balance in favor of the "new" capital. This raises the question of why Qahira did finally supplant Fustat when neither al-Askar nor al-Qata'i ever truly took hold and instead remained dynastic cities whose development was arrested. The

Mustansir Crisis and the events of 1168 were factors but probably not deciding ones. It appears that the large dimensions of Jawhar's initial city and the numerous populations the conquerors brought with them did, from the start, set the stage for Qahira's urban development. The considerable distance between the earlier center and the new capital also made Qahira's transformation into a full-fledged city almost inevitable, Fustat being unable wholly to supply the new foundation's needs. Finally, time was a decisive factor, as the two centuries of Fatimid rule gave Qahira the leisure to take root as a city. The Ayyubids, who brought an end to Qahira's political role as a caliphal city and made it into an "ordinary" city, would put the finishing stamp on a development already begun in the Fatimid era.

# 3

# Cairo under the Ayyubids

IT TOOK SALADIN only two years to rise from vizir under the Fatimid caliph al-Adid (1169–1171) to undeclared ruler of Egypt. He first brought Egypt within the Abbasid sphere of influence by means of a perfectly achieved coup d'état (10 September 1171). The caliph's death on 12 September left the reins of power in his hands, under the suzerainty of Nur al-Din. This situation could not have lasted indefinitely, but the death of Nur al-Din on 15 May 1174 allowed Saladin, as the sole ruler of Egypt, to assert his right to the throne, conquer Damascus (30 October) and Syria, and prevail on the caliph of Baghdad to invest him with legitimate authority (May 1175). Saladin thus founded a dynasty that was to seem relatively short-lived (a little less than a century) if compared to the Fatimid dynasty (two centuries) and the Mamluk sultanate (more than 250 years). The Ayyubid dynasty would nonetheless constitute a decisive era in the long history of Egypt and its capital.[1]

The return of Egypt's rulers to Sunni orthodoxy constituted an event of considerable importance. The Ismailis, despite their long rule, had failed to impart their faith to the mass of the Egyptian population. Saladin and his successors addressed the task of making Egypt once more a center of orthodox belief. The al-Azhar Mosque, built as a center of Shiite propaganda, henceforth began to play a role in the orthodox Muslim world, as it has ever since. The founding of madrasas, an experiment tried elsewhere for the maintenance of or-

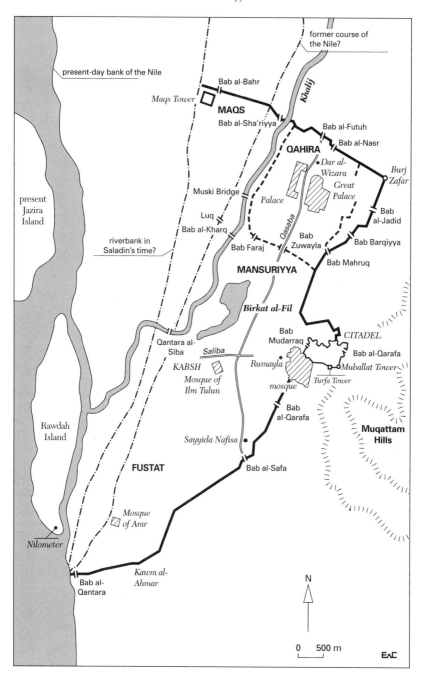

former course of
the Nile?

present-day bank of the Nile

Bab al-Bahr

*Maqs Tower*

**MAQS**

Bab al-Sha'riyya

*Khalij*

Bab al-Futuh

Bab al-Nasr

**QAHIRA**

• *Dar al-
Wizara*

*Great
Palace*

*Burj
Zafar*

Muski Bridge

*Palace*

*Qasaba*

Luq

Bab al-Kharq

present
Jazira
Island

riverbank in
Saladin's time?

Bab Faraj

Bab
Zuwayla

Bab
al-Jadid

Bab Barqiyya

**MANSURIYYA**

Bab Mahruq

*Birkat al-Fil*

Bab
Mudarraq

*CITADEL*

Qantara al-
Siba

*Saliba*

*KABSH*

*Mosque of
Ibn Tulun*

*Rumayla*

*mosque*

Bab al-Qarafa

*Muballat Tower*

*Turfa Tower*

**Muqattam
Hills**

Bab
al-Qarafa

Rawdah
Island

*Sayyida Nafisa* •

**FUSTAT**

Bab al-Safa

*Mosque
of Amr*

*Nilometer*

Bab al-
Qantara

*Kawm al-
Ahmar*

N

0    500 m

E∧C

Map 3. Saladin's Cairo (after Casanova)

thodoxy and now transposed to Egypt, contributed largely to the movement's success.

During this period Egypt continued to be an entirely independent state, sometimes ruling the province of Syria after the example set by Saladin during the twenty years of his reign. Syria played a central role, to some extent casting Egypt into the shadows. One reason was that Saladin, who strove to reconquer the areas occupied by the Franks (Jerusalem above all, capturing it in 1188), was often away from Egypt. Of the twenty-four years of his reign, he spent only eight in his capital, which he left for good in 1182 and never revisited before dying in 1193. After his reign, relations with the Franks (sometimes hostile, sometimes peaceful) remained the chief issue. The Syrian states also maintained a fundamental importance in Ayyubid politics. With Saladin gone, his relatives were saddled first with the problem of succession, then with intrafamilial relations, and tried several times to rebuild their family unity around Damascus. The Egyptian rulers were absorbed in the ups and downs of a national history marked by divisions, by tribulations, and at times by a successful return to the "Saladinian" state, notably under Malik al-Adil (1199–1218), Saladin's brother; Malik al-Kamil (1218–1238), Adil's son; and Salih Najm al-Din Ayyub (1240–1249), Kamil's son. These rulers, each remarkable in his own way, had thus to devote considerable attention to Syria, where the greatest threats to the dynasty surfaced: the arrival of the Khawarismians, a people originally from Central Asia whom the Mongol advance had driven west (from 1225 on), and the approach of the Mongols themselves. Egypt was to remain safe from external dangers, with the sole exception of the Crusade of Louis IX of France in 1248 and 1249. In writing to his secretary and adviser al-Qadi al-Fadil, Saladin exaggerated little when he described Egypt as "a mistress who tried in vain to separate me from my faithful spouse [Syria]."

At the end of the Ayyubid period a new military system appeared that was to prove of great importance to Egypt. Until then tribal armies had undertaken the conquest of Egypt and the settlement of Fustat, the Fatimid conquest and the settlement of Qahira, and finally Saladin's takeover of Egypt (with the help of Kurdish troops). These were replaced by slave troops from Turkey who were later granted their freedom, the mamluks (*mamluk* means "possessed" by one's master). The last Ayyubid sultan, Salih Ayyub, experiencing difficulties with the Kurdish troops who had faithfully served the dynasty until then, bought Turkish slaves and used them to form his guard and the main part of his army. Thierry Bianquis observes that the tribal forces were expensive, and the kinship ties they maintained were incompatible with a permanent army. "By contrast, the armored horsemen, who were few in number and had no families, were more effective and less costly."[2]

The Ayyubid period was a decisive one in the history of Egypt's capital, influencing its fate for six centuries by the construction of a citadel that would become the center of Egypt's official, political, administrative, and military life. This decision completed Qahira's transformation into a city and promoted the evolution of the twin cities of Qahira-Fustat into a unique conurbation in which Fustat would inevitably decline.

### THE BUILDING OF THE CITADEL AND THE WALL OF CAIRO

Many reasons could be cited to explain why, in 1176, Saladin decided to build a citadel on a projecting spur of the Muqattam Hills, one kilometer from the south wall of Qahira, and encompass all of Qahira and Fustat within a wall protected by this citadel. The traditional "dynastic" reasons informing the precedents of Askar, Qata'i, and Qahira, namely, the desire of a new government to build itself a new capital, are entirely plausible here. Saladin's antipathy toward the Shiite caliphate and his repugnance at settling into a city and palaces that bore the strong mark of his predecessors must have been keen. "It is the custom of kings," Maqrizi observes, "always to eliminate the traces of those who have preceded them. That is why they have destroyed so great a number of cities and fortresses."[3]

Concerns about the security of the new government also prompted the project. The main threat was naturally to external security. The presence of Franks in Palestine and Syria constituted a permanent danger to Egypt and its capital. Amalric's various incursions, in particular his expedition of 1168, had shown the vulnerability of Fustat, which had no protective walls, and the threat this posed to the safety of Qahira. But there was also a threat to internal security, as Saladin could reasonably expect the partisans of the fallen dynasty to mount a hostile reaction. In August 1169 Qahira saw a bloody rebellion of the black slaves, and Saladin was obliged to destroy their military quarters beyond Bab Zuwayla. A plot to overthrow Saladin and put one of al-Adid's sons on the throne was discovered in 1174. In 1188–1189 there was an explosion of pro-Fatimid propaganda, with men passing through the streets of Cairo shouting slogans in support of the Shiites in the hope, ultimately disappointed, of inflaming the masses. Though carefully guarded, the descendants of the last caliph might always arouse a tide of Fatimid loyalism. The Ayyubid chronicler, Ibn Wasil (1208–1298), reports the death in 645 A.H. (1247–1248) of Badr al-Din, the grandson of Adid. His father was Dawud, to whom Fatimid sympathizers had managed to smuggle a woman in the Citadel and smuggle her out again with the child she had conceived. The child was later arrested by Kamil, however, and imprisoned in the Citadel, where he died. Maqrizi comments: "Living in what he considered a conquered country, and fearing uprisings led by Fatimid sympathizers, who had the support of the Christians, Saladin very prudently chose the same course of action as the founders of al-Askar, Qata'i, and Cairo . . . It was a question of security."

Saladin may also have thought it necessary to isolate himself from the cities of Qahira and Fustat with their large and sometimes turbulent populations. The cities of Syria, each with an impregnable fortress where the ruler could barricade himself in case of danger, provided a model solution. In Damascus, which Saladin knew well, Nur al-Din (1154–1174) had undertaken the vast labor of reinforcing the walls and the citadel. And finally, Saladin had arrived with his own army of "Ghuzz," as the Turks were called, and of Kurds, for whom quarters had to be found.[4]

Saladin's defensive concerns were initially manifested in a project of limited scope: the ruler had not yet achieved his full independence, and to undertake large-scale projects might well have raised eyebrows in Damascus, where his powerful suzerain reigned. In 1171, perhaps following a May visit to Alexandria, during which he commissioned new fortifications, Saladin decided to rebuild in stone the wall originally constructed by Badr al-Din al-Jamali, a large section of which had been destroyed. The man put in charge of repairing the destroyed or damaged parts was Baha al-Din Qaraqush, a eunuch who had been one of Shirkuh's mamluks and became the marshal of the court and Saladin's trusted adviser. Remnants of a portion of the rebuilt wall, along what was the Cairo Canal on the western edge of Qahira, bear witness to these early efforts, and an inscription in Saladin's name, at a time when he was still the caliph's vizir, specifies the date.[5]

In 1176 Saladin launched an undertaking on a different scale altogether, building a citadel southeast of Qahira that would be the keystone in a wall encompassing the cities of Qahira and Fustat. According to Imad al-Din al-Isfahani, his secretary and historian, Saladin observed that the two cities were poorly protected and decided to join them behind a single defense: "With a wall I will make the two into a unique whole, so that one army may defend them both; and I believe it good to encircle them with a single wall from the bank of the Nile to the bank of the Nile."[6] He also ordered that a citadel be built at the center. The site, so legend has it, was chosen for hygienic reasons: Saladin had bits of meat placed in different parts of the capital; seeing that those hung on the Muqattam Hills stayed fresh longest, he decided to place his citadel there, where the air was healthiest.

It does not take an experiment of this kind to realize the appropriateness of the chosen site. The Citadel sits on a rocky spur projecting outward from the Muqattam Hills (which a later quarry, dug into the flank of the mountain behind the Citadel, divides even more sharply from the surrounding terrain). It dominates the elevated land where Qahira was built, having both a strong position and one that is relatively close to Qahira, given that a site farther north was impossible because of the mounds of debris. This spur was higher than Jabal Yashkur, chosen by Ibn Tulun as the location for his mosque and the Qata'i district. That the Muqattam Hills rose above it put the Citadel at a military advantage in Saladin's time, when no artillery piece was capable of bombarding the Citadel at that range.[7] The site had previously been built on; though the Dome of Fresh Air had been destroyed after the fall of the Tulunids, there were a cemetery and some mosques on it.

For a building site on the scale envisioned by Saladin, Qaraqush, who was again in charge of construction, marshaled extraordinary means. Abd al-Latif, a visitor to Egypt in 1192, writes how this "man of genius," responsible for "overseeing the buildings of the capital," demolished "a considerable number of pyramids, small ones," in Giza. To transport the stones, Qaraqush built a raised causeway starting near the pyramids and ending in Giza, perhaps along the path of the present road. Abd al-Latif describes it as being "like arches," such as those presently seen in Giza. They should be counted, he continues, "among the structures worthy of the greatest admiration, and they deserve a place among the works of the Titans. There were more than forty similar arches." The stones had to be brought from the region of Abusir, 25 kilometers south of present-day Cairo. Sailing up the Nile from Fustat toward Upper Egypt in May 1183, Ibn Jubayr recounts that on the second day he saw "the ancient city of Joseph the Truthful [Abusir] where is the prison in which he was confined, which is now being demolished, and its stones removed to the citadel being built in Cairo; a strong and impregnable fortress." Most of the Citadel, however, appears to have been built, as J. M. Rogers has noted, with "soft Muqattam limestone quarried on the site."

To realize his undertaking, Qaraqush apparently used the large and unpaid labor force provided him by Saladin's Christian prisoners, whose numbers had been recently swollen by Reginald of Châtillon's disastrous defeat in the Red Sea, where he had undertaken a naval raid against the Land of the Prophet. On his passage through Alexandria, Ibn Jubayr witnessed the crowds hurrying out to see the prisoners arrive, tied to camels, ignominiously bound facing the tail, a spectacle that was greeted with great enthusiasm mixed with retrospective fear. "We asked their story and were told a case," writes the chronicler, "that would rend the heart in compassion and pity. Allah had once again intervened to protect Islam and, by his beneficent works, restored peace to the hearts of good Muslims." Some time later, the traveler saw Christian captives working on the sultan's construction site:

> The forced laborers on this construction, and those executing all the skilled services and vast preparations such as sawing the marble, cutting the huge stones, and digging the fosse that girdles the walls noted above—a fosse hollowed out with pickaxes from the rock to be a wonder amongst wonders of which trace may remain—were the foreign Rumi prisoners whose numbers were beyond computation. There was no cause for any but them to labor on this construc-

tion. The Sultan has constructions in progress in other places, and on these too the foreigners are engaged, so that those of the Muslims who might have been used in this public work are relieved of it all, no work of that nature falling on any of them.[8]

The Citadel was used as the governmental center of Egypt from the Ayyubid period to the mid-nineteenth century, and successive architectural alterations have made reconstructing its original aspect difficult. The construction, too, spanned a relatively long period. The historian Ibn Wasil cites construction on the wall and the Citadel at the end of *rabi* 572 (before 6 October 1176), which is the probable starting date for the work. An inscription discovered on the Citadel's west gate (Bab al-Mudarraj) celebrates its foundation and, in principle, its completion in 1183–1184:

The foundation of this resplendent citadel, close to [the city of] Cairo the well protected, was ordered built, in accordance with a resolution to unite usefulness with beauty, and this space with the protection of all who might seek shelter in the shadow of his kingdom, by our master, al-Malik al-Nasir Salah al-Dunya wal-Din . . . Yusuf, son of Ayyub, the vivifier of the empire ruled by the emir of the faithful [the caliph of Baghdad], under the oversight of his brother and presumptive heir, al-Malik al-Adil . . . and by the hand of the emir of his principality and the pillar of his empire, Qaraqush, son of Abd-Allah, servant of al-Malik al-Nasir, in the year 579 [1183–84].

Presumably the reference is to the beginning of 1184, as Ibn Jubayr described a work site still operating at full bore in 1183. In his study of the walls of the Citadel, K. A. C. Creswell notes several distinct phases in the construction attributed to Saladin and al-Adil, his successor, who acted as regent (and director of construction) during Saladin's absences and after his final departure from Cairo. Certain elements, particularly those on the southern wall, are clearly of a later date.[9]

The northern enclosure is the military portion of the Citadel. Built directly into the rock, it forms a vast irregular four-sided polygon, measuring 560 meters from east to west and 320 meters from north to south. The combined length of the walls and towers is 1700 meters, and the enclosed area measures approximately 13 hectares. Its towers, some round (with dressed stone) and some square (with embossed stone), attributed respectively to Saladin and Adil, are large enough to contain several hundred soldiers and were intended to provide for the defense of each section of the wall, which was also protected by a ditch. On the ramparts was a sentry path protected by rounded battlements.

This enclosure had four gates. The two main ones, designed by Saladin, were located on the east and west. The west gate, Bab al-Mudarraj (Gate of the Stair), faced toward the city and is today obscured within additions built under Muhammad Ali (early nineteenth century). It is here that the foundation inscription was discovered, confirming it as the main entrance to the fortress. The east gate (known as Bab al-Qarafa because it looks down onto the cemetery, but also as the Gate of the Mountain, Bab al-Jabal) is located opposite the first and faces the Muqattam Hills. It was little used because of its difficult approach, and was reinforced, probably by Adil. The southeast and northeast portions of the wall still exist in something like their original state: the wall on the southeast is 2.8 meters thick, and the tower of Burj al-Muballat on the southeast corner rises to 16.8 meters above the rock, which is itself 9 meters high.

The Citadel's north enclosure is remarkable for both its size and the quality of its construction. The fortified citadel of Krak des Chevaliers, the standard by which all works of military art in the Levant are judged, measures only 200 by 140 meters, for an area of 2.5 hectares. The al-Turfa Tower on the Citadel's encompassing wall, which dates from the time of al-Adil, measures 30 meters on a side, almost the size of the Tower of London. On the outside are four vaulted chambers or casemates measuring 4.5 by 7.2 meters. The fortress incorporates architectural innovations that were brought back from the campaigns in Syria and Palestine against the Crusaders. For instance, the entrances to the Citadel were elbow-shaped, the better to defend the fortress; and thanks to machicolations projecting outward above the entrances, boiling liquids could be poured down onto the heads of assailants.[10]

The northern section of the Citadel was completed in the main by Saladin and dates from his lifetime; the southern section had only

Wall of the Cairo Citadel (*top:* photo Doris Behrens-Abouseif;
*bottom: Description de l'Egypte,* Bibliothèque Nationale)

been sketched in by the time of his death. According to the archaeologist K. A. C. Creswell, a wall much smaller than the north enclosure
wall was built on the southeast, in an area where the Mamluk sultans
would later build. It was there that a palace complex was to be
erected, looking out over the capital, its elements gradually set in
place by Saladin's successors. The two enclosures communicated at
the place where Sultan Baybars (1260–1277) would later build the
Gate of the Tower (Bab al-Qulla). A mosque probably stood nearby,
to be replaced in 1318 by the Mosque of al-Nasir Muhammad.

Saladin may never have lived in the Citadel, but he did concern
himself with providing for its water supply. He excavated a giant well,
the Well of Joseph (Bir Yusuf), a public work that never fails to impress visitors—hence no doubt its popular attribution to the patriarch Joseph (when in fact it bears one of Saladin's names). It is rect-

angular in shape (5 by 7.8 meters at the top, and 3.4 by 4.4 meters at the bottom) and 90 meters deep. It was divided into two parts, with the water raised by waterwheels to a cistern midway up the shaft, then brought to the surface by another set of wheels. The oxen that turned the wheels stayed in the well all their lives. One entered by a stairway consisting of 300 steps, whence the name Well of the Spiral. An aqueduct was also built to carry water to the Citadel, portions of which were incorporated into later constructions by al-Nasir Muhammad.

It appears that work on the Citadel stopped at the time of Saladin's death, to be resumed under al-Malik al-Kamil, the first Ayyubid ruler to live there permanently. He completed its plan and built the royal residences in 1207–08. Little is known about these buildings. The palace looked out over Cairo: an anecdote recorded by Ibn Wasil has Kamil looking down from his palace at the funeral cortège of a shaykh he had invited to Cairo and waxing indignant that the man did not have a greater following among his colleagues. The royal residence included a hall (iwan), later reworked by Qalawun (1279–1290), a library (a relic of the library of the Fatimids), a palace of justice (founded in 1240), and the royal stables. The last Ayyubid sultan, Salih Ayyub, abandoned the Citadel to set up residence on the island of Rawdah, yet he built a hall in the Citadel that would burn down in 1285 after having served as a residence for several Mamluk sultans. Salih Ayyub's wife and successor, Shagar al-Durr, also built a hall, called the Hall of the Columns, which survived for several centuries.[11]

The construction of a wall to encompass Qahira and Fustat within a single enclosure, two cities separated by a broad empty space, represented an even more gigantic feat. It is therefore not surprising that neither Saladin nor his successors were able to complete it in their lifetimes. The historian Abu Shama, who lived almost contemporaneously with these events (he was born in Cairo in 1203 and died in Damascus in 1268), had access to firsthand sources and describes in some detail the plan for this enormous construction. The wall was to go from the Nile to the Nile, connected and fortified by the Citadel at its center. It would measure a total length of 29,302 cubits, or almost 20,000 meters.[12]

Construction began on the wall at the same time as on the Citadel, around October 1176, and also extended over a long period. Ibn Jubayr describes the work site in 1183. Maqrizi mentions several phases of construction: he notes that construction began on a stone wall around Fustat in 1185–86; work was proceeding on the trench between Bab al-Futuh and al-Maqs in 1192; and in January 1200 the regent ordered the Citadel to be readied for defense and the remaining parts of the Fustat-Qahira wall to be dug down to the rock, in particular between the river and al-Maqs "in order that there be no road to the city other than through the gates." But we know that work on the walls was still in progress in 1238, forty-five years after Saladin's death.[13]

The northern and eastern sections (as far as Darb al-Mahruq) were started and completed first. The east section (from Darb al-Mahruq to the Citadel and from there to Fustat) was started later. Creswell has been able to identify and study the sizable remains of these fortifications. The wall, built of stone, varied in thickness from 3.33 to 3.85 meters and incorporated projecting towers, as well as larger structures, such as Burj al-Zafar on the northeast corner, measuring 16 meters in diameter and having seven casemates. Eight gates have been identified: Bab al-Bahr and Bab al-Sha'riyya to the north; Bab al-Jadid, Bab al-Barqiyya, and Bab al-Mahruq to the east; Bab al-Qarafa, Bab al-Safa, and the Fustat Gate.

The section of the wall intended, according to written sources, to follow the bank of the Nile from Maqs to Kawm al-Ahmar was certainly never built—not surprisingly, since the river itself offered protection on this side. But the section intended to protect Fustat, long thought to have been left incomplete, actually was built. A large segment of this wall has been discovered by Ali Bahgat in the course of his excavations in the residential sector of Fustat. The rampart was apparently built through the long-since-abandoned rubbled area (*kawm*). The wall cuts arbitrarily through blocks of houses, following a wide channel dug for the wall's foundations. Abd al-Latif's testimony on this point is unmistakable: it was Qaraqush, he writes, "who raised the wall of stone that encloses Fustat, Cairo, all the ground between the two cities, and the Citadel."[14]

The imposing character of this structure leads us to ponder its military and political significance. We cannot attribute to Saladin the thought that by enclosing Qahira and Fustat behind one wall he was laying the foundations for a "Greater Cairo"—the concept is an anachronism. Seven centuries after Saladin, the two cities joined in this way would still constitute separate entities, divided by a considerable distance. That it was intended as a giant defensive installation for Cairo must therefore suffice. The only potential aggressor within striking distance was the Crusaders' kingdom, which was even then in decline. Aside from the mad raid by Louis IX, European aggressors would not be seen again on Egyptian soil until 1798. While the wall was painstakingly being built, Saladin was pursuing a military operation in Palestine that would ultimately lead to the recapture of Jerusalem. The Mongol threat would declare itself only a half-century later. No external danger would trouble Egypt until the victorious expedition of the Ottoman sultan Selim in 1517. But Saladin's walls, greatly deteriorated in the meantime, were of no help to the Mamluks. It is therefore as a superb construction, somewhat outsized and of dubious usefulness, that we must judge the enclosing wall Saladin gave Cairo starting in 1176.

### QAHIRA'S TRANSFORMATIONS

Saladin's wall did not turn the two cities of Qahira and Fustat into a single conurbation. Rather, the two evolved in separate and contrasting ways. The building of the Citadel and the (relatively late) displacement of the political and military centers to it cannot explain Qahira's urban development and the gradual decline of Fustat. These trends were already under way when the Ayyubids ascended to power in Egypt. The events of 1168 may have accelerated these trends, and the great crisis of the years 1200–1201 also contributed to them.

The high prices and famine that beset Egypt at that time are attested in the eyewitness account of Abd al-Latif. In 1200 the river crested at twelve cubits and twenty-one fingers, "an extremely rare occurrence." Only once since the Arab conquest of Egypt, in 967, had the Nile's flood level been lower. The customary sequence of events following an inadequate flood was rapidly reenacted: rising prices due to precautionary buying, scarcity, famine, epidemic, and death. "The year 597 [which began on 12 October 1200] swept in like a monster bent on destroying all the resources of life and every means of subsistence." The apocalypse had arrived: "The poor, driven by a rising tide of hunger, ate carrion, corpses, dogs . . . They even ate small children. It was not rare to come across people with small children who had been roasted or boiled." Inhabitants fled the cities. Abd al-Latif asserts that 111,000 dead were recorded in Qahira and an even greater number in Fustat, which, after visiting it in 1202, he describes as an abandoned city: "We saw streets and markets that had previously been choked with bustling crowds. Now they are all empty. No living beings are to be found there, other than a passerby from time to time. So deserted are these places that one crosses them today with terror." The extent of the crisis is confirmed by the Geniza documents, which record the high prices (three dinars for an irdabb of wheat in 1201) and the decline in commercial activities (the apartments belonging to the religious foundations fetch only half the customary price or stand vacant). The documents also suggest a mass exodus toward Cairo.[15]

The process Maqrizi describes ("al-Qahira became, after being a fortified site and the seat of the caliphate, a middle-class city, sought after as a shelter") was in all probability slow and gradual. In the first instance, the Ayyubids expelled the Fatimids and substituted their own troops for them. On the death of al-Adid, Saladin is said to have evicted 18,000 people from the palace, including 252 males of the caliph's family, dispersing them to various residences and keeping the sexes segregated in order to ensure that the race would die out. The palace was thoroughly looted of its valuables, including the famous 120,000-volume library, which was given to Saladin's chancellor, the *qadi* al-Fadil. Despite their revulsion against their predecessors the Ayyubids did not hesitate to use their palatial buildings: troops were billeted in the Fatimid palaces, the Turks in the Western Palace. Saladin took up residence in the Great Hall of the Vizirate (Dar al-Wizara) northeast of the Great Palace. His successors up to Adil (1199–1218) resided there as well. When Kamil moved to the Citadel, the Dar al-Wizara became a house for high dignitaries such as the heir to the sultanate or important guests. And the palace went on being used by Ayyubid princes: before his accession al-Malik al-Adil lived there in 1194, and the son of al-Kamil, Mas'ud, lived there in 1223 during a visit to Cairo.[16]

But it was not long before changes were made to these palaces, and new buildings were raised. In 1182 Saladin ordered a hospital to be installed in the hall (qa'a) of the Great Palace, reachable by the Qasr al-Shawk gate. This hospital was therefore near the present-day Sanctuary of al-Husayni. Saladin endowed this institution with a monthly revenue of 200 dinars along with grain from Fayyum, and he staffed it with a large number of doctors, surgeons, and orderlies. We have a detailed and enthusiastic description of it by the traveler Ibn Jubayr, who visited the hospital in 1183 shortly after it opened:

> Another of the things we saw, doing honor to the Sultan, was the hospital [maristan] in the city of Cairo. It is a palace, goodly for its beauty and spaciousness. This benefaction he made so that he might deserve a heavenly reward, and to acquire merit [in the next world]. He appointed as intendant a man of science with whom he placed a store of drugs and whom he empowered to use the potions and apply them in their various forms. In the rooms of this palace were placed beds, fully appointed, for bedridden patients. At the disposal of the intendant are servants whose duty it is, morning and evening, to examine the conditions of the sick, and to bring them the food and potions that befit them.
>
> Facing this establishment is another specially for women, and they also have persons to attend them. A third which adjoins them, a large place, has rooms with iron windows, and it has been taken as a place of confinement for the insane. They also have persons who daily examine their condition and give them what is fitting for them.[17]

This exception aside, however, it seems that in the first decades of their rule, the Ayyubids created buildings of this sort on the margins of the palace area. The first convent for mystics (khanqa; pl. khawaniq), an institution that was to have a great flowering under the Mamluks, was established by Saladin in 1173 in the palace of Sa'id al-Su'ada, a eunuch of the caliph Mustansir, just across from Saladin's residence in the Palace of the Vizirate; it housed 300 Sufis. The same pattern was followed for the seven schools built in Qahira between 1175 and 1225 to speed Egypt's return to orthodox Sunnism. It was only in 1225 that a madrasa was sited in the Between the two Palaces area by Sultan Kamil, inside the palace zone but on a vacant site. And it was not until 1243, in the reign of the last of the Ayyubids, Salih Najm al-Din Ayyub, that a madrasa was built on land occupied by the Western Palace, a part of which therefore had to be demolished. A few years later, in 1250, the regent, Shagar al-Durr, the widow of Sultan Salih, built a mausoleum for her late husband adjoining his madrasa. The prohibition, as it were, around the perimeter of the Fatimid palaces dissipated only as the Ayyubid dynasty was coming to an end. Under the next dynasty, destruction of the palaces accelerated.[18]

Qahira, where the members of the ruling caste lived, retained a special dignity, at least in the eyes of Ibn Sa'id, an Andalusian traveler who lived in the capital from 1241 to 1249 and again from 1260 to 1277: "[Qahira] is more prosperous and more luxurious than [Fustat] because it has finer schools, busier caravanserais, and more emirs' mansions. The sultan and his followers prefer it because it is close to the Citadel." Yet at the end of the Fatimid era, the city had been opened to a great influx of the Egyptian populace, accompanied by the development of commercial and artisan activities, in part as a result of the sultan's having installed his troops there. Ibn Sa'id's impressions therefore reflect the progressive change, seen by the traveler as a deterioration, of the former sultanic order. Between the Two Palaces Square, reflecting "a sultanic conception," was designed to serve as a setting for a military parade. And yet, as Ibn Sa'id notes deploringly, it was at the time no more than

a cramped space from which you cross a narrow passage; you find yourself in a dirty place, repulsive, with stalls on either side; when horsemen and spectators gather there, the sight wrenches one's heart and hurts to see. One day, with my own eyes, I saw the great vizir and all the government emirs arrayed in a magnificent procession stopped by a wagon carrying stones that obstructed the street in front of the stalls. Unable to advance, the vizir was caught in a growing confusion, directly across from the food stalls, whose smoke blackened his face and clothes.

There is the same impression of hasty and disorderly development outside the center of Qahira:

> Most of the streets . . . are narrow, dark, and strewn with dust and detritus. The buildings lining them are made of reeds or mud clay; they are tall, poorly ventilated, and ill lit. I never saw anything as miserable as these buildings in the Maghrib . . . When I walked through these streets, I felt uncomfortable, prey to a strong unease, until I was once more at Between the Two Palaces.

The city he describes is already a large and densely populated one, a bustling city where the individual lives in anonymity:

> An ideal place for the poor man, who needn't fear that he will be assessed for the *zakat* or ever face arrest . . . The poor man lives without a worry or care because of the low price and abundance of bread . . . He feels at ease there because nothing stops him from doing whatever he pleases. He is free to dance in the markets, dress in rags, grow drunk on hashish or other products, and run with scoundrels—the opposite of what happens in the Maghrib.

In the former city of the caliphs, economic activities were developing. Ibn Sa'id enumerates some of the products of Cairene manufacture: leather goods for export to Syria, woven goods, dyestuffs, luxury items for the elite. Maqrizi confirms the extent to which tradesmen have invaded the center of Qahira: "After the fall of the Fatimid dynasty when the palaces, emptied of their residents, were occupied by the emirs of the Ayyubid family, and when these emirs altered their character, the site became used as an ordinary market . . . The shopkeepers came there with victuals of all sorts, various meats, heaps of pastries, fruits, and other edibles."

In the years following the fall of the Fatimids, shops and stables were similarly built in the vicinity of al-Azhar; an order to demolish them was given in 1194. Before 1195, the emir Gaharkas built a covered market (*qaysariyya*) and a building for communal residence (*rab;* pl. *urbu*) on the Qasaba. And in 1229 some shops and two *urbu* were built a little farther north. The many Christians and Jews observed by Ibn Sa'id in Qahira, identifiable by their distinguishing signs and notable for their prosperity ("they ride mules and wear sumptuous clothes"), provide a further clue that Qahira had evolved into a "large and highly populated" city. The dissolute morals of Qahira confront the traveler pell-mell: drunkenness, resulting in crime; the plucking of stringed instruments; the presence in the streets of brazen women, their faces unveiled; hawkers crying plea-sure-haunts—all of which elicited a frown from the stern Maghribi moralist.[19]

There are no credible indications to suggest that the tide of ur-banization extended beyond the limits of Qahira, which was spacious enough to absorb the population that came to live there under the Ayyubids. Saladin's building projects to the north, a maydan for equestrian exercises and some pavilions, tend to confirm that the area was in fact little built up. To the west, there is no mention of the par-celing out of Kafur's gardens, a resort ground for the caliphs, until 1247–1248. Nothing suggests that active expansion was occurring be-yond the Khalij. Saladin's wall had encompassed the al-Maqs area, which was inhabited mostly by Copts and functioned as an outer port for Cairo. Communications with al-Maqs were improved by the building of roads in 1177 and the Muski Bridge (I 9) over the Khalij prior to 1188. But the Nile's shift westward, which appears to have accelerated around 1200 in this area, made using the port of Maqs difficult, and it always remained small in comparison to Fustat. Sul-tan Salih Najm al-Din's interest in the Luq area (M 13) led him, in 1241, to build another bridge at Bab al-Kharq (M 9). But the con-struction of a polo ground and of magnificent pavilions does not con-stitute evidence of urban development.[20]

It is only in the large zone between the southern boundary of Qahira and the Citadel that we can speak of the beginnings of urban-ization. Saladin's reign started off badly in this respect: the great re-bellion of the Sudanese troops in August 1169 resulted in the de-struction of the Mansuriyya quarter south of Bab Zuwayla where they had their barracks. The area was then turned into gardens and parks. It is said that Saladin, proceeding several years later from his palace to the Citadel, "passed between trees and flowers and, standing at the Mosque of Ibn Tulun, could see the Zuwayla Gate without a single building obstructing his view." The abandonment of the Mosque of Ibn Tulun, which Saladin made into "a retreat for the foreigners from the Maghrib, where they might live," indicates plainly that, at the time of Ibn Jubayr's visit, it stood in an uninhabited area. The construction of the Citadel and its election as a residence by Sultan Kamil (1218–1238) must have brought an increase of activity to this area. Al-Malik al-Kamil decided to move the livestock market (horses, camels, and donkeys) to Rumayla Square, at the foot of the Citadel, where it would stay until the end of the eighteenth century. And we should suppose that all the activities that traditionally developed "below the Citadel" *(taht al-qal'a)* in medieval Arab towns also gradually developed there.[21]

A place of residence for the court and the military personnel around the sultan, the Citadel also became a center of attraction and festivities. In October 1239, to celebrate his return to Cairo, Sultan Adil II ordered the decoration of Qahira and Fustat for a great entertainment to be held on the Black Esplanade (Qaramaydan) below the Citadel on the mountain. Maqrizi relates: "There were castles made of sugar, tanks full of lemonade, 2,500 sheep's heads and other food of this kind. One thousand five hundred loaves of sugar were eaten. Adil invited the entire population to the festivities, and they all came, both great and small."

The Ayyubid princes also built pleasure houses on Kabsh Hill and toward the pond known as Birkat al-Fil. We can infer that some urbanization was occurring in this southern region because a mosque was built before 1244 in the Saliba quarter. But in the 1240s, according to Maqrizi, "there were no buildings along the Birkat al-Fil, nor on the banks of the Khalij al-Gharbi from the Bridge of Lions (Qanatir al-Siba) [U 12] to al-Maqs." The zone between Ibn Tulun's Saliba (T 7) and Bab Zuwayla consisted of parks and gardens. From all the evidence, the area south of Cairo did not truly start to become urbanized until the advent of the Mamluks.[22]

## THE CONTRASTING DEVELOPMENT OF FUSTAT

Gravely affected by the events of 1168, which caused destruction and a mass exodus, and hard hit by the crisis of 1200–1201, Fustat saw a period of marked contrasts under the Ayyubids. In the midst of ruins that had been growing since the time of Mustansir, the city, though weakened by emigration toward Qahira, remained a great commer-

Rawdah Island (*Description de l'Egypte,* Bibliothèque Nationale)

cial and economic center. The building of the Citadel, which was nearer than the Fatimid city had been, offered the possibility of a new stimulus. At the very end of the Ayyubid period, the transfer of the center of government to Rawdah Island held out a final opportunity for development; but it was not to be.

The westward shift of the Nile's main channel and the slow advance of the river's eastern shore seem to have accelerated during the Ayyubid period. At times (in 1181, for example, and again around 1240), the eastern branch of the Nile almost dried up, attaching the Rawdah Island to dry land. Considerable work was done by Kamil in 1231 and by Salih after 1240 to bring the Nile's water back into the Rawdah channel and ensure that the Nilometer would not be left high and dry. The withdrawal of the Nile, though inconvenient, also left new land exposed for Fustat to build on. The port facilities were so primitive that the shifting of the river hardly created difficulties; commercial activity and shipbuilding continued in Fustat without interruption. In 1181, when there was fear that the Nile might dry up, four light boats for carrying troops to Yemen were being built in Fustat's shipyards.[23]

It is uncertain whether the following unflattering description, written by Ibn Sa'id in the 1240s, should be taken as a sign of Fustat's decline. He had set out from Bab Zuwayla in a dusty procession of rented donkeys and was arriving at his destination:

> As we neared Fustat, my heart fell. I could see cracked, blackish walls and dusty vacant lots. The gate had been left agape and opened onto a field of ruins dotted with buildings of several stories. These were disorderly structures, lining poorly laid-out streets, and built of mud, of grayish fieldstone, of reeds, and of palm stalks. Before the doors of these houses grew piles of refuse and detritus that made one want to turn one's eyes away in nausea.

We have seen that Qahira also found no favor in the eyes of our critical Andalusian traveler, in comparison with the "large markets of Seville and Marrakesh." Crossing the *kawm* was undoubtedly depressing. In the center of the city, where he found the streets and markets quite confined ("narrow markets . . . a maze of [cramped] bazaars"), the traveler was nonetheless struck by the animation of the scene: "I was swept up . . . in the bustle of people making small purchases and going about their business, while camels brushed against me carrying full water skins." At the cathedral mosque of Amr, the traveler strongly felt the structure's magnificence and spiritual aura, "which is not to be found in the mosque of Seville, despite its ornaments." But even this mosque is an important passageway: "In this shrine, vendors sell cakes and tarts of all sorts. People eat in every corner of it, shamelessly . . . Children go about carrying water containers, making the rounds of the eaters."

Despite the dilapidation of the city, the traveler was most struck in the end—like all who traveled there before him—by the commercial activity of Fustat. The riverbank was "unclean, soiled, narrow," but it was also

> full of ships and goods hailing from every part of the earth and the Nile Valley. If I were to say that nowhere else have I seen what I saw on this riverbank, it would be no more than the truth . . . What arrives in Fustat from the Alexandrine [Mediterranean] and Hejazian [Red] Seas beggars all description. It is in Fustat that all of this is gathered, not in Qahira . . . Fustat has more goods and at better

prices than Qahira because the Nile is nearby . . . so that vessels laden with merchandise may land there.

Ibn Sa'id also remarks on all the industrial activities centered in Fustat, especially the refining of sugar and soapmaking. Fustat apparently still had considerable vitality. Yet S. D. Goitein points out that while the number of Geniza documents did not decline with respect to the period before 1168, they primarily concern local Egyptian business and hardly any international trade at all between 1160 and 1250. The change may have been due to a declining Jewish community in Fustat. Many of its members were relocating to Qahira, where the greater share lived by 1250. It is also possible that, having reached its apogee in the Fatimid period, Fustat was starting to experience a relative decline, whose extent would become apparent under the Mamluks.[24]

Fustat's fate might, however, have been modified by Sultan Salih's decision to abandon the Citadel and, for reasons of security, establish his residence and the barracks for his Turkish mamluks on Rawdah Island. Work on a new fortress began on 20 February 1240. It was to have palaces and a barracks for the military, who were known as the Bahris (from the common term for the Nile, *bahr*, or "sea"), a name subsequently borne by the first Mamluk dynasty. Rawdah's citadel, palaces, and barracks were built in three years on a site where there had stood houses and pavilions, particularly during Kamil's reign. Work was done to ensure that the east branch of the Nile would always carry water and keep the island isolated. A bridge was built between the island and Fustat so that the emirs and soldiers in the sultan's service could come and go. So grand a complex and the proximity of the sultan's court and his troops (among them 1,000 Turkish mamluks) might well have altered Fustat's fate for the better. The comments of Ibn Sa'id, who was visiting Egypt when the new citadel was being built, are very much to the point: "a new wind" had entered Fustat. The town adjoined Rawdah,

so that many soldiers have moved back to Fustat to be near their post, and a number of them have even built pleasant belvederes on the encircling wall . . . At the present moment, with the sultan building the new citadel on the island opposite Fustat and making it the seat of government, Fustat is becoming increasingly prosperous and many emirs have moved there. Its bazaars have grown in size and, opposite the bridge leading to the island, they have built a gigantic *qaysariyya* to which the suqs for the soldiers have been transported from Qahira, where they sell leather, cloth . . .

Salih's early death in 1249 put an end to the undertaking. In 1251 the Mamluk sultan Aybak ordered the evacuation of the Rawdah castle. Of this building complex, which Maqrizi considered one of the most magnificent ever erected in Egypt, nothing has survived. Only the four enormous columns in the mausoleum of Qalawun in central Cairo remain to give us an indication of the Rawdah palace from which they were taken.[25]

### THE MADRASAS AND THE RETURN TO ORTHODOXY

In the sphere of religion, the fall of the Fatimid dynasty resulted in Egypt's return to Sunni orthodoxy. Sunnism was once again on the ascendant in the Middle East, a fact also expressed in the resumption of active opposition to Frankish settlement. The restoration of the Friday invocation *(khutba)* in the name of the Abbasid caliph and the return to a call to prayer in line with Sunni practice symbolized the end of Shiite dominance in Cairo.

The return to strict Sunnism may have been followed by greater hostility toward the *dhimmi,* the pendant on the domestic front to the renewed struggle against Western Christians. One of Saladin's first rulings as vizir was to deny Christians the right to hold administrative office. This move was probably intended mostly to purge Fatimid elements, as it was apparently not applied with any strictness. Maqrizi notes, somewhat later, that the Christians who worked for the Turks were left untouched "because their masters refused to dismiss them, saying they were well-trained to manage their affairs, and that dismissing them would be harmful to their own interests." The harassment of Christians under the Ayyubids (through various forms of discrimination, and through rules governing places of worship or the sale and distribution of wine) never reached the level of outright persecution. There may have been less tolerance in the Ayyubid period than in the preceding one; nevertheless, Christians were allowed to pursue their religion and to restore, and even build, churches.[26]

Shiism had been dominant in Egypt for two centuries and threatened to divide the Muslim community. To ensure the restoration of Sunnism, Saladin and his successors established a system of education that had proved highly successful in Syria. It centered on the madrasa (school or college) rather than the congregational mosque— the Shafi'i Sunnism of the Ayyubids held that there could be only one such mosque per city anyway. An inscription celebrating the construction of a madrasa in Cairo in 1180 conveys the character of this movement well: "This college [*madrasa*] was built at the instance of the shaykh, doctor [*faqih*], imam . . . and ascetic Najm al-Din, the pillar of Islam . . . Abul-Barakat al-Khabushani . . . for the benefit of those learned doctors, disciples of al-Shafi'i, who are distinguished by their firm doctrinal base . . . [in contrast to] other vain reasoners and innovators." Significantly, the text stigmatizes the doctrinal errors of the previous regime and acclaims the Shafi'i school of religious law, which remains that embraced by the greater number of Egyptians even today.

To a certain extent, the madrasas resembled the institutions created by the Shiites to spread their own propaganda. They were intended to teach theology and law in accordance with orthodox belief, following one of four schools of canonical law, and their students received free food and clothing. The college had its own teachers. It was built and financed by the sultans and members of the ruling caste, along with some civilians. Also developed in Cairo under the Ayyubids was the *khanqa*, or convent, an establishment intended as a retreat for Sufi mystics. Saladin founded the first madrasa, known as Qamhiyya, for the Malikis in 1170 and the first *khanqa* on the site of a Fatimid town mansion in 1173. Ibn Jubayr, ever enthusiastic in his praise for Saladin's undertakings, describes the first madrasa in these terms: "Behold yet another generous institution witnessing the sultan's concern for the interests of Muslims . . . He has organized gatherings and appointed professors to teach the Book of God, especially to the sons of the poor and orphaned, in exchange for payment."

Saladin played a determining role in the development of the madrasa; he steered the institution away from adherence to any one school of Sunni law (the Shafi'i in particular) and toward a unified "pan-Sunnism" that brought together all the different schools on an equal footing.

Saladin himself founded five important madrasas in Cairo between 1170 and 1176. Each was devoted to a single school of law, with three of the five embracing Shafiism. During the rest of his reign nine madrasas were founded, four by emirs. Between 1193 and 1225 seven new madrasas were established, but none by a sultan—the first Hanbali madrasa was probably also the first private foundation. From 1225 to the end of the Ayyubid dynasty, five madrasas were built, two by sultans (Kamiliyya and Salihiyya). These two were also unusual in catering to Sunnism generally, the former being devoted to the teaching of the Tradition *(hadith)*, which the schools follow in common, and the latter offering instruction, for the first time in Egypt, to all four schools of Sunni law (Shafiʻi, Hanafi, Maliki, Hanbali).[27]

Few monuments survive from the Ayyubid period other than the military constructions described earlier—no mosques, and few madrasas, though they were the characteristic structure of the time. Despite the political and ideological break with the Fatimid period, the architecture and decoration were largely inspired by earlier models, with some adaptation for the new institutions that prevailed under the Ayyubids. For the madrasas and *khawaniq*, where students and Sufis would live, it was necessary to provide service areas and halls: the iwan, a vaulted or ceilinged room that opens onto a courtyard, was a staple of domestic architecture that became widely used in madrasas. Two iwans facing each other across a courtyard, modified toward the end of the century to four iwans of unequal size around the courtyard with living quarters in the corners—this was the "cruciform" plan that became such a classic form in Cairene architecture. The facade with recessed panels of the Sahiliyya madrasa is modeled on the facade of the Mosque of Tala'i (1160), and the minaret in the form of an incense burner *(mabkhara)*, of which several Ayyubid examples survive, was also not without precedents. One of the most notable innovations was the phasing out of Kufic writing in inscriptions and its replacement by Naskhi, the more rounded cursive script, imposed by Nur al-Din in Syria and introduced to Egypt by Saladin. This writing style was to attain its apogee under the Mamluks.

Decoration at the entrance to the madrasa of Salih Ayyub, 1243
(photo Doris Behrens-Abouseif)

The best-preserved Ayyubid monument is the double madrasa
built on the Qasaba, the main street in Fatimid Cairo, on a site that
was once part of the Fatimid Great Palace, by Sultan Salih Najm al-
Din Ayyub in 1243. Today only its minaret is visible above a facade
that is almost totally hidden by a row of shops. This brick minaret is
topped by a *mabkhara* with stalactites. It was built above a porch and
passageway separating the two parts of the monument. The madrasa,
whose plan has been reconstructed by K. A. C. Creswell, consisted of
two wings separated by a public passageway; each wing was organized around a courtyard having two iwans facing each other, one
backing onto the street while the other, larger one was oriented toward Mecca. Along the sides were two stories of quarters for the students. The south wing of the monument has disappeared. In the
north wing, only the northwest iwan has survived, along with the west
facade, decorated with recessed rectangular panels that include a
window (a device seen earlier in the Mosque of Tala'i), and a panel
surmounted by a keeled arch at the entrance to the monument.

A few years after the madrasa's construction, the regent Shagar

Mausoleum of Salih Ayyub, 1250 (photo Doris Behrens-Abouseif)

al-Durr built a mausoleum for her late husband. Located in the northwest corner of her madrasa, this monument is the first instance in which a sultan's funerary structure was attached to a religious foundation, a practice that was to become a constant in Mamluk architecture. The mausoleum's facade, protruding from the madrasa which it extends, has three recesses with a window at street level; the panel is crowned by a keel arch. A dome covers the funerary chamber. Begun in 1249 after the death of Salih on 23 November in al-Mansura, where he was battling the French Crusaders, the monument was completed in 1250 after the surrender of King Louis IX. After the short reign of Salih's son, Turan Shah (assassinated on 30 April 1250 by his father's mamluks), Shagar al-Durr was acclaimed sultan (6 May 1250), with one of Salih's mamluks, al-Muʿizz Aybak, as regent. But on 30 July the mamluk emirs decided to confer the sultanate on Aybak. It was therefore Aybak, the first Mamluk sultan, who presided over the transferral of Salih's remains from Rawdah Island, where they lay in the mausoleum: "He was followed by the emirs and dignitaries, all dressed in white, their hair shorn in sign of mourning. They carried the banners, clothes, and weapons of the dead sultan and deposited them in his tomb."[28]

⁓

AFTER THE FOUNDING of the various earlier cities and the construction of the Citadel, all the elements that were to constitute "Cairo" were finally in place. It is only in retrospect, of course, that we can discern any logic in the successive stages: the shift north between 642 and 969, as though the "founders" were drawing closer to the Nile Delta in anticipation of the twentieth-century expansion onto the agricultural land of Qaliyubiyya province. Actually, for nearly seven centuries, from the Ayyubids (1169) to the Khedive Isma'il (1863), the future of the capital lay in the area between the Fatimid city and the Citadel, and on the lands between the Khalij and the Nile. It was within these zones that first the Mamluk, then the Ottoman city would appear, but only toward 1900 would the area between Bulaq and Fustat become fully urbanized.

The changes in the structure of the city between 642 and 1250 are reflected in the changing names of its constituent elements. At the time of the Arab conquest, the name for Egypt, Misr, was applied to the Arab foundation, in the form Fustat-Misr. When Qahira became a full-fledged city in the thirteenth century, spilling beyond the limits of the Fatimid foundation, it became the usage to apply the name Misr to the developing conurbation, just as Tunis referred both to Tunis and Tunisia, and Shams to both Damascus and Syria; Fustat meanwhile became Old Misr (Misr al-Qadima). Western travelers of the Middle Ages established the names Cairo and Old Cairo for the two cities, a usage we will henceforth follow, reserving Qahira to denote the Fatimid foundation. The new nomenclature reflected the new urban topography, ushered in by Saladin.

# II
# MEDIEVAL CAIRO
# (1250–1517)

*The Mamluk city flourished between the period of the foundations, which spanned the first six centuries of Egypt's history after the Arab conquest (642–1250), and the "modern" period, which begins with the Ottoman occupation in 1517. The supposed "changelessness" of Cairo from the high point of Islamo-Arabic civilization to the nineteenth century, when the Arab city was transformed into one strongly marked by Western influence, is an illusion. Whereas the city of the Ottoman period has left extensive remnants even to this day in Cairo's old quarters, we must reconstruct Mamluk Cairo through its few surviving vestiges and through the collation of data from the* Description de l'Egypte *(late eighteenth century) and the historian* Maqrizi *(early fifteenth century) to "rediscover the medieval reality."*[1]

# 4

# The Mamluks

## MAMLUK ORGANIZATION

THE PRINCIPLES OF THE SYSTEM that were instituted in Egypt in 1250 and were to last, with some adaptations, until 1517 were not entirely new. Muslim countries had been using slaves (Turks in particular) in their military and administrative organizations for a long time. In Egypt, the idea of having the state rely for its army and administration on a caste recruited as slaves from abroad and then freed was first developed during the Ayyubid period. It was the Mamluks, however, who institutionalized the system, devising a strict hierarchy that extended from the lowest military and administrative ranks to the sultanate.[1]

Western historians have expressed their surprise at this system, deeming it exotic. But with regard to the foreign origins of the ruling caste, Paul Veyne has rightly observed that "the nationalist pride that bizarrely identifies the state with an ethnic group and requires the ruler to be a native is a strange and very recent phenomenon." The fact that some non-Egyptian Mamluk sultans and emirs spoke Arabic poorly should surprise us no more than that the Hanovers, at least until George III (1760–1820), were more German than British. We should also keep in mind that the slavery practiced in antiquity and in the West until the nineteenth century was very different from the slavery practiced in Islamic societies, where it was not considered an indelible moral or religious stigma. The practice generally did not lead to a system of collective forced labor and harsh treatment, but often resulted in the freeing of the slaves. The Qur'an and hadith in fact enjoin Muslims to treat slaves fairly, and Islamic law establishes protections for them.[2]

Slaves were recruited by preference from among the Circassian, Turcoman, Mongol, and especially Turkish peoples of the Caucasus and the Russian steppes, because of their long-admired warlike natures. The Mongol invasions, driving the peoples of the steppe before them, created a vast reservoir of slaves on which the sovereigns of Egypt and Syria might draw. In the first period, the Mamluks were of Turkish origin, like those recruited by the last Ayyubid sultan, Salih, and settled by him in barracks near the Nile (the Cairenes' "sea," or *bahr*), whence the dynastic name of the Turkish or Bahri Mamluks (1250–1382). After 1382 the sultans recruited mostly Circassians, who like their predecessors lived in the Citadel. The second dynasty took the dynastic name of Circassian Mamluks (also Burji Mamluks, from the word for castle) (1382–1517).

The slaves were captured in the course of campaigns against the tribes, sold in the wake of intertribal raids, or voluntarily turned over to slave merchants. The slave trade, in which Europeans took an active part (by providing sea transport for the slaves), was conducted by specialized merchants, who arranged to ship the slaves to likely markets. The purchase of slaves required considerable means: in 1468 Qaytbay bought 500 boy recruits for 10,000 dirhams apiece. The emirs had means at their disposal proportionate to their rank in the social hierarchy and their fortunes. A country's capacity for importing slaves was therefore dependent on its political and economic fortunes and the prosperity of its ruling class.

Once slaves entered the house of a sultan or emir, they received an education that prepared them for the role they would later play in the army and the administration of the state. Their schooling included a classical Muslim education and rigorous training in arms and military sports to form them into armored horsemen. The study of Arabic was an element of the curriculum as well. We have exercise books in which young mamluks transcribed Turkish and Arabic works during their stays in barracks. Perhaps the chroniclers' examples of mamluks who could speak no Arabic were rather the exception. Describing the rank-and-file mamluk who never rose to the higher levels, Maqrizi remarks that "at least he had received a good education, acquired good manners, and had lodged in his heart a [solid] respect for Islam and its believers." Indeed, the education of a mamluk was a costly investment on his master's part. Once the slave completed his education and reached manhood, he was freed and became officially *mamluk*. In the case of the sultan's mamluks, several hundred individuals sometimes underwent this rite of passage together, receiving their horses and equipment from the sovereign in a solemn ceremony performed in the Citadel.

The second fundamental principle of Mamluk organization, a corollary to the requirement of slave origin, was the ban on inheritance. This condition was crucial to the maintenance of the system, which was intended to produce a caste without social or political ties and therefore bound exclusively to its masters, forming a cohesive group held together by internal solidarity. The Mamluks' descendants, the *awlad al-nas* (children of the [Mamluk] elite), were in theory prohibited from holding political or military office. The rule, however, was subject to exceptions (notably the sultans' desire to pass on the sultanate to their offspring) and in any case did not forbid the *awlad al-nas* from taking part in government organizations, for example the *halqa,* a kind of reserve corps. This prohibition may have encouraged charitable (and architectural) activity on the part of the mamluks, since they could not normally hope to pass on an inheritance to their descendants.[3]

Army officers came from the mamluk ranks. High government officials were also recruited from their number. The Mamluk army had three components: the sultanic mamluks (an elite corps), the troops of the emirs, and the *halqa.* The emirs were ranked according to a strict hierarchy, with their titles corresponding to the number of troops they put in the field: emirs of ten, of forty, of one hundred (or a thousand). Mamluks received endowments of land consisting of villages or fractions of villages (*iqtaʿat*), whose revenues paid for their upkeep and that of their men, with the size of the endowment a function of the mamluk's rank. Although the *iqtaʿat* were rural holdings, the mamluks lived in Cairo and were an urban class, which explains their role as builders in the city.

Promotions were granted according to precise rules and could lead to the highest positions in the government, both military (*atabak al-asakir,* general-in-chief; *amir silah,* director of the arsenal; *amir akhur,* supreme commander of the army) and administrative (*amir majlis,* emir of the audience; *dawadar,* chancellor), as well as to the governorship of the provinces. The career of Sultan Inal (1382–1461) allows us to review these titles and functions: a Circassian slave bought and subsequently freed by Sultan Faraj, he was first an emir of ten (1426), then of forty, then governor of Gaza (1428), an emir of one thousand, *dawadar* (1442), *atabak* (1445), and finally sultan (1453). To be acclaimed sultan was naturally the chief career objective of a capable and ambitious emir. One might reach it through seniority, merit, cabal, intrigue, or violence. But within the group of great emirs in the government the sultan was in theory only the first among equals, and the threat of being overthrown was never far away.

In fact, however, there was almost a century during the Mamluk period when the rule of Egypt was inherited. From 1290 to 1382, seventeen descendants of Sultan Qalawun (1279–1290) succeeded to the throne, from Khalil (1290–1293), Qalawun's son, to Hajji (1381–1382), the great-grandson of Nasir, who was himself a son of Qalawun. It is true that, after the death of Nasir in 1340, the power of the throne was generally wielded by high emirs in the name of sovereigns who had no real power—emirs such as Qusun, Shaykhu, and Sarghatmish. But the desire to transmit power hereditarily was so strong that, after the fall of the Bahri (or Turkish) dynasty in 1382, many sultans of the Burji (or Circassian) dynasty tried, with admirable doggedness, to have their sons succeed them. These efforts were invariably unsuccessful, with the exception of Barquq and his son Faraj (1399–1412), whose reign was a disaster.[4]

The faults of this system have often been pointed out: a troublesome foreign soldiery, who governed the country only to exploit it; a violent political culture driven by the search for power and marked by factional struggle; an unstable power structure that extended to the highest levels—there were no less than fifty-five rulers in 267 years and, once the Qalawuns were gone, a rapid and apparently anarchic succession of sultans at the head of the government. Yet the instability in the fifteenth century is more apparent than real. True, there were twenty-six different rulers between 1382 and 1517, but if we discount the most "meteoric" of them we find that nine of those sultans occupied the throne for 120 years and almost all of them were honorable or even first-rate men. It would then seem that the Mamluk system allowed the country to be reasonably run and to maintain a degree of prosperity over long periods, explaining the extraordinary material and artistic brilliance of this "dynasty."

The military strength of the Mamluks enabled them to fend off four separate Mongol invasions led by Genghis Khan's successors in the first decades of the Bahri dynasty: in 1260, 1273, 1281, and 1303. The Mamluks successfully dismantled and swept away the last Christian possessions in Syria and Palestine. They built and to the very last maintained a mighty empire that extended to the Hijaz, Palestine, Syria, and a large part of western Anatolia. The removal of the Abbassid caliphate from Baghdad to Cairo after the sack of Baghdad by the Mongols in 1258 was a de facto recognition of the prestige and power of Egypt, a state that, until the sixteenth century, was the heart of the Islamic world.

In domestic policy, the Mamluks established an administration that was staffed preponderantly by the military but also had wide recourse to civilians and Christians. Because of the system's efficiency, the Mamluks were able to marshal the resources needed to maintain the ruling caste and embark on a program of building whose magnitude and sumptuousness can be appreciated down to the present day, thanks to the monuments still surviving in Cairo.

### THE GREAT PERIODS OF MAMLUK HISTORY

The political success and artistic flowering under the Mamluks rested on a material prosperity that lasted over a good part of the fourteenth century. It was an era of general expansion for the eastern Mediterranean. The Genoese, operating from their base on the Sea of Azov, brought goods from China, while the Venetians traded with Syria and Egypt, and Alexandria established itself as a great market for pepper and spices. On the Egyptian side, a group of important traders, the Karimis, who appeared under the Fatimids and Ayyubids and specialized in importing goods from Asia through their ties in Yemen (pepper and spices in particular), established themselves solidly in Egypt. They appear to have reached the height of their prosperity in the first half of the fourteenth century. During the reign of Sultan al-

Nasir Muhammad, there were 200 Karimi merchants, who had commercial interests in Yemen, Jidda, Aydhab (on the western shore of the Red Sea), Qus, Cairo, Alexandria, and Damietta, and sometimes ranged as far as Sudan and the Indian Ocean. The Karimi Nasr al-Din Muhammad al-Balisi (d. 1375), who was said to have a fortune of 10 million dinars, an impossible figure, had representatives in India, Yemen, Ethiopia, Mali, and Takrur (in Senegal). The great merchant and trader Ibrahim Mahalli (d. 1403) was rich enough for Sultan Faraj to confiscate 100,000 dinars from him. In the fourteenth century, the state's annual revenue came to 9.5 million dinars, higher than at almost any other time since the Arab conquest.[5]

The zenith reached during the fourteenth century, corresponding to the long reign of Nasir Muhammad, was interrupted by the Black Death of 1348, which started a demographic decline that ended only with the Ottoman conquest and brought about a corresponding economic downturn, visible in the falloff in state revenues. While the reliability of the numerical data is uncertain, it is worth noting that Ibn Iyas estimated Egypt's revenues in 1521 at only 1.3 million dinars, plus important receipts in kind (wheat and barley). The country's material decline coincided with an erosion of the fundamental bases of the Mamluk system: a weakening of the sultanate (less severe probably than has often been stated); and a decline in the Mamluk institution, the army proving a heavy expense while its effectiveness was ever more uncertain and a source of continual unrest, largely responsible for the troubles and instability that affected Cairo during a good part of the fifteenth century. Yet this decline occurred at the moment when, for the first time since the Mongol invasions, Egypt faced an urgent need to ensure its external security. Tamerlane's incursion of 1400 was luckily stopped on the threshold of Egypt, but it was to be the first of a succession of military incidents that would grow more and more threatening for the country.

The traditional division of the Mamluk period into a Bahri/Turkish dynasty (1250–1382) and a Burji/Circassian one (1382–1517) is an inheritance from medieval chroniclers, but it corresponds to no fundamental changes in the organization of the Mamluk state or in Egypt's fortunes. A chronological division responsive to the vagaries of history seems preferable: first, a period of expansion and prosperity, encompassing particularly the reign of Nasir Muhammad, which may be said to end conveniently (if somewhat arbitrarily) in 1348. Next comes a period of crisis starting with the great plague epidemic of 1348, encompassing Tamerlane's expedition, which brought ruin to Syria and decline to Egypt, and ending with the crisis of 1403 and the disastrous reign of Faraj. There follows a period of relative recovery, with a return to normality and periods of brilliance, even as the factors of decline (demographic stagnation in particular) continued to exercise their effects, and clouds gathered in the northern Mediterranean, whence the storm that the Ottomans were brewing would erupt.

Along the way we will pause to look at Cairo through the window provided us by a particularly attentive historian of the city, Ahmad al-Maqrizi (1364–1442), which is almost as detailed a view as another of the great descriptive works that signpost the history of Cairo, the French Expedition's *Description de l'Egypte* (written in 1798–1801).

# 5

# The High Point of Mamluk Cairo
# (1250–1348)

THE LONG REIGN of Sultan Nasir Muhammad (1293–1340) dominated the century extending from the fall of the Ayyubids to the great
plague of 1348, when Egypt entered a period of crisis. It is not that
the years before his reign were unimportant. Two great sultans ruled
during that time. Baybars (1260–1277) set Egypt on its feet again. After the great victory won by Kutuz over the Mongols at Ayn Jalut in
1260, Baybars restored Syria to Egyptian suzerainty and attempted to
win back Palestine from the Crusaders. His two sons ruled briefly
after him before Qalawun seized the throne (1279–1290), fought the
Mongols victoriously at Homs in 1281, seized Tripoli, and planned
the capture of Acre, which was executed by his son and successor
Khalil, ending the Crusades (1291). His reign, as Gaston Wiet puts it,
was "to the end glorious and fertile." But whatever projects these sovereigns may have undertaken in their capital, we really pick up the
thread of Cairo's history only with Nasir Muhammad, Qalawun's son,
whose reign spans a half-century. Set on the throne in 1293 at the age
of eight, removed from power between 1294 and 1298, he recovered
the throne, lost it again from 1309 to 1310, and resumed power once
and for all from 1310 to 1340.

Thanks to the climate of international peace, clinched by a decisive victory over the Mongols at Marj al-Suffrar, near Damascus (20
April 1303), and to Egypt's domestic tranquillity, the nation experienced a period of economic prosperity. A contributing factor was undoubtedly the country's strong demographic growth throughout the

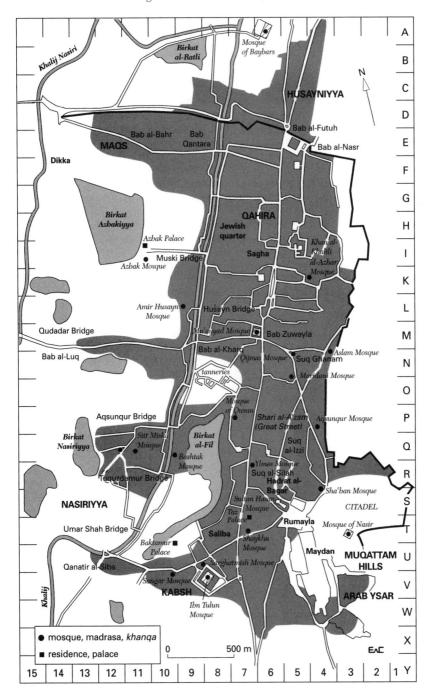

Map 4. Cairo in the Mamluk period (from *Description de l'Egypte*)

fifteenth century. Other than the epidemics of 1258–1259 and 1294, Egypt met with no serious accident until the plague of 1348. Its population increased from 2.4 million under Saladin to 4 million in 1348. An active international trade favored Cairo's development. Arriving in the city in 1325, exactly at the midpoint of Nasir's reign, the Moroccan traveler Ibn Battuta celebrated the power of Cairo with an enthusiasm that goes beyond rhetoric:

> Mistress of broad provinces and fruitful lands, boundless in the profusion of its people, peerless in beauty and splendor, she is the crossroads of travelers, the sojourn of the weak and the powerful . . . There are reported to be twelve thousand water carriers and thirty thousand *mocaris* [renters of beasts of burden]; thirty-six thousand watercraft on the Nile belonging to the sultan and his subjects that do nothing but come and go, ascending the river toward the Sa'id or descending it toward Alexandria and Damietta laden with merchandise of every kind.[1]

Nasir Muhammad played a personal role in the development of Cairo. Thanks to the general prosperity, he disposed of enormous resources. At the time of the great land registry of 1316, the country was divided into twenty-four parts, ten of which the sultan claimed for himself, while fourteen went to the emirs and the soldiers of the royal guard. These conditions allowed Nasir to give free rein to his evident love of building. Maqrizi estimates that he spent an average of 100,000 dirhams a day on his construction projects, or approximately 36 million dirhams per year. He also encouraged his principal emirs to follow suit—successfully, as may be judged from the works attributable to Emir Husayn, to Qusun, to Bashtak, and to many other high officials.

The register of historical monuments lists no fewer than eighteen mosques and madrasas dating to Nasir's time. But Maqrizi cites thirty-three of them, and I have been able to identify and locate a total of fifty-four mosques and madrasas built between 1293 and 1340, accounting for more than a quarter of the 198 monuments of this kind ascribed to the entire Mamluk period. Just as striking is the distribution of these buildings, with every area of the city seeming in a fever to push back the limits of the Ayyubid city in every direction.[2]

The urbanization of Qahira, which began at the time of the Ayyubid conquest, continued under the Mamluks. Spectacular building projects soon transformed the traditional center of the city. Baybars started the process in 1262 by building a madrasa next to Salih's monuments of a few years earlier on the east side of the Qasaba (H 6 on Map 4). But it was under Qalawun that construction started on the great sultanic foundations. Within a century they would occupy the whole west side of the Qasaba, in what was once Between the Two Palaces Square (Bayn al-Qasrayn). His hospital *(maristan)*, built in 1284 (H 6), was certainly an impressive facility, both as a building and as a health-care institution.

The hospital was divided into two sections, one for men and one for women. Each patient had a wooden bed with bedclothes and a chamber pot, and his laundry was washed by the hospital. An administrator saw to it that the patients received the necessary food (prepared in the hospital's kitchen) and medicine (made in the hospital's laboratories). Four thousand patients are thought to have been treated there every day. The hospital had doctors, including ophthalmologists, who followed the patients' progress. All services were provided free of charge, and even funeral costs were paid by the hospital when necessary. The foundation had considerable revenues, estimated generously by Ibn Battuta, a great admirer of the hospital ("it would be impossible," he wrote, "to describe its beauties"), at 1,000 dinars a day.

The hospital building, which has almost wholly disappeared, was apparently impressive and magnificently decorated. The structure was part of a complex that also included a madrasa and a mausoleum, the latter surviving today as one of the most remarkable monuments of Arab Cairo. The facade extends for approximately 70 meters along Great Street and is surmounted by a superb minaret. This complex was afterward completed by the construction of the other Mamluk monuments that make up the wonderful panorama still visible today in this portion of the Bayn al-Qasrayn: a mosque and mausoleum built by Nasir Muhammad (1304) and the later mosque of Sultan Barquq (1386). This sumptuous locale served as a setting for official ceremonies, processions, and investitures, whose regalia and luxury confirmed the power of the sovereign. It is thus that, in 1321–1322, a number of mamluks who had just been made emirs by the sultan came to the Mansuriyya madrasa (built by Qalawun) at Bayn al-Qasrayn. Maqrizi recalls: "Qahira was lit up in their honor. Female singers performed from shops in various places; and a sumptuous banquet with fruits and drinks was prepared for them in the madrasa. It was a memorable day."[3]

The Mamluks continued the gradual transformation of the Fatimid palaces that had begun under the Ayyubids. In 1262, for example, Baybars drew up a document for signature by the descendants of Caliph al-Adid stipulating that a certain number of the parts of the palace belonged to the public treasury. They were then sold, lot by lot, and new buildings were raised there. The palaces disappeared bit by bit, replaced by religious buildings, commercial spaces, or even residences. Emir Baktash was thus able to buy a part of the Eastern Palace and build a residence and stables on it. After his death, Emir Bashtak bought the palace (qasr), received a plot of ground from Nasir, demolished eleven mosques from the Fatimid period, and, in 1339, built a vast palace (H 6). By Maqrizi's time there remained only a few vestiges of the Great Palace, sometimes brought to light by the ongoing construction. Thus the historian reports that in July 1375 two enormous columns were discovered buried under rubble at the Bab al-Zumurrud (Gate of the Emerald) and brought to the sultan's construction site. Outside the palace area, people moved into the space between the Fatimid quarters and also rearranged those quarters. Among those settling in Cairo were of course the Mamluks: in 1279–1280, during the civil disturbances, the emirs living in the Citadel asked that the gates of the city be opened "so that the soldiers may return to their homes and see their children, from whom they have been separated for so long."

At last Qahira experienced a period of rapid development for businesses, shops, and caravanserais. The Qasaba was packed with them at the beginning of the fifteenth century, and they even overflowed into the neighboring areas. Maqrizi relates that before 1340

Emir Qusun built a large caravanserai *(wakala)*, with a *rab* (apartment complex) above it, on the site of a private house (F 5):

> The emir built a *funduq*, vast in area, and surrounded it with shops. He stipulated that the renter of any shop should pay no more than five dirhams . . . I visited this [*wakala*]: its exterior and interior aspects are a source of wonder, because of the abundance and diversity of the goods stored there, the affluence of its clientele, the cries of the porters carrying merchandise and delivering it to the river barges . . . The upper stories contained 360 apartments, which I learned to be entirely occupied: the number of residents could be estimated at approximately 4,000 people, men and women, children and adults.[4]

### NORTHWARD EXPANSION FROM QAHIRA

While Qahira completed its transformation, the Mamluks developed the outlying areas, undoubtedly responding to the needs of a growing population but also to the ambitious policies of Sultan Nasir. The results were uneven.[5]

In 1269 Baybars built a large mosque 700 meters northwest of the Bab al-Futuh, opening the way for the urbanization of the Husayniyya quarter. The mosque was sited on a large open space, a maydan, in an area that was still sparsely inhabited though well situated on the road to Syria and on the route of the annual pilgrimage. It was to become the city's northern suburb. This development benefited from the digging of a new canal in 1325, the Khalij al-Nasiri, which lay 1,200 meters west of the old canal, joining it at the height of the Mosque of Baybars. Though probably somewhat exaggerated, Maqrizi's enthusiastic description of Husayniyya and its markets, which he contrasts to its decline in the late fourteenth century, gives an indication of the city's extension into a zone bounded on the north by the Khalij al-Nasiri:

> Husayniyya was the most prosperous artery of Old Cairo and Cairo. An elderly man in whom I have complete trust described it to me [thus]: "Husayniyya was full of suqs and residences, and the streets

were full of vendors, pedestrians, food sellers, jugglers and acrobats, to the point where, for a considerable distance, you could advance on this long, large road only at the cost of great effort . . . on the day the pilgrimage left Cairo."

Maqrizi also mentions a small number of nonspecialized markets (*suwaqqat*), which likewise indicate the urbanization of this area. He states that toward 1360 the small Market of the Arabs next to Husayniyya on the Raydaniyya side had an oven where "around 7,000 breads [were baked] every day for the large number of inhabitants in the neighborhood." Ten mosques were in fact built in Husayniyya between 1250 and 1340, eight of them during Nasir's reign alone. The settlement there of several hundred Tatar refugees in 1262 and 1296 probably contributed to the growth of the suburb and its character as a popular neighborhood, which it retained into modern times.

In the area beyond Husayniyya on the road to Syria, the sultans and emirs concentrated their energies on religious institutions and royal palaces. A limited urbanization resulted at isolated points: the mosque erected at Raydaniyya in 1301, the accommodations built at Birkat al-Hajj on the orders of Nasir to allow him to hunt crane, and especially the *khanqa* built in 1325 in Siriyaqus some 30 kilometers beyond Cairo's northern gate. This institution, intended for a hundred Sufi priests, consisted of a mosque and a bath. Pavilions were constructed there for the sultan and his emirs, and each year from 1322 on the sovereign spent a few days there in November and December. These regular visits occasioned a considerable influx of people, and Nasir had a maydan and a market built there, while the new Nasiri Canal was intended to allow grains and food to reach the *khanqa* by water. A village grew up around Nasir's core construction, described somewhat hyperbolically by the historian Ibn Taghribirdi as "a large town." Nothing of all this should be taken to indicate that a town formed north of Cairo, nor that—except for distinct settlements at Siriyaqus, Ayn Shams, and Matariyya, and some polo grounds, religious monuments, cemeteries, and tombs—a densely urbanized strip has been found stretching from the gates of Cairo north along the road to Syria.

## DEVELOPMENT TO THE WEST

There seems in fact to have been a will to develop the area westward of Cairo, and various means were deployed to this end: a suitable legal framework was devised, and major construction was undertaken on the infrastructure. The westward shift of the Nile had opened a huge area to urbanization, leaving large ponds that would later be sought out as sites for country villas and residences, such as the Birkat al-Azbakiyya and Birkat al-Nasiriyya.

The digging of the Nasiri Canal may have had other justifications besides supplying the *khanqa* at Siryaqus. Wanting to bring a source of water toward Cairo to supplement the Khalij (which was often silted up) could have been a factor weighing in the deliberations. At any rate, the work was entrusted to Emir Arghun and completed between 15 April and 12 June 1325. The canal left the Nile at Mawridat al-Balat, opposite the northern tip of Rawdah Island. It flowed north, parallel and 150 meters to the west of the Khalij al-Hakimi, veered northeast at Maqs, and joined with the old canal not far from the Mosque of Baybars.

This canal, which was more than 5 kilometers long, was also large enough for boats carrying cargo for Siriyaqus to navigate it and, when the Nile was in flood, even pleasure boats. Their presence on the old canal in the middle of Cairo had been the subject of scandal: "Women showed themselves on these boats, in full regalia, sitting next to men, their faces uncovered . . . and brazenly drank wine," writes Maqrizi in reference to events of 1306. It also made it possible to install waterwheels for irrigating gardens and brought water to Birkat al-Ratli, which would become an area of summer residence. The excavation of the canal might thus contribute powerfully to the urbanization of the areas it crossed. Seven bridges were constructed over the new canal between 1325 and 1376. Bridges were also built over the old Khalij to supplement those created in Ayyubid times: the Bridge of Lions (Qanatir al-Siba), built by Baybars and rebuilt by Nasir in 1331 (U 12), the Amir Husayn Bridge of around 1319 (L 9), the Aq Sunqur Bridge of before 1339 (P 10), and the Tuquzdamur Bridge of before 1345 (R 10). All these were in Qahira, and there were five more between Cairo and Siriyaqus.[6]

To promote urban development in the more than 600 hectares between the two canals, the sultan conceded grants to several of his emirs. In return they were to make certain improvements, construct basic buildings (mosques, baths, shops), and encourage settlement on leased parcels of land. Maqrizi estimates that more than sixty such grants were bestowed, varying in size from fifteen feddans (6 hectares) to Emir Qusun, to thirty feddans to Emir Tuquzdamur. The grant holders raised buildings and installed facilities according to a schedule we can actually follow in the case of Emir Tuquzdamur. The emir built a bridge over the Khalij to facilitate settlement, and a *hammam* (bath) and shops. He cut down the trees in the garden he had received and authorized people to build. Houses went up, and the *hikr* became a place of residence for emirs and military officers. It was probably under these same terms that Emir Aq Sunqur (d. 1339) built a bridge on the Khalij, a mosque nearby (Q 11), and two public baths, in the area of the Nasiriyya Pond.

This parceling and development seems to have been particularly active in the south part of the zone between the two canals, the area near Birkat al-Nasiriyya, where three of the four bridges built under Nasir can be found. The facts that the area boasted a polo ground (Maydan al-Mahar), built by Nasir in 1320 between the Khalij and the Nile, and that the sultan maintained an active interest in it (going there to play polo with his emirs) may explain the zeal of his courtiers. However, we have uncovered only two mosques built in this zone, Aqsunqur and Sitt Miska (1339, Q 11), a pace of development far short of the rapid one described by Maqrizi. In the entire western zone "between the two canals" only six mosques were built during Nasir's reign, leading us to a similar conclusion.[7]

Farther west, Nasir's efforts at urban development seem to have had only modest success. The settlement of Tatar refugees in the Luq area (M–N 13) in 1262 certainly promoted development there. Buildings also went up beyond the Khalij al-Nasiri to the banks of the Nile, between what would become the port of Bulaq and Old Cairo. But settlement was relatively sparse and included many gardens, with residences often intended largely for summer use during the hot months when the rich traditionally migrated to the countryside, a custom that would remain typical of Cairenes until the eighteenth century. The course of the Nile being unstable, with violent phases of drying and flooding, and with islands appearing and disappearing, conditions did not favor settlement in the areas closest to the river. In 1281 the east branch of the Nile dried up and the Island of the Elephant was connected to Maqs by dry land. Yet in 1322 the flood crested so high that the riverbank was submerged between the mouth of the Khalij al-Nasiri and Bulaq, and a dike was built to protect Qahira. In 1337 the rising Nile again threatened the riverbank at Bulaq, and construction was undertaken to direct water toward the west bank (Imbaba) with what Maqrizi assures us were 23,000 boats to carry stone from the mountain. In 1348 the Nile dried up between Misr and Bulaq, and dikes were built opposite Giza and the Nilometer, but in the same year the floodwaters rose so high that they caused houses built along the Nile at Bulaq to collapse.[8]

Maqrizi is always an optimist in describing the expansion of Cairo during Nasir's time (and always a pessimist in describing the period that followed). As an instance, in reference to the sultan's plans for building in 1313, he writes: "The people began to build toward Luq, on the far side of Maqs, and to build on the land of Bustan al-Khashshab between Luq and Manshiya al-Mihrani along the Nile," that is, between the mouth of the old Khalij and the Luq area. In reference to the digging of the Khalij al-Nasiri in 1325, he writes that building proceeded until "the area that extended in width between the bank of the Nile at Bulaq and Bab al-Bahr [E 11] and in length between Manshiya al-Mihrani and Minyat al-Shiraj [was organized]. The banks of the Khalij on either side were covered with houses, while behind them were gardens, markets, public baths, and mosques." The region west of Qahira had become "a series of towns."

In actuality, Cairo's westward expansion seems to have been limited at the time to a fringe of plots neighboring the Khalij al-Hakimi; corridors of urbanization along the roads leading to the Nile from Bab al-Bahr, Bab al-Luq, and the Bridge of Lions; and fairly sparse settlements along the Khalij al-Nasiri and the bank of the Nile. For the period 1293–1348 our sources mention only two emirs' residences in the western zone and two more near the Nile, in contrast to twenty-seven in Qahira and eighteen in the southern district. Bulaq was only starting to develop. Sultan Nasir sold courtiers parcels of land recently uncovered by the Nile for them to build on, but the first large religious foundation, the al-Khatiri Mosque, was built by Emir Aydamur (along with a *funduq* and a *rab*) only in 1336. Even so, it was almost immediately damaged by the flooding of the Nile, built as it was on the immediate shore (though it now stands some 200 meters from the river).[9]

CONSTRUCTION ON THE CITADEL

Nasir's efforts to promote urban development met with more lasting success in the southern zone, perhaps because they coincided with Cairo's natural evolution and continued a development already sketched out under the Ayyubids.

After Salih's brief interlude on the Nile, the Citadel once more became the residence of the sultans. New buildings went up under Baybars, Qalawun, and especially Nasir to make a palace zone, a "setting for Mamluk ceremonial," in Doris Behrens-Abouseif's felicitous phrase. Baybars built the "House of Gold" there, the Hall of Justice (Dar al-Adl), and quarters for the mamluks. Qalawun, for his part, built a dome *(qubba)* and the residence of the *na'ib* (viceroy). But it was Nasir who was the primary builder of the southern enclosure of the Citadel, the residential complex, whereas the northern enclosure housing the soldiery had by and large been organized under the Ayyubids. The Mosque of Nasir augmented the structure built by the Ayyubids; it was rebuilt in 1318 and altered significantly in 1335.

The Great Iwan (1315), or main reception hall, stood on the present site of the Mosque of Muhammad Ali, replacing the iwan built by Qalawun. It had three primary functions: a hall of justice, a reception hall for ambassadors and important guests, and the ceremonial site where the sultan's review of the Mamluks culminated. This monument, which was greatly admired and often described by travelers (who knew it as the "Divan of Joseph"), consisted at the time of the French Expedition of thirty-two columns of red granite 8 meters high, supporting stone arches and a dome. It was open on three sides. In its architecture, it was thought to surpass every mosque in Cairo, including the Mosque of Sultan Hasan.

The Qasr, built in 1313, was another royal reception hall, less ceremonial, where the sultan held his daily audience except for the two days when he sat in the Great Iwan. It was known as the Qasr al-Ablaq, or Striped Palace, because its facade was built of alternating

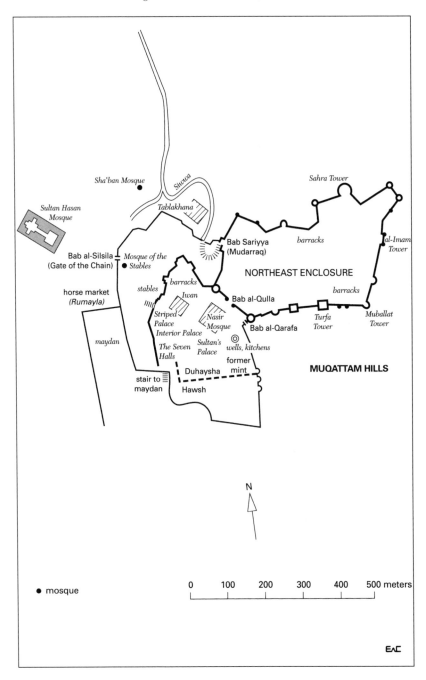

Map 5. The Citadel in the Mamluk period (after Casanova)

Mosque of Nasir Muhammad in the Qasaba, 1304

courses of dark and light stone. It was built like the Palace of Baybars in Damascus, and artisans from Syria had in fact been imported to work on it. It was there that the investiture ceremony for new sultans was performed. In ruins at the start of the Ottoman period, it survives only in fragments.

The south end of the Citadel contained the Courtyard (Hawsh). This was the private part of the royal residence, including the harem. Later, ceremonies would also occur there, the Iwan and the Qasr being used only on exceptional occasions. In 1337 the sultan installed a livestock pen there for sheep (there were reportedly 30,000 at his death), cattle, and geese in a space that had been used as a quarry in building the Citadel. We can only suggest the private buildings that included, notably, three palaces and seven halls. The great serai at one time housed 1,200 slaves. Finally, residential quarters were built for the mamluks. Of all this gigantic complex, only the mosque has survived intact. By Maqrizi's report, its luxury and high cost provoked lively criticism among the people.

The necessary complement to these buildings, in a society in which horsemen played such a prominent role, were the stables and maydan where men and horses trained. The stables were arranged in such a way that the sultan could observe them from the Qasr. Nasir, who had a passion for horses as strong as his passion for sheep and geese, probably had the stables refurbished. A loggia (maq'ad) was used for ceremonies; later it would also be used by the Circassian sultans. The stables were outside the main wall of the Citadel but communicated with it; hence their importance in the event of unrest, when access to the Citadel was cut off. From the stables, the sultan could reach the maydan, which was below the Citadel. Known as the Black, or Qara, Maydan, it dated back to Ibn Tulun. The mamluks trained on it, and the sultan himself played polo there with his emirs every Tuesday. But it was also used for various celebrations, including prayers for the Two Feasts, which were followed by a banquet in the Iwan and the distribution of robes of honor. In 1313 Nasir had significant improvements made to it. Soil was brought by the emirs, palm trees and shade trees were planted, wells dug, and waterwheels installed. A stone wall was built to encircle it, part of whose western section appears in the *Index to Mohammedan Monuments*.[10]

As a considerable number of soldiers and courtiers resided in the

Citadel, a water supply was needed. In 1313 Nasir built four water-wheels on the Nile. From this site, probably corresponding to where Sultan Ghuri much later placed the intake for his aqueduct, the water was carried to Saladin's wall, whence channels led it to the Citadel.[11] Nasir had plans for even more substantial constructions: in 1327 he thought to "make the Nile pass under the Citadel," writes Maqrizi, by diverting it from the area near Hilwan, 20 kilometers south of the Citadel. He sent the supervisor of monuments (shadd al-ama'ir) to Hilwan to draw up plans for the canal. The project's costs and labor, however, forced him to renounce it. In 1340 Nasir took up the project again in a more modest form. In the company of his engineers he visited Birkat al-Habash, somewhat to the south of Old Cairo, and ordered ten wells to be dug there, each forty cubits deep, and mechanisms installed to bring the water to the Citadel. Work began on a canal starting from the Nile north of Ribat al-Athar, this time only 5 kilometers from the Citadel. The death of the sultan brought an end to the undertaking, which had been typical of the outsized ambition of Nasir's projects.[12]

## THE URBANIZATION OF THE SOUTHERN DISTRICTS

The development in and around the Citadel could only reinforce the urbanizing trend started under the Ayyubids in the districts south of the Fatimid city. Indications of urban development in that area from the time of the earliest Mamluks survive. One example is the parceling into lots of a quarter northwest of the Citadel that had once contained cemeteries, and whose small market took the name of Emir Izz al-Din Aybak al-Izzi, an inspector of the army who died before Acre in 1291—the Suwayqa al-Izzi (Q 5–6) would remain one of the busiest markets in Cairo right to the end of the eighteenth century. Then there is the renovation by Sultan Lajin (1296–1298) of the Mosque of Ibn Tulun, which had lapsed into ruin and lain quasi-abandoned. He apparently invested 20,000 dinars in the enterprise, enlarging the mosque and building the handsome domed structure that now occupies the center of the courtyard. With the monument thus renovated, the district around it came back to life. It was certainly in the context of this renaissance that Sultan Kitbugha (1294–1296) built a maydan between the Birkat al-Fil and Kabsh Hill and, shortly after, built the beautiful madrasa and double mausoleum of Emirs Sangar and Salar (1303–04, V 10).[13]

To this gradual development, Nasir Muhammad gave a vigorous boost by his policies, reminiscent of the methods he used to promote expansion in the western district. Once again grants were given to encourage the parceling and settlement of land near the large Birkat al-Fil, which was to become one of Cairo's chic quarters. Referring to one of the developments, this one managed by Emir Aqbugha on the site of gardens near the pond, Maqrizi notes that many houses were built and that a "large town" *(madina kabira)* grew up on a desert spot with little security. As part of the urban development of the area, the main emirs founded mosques there: the Mosque of Ylmas in 1329 (R 7); the Mosque of Qusun, also in 1329 (P 8); the Mosque of Bashtak in 1337 (R 10); and finally the mosque of Altunbugha al-Maridani in 1339 (O 5), of which Sultan Nasir himself underwrote the costs and oversaw construction. These congregational mosques have survived to our day. They are among the most remarkable of Nasir's time, the last in particular, built in honor of a mamluk whom the sultan held in great affection. This program would continue actively after Nasir's death: the Mosques of Aslam al-Silahdar in 1344 (N 4); of Aq Sunqur in 1346 (P–Q 5); of Shaykhu in 1349 (T 7); of Sarghatmish in 1356 (U 9); and finally of Sultan Hasan in 1356–1361 (S 6).

This mushrooming of monuments by all accounts accompanied and, in some cases, promoted urban development along the main arteries of the zone south of Cairo. To encourage this trend the sultan urged his emirs to build large mansions in the area, thinking they would become the core around which people clustered. Maqrizi attributes the building of several palaces to the sultan. These were intended for his favorite mamluks: the palace of Emir Taqtamur, built on the Rise of the Oxen (Hadrat al-Baqar, S 7) at a cost of 300,000 dirhams; the palace of Emir Baktamur on the Birkat al-Fil, which cost one million dirhams; the palace of Yalbugha al-Yahiyawi, whose construction the sultan saw to personally and which cost 460,000 dirhams, the most beautiful of all, according to Maqrizi. Unfortunately it was later destroyed to make room for the Mosque of Sultan Hasan.

Kabsh Hill, rising behind the Mosque of Ibn Tulun, became a

Mosque of Maridani, 1340

residential area for members of the sultan's family, emirs, ambassadors, and, in alternation with the Citadel, the Abbassid caliphs. In 1322 Nasir refurbished the pavilions on Kabsh for his daughter's wedding to the son of the great Emir Arghun. Maqrizi writes that pavilions surrounded the Birkat al-Fil "as leaves surround the bark," and "they appear to the eye as no less than the stars scattered around the moon"—not just a poetic phrase. Of the sixteen emirs' residences we have located in the area south of Qahira, representing 35 percent of all residences located for the period from 1293–1340, six were in fact situated on the *birkat*.[14]

The establishment of handsome mansions certainly promoted settlement in the area. Maqrizi describes the many houses built along the "avenue" joining the Zuwayla Gate to Saliba and mentions several suqs having "a certain number of shops, although," he adds, "they are far from being as large as the suqs of Cairo and much less affluent." Other sources speak of markets, caravanserais, and apartment houses in this district, confirming its gradual urbanization along the main axes: the Hall of the Apples (Dar al-Tuffah) and the *rab* above it, built by Emir Tuquzdamur just outside the Zuwayla Gate, where Cairo's fruits were sold, their sight and smell suggesting paradise, according to Maqrizi; and the *qaysariyya* built in 1349 by Taj al-Din al-Munawi near the Mosque of Ibn Tulun, which contained thirty shops and whose success was due to a supernatural event: "During the night of [27 November 1349], the messenger of God appeared in a dream to a pious man standing at the door to this covered market and spoke to him thus: 'God bless those who live in this market!' He repeated this sentiment three times. The man told of the apparition, and the demand for rentals rose."

Settlement in the area is characterized by Maqrizi with his customary emphasis: people started to build as though they had been called upon to do so "all without exception," and constructions stretched uninterruptedly "from outside Qahira to the Mosque of Ibn Tulun."[15]

NASIR'S LEGACY

What is the tally, finally, of Nasir's urban achievement? Historians have generally adopted Maqrizi's sanguine appraisals, tempering them somewhat in recognition of the fact that Maqrizi lived well after the death of Sultan Nasir and in a period of crisis that led him to describe the past in the rosiest terms. In a chapter of his book on Cairo significantly titled "The City of a Thousand and One Nights," Stanley Lane-Poole describes the expansion of the city under Nasir "in every direction," concluding that "Cairo had reached its size of approximately fifty years ago before the development of new European suburbs along the Nile." Marcel Clerget describes a Cairo "full to bursting," where "the empty lots . . . are rented out and immediately overrun with buildings; the gardens that surrounded houses during the Fatimid period are being filled with several-story apartment houses. The public squares are disappearing." He estimates the minimum population of Cairo in around 1350 at 600,000. Janet Abu-Lughod suggests 500,000 as a maximum. These estimates are based on no concrete data, such as the total built-up area, and it is therefore difficult to decide between this rosy picture and David Ayalon's very negative view of the long-term effects of Nasir's construction policies.[16]

One way to appreciate Cairo's expansion under Nasir is to survey the number of mosques and schools built in the various districts between 1293 and 1340: one in the north, eight in Husayniyya, six in the western zone (including Bulaq), ten in Qahira (already well supplied with religious edifices), sixteen in the zone between Bab Zuwayla and the Mosque of Ibn Tulun, six in the zone between the two canals, three in the south (Rawdah Island and Misr), four in the south cemetery. These figures indicate that expansion at a distance from the city (north of Husayniyya and west of the Khalij al-Nasiri) should be regarded not as true urbanization but at most as the establishment of "networks" of population along the major axes and a fairly sparse residential settlement along the Nile and the Khalij al-Nasiri. So too the zone between the two canals saw a beginning of settlement, limited to the main routes of circulation. The Husayniyya district developed actively but suffered a serious decline when Cairo experienced a crisis in the second half of the fourteenth century. The expansion of the southern zone between Qahira and the Citadel was considerable, though probably somewhat uneven except along the principal axes. The data available to us (location of mosques) suggests that the built-up area in 1348 was more extensive than can be supposed from Maqrizi's information, but less extensive than is indicated by the *Description de l'Egypte*.[17] As to Cairo's population, it probably did not exceed 200,000. Paris had a population of only 80,000 in 1328 (in a built-up area of 437 hectares), and London a population of 60,000 in 1377 (on 288 hectares). Of the cities in the West at this period, only Constantinople could claim a greater population.[18]

That Cairo under Nasir was a city bursting with prosperity and beauty is attested by all who described it at the time. Writing in 1325, Ibn Battuta claimed that one found everything one could want in Cairo,

> the learned and the ignorant, the grave and the gay, the mild and the choleric, the noble and the base, the obscure and the illustrious. Like the waves of the sea she surges with her throngs of folk, yet for all the capacity of her station and her power to sustain can scarce hold their number . . . Speaking of Cairo the poet said: ". . . Misr [Cairo] is not *misr* [a large city] but paradise here below . . . Its children are angels, and its doe-eyed girls are houris."[19]

It cannot be denied, however, that some aspects of Nasir's construction and urbanization policies exhibit megalomania, which would explain why certain of his undertakings withered on the vine. It is not certain, for instance, that the Khalij al-Nasiri corresponded to any real need. The same goes for the project of bringing a canal to the Citadel. The urbanization of the western zone at a forced pace was probably premature, and a period favorable to Bulaq's development would come only much later, when Egypt's geopolitical situation had changed. But it is also true that several of Nasir's enterprises failed because of an economic and demographic crisis that developed only after his reign. The sultan's projects existed in the context of a rising demographic base, which justified opening up new areas to Cairo's expansion. At least Sultan Nasir prepared the way for urban development in the south, where it would continue unabated, and in the west, where it would be resumed much later. In any case, the expansion he began and encouraged and the interest he brought to bear on constructing monuments profoundly transformed the physical aspect of Cairo, which experienced, after the splendor of the Fatimids, a new climax under his reign.

# 6

# The Great Crisis
# (1348–1412)

A FEW YEARS AFTER the peaceful and brilliant reign of Nasir Muhammad ended, Egypt was hit by a catastrophic demographic event, the great plague epidemic of 1348. The country entered a decline, which Tamerlane's invasion of Syria in 1400 would exacerbate. It culminated in the disastrous reign of Faraj, "a long and painful story of terrible atrocities" leading to a civil war replete with "burlesque and bloody incident."[1] The savage assassination of the sultan by his footmen in Damascus in 1412 marked the end of the crisis. With Egypt's fortunes at a low ebb, the transition from the dynasty of Turkish (Bahri) sultans to that of Circassian (Burji) ones in 1382 does not seem to have signaled a decisive change.

### THE BLACK DEATH OF 1348

"It was then that an epidemic of plague exploded such as was never before seen in the Islamic era," writes Maqrizi.

It entered Egypt at the end of the season when the grasslands turn green, hence in the autumn of the year 748 . . . This epidemic was distinctive in that it did not particularly affect one region and leave another untouched but spread to all parts of the Earth, in the East as in the West . . . Furthermore, it encompassed not just the human species but also the fish in the sea, the birds in the sky, and the animals in the field . . . A letter from the governor of Aleppo arrived in

Cairo saying that a devout man had seen the Prophet in a dream. When he complained to Muhammad of this plague . . . the Prophet advised him to tell the people to repent, reciting the following prayer: "O God, soften the terrible trial caused by the All-Powerful Master . . . We cling to the coattails of Thy Bounty that Thy intercession may protect us against Thy oppression."

The Black Death originated in the steppes of Central Asia where there existed a permanent reservoir of infection. The epidemic reached the Black Sea in 1338–39, and the rats that are its vector were transported from there to Egypt probably by Christian merchant ships. Infected flies may also have transmitted the disease, such as those traveling in the furs that were actively traded between southern Russia and Mamluk Egypt. The epidemic reached Egypt's shores in the early autumn of 1347 (at the same time that it arrived in Sicily), spread throughout Lower Egypt in April 1348, and soon made its way to Cairo. The plague was at its height from October 1348 to January 1349 and ended in February 1349. Maqrizi describes its onslaught:

Cairo became an empty desert, and there was no one to be seen in the streets. A man could go from the Zuwayla Gate to the Bab al-Nasr without encountering another soul. The dead were so numerous that people thought only of them. Rubble piled up in the streets. People wore anxious expressions. Wailing could be heard on all sides, and you did not pass a house without being assailed by shrieks. Corpses lay piled along the public way, burial trains jostled one another, and the dead were carried to their graves amidst commotion.

It is obviously difficult to evaluate the number of victims. Maqrizi writes that they numbered from 10,000 to 20,000 per day. Ibn Battuta, who was in Cairo in 1348 and 1349, reports 24,000 dead in a single day in Cairo and Misr. The total number of 900,000 dead suggested by Maqrizi, "not counting those who died on vacant lots, or those from the districts of Husayniyya or Saliba, or from the streets in the immediate suburbs of Cairo, who would more than have doubled the number," is highly improbable. Sifting all of the available information, Michael Dols concludes that the total number of deaths came to one-third or two-fifths of the population of the city, a proportion that seems plausible given what we know about mortality from the Black Death in other localities (Europe, for example) and from other epidemics in other periods. We may therefore estimate that a reasonable figure would be 100,000 dead.[2]

## THE CRISIS IN EGYPT

The plague epidemic decreased the population of Egypt and Cairo significantly. Maqrizi writes: "Many streets stood empty of their inhabitants. In Barjawan Street [his own quarter], forty-two empty houses were counted. Small streets and impasses became deserted, despite their many dwellings. The furniture abandoned in these places found no takers—an inheritance might pass through the hands of four or five people in a single day."

This brutal letting of the population made itself felt for a long time afterward. Given the slow rates of population gain that were the rule, only a long period of demographic tranquillity could have made up the difference, but Cairo and Egypt were not to see another such period. The degeneration of the city at the start of the fifteenth century was in large part due to the hemorrhage of its population. The consequences were equally grave for the army, whose decimated ranks never entirely recovered from this and subsequent crises. One thousand mamluks died during the epidemic of 1437–38, and 1,400 in 1460. The depopulation of the countryside, as significant as in the city, entailed a noticeable decrease in revenues—moneys used to support the elite caste. Of the 2,200 villages in Egypt, 40 were abandoned, and 462 saw their tax burden reduced. Tax revenues are estimated to have declined 12 percent overall between 1348 and 1420. Clearly, Egypt's entire economy suffered from the consequences of this crisis. The scarcity and high price of labor occasioned lower agricultural production, while the output of skilled urban craftsmen declined as foreign competition stepped into the gap (textile manufacture, for instance).[3]

The Black Death, as it turned out, was only the first in a series of crises that prevented the country and city from making a lasting recovery. The plague returned again and again, in 1374–75, and in 1379–1381.[4] The frequency and intensity of these outbreaks prevented the earlier losses from being rectified, occasioning an absolute decline in the population. Egypt and its capital were therefore faced with an ongoing demographic crisis after 1348, with the outbreaks of epidemic sometimes exacerbated by other natural disasters: an abnormally high rise of the Nile in 1354, which flooded areas north of Cairo; a famine in 1375 so severe that the poor had to be divided among the emirs to provide them subsistence; an inadequate flood and grain shortage in 1394.[5]

In the second half of the fourteenth century, serious political difficulties arose to make the situation worse. Although the principle of hereditary succession within Qalawun's line was maintained after the death of Nasir (twelve of whose sons, grandsons, and great-grandsons succeeded him to the throne between 1340 and 1382), the reigns of sovereigns too young to govern were in fact overseen by prominent emirs. Most reigns were brief, with only Hasan (1347–1361) and Sha'ban (1363–1376) reigning for any length of time. The dominant figures were therefore the great emirs, who imposed their will on the country and were also its great builders: Taz, Shaykhu, Sarghatmish, Ylbugha, and Barquq, who became sultan in 1382 and founded the Circassian "dynasty." Barquq's reign (1382–1399) was relatively prosperous, but the country experienced severe domestic disorders: a civil war in 1389 during which Barquq was unseated, and an open struggle between the two leading emirs, Mintash and Ylbugha, which divided the population of Cairo. At the same time, the difficulties the sultans encountered in Syria (border conflicts, rebellious emirs, Mongol invasion) indicated that the external security Egypt had enjoyed under Nasir was now a thing of the past.

### THE RUIN OF CAIRO

The calamities that swept Egypt from 1348 on did not, for all that, engender an immediate and irreversible decline. Only a few years after the ravages of the Black Death, Sultan Hasan—a relatively obscure ruler, controlled by officers who deposed him in 1351 after he had reigned for four years and restored him to rule in 1354—had the power to build, from 1356 to 1361, the gigantic mosque that bears his name and is considered one of the most remarkable monuments of the Islamic world. It is true that because of the gigantic size of the

North facade of the Mosque of Sultan Hasan, 1362
(*Description de l'Egypte*, Bibliothèque Nationale)

building (intended for 400 students) it was neither completed or decorated, yet it remains the most majestic testament to Mamluk art. How are we to explain the profusion of religious monuments erected in the same area between 1350 and 1380, most of which still survive? These buildings called for substantial means, which a government in utter bankruptcy could never have mobilized. Maqrizi estimates that the construction of the Mosque of Sultan Hasan cost 20,000 dirhams per day for three years (totaling more than 20 million dirhams), which would make it the most expensive monument ever built in Cairo. Paradoxically, the countless deaths from the plague epidemics allowed the government to collect death duties and make confiscations that in all likelihood substantially increased the rulers' resources and enabled them to implement ambitious architectural programs. But the land registry of 1376, replacing that of 1315, cites revenues of 9.5 million dinars, a considerable sum.[6]

Thus economic activity did not come to a standstill in Qahira during this period. Several commercial structures were built, among them the caravanserai that, taking the name of its builder, Emir Jaharkas al-Khalili al-Yalbughawi, was to become the most famous center of commerce in Cairo, and the present-day symbol of its old suqs, the Khan al-Khalili (before 1389). On the Qasaba, Sultan Barquq built a mosque in 1384–1386 that would complete in an almost definitive manner the prestigious setting of the Bayn al-

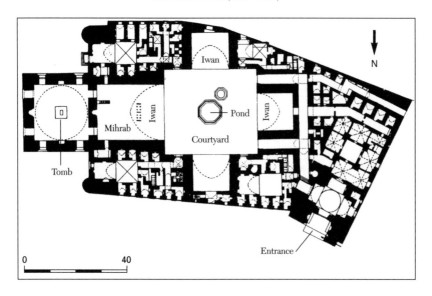

Plan of the Mosque of Sultan Hasan (Antiquités du Caire)

Qasrayn. The account by a Muslim traveler of the spectacle that greeted him at the center of Cairo on his arrival in 1390 offers no indication of a decline, but rather of ceaseless activity:

> The first time I entered Between the Two Palaces Square, I thought a wedding procession was passing or an important funeral, so great was the unbroken flow of passersby. I inquired to discover what led people to walk thus across the square and was told it was the custom in the city. I have heard that people walking at night in Between the Two Palaces Square pursue young boys and women. They engage in intimacy even as they walk without anyone noticing, so intent is each on his own pleasure. But I never had any difficulty in moving through the square, no matter how great the crush, and someone pointed out to me that people walked to the left . . . The idlers on Between the Two Palaces . . . formed two lines, each like a raging torrent flowing left. My informant gave me the following reason for it: since the heart is on the left, strollers lean toward the side their heart is on, and that explains why they incline to the left.[7]

Just as significant was the development of the zone south of Cairo, particularly the area between the Mosque of Ibn Tulun and

Courtyard of the Mosque of Barquq, 1386

the Citadel. We have mentioned the imposing religious buildings that were built in succession after 1340. The trend continued after the construction of the Mosque of Sultan Hasan. Maqrizi has no hesitation in comparing the madrasa of the Sultan Sha'ban Mosque, built in 1375 (S 4) and destroyed in 1411, with the magnificent madrasa of Sultan Hasan. Nineteen of the forty-nine mosques built during the period 1341–1412 were built in the southern zone (fourteen of them around the Citadel), which is more than were built in Qahira during Nasir's reign.

Urban development in this part of Cairo was also notable, as under Nasir, for the building of large residences for the emirs. Seventeen of the forty palaces dating from 1341 to 1412 were built in the area south of Qahira—more than in Nasir's own time, showing that the trend he had set in motion was actually growing stronger. We are fortunate to have the imposing remains of the palace that Emir Taz built for himself in Saliba in 1352 (S–T 7), whose inaugural banquet on 30 July 1353 was attended by Sultan Salih, the last of Nasir's sons to rule (1351–1354). This was a very great honor to Taz, as Maqrizi notes somewhat ruefully: "Before this, no Turkish sovereign had ever descended [from the Citadel] to the residence of an emir." Sultan Barquq was to undertake construction and restoration in the Citadel and its immediate vicinity (thus the maydan was restored) that testify to the ongoing activity in this area.[8]

Other parts of the city, in the north and west particularly, were perhaps stagnating, even regressing (though as much because of the venturesome expansion under Nasir as because of the economic climate). But on the whole the city presented an impressive front, enough to arouse the enthusiasm of the celebrated Maghribi traveler Ibn Khaldun. Arriving in Cairo in January 1383, he echoed Ibn Battuta's enthusiasm:

> I beheld the metropolis of the World, orchard of the Universe, hive of nations . . . human anthill, portal of Islam, throne of royalty, bursting with palaces and portals within, shining on the horizon with convents and schools, illuminated by the moons and stars of its learned doctors, which appeared on the bank of the Nile, River of Paradise, flowing with the waters of the sky.[9]

The situation in Cairo was to decline precipitously in the last decades of the fourteenth century and the first decades of the fifteenth, as the crisis that had started to affect Egypt became more generally felt. The change of dynasty in 1382, with the advent of the "Circassian" (Burji) Mamluks, played only a secondary role in the deterioration. The system of government did not change, and Barquq did not fail, at the end of a basically calm and fruitful reign, to try to reestablish hereditary succession to benefit his son Faraj, who was then eleven years old. His extreme youth provoked the same difficulties encountered by Nasir's successors, but Faraj was a somewhat unstable individual whose faults would reveal themselves only gradually, and he was incapable of coming to grips with the enormous difficulties that beset Egypt: domestic problems due to the insubordination of the emirs, and Tamerlane's invasion of Syria in 1400. Aleppo suffered extraordinary carnage. Then, after meeting amiably with Ibn Khaldun, Tamerlane allowed his troops to sack Damascus. Luckily the Mongol conqueror stopped at the gates of Egypt, but his brief passage left several countries in ruins.

All these difficulties unfolded against a backdrop of natural catastrophes that finally ruined the Egyptian economy: a weak flood in 1403, followed by a famine (no doubt horrific, as Maqrizi dates from 806/1403–04 the era of "events" and "trials" during which, to hear him tell it, Egypt was ruined, two-thirds of its population lost, and more than half of the buildings in Cairo and its surrounding area destroyed). And though the historian's confirmed antipathy to Faraj and his severe judgment of Faraj's reign may have caused him to blacken the picture somewhat, we must suppose that his interminable litany of complaints aptly reflects the disastrous situation of Egypt and Cairo.[10]

The signs of Cairo's ruin are amply recorded by Maqrizi, who wrote his description, it would appear, mainly between 1415 and 1424 at a time when the wounds from Egypt's time of crisis were still visible and its eventual recovery still largely in the future. Maqrizi cites a census of the looms in Alexandria, whose number fell from 14,000 in 1388 to 800 in 1434. The decline of the local textile industry is no doubt reflected in the vogue for European woolen fabric (*gukh*). Traditionally worn only by the poorer classes, *gukh* seems to have come into general favor in the fifteenth century. It was cheaper than Egyptian cloth, which was at one time more highly prized, and also owed its penetration of the Egyptian market to the growing dominance of Western merchants. The decline of luxury handicrafts in a city boasting a wealthy elite who were strong consumers of luxury goods can best be symbolized by the dwindling of the art of silver- and gold-inlaid copper objects, once highly valued in Cairo. Maqrizi reports that these objects had disappeared almost entirely as a result of a falloff in demand, the general impoverishment, a shortage of workers, and the difficulty of obtaining the necessary metals—all factors that related to the crisis in Egypt.

But it is in Maqrizi's description of the city and its centers of economic activity that we no doubt find the most obvious signs of Egypt's decline. The situation on the Qasaba, where the city's main commercial activity transpired, "has become lamentable. It is nothing more than a ruin, for most of the shops are in ruins, though they were once too narrow for the shopkeepers . . . There were suqs on this boulevard—some now abandoned, though others still exist." The Bab al-Futuh suq "has diminished in size since the events." Most of the shops in the suq of the caravan outfitters had been destroyed; "those remaining, few though they are, are bare of merchandise." The suq in the Barjawan quarter, once "the most substantial in Cairo," shut down entirely in 1403 and "has become more solitary than a stake at the bottom of a deep pit." In the Waxmakers' Suq "there are hardly five shops" where there were twenty before. Finally, the Between the Two Palaces Suq: "The sadness I feel at the mediocre vestiges to which it has been reduced is keen." Maqrizi offers the same desolate picture of the caravanserais. The Masrur Khan "was one of the largest and most renowned . . . From the time that calamities rained down on Syria in the year after Tamerlane's destructive invasion, which also caused Egypt's ruin, the number of merchants has declined . . . The upkeep of this khan . . . was neglected to the point where a number of rooms fell to ruins." On the Funduq of Bilal al-Mughithi: "At the time of Tamerlane's invasion . . . the *funduq* foundered: only remnants of it subsist." And so on.[11]

The ruin described by Maqrizi affected entire sections of Cairo, and in some cases these were sections where the urban development fostered in Nasir's reign rested on too shaky a foundation to survive in adverse times. Thus on the fate of Husayniyya north of the city, Maqrizi brings an odd mixture of political and natural circumstances to account. He first launches into his usual panegyric on the quarter's prosperity during the golden age: "Husayniyya was the most prosperous artery of Old Cairo and Cairo . . . [It] was full of suqs and residences, and its streets were full of vendors, pedestrians, food sellers, jugglers and acrobats." Then came "the lamentable events of 1403" and the following years: "Its quarters fell into ruin, its buildings turned to rubble, which was sold for materials, the beams especially, and its population moved away." At that point, "a calamity from heaven" crowned the disastrous situation: an invasion of worms, first appearing north of Cairo in 1388, descended on Husayniyya. "The worms attacked the roofs of houses . . . the infestation reached the beams . . . The worms multiplied and gnawed even the walls, so that the inhabitants of the quarter considered demolishing what was left of their houses." The withdrawal from the western areas of development was no doubt a gradual result of the contraction of the city back into its old urbanized zones, which were less hard hit by the demographic and economic crisis. Maqrizi reports that mosques near the Khalij al-Nasiri were abandoned and in some cases destroyed. The city seems to have returned to its former equilibrium in this area and retracted to the district near the old Khalij.[12]

Inside Qahira itself, the demographic decline can be gauged by the large number of public baths that were abandoned. These generally provide an accurate index of urban development, and we find that of the fifty-one baths that Maqrizi mentions in Cairo, only twenty-nine were operating during his own day. This effect was concentrated almost entirely within Qahira, where only twenty-five of the forty-six baths mentioned were in operation. In nearly every case (nineteen), Maqrizi speaks of the "ruin" of the bath, and in several instances he specifies that the bath ceased to be used after 1340, therefore during the crisis. In certain quarters of Cairo, whole sectors were probably abandoned for a long time. Discussing the road that led to Juwaniyya and al-Utufiyya (F 4), Maqrizi writes: "These localities are in ruins." The city that emerged from the crisis triggered by the epidemic of 1348 was therefore a city whose population and built-up area had shrunk significantly.[13]

# 7

# Maqrizi's Cairo

IT MAY SEEM PARADOXICAL to look in Maqrizi's work for "the evoca-
tion of a city's greatness, when he witnessed mainly its ruin," but the
choice is a reasonable one all the same. Maqrizi, one of Egypt's greatest historians, is also the only one to have given us a complete description of Cairo until the scholars of the Napoleonic Expedition
produced their *Description de l'Egypte* at the end of the eighteenth
century. Maqrizi's life was a long one (1364–1442). His *Khitat* is a
geographic and historical description of Egypt and especially Cairo,
examining its religious monuments, economic structures, streets, and
quarters. The work was written at a crucial period in Egypt's history, namely the period of transition between the Bahri (or Turkish)
Mamluk dynasty (1250–1382) and the Circassian Mamluk dynasty.
Although the historian dwells on the negative aspects of the reign of
Faraj (1399–1412), his description of contemporary Cairo contains
enough elements antedating 1400 that a balanced picture of the city
can be formulated.[1]

## THE CITY'S EXPANSION

Maqrizi's history gives us the location of Cairo's public baths, its self-
contained residential quarters, and its mosques and madrasas, thus
providing a set of indicators from which a map of the inhabited areas
of the city can be drawn.

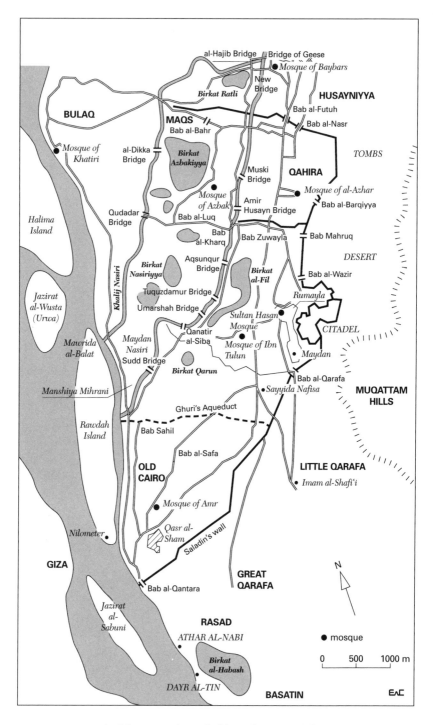

Map 6. Cairo and Old Cairo in the early fifteenth century (after Meinecke-Berg)

| | MOSQUES | PUBLIC BATHS | RESIDENTIAL QUARTERS |
|---|---|---|---|
| Husayniyya | 5 (3.4%) | — | 1 (2.6%) |
| Qahira | 69 (47.3%) | 46 (90.2%) | 27 (71.1%) |
| Southern zone | 49 (33.6%) | 4 (7.8%) | 9 (23.7%) |
| Western zone | 23 (15.7%) | 1 (2.0%) | 1 (2.6%) |

*Note:* Husayniyya = the suburb north of Fatimid Cairo; Qahira = the Fatimid city bounded by the walls and the Khalij; southern zone = the area from Qahira's Fatimid wall to Kabsh Hill and the Citadel; western zone = the area from the Khalij to Qanatir al-Siba.

These data give us some idea of the distribution of Cairo's population. The main concentration remained in the oldest zone of development, Qahira, where most commercial and religious activities were centered and where most of the native population lived. The southern zone developed considerably in the fourteenth century. The effort made to promote its urbanization explains the number of religious edifices there. Fashionable residential quarters were growing up around the Citadel, the center of military and political power, and the Birkat al-Fil, a pleasant residential area. The Egyptian population had settled along the main axes of communication, but there remained large blank sections, for instance in the area around the tanneries (*madbagha;* O 8–9 on Map 4), which would not become densely occupied until the late sixteenth century; in the neighborhood of the Sheep Market (Suq al-Ghanam, N–O 5), which would eventually be displaced farther south; and finally in the area between the Birkat al-Fil and the Khalij. Various texts give the impression that the southern zone consisted of relatively separate centers of population: Saliba, the Citadel, Qanatir al-Siba.

In the western zone, despite the definite push to urbanization signaled by the building of numerous mosques, settlement remained limited to a fringe along the Khalij, to corridors along the main routes of travel (from Bab al-Qantara to Bab al-Bahr, and from Bab al-Kharq to Bab al-Luq), and to a cluster between the Qanatir al-Siba and Birkat al-Nasiriyya. The suburb of Husayniyya had contracted greatly since its high point during Nasir's reign.[2] The Husayniyya and Qahira quarters (which would hardly change under the Ottomans) covered an area of 150 hectares; the southern zone covered less than 200 hectares, in contrast to the 266 hectares it occupied in 1798; and the western zone covered only 100 hectares—for a total built-up area of no more than 450 hectares. If we estimate the population density at 400 residents per hectare—a plausible average for classical Arab cities—we obtain a total population in the neighborhood of 150,000 residents, a distinctly lower estimate than the (admittedly hypothetical) estimate we reached for the city in the middle of the fourteenth century. No credence can be given, as usual, to the impressions of travelers: d'Anglure (in 1395) reported 12,000 mosques; Gucci du Dino (end of the fourteenth century) assigns Cairo and Qasr al-Sham 3 million.[3]

### THE ADMINISTRATION OF THE CITY

The sultan and his officials normally governed the city, both in terms of daily administration of the city and in terms of high-level decision-making concerning urban development and new constructions. The wide range of matters in which the sovereign was concerned can be inferred from a memorandum Sultan Qalawun addressed on the eve of his departure for Syria in 1280 to his viceroy (na'ib al-saltana), to whom he entrusted the governance of Egypt and Cairo during his absence. These injunctions, which have been studied by Leonor Fernandes, were intended primarily to maintain public security but also to uphold the moral order, which remained an important preoccupation of the viceroys. They also give us an idea of the way the sultans conceived their responsibilities in the capital.

> No one is to be abroad in the City or its environs . . . at night except in an emergency . . . Women may not circulate in the streets . . . The prisons must be guarded and protected day and night. All prisoners of war (Franks, Antiochans, and others) must shave their beards [presumably to distinguish them from Muslims] . . . Soldiers must be assigned to patrols in the City to police the streets and close the gates [of the quarters], to inspect the landlords of the *urbu* and see to the maintenance of order . . . The security of the gates [of the city] must be strictly ensured. Patrols must make the rounds at night, both inside and outside . . . Places where the young congregate, places of ill repute where debauchery and prostitution occur must not remain open. No one is authorized to visit such places either by day or night . . . Sentinels must be posted around the two

cities of Qahira and Misr, as is the custom. Some must also be posted at the Qarafa behind the Citadel, along the Nile, and outside Husayniyya at night . . . Men and women must not congregate in the two cemeteries on Friday night . . . The work [of maintenance] on the Qahira and Misr canals must be carried out satisfactorily.[4]

The administration of Cairo and its inhabitants was in the hands of three traditional magistracies. The judges (*qudah;* sing. *qadi*) had a very broad jurisdiction that covered matters of civil law, and many urban problems were addressed in their courts. The police prefects (*wulah;* sing. *wali*) saw to public order and security. They were particularly responsible for making the rounds at night and therefore also of fighting fires. Describing the Suq of the Great Jamalun, located right in the center of Qahira, Maqrizi observes that two gates were built at either end after 1388 and were kept shut at night:

The chief of the sergeants of the watch, whom the people today call the duty officer [*wali al-tawf*] sat across from the entrance each night, starting at the time of the evening prayer. A torch was placed in front of him that lit up the darkness all night. He was surrounded by policemen, as well as by many water carriers, carpenters, fullers, and demolitioners, who served on a rotating basis, to deal with the dangers of nighttime fires in Cairo and put out the blaze. Anyone discovered taking part in a brawl, or found in a state of drunkenness, or caught red-handed in the act of committing a theft was placed under arrest by the commander of the watch, who decided his fate according to his crime.

Maqrizi describes one particularly energetic *wali*, Dawlat Khuja. His severity had an excellent effect on thieves, who feared him greatly, but he aggravated the people of Cairo by his ordinances, which were thought to be excessive. Dawlat Khuja obliged shopkeepers to sweep the streets, to sprinkle them with water, and to hang lamps above their shops, and he tried to prohibit women from making the traditional Friday visit to the cemeteries. His death in 1438 moved the historian Ibn Taghribirdi to a vituperative enumeration of his traits in place of an epitaph: "He was tyrannical, mean, sinful, violent. He was an abominable and tyrannical old man." Cairo was remarkably safe from crime, presumably because it dealt severely and publicly with offenders. In 1386, Maqrizi recounts, eighteen thieves were nailed onto camels, and three more had their feet nailed to wooden boots. The thieves were paraded through Cairo in this way, after which all were cut through the middle except one, who was kept to witness the others' torture.

The third city official was the overseer of the market (*muhtasib*). His duties traditionally included the supervision of professional activities (hence the right to levy monthly and weekly taxes on the shopkeepers, which, though highly unpopular, were always reinstated after a revocation), as well as the maintenance of public morality and religious observance. In 1388 the *muhtasib* sent a number of doctors of law (*fuqaha*) to the shopkeepers in the suqs to instruct them in the basic elements of the Qu'ran necessary for the ritual prayer, and this rudimentary religious instruction cost each shopkeeper two fals (a small copper coin) per day.[5]

There were naturally no "municipal services" in the Cairo of that day. When great public works were called for, as when the Nile wandered in its course, the sultan organized the effort, placing it under the management of his emirs. Maintenance of the Khalij was similarly carried out by the authorities, probably at the expense of the local residents. All the streets except the main arteries had developed in a relatively anarchic way; they were narrow and irregular, and the authorities intervened in only the most flagrant transgressions of public order. Maqrizi tells the unedifying story of Emir Baktamur, who built a stable in the middle of a street. For a time, people continued to pass through his stable. Then one of the doors was shut and communication between the quarters of Barjawan, Khurushtuf, and Kafuri (F, G, and H 7) was cut off.

One of the many travelers who have evoked the streets of Cairo is Simon Simeonis, who described them in 1322 as "narrow, tortuous, dark, rich in recesses, full of dust and other refuse, and unpaved." But they must not have been so very different from those in his native Europe. Since wheeled vehicles were not in use, streets had to be only wide enough for two laden camels to pass each other, hence the contemporary interest whenever an "exceptional convoy" was crossing Cairo. In 1369 two marble columns had to be brought through the streets by means of rollers and winches. The official chronicler described the event, popular poets wrote epigrams about it, and the scene was even embroidered onto scarves. The cleaning and lighting of a street was attended to in proportion to its size. The Qasaba and the large suqs were probably cleaned regularly, secondary streets only episodically. It was sometimes necessary to issue public reminders of the need to remove garbage, dust, and accumulated soil from the streets, lest the ground level rise and the streets be obstructed. Barquq ordered such a cleaning in 1381, but he limited the requirement to "open" streets. For a special occasion, such as the celebration of a sultan's return, the authorities might order that shops and house fronts be whitewashed and that lanterns be hung at night above the shops. Such was the case when, in 1400, Sultan Faraj returned to Cairo from Damascus.

For its water supply Cairo depended on the carriage of water from the Nile and its distribution to streets and houses, a service paid for by the user: "One encounters many strong, handsome pack camels, used solely to carry water from the Nile, which is then sold throughout the city," noted Frescobaldi in 1384. In 1436 Pero Tafur recounted: "Innumerable water carriers pass through the streets, selling the water they carry on their backs, or else carried by camels and asses, for the population is very great and water can be got only at the river."[6]

### THE STRUCTURE OF THE CITY

Areas of the Mamluk city were already becoming differentiated according to their function, prefiguring the organization of the "traditional" city. Maqrizi's account leaves us in no doubt that there existed an economic center where business activities and artisan manufacture were grouped. From his chapters listing and describing the suqs and caravanserais (which he also locates with precision) we learn that along the Qasaba from the Bab al-Futuh to the Bab Zuwayla, an area of 38 hectares, there were 48 suqs (of 87 that Maqrizi locates in Cairo) and 44 caravanserais (of a total of 58). Economic activity was particularly dense in a sector 100 meters wide by 400 meters long between the Quarter of the Goldsmiths (Sagha) to the north and the Market of the Biscuit Merchants (Ka'kiyyin) to the south, where there were 21 suqs and 18 caravanserais within an area of 4 hectares.

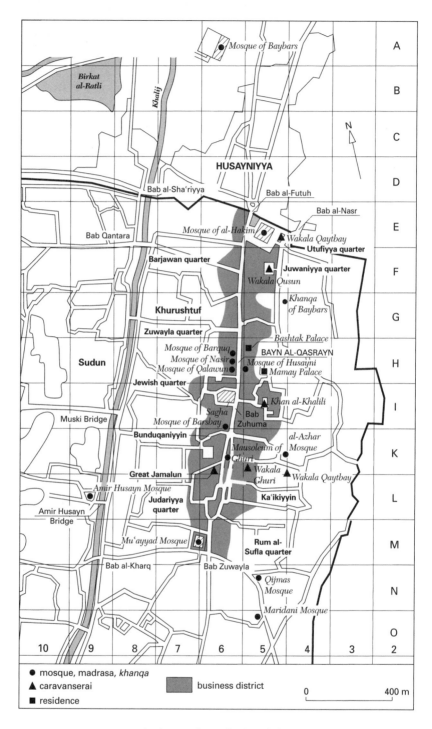

Map 7. The Qasaba in the Mamluk period

The Qasaba

This was where Egypt's major trading occurred: cloth (often imported), spices, exotic products, and the manufacture of luxury goods (including weapons). Other specialized markets existed along a few large arteries leading out of the city starting from Bab al-Qantara, from Bab al-Kharq, and from Bab Zuwayla to Saliba near the Mosque of Ibn Tulun and the Citadel. In the rest of the city there were mainly local suqs, unspecialized secondary markets intended to supply common items, especially foodstuffs, to the inhabitants of the residential quarters.

The markets were open structures on either side of a street at a crossroads, in most cases simply a series of shops. Generally grouped according to occupation, they were most often spontaneous developments, although some were built by powerful personages. They customarily had no buildings as such, and if they were covered it was most likely in a rather rudimentary way, with reed mats over a wooden frame.

The caravanserais, on the other hand, were monumental structures. Unfortunately, the surviving examples are of a later date—only the portal of the *wakala* of Qusun (around 1341) has been preserved (F 5). These structures have been described in detail in numerous documents belonging to religious foundations. The building was square or rectangular with a monumental covered entry opening onto a central court. All around the court on the ground floor were shops, while on the second floor were living quarters for the merchants, who often hailed from beyond Cairo. These caravanserais have been known by various names, though their structure and function remained constant. The oldest term, *funduq* (pl. *fanadiq*), is probably of Greek origin and appeared in Syria under Saladin before spreading to the Maghrib, where it is still current. The Persian word *khan* (pl. *khanat*), which replaced the preceding term in writings of the thirteenth and fourteenth centuries, was much used to designate way stations along the great trade routes in the Middle East. The word *wakala* (pl. *wakalat*) is a shortened form of *dar al-wakala* (depot hall), which perhaps referred to the place where import duties and taxes were paid. This word was to enjoy great currency in Egypt. The word *qaysariyya* (pl. *qayasir*) (from the Greek) originally meant a covered market where precious objects were traded. But these different terms, used with varying frequency, seem to refer to establishments between which there is little to choose: in Cairo Maqrizi locates 13 *fanadiq*, 32 *qayasir*, 9 *khanat*, and 4 *wakalat*.

The multistoried apartment complexes *(urbu)*, which caught the interest of travelers to Fustat from an early date, were often located above caravanserais. The apartments were duplexes and triplexes. While we again have only relatively late examples of these buildings, we know their structure in great detail thanks to the records of religious foundations, as the buildings were often used as real-estate investments, whose income was used to support charitable works or maintain church buildings. Generally located near the central business district, the *urbu* were mainly intended as housing for the middle class of skilled craftsmen and shopkeepers. The chronicler Ibn Iyas, who was active in the late Mamluk period, writes that *rab* residents were in fact "of the people" *(al-awamm)* and usually rented their lodgings.[7]

The city's residential areas were situated around the zone of commercial activity, where the density of buildings devoted to business and artisan manufacture was so great that it was difficult to find space for any other forms of residential housing than the apartment building. The residential areas were organized into quarters [*harat*], defined by Maqrizi as "a place where the houses are close together." He draws up a list of 38 *harat*. The majority (27) were in Qahira, where they formed a ring around the center, or in the zone between Bab Zuwayla and the Birkat al-Fil (9), an older urbanized area, but there was only one in the western district. These quarters could often be closed off, as witnessed by the mention of barriers and gates—the fourteenth-century gate of a quarter has been preserved in the Darb al-Labban not far from the Citadel (S 5). During periods of disturbance, which were common in the fifteenth century, the *harat* were closed, often on orders from the authorities, who were anxious to avoid the spread of disturbances from the city. The quarters were kept in order by guards *(khufara)*, organized in 1323 by a *wali* to deal with problems of civil unrest. Heads of quarters *(ru'ah)* are also mentioned.

Other than their occasional use for defense, the *harat* no doubt played an administrative role, particularly in the levying of taxes and the usual policing of the city, and the fact that they were closed made it easier to inspect them and perform searches. The *harat* were held to have collective responsibility, so that when the authorities were seeking Emir Janibak in 1424 they threatened to burn down the *hara* in which he lived, and two years later they ordered the expulsion of the residents of the Judariyya area, where they suspected the emir was hiding. The quarters had a kind of self-defense militia, the *zu'ar,* groups of young people who played a very active role during Cairo's periods of turmoil in the late fourteenth and fifteenth centuries. Emirs competing for power made use of the *zu'ar,* and the chronicles represent them as having been dangerous and uncontrollable elements because of their strong ties to the popular quarters of the city. It is likely that they represented their *harat* and defended them in cases of armed struggle, of which some episodes have come down to us through the chronicles. In August 1511, during the public celebrations that accompanied the breaking of the dike and the annual flood, people crowded onto the roof of a house at Qantara Sunqur to watch, in this case, a friendly combat between the militias. The great press and disorder caused by the mamluks turned the celebration into a bloody incident: the death of seventeen people explains why it was reported by Ibn Iyas.[8]

Was the population in each *hara* homogeneous? There certainly existed quarters that were relatively well-off. Maqrizi boasts of the advantages and amenities of his native quarter of Barjawan (F 7): "In our youth, we constantly vaunted the merits of the Barjawan *hara* to the residents of all the other quarters in Cairo. We said, 'In Barjawan there are [two] baths . . . two ovens, and a suq so well stocked that nearby residents have no need of any other.'" In a robbery in the Zuwayla quarter (G 8 on Map 7) in 1502, 12,000 dinars were stolen from funds collected in the *hara,* indicating the prosperity of a quarter where leading citizens (shopkeepers and bourgeois) lived. On the other hand, the quarters where *zu'ar* were recruited were plainly poor.

While residential stratification is difficult to discuss because of our limited knowledge of Egyptian society and its residence patterns, we know that certain fashionable neighborhoods developed south of Qahira in the fourteenth century, when emirs settled there. We have already noted the main stages of this development in the area north of the Mosque of Ibn Tulun and the Citadel and in the vicinity of the

Birkat al-Fil, a trend that would only increase in the fifteenth century. The Egyptian population lived mainly in Qahira but was starting to move into some parts of the southern district, near and to the south of Bab Zuwayla and also along the newly developed roads linking Bab Zuwayla to the Citadel and the Mosque of Ibn Tulun. The highest class of citizens (shaykhs and merchants) seem to have preferred living in the northern section of Qahira, probably because it put them closest to the large markets and great centers of religion and learning. In fact 63 percent of the members of this upper echelon for whom we have located houses between 1349 and 1425 lived there.

We know little about the dwellings of the poorest classes, who remain outside history except when exceptional events, often provoked by an economic or political crisis, thrust them into the forefront. Only then, and fleetingly, do they catch the attention of chroniclers, whose ties are to the upper-middle class and the ruling elite and who are uncomfortable with the popular movements rising up from the depths of the city. On 28 March 1458, Sultan Inal went to the waterfront at Bulaq, where he observed a proliferation of miserable structures, huts made of brush, the equivalent of our modern shantytowns, whose poverty offended his sight. In 1491, collecting a levy imposed by Qaytbay, a tax collector visited a woman in Husayniyya who lived in an "enclosure" (hawsh), probably one of those very poor communal residences that we find again in Ottoman times. The woman possessed "literally" nothing and was unable to pay even the negligible sum of 20 nisfs—all she found to offer was the jujube tree that shaded her from the heat of the sun.[9]

That religious minorities were segregated into different quarters is certain. In the fourteenth century, the Copts went from being a still populous community to a minority. Their large-scale conversion to Islam owed more to pressure from the Muslim population than to pressure from the Mamluk rulers, who were well aware of the important part played by Copts in the administration of the Egyptian state. The events of 1293 and 1301 resulted in a resumption of the various forms of discrimination against the Christians, though as usual these were temporary. These disturbances were only a prelude to the violent riots of 1321, when many churches were destroyed (eleven in Cairo, eight in Misr, and sixty in Egypt all told). Sultan Nasir, clearly acting against his will, then took measures against the Christians and closed some churches and convents, which provoked a first wave of mass conversion.

But it was particularly in 1354, after a new outbreak of anti-Christian demonstrations and violence, and a new round of harsh regulations, that an overwhelming trend to conversion occurred. The year 1354, writes Donald Little, "can be considered a turning point in the religious history of Egypt, as the moment when the second great transformation in Egypt's religion became virtually complete." The harassment of the authorities and the Copts' concern for their safety explains why Christian quarters were located at some distance from the center, mainly on the west bank of the Khalij in the Nasiriyya quarter near al-Dikka, and near Bab al-Bahr not far from the Canal (Sudun quarter), in areas where Muslims were then few. In Maqrizi's time, only two Coptic churches were left in Qahira, one in the Zuwayla quarter where the Coptic patriarch lived, and one in the Harat al-Rum al-Sufla. Although many Copts had moved to Cairo, there was still a sizable Christian community living in Fustat.

Fustat's Jews had relocated to Cairo in the thirteenth and fourteenth centuries. In 1400 the majority of the community lived there, and Cairo had four synagogues as against Fustat's three. Most of the Jews were grouped in a quarter right in the heart of Qahira (H 7), just west—not coincidentally—of the quarter of the goldsmiths and moneychangers (Sagha). Ibn Iyas, reporting on the construction of the Mosque of Barakat Ibn Quraymit in the middle of the Sagha quarter in 1499, remarks significantly: "It was a building of great beauty, especially in this neighborhood."[10]

### THE SUBURBS

Misr and Bulaq were satellite urban clusters separated from Cairo by large spaces that were practically bare of construction. Misr was an autonomous city with all a city's attributes: it had a judge *(qadi)*, a prefect of police *(wali)*, an overseer of the markets *(muhtasib)*.[11] But Old Cairo (Misr al-Qadima), as it came more and more to be called, was now a city in decline.

At the start of the fifteenth century, Misr occupied a quadrilateral defined by the Gate of the Riverbank (Bab al-Sahil) in the north along the river, the Bab al-Safa to the northeast, and the Bab al-Qantara to the south. The city abandoned vast areas to the east to ruins *(kharab)*. The gains made to the west, owing to the gradual retreat of the Nile (a maximum distance of 200 meters to the end of the Mamluk period, according to Paul Casanova), did not entirely compensate for these losses. The city's built-up area in the fourteenth century must therefore not have exceeded 200 hectares. But many areas for which streets were recorded were in fact abandoned: Sylvie Denoix observes that of 132 listings of streets by Ibn Duqmaq, 39 are described as "prosperous" and 44 as in a state of ruin. Everything suggests that the ruin was related to the crisis of the second half of the fourteenth century, which was at its height when the chroniclers Ibn Duqmaq and Maqrizi were writing their histories. The population of Misr could thus have been no more than 40,000 or 50,000. This necessarily uncertain estimate nonetheless gives us some basis for comparison with Cairo at the time (around 150,000 residents) and with Fustat's period of greatest prosperity (120,000 residents in the eleventh century).

In the area reclaimed from the Nile, the city was traversed by a network of large and quite regular north–south streets, cut across by almost perpendicular east–west streets. The network of streets became more irregular as one moved eastward toward the older sections. The great markets and caravanserais were grouped in a central district to the west, where commercial activities that were practically nonexistent in the eastern, more residential part of town predominated. We do not know if the residential area was divided into quarters of the *hara* type. Minority communities still lived in the city, the Jews grouped together in a few streets and the Christians seemingly mixed more freely with the Muslims. Qasr al-Sham is an exception, though even there one found Muslims and Jews, so it cannot be called a strictly Christian quarter.[12]

The port continued to bring prosperity to Misr al-Qadima, and the very primitiveness of the installation—the boats, being of small tonnage, were hauled right to land—meant that the retreat of the Nile had little or no effect on the activities of the port. But the silting of the arm of the Nile running between Rawdah Island and the Fustat shore did pose a threat that may in the long run have had an unfavorable effect on Old Cairo and contributed to the rise of Bulaq.

There continued to be boatbuilding in Misr, however: in 1386, eight armed naval vessels were completed. The main traffic was in wheat and other grains (stockpiled in vast granaries), but there was also trade in precious goods, spices in particular, hence the presence in Old Cairo of several important Karimi merchants. Burhan al-Din Ibrahim al-Mahalli, who died in 1403, traded with Yemen, having been provost of merchants in 1385. Immensely wealthy, he founded a college in Old Cairo and paid the costs of restoring the Mosque of Amr. His personal residence on the Nile cost more than 50,000 dinars. He participated in government councils, where he required the use of an interpreter because he spoke no Turkish. But Misr was visibly declining as a center of international commerce. Of the forty-six Karimi merchants cited by Gaston Wiet, only four were unequivocally linked to Misr (and none after al-Mahalli). The situation had clearly changed since the end of the thirteenth century when, to receive payment of funds owed by residents of Damascus, the Karimi merchants of Misr were called together and ordered to advance the sum. According to Ibn Duqmaq, Old Cairo at the end of the fourteenth century had 23 suqs, 15 *qayasir*, and 16 *fanadiq*, at a time when Cairo had 87 markets and 58 caravanserais.

Old Cairo, finally, continued to be an active "industrial" center. Ibn Duqmaq mentions sixty-six sugar factories, but only nineteen were functioning at the time. Among its other noteworthy commercial activities were mills and bread ovens that transformed the grain carried to Misr, paper mills (located near the Bab al-Qantara), and potteries. Despite its decline, Old Cairo remained an active center of commercial and artisan activities, as yet unsupplanted by Bulaq.[13]

The rise of Bulaq, situated along the Nile northwest of Cairo, had started in the reign of Nasir, presumably to replace the port of Maqs, which had been left high and dry by the retreat of the Nile. Bulaq was starting to play a role of some importance in the grain trade. However, the erratic behavior of the Nile (in 1398 the island of Khurtum appeared between Bulaq and Imbaba, and Bulaq's shoreline silted in) must have militated against the port's development. Only in the fifteenth century would Bulaq's star truly rise.[14]

# 8

# The End of an Era
# (1412–1517)

## THE DECLINE OF THE MAMLUKS

THE FINAL CENTURY of the Mamluk dynasty opened with the disastrous reign of Faraj (1399–1412) and ended with the Mamluks' unconditional defeat at the hands of the Ottomans (1517). It is considered a period of decline, interrupted only by remissions during the reigns of Barsbay and Qaytbay: the great Mamluk institutions experienced irreversible deterioration; the country faced external problems to the north that would bring about its fall, its demographic and economic bases collapsed, disorder and insecurity reigned—and the city naturally felt the effects of these disastrous developments. Although there is nothing inaccurate about this picture, it lacks nuance.[1]

After the reign of Faraj, whose course and tragic end brought great harm to the institution of the sultanate, we cannot say that the twenty-one succeeding reigns were marked only by instability, violence, and ineptness. Almost to the end, a persistent desire for hereditary succession is visible, as one ruler after another sought to organize the sultanate along the stable lines that Egypt had apparently known in the preceding century under the descendants of Qalawun and Nasir. Hereditary legitimacy is clearly what Sultan Barsbay, a former Circassian slave, sought in attributing to himself a genealogy linking him to Barquq and the Qurayshi (the tribe of the Prophet).

After Faraj, who with difficulty maintained the throne he inherited from Barquq (he was deposed from 1405 to 1406), there were six sultans who tried to establish their sons as their successors. This obstinacy was all the more remarkable, as the historian Ibn Taghribirdi has noted with some irony, in that they had generally toppled their predecessor's son from the throne: "If you wish to know what the world will become after your death, examine what it became after the death of another." Despite some ingenious scenarios (in 1453, shortly before his death, Jaqmaq abdicated in favor of his son Uthman; Inal did the same in 1461 for his son Ahmad, whom he had earlier brought into his administration as Emir of the Pilgrimage), these sons of sultans were invariably ousted after a brief reign and replaced by more powerful emirs. These machinations certainly caused disturbances at times, as in 1453 during the struggle to succeed Jaqmaq, and in 1497 after the death of Qaytbay. This was the exception, however. From 1412 to 1517, a period of 105 years, seven sultans reigned for 97 years. Almost all were capable rulers (Jaqmaq, 1438–1453; Inal, 1453–1461; Khushqadam, 1461–1467; Ghuri, 1501–1516) and in some cases even exceptional ones (Barsbay, 1422–1438; Qaytbay, 1468–1496). Maqrizi was therefore incorrect in branding all the sultans of the first half of the fifteenth century as poor rulers.[2]

On the other hand, the mamluk institution was in decline. The system of recruiting slaves was proving costly and growingly less efficient. Buying Circassian mamluks imposed a heavy financial burden. The slave trade was mainly in the hands of the Genoese, who annually transported 2,000 young males between the ages of ten and twenty down the Bosporus from the Crimea. Barsbay alone bought more than 2,000 of them. These slaves were expensive (the Circassians sold for from 100 to 200 ducats); their education, which was lengthy, and their upkeep (10,000 dirhams per mamluk per year in 1498) were also costly. Military wages rose from 11,000 dinars per month under Mu'ayyad (1412–1421) to 46,000 under Qaytbay in 1468. The preparations for an expedition represented a veritable financial chasm, particularly as the mamluks became more and more demanding and wanted bonuses both at the departure of an expedition and at its return. (Qaytbay's sixteen campaigns are estimated to have cost 7 million dinars.) Sometimes they asked for a bonus at the investiture of a new sovereign. The sultans, because of their financial difficulties, did not always pay military wages regularly, and monetary devaluation was meanwhile reducing the wages' true value. This was a frequent cause of mutiny among recruits and of disturbance in Cairo, particularly as the economic crisis reduced their traditional revenues from the *iqta'at*. Finally, the succession of relatively short reigns promoted party factionalism and conflict between the new recruits and the troops of the preceding sultan (or sultans).

Meanwhile these professional soldiers, now grown so costly, had greatly diminished in value. For one thing, they were less and less inclined to perform the military role for which they had been recruited. It became harder to mobilize them (hence the increase in bonuses) and to get them to fight with conviction. For another, military technology had progressed, and the spread of firearms made infantry troops superior to armored cavalry equipped with swords and bows—though superbly trained, the cavalrymen were using obsolete combat technology. The problem was to become particularly serious when the Mamluks faced their most threatening opponent, the Ottomans, whose janissary army of infantrymen equipped with firearms dominated battlefields from Europe to the Middle East. Recognizing the problem, the Mamluk sultans endeavored to modernize their army, experimenting with cannons as early as 1464 and, at their last gasp, after Ghuri was crushed at Marj Dabiq (24 August 1516), organizing a corps of portable artillery and mounted gunmen. But it was too late. These innovations were in any case not adapted to the mamluk soldiery or to their combat tactics. The combat weapon that had ensured Egypt a long period of external security was now usable only with difficulty and was, in some respects, no longer viable.[3]

Epidemics contributed to Egypt's material decline. The country suffered continual outbreaks of plague after the great pandemic of 1348; those of 1416, 1430, 1437, 1448, 1459, 1469, 1477, 1492, 1498, 1505, and 1513 were especially severe. In 1430 there were a reported 2,000 dead per day, and Maqrizi estimates the total number of deaths in Cairo and Old Cairo that year at 100,000; for the year 1460, Ibn Taghribirdi reports a toll of 4,000 dead per day at the height of the outbreak; for the years 1492 and 1498, Ibn Iyas reports 200,000 deaths. These figures, of course, should be taken as no more than indicators of the gravity of the epidemics. What is certain, though, is that Egypt, swept by recurrent epidemics, was caught in a downward demographic spiral, with inevitable repercussions for its economy.

Egypt's economic depression in the fifteenth century is variously explained by scholars: it was due to demographic decline (J.-C. Garcin), to technological stagnation (Eliyahu Ashtor), to bad political leadership, starting with Baybars, particularly in allowing monopolies and the sale of official titles (Ahmad Darrag). Finally, the competition from European trade undercut Egypt's own ports and threatened its domestic production. The European discovery of sea routes around Africa after the voyage of Vasco da Gama in 1497–1499 would in the long run have an inevitable effect on the great trade with the East. But even by the end of the fourteenth century, Western currencies dominated the market in Cairo to an extraordinary degree, showing Egypt's relative decline with respect to its European competitors and the reorientation of its trade toward the Mediterranean. The decline of large-scale trading is reflected in the waning influence of the Karimi, visible in the fifteenth century.

All these combined elements, along with the probable difficulties faced by certain Egyptian industries (textiles, sugar) and the reduction in farmland owing to Egypt's depopulation, diminished the resources the sultans were able to extract from the country. (Revenues from the land registry, for example, fell from 9.5 million dinars in 1375 to 1.8 million in 1517.) The rulers were forced to use a number of expedients. They had recourse to monopolies and to the sale of high offices (the most extreme example of which was the "tax-farm of the bald," created by Barsbay in 1427). And the sultans ordered exceptional taxes, such as the collection of five months' revenue on all property under Qaytbay in 1491, or the tax of a year's revenue on religious foundations and ten months' rent on private houses, rental buildings, shops, and public baths, exacted by Ghuri in 1501.[4]

The economic decline and the state's financial difficulties caused or exacerbated the conflicts that became increasingly frequent in Cairo in the second half of the fifteenth century and the first years of the sixteenth: conflicts between mamluks with different allegiances (recent recruits against the troops of the previous sultan or sultans) or of different origins (Circassians against Georgians, Tartars, and Greeks), between mamluks and sultans (usually for financial reasons), or between mamluks belonging to the parties of different emirs contending for power. Ibn Iyas cites eleven troop revolts between 1473 and 1493, and nine between 1497 and 1515. Cairo experienced several serious "revolutions": at the accession of Sultan Inal in 1453 (when the Citadel was under siege for seven days); the succession struggle after the reign of Qaytbay in 1497 (the Citadel was under siege for thirty-one days); and at Sultan Ghuri's assumption of power in 1501. Sometimes the city emerged undamaged. Ibn Taghribirdi notes with surprise that the city remained calm in 1453 while the fighting raged around the Citadel between the supporters of Sultan Uthman (son of Jaqmaq) and Emir Inal (the future sultan). People went about their business and even went to Rumayla Square to "enjoy the sight of the battle." More and more often, however, the disturbances provoked looting of markets and shops, which were closed both to protect them and to put pressure on the combatants.

The rulers' inability to observe discipline among themselves and the poverty caused by the crisis created an atmosphere of insecurity that is well documented from the last decades of the fifteenth century on: confrontations between "gangs" (the zu'ars in particular); looting and robbery of the markets by bands of brigands—the Jarkas Qaysariyya in 1482, the suq of Bab al-Sha'riyya in 1486, the suq of Bab al-Luq in 1494, and the Suq of the Merchants near the Mosque of Ibn Tulun in 1496. In addition to these internal threats there were incursions by Beduin, who were seen prowling outside the gates of Cairo in 1457, in 1471, and in 1474, when a group of Beduin horsemen, after riding up from the direction of the Chamberlain's Bridge (Qantara al-Hajib), attacked strollers and robbed passersby, including an emir of ten, whose coat they stole.[5]

The period was not without its moments of reprieve, even brilliance. But it is clear that domestic difficulties were mounting as external dangers cropped up in response to Egypt's changed geopolitical situation.

THE "MEDITERRANEANIZATION" OF MAMLUK EGYPT

After a period when the country was strongly centered on the Nile, with Syria forming essentially a buffer zone, there developed in the second half of the fourteenth century a new geography of Egyptian space. The ancient trade route to the Red Sea now shifted to Suez, the Nile delta grew in importance, and Mediterranean issues became more significant. Egypt's new orientation revealed itself fully in the fifteenth century. "A Levantine Egypt appeared," writes Jean-Claude

Garcin, "a coastal Egypt . . . [its] Mediterranean facade masking the Egypt of the interior."[6] These changes were of great importance in Cairo's history.

Egypt's redirection toward the Mediterranean was due to several new factors. The growth of trade with the Christian West had a considerable effect on the Egyptian economy, one sign of which was the dominance of European currencies. It opened the door to more sustained political relations—embassies were formed to settle the commercial disputes that arose in consequence of these relations—and also led to a remarkable opening of Egypt to the rest of the world: in the "state of the world" laid out in his *Hawadith* in 1456, Ibn Taghribirdi encompasses not only the Muslim states but those of the Christian West—an extraordinary broadening of horizons for an Egyptian intellectual.

Closer ties with the West also had negative consequences. Starting in 1422, Egypt and its shipping became the target of corsairs, Catalonian rovers in particular, and the Mamluk sultans were obliged to erect protections against raids (constructing towers in Alexandria and Rosetta, installing a chain barrier across the Nile at Damietta), build a fleet of warships for naval reprisals (the shipyards would be in Bulaq), and counter Frankish aggression with a vigorous military action in the eastern Mediterranean basin. The expeditions against Cyprus, which resulted in an Egyptian protectorate of the island in 1426, constituted one of these retaliations. With Egypt's increased demand for wood to build its fleet, the sultans saw themselves obliged to mount yearly expeditions to Ilgun, in southern Anatolia, starting in 1452. And Egypt's constant engagement in Asia Minor led to a more active foreign policy and to long-range military campaigns requiring large armies (Qaytbay owned no fewer than 8,000 mamluks). The influence of Egypt would be strongly felt in Anatolia.

But these campaigns also contributed to the further decline of the military establishment and, in the end, brought Egypt into contact with the Ottomans. The great expedition of 1488, led by Azbak, brought together 4,000 mamluks and cost one million dinars. It ended with a victory over the Ottomans on 16 August 1488, and peace was concluded in 1491. But the mortal danger threatening the Mamluks had only temporarily been held at bay, and it was in fact from this quarter that the final catastrophe was to descend on Egypt in 1516. The city meanwhile, which according to J.-C. Garcin "turned its back on the south in the building of its quarters, its commercial activities, and its residents' preoccupations," had decisively reoriented itself. The Ottoman conquest would only reinforce its new orientation.[7]

## URBAN RENEWAL

Despite Egypt's mediocre circumstances, Cairo recovered in the century following the great crisis of 1348–1412. Western travelers were prodigal in their expressions of admiration. Cairo "is certainly the largest city in the known world," wrote Joos van Ghistele in 1482. "It is so large that one could scarcely ride around it on horseback in twelve hours." And Felix Fabri, writing in 1483, concurred: "We finally entered this enormous city, the most formidable in the world." The disappointment expressed by Domenico Trevisano is entirely relative: Cairo "is a city that is in every way inferior to its reputation. It is true, however, that it is very rich . . . Its population is thought to be one and a half million people but is not half that number."[8]

A certain awareness of the city and its problems is discernible. It would be an anachronism to talk of urban planning, but it is striking to see how city problems were identified and addressed with somewhat more coherence than in the past. Chroniclers expressed their skepticism at these measures, but this reflected the population's disapproval of regulations that upset its settled habits and whose costs, moreover, it stood to bear. The orders given from time to time to clean the city by removing earth from the streets were not new, any more than the cynical comment they provoked—Maqrizi mentions these operations in 1426 and Ibn Iyas in 1503 and 1516 only in terms of their general inconvenience and cost. Ibn Iyas quotes two verses of doggerel that presumably reflect the response of the masses, citing "the poor security and the street cleaning" as causes of complaint under Ghuri.

Just as frequent was the reminder, several times repeated, that shops were to be lit by lamps: in 1432, 1498, 1514, and 1516. Issued by Nasir Muhammad, Qaytbay's son, whose brief reign (1496–1498) is known above all for its bloody excesses, the 1498 order appeared reasonable: owners of shops and buildings facing onto the street were to hang out lamps at night. But the rounds made at night by the sultan to see that his order was carried out and the severity of the punishment for failure to do so (at which he himself presided) aroused the chronicler's ire: "All this indicated a great meanness of spirit." The same Nasir Muhammad ordered, also in 1498, that the facades of all shops and *urbu* giving onto the street be whitewashed. This measure found no greater favor with Ibn Iyas: "All these measures were an initiative on the part of people of the lowest class and intriguers in the sultan's entourage."[9]

More significantly, other initiatives indicate that the street system, whose irregularity and narrowness were due to individual infringements, was being viewed in a new light. In 1457 Sultan Inal, while constructing a *rab* and two public baths in the Between the Two Palaces district, decided to enlarge the Qasaba—its narrowness was an inconvenience to the people. The old structures, Ibn Taghribirdi observes, projected into the middle of the street. The sultan had them demolished and set back the street line. For once, the chronicler approved the decision, for it benefited the public generally and not just the builder. In 1458 the same Inal went to the bank of the Nile at Bulaq and discovered that extensive building had occurred on Arwa Island and the Bulaq shore. On 29 March he forbade construction on both sites because of the narrowness of the road; he also ordered the demolition of several structures, particularly the huts and shops that had proliferated along the road. This new manifestation of the sultan's concern with urban planning and aesthetics met with some reservations from his council, but Ibn Taghribirdi once again approved, for, as he said, each must have access to the shore, and the liberty of the individual must not infringe on that of others.

A few years later the secretary of state, Yashbak, who governed while Qaytbay was campaigning in northern Syria, undertook to enlarge Cairo's avenues, streets, and alleys. He gave orders to the *qadi* al-Suhaji to demolish "all structures in the streets and markets that had not been constructed legally, rental buildings, shops, stalls, projecting balconies, benches." This undertaking, from May 1477 to April 1478, put the city in an uproar because of all the houses torn down in consequence. On this point, Ibn Iyas sides with the shopkeepers and building owners. He informs us that three *urbu* belonging to the princess Shaqra, daughter of Sultan Faraj, were destroyed in the Quarter of the Sellers of Scales (al-Mawaziniyyin) south of Bab Zuwayla, which tells us that Yashbak's activities were not limited to Qahira. Yashbak not only enlarged the streets but also ordered the facades and portals of mosques restored and whitewashed, and more generally had the shop fronts and facades of the buildings facing the street refinished. He then appointed an "inspector of streets" (*mushadd al-turuqat*), whose job it was "to harass the owners of buildings, to urge on the work of replastering and painting." Thus, concludes Ibn Iyas, fulsome as usual, "the city became as beautiful as if newly founded, as splendid as a betrothed at the instant of unveiling her face." Is it not remarkable that, at the end of the fifteenth century, an Egyptian manuscript should have been written on the street system (*An Exposition of the Rules Concerning the Streets of Cairo*), which, despite its traditional outlook, takes a significant interest in the problems of the city, paralleling the initiatives of several Mamluk sultans and emirs?[10]

## THE CENTER

Cairo's revival was probably linked to the slow immigration of people from the countryside, who came to fill the vacuum left by the plague epidemics. Noting the settlement of rural immigrants in the northwest sector of the city near Bab al-Sha'riyya in the second half of the fifteenth century, Jean-Claude Garcin has made the connection between this movement and an outbreak of popular religious fervor in that sector which would reach its height with the preaching of Shaykh Sha'rani (1491–1565). Facts seem to indicate that Cairo was repopulating after the crisis: in 1424, for instance, an edict ordered all rural immigrants (*ahl al-rif*) to leave Cairo and Misr; and after a site near Bab al-Zuhuma was preempted for construction, it proved difficult to resettle the former occupants, as Maqrizi reports, "by reason of the unavailability of lodging."

The old center was also being rehabilitated, and monuments that had been neglected during the crisis were being restored to their former condition. In 1441 work began on the restoration of a series of mosques both in Qahira (al-Hakim in particular) and outside the center. Monuments were raised, such as the Mu'ayyad Mosque (1420) and the Mosque of Barsbay (1425), which are among the most remarkable buildings in Islamic Cairo. The same period saw the building of caravanserais, rental buildings, shops, and public baths belonging to religious and charitable foundations. The constructions of Barsbay (1422–1438), some of them linked to his mosque, form an impressive set and include three *khanat*, five *wakalat*, four *urbu*, six *qayasir*, and one *tarbi'a* (square plaza), most of which were in Qahira. Some of these buildings were located on the site of "ruins," which indicates that the center was being restored and restructured.[11]

Sultan Inal (1453–1461) undertook similar enterprises, though on a lesser scale, but it is Qaytbay (1468–1496) and Ghuri (1501–1516) who must receive credit for the most ambitious undertakings. The monuments left in their wake are imposing. The charter governing Qaytbay's religious foundation runs to no fewer than 383 pages, to give some idea of the vast scale of the sultan's undertakings and the effect they would necessarily have on the city. Qaytbay built a number of *urbu* in Qahira whose revenues were to finance a foundation for the benefit of the inhabitants of Medina. Four of the buildings are known to have been in Bab al-Nasr, Bunduqaniyyin, Dajjajin, and Khashshabin. We also know of two *wakalat* built near the Mosque of al-Azhar (1477) and Bab al-Nasr (1480), and of a *khan* built near the Khan al-Khalili.

Ghuri's constructions seem to have been intended to renovate a particular district in the center of town. At the intersection of the Qasaba (where it becomes the Market of the Sharbush Sellers, Sharabishiyyin) and the street leading to the Mosque of al-Azhar, the sultan built a mosque and madrasa, inaugurated on 5 June 1503, and a complex facing it that included a monumental fountain, a mausoleum, and annexes. The result was a small square 13 meters wide that remains to this day one of old Cairo's privileged sites. We can only share Ibn Iyas' enthusiasm: "It was a splendid structure, sumptuously elegant . . . The college became one of the wonders of its age." It was perhaps during its construction that the avenue was widened to eight meters and regularized. Ghuri's public works extended to the street perpendicular to the Market of the Sharbush Sellers, where he built houses and, in 1504, a great caravanserai *(wakala)*, which again led to regularizing the street over a distance of more than one hundred me-

Entrance to the Ghuriyya (engraving by David Roberts, *The Holy
Land . . . Egypt and Nubia,* 3 vols. [London, 1842–1849])

ters. Ghuri built many other caravanserais and rental buildings in the center, and demolished the Khan al-Khalili and had it rebuilt in 1511. From what we know of its layout, its monumental doors, and its streets at right angles it resembled the covered markets (*qayasir*) where the most precious goods were bought and sold, known in Ottoman cities as *bedestanlar*. In fact, as early as Ghuri's own time this *khan* had ties to the Turkish element, as if a center had been built for Turkish merchants on the model of the establishments they knew from their own country.[12]

There still exist a few of the magnificent commercial edifices that mark the urban and economic revitalization of Cairo's ancient center in the late fifteenth and early sixteenth centuries. The two *wakalat* by Qaytbay and the one by Ghuri are examples of a perfect balance between function and architectural quality. Nothing comparable is found outside of the great *khanat* of Aleppo, as the Cairene *wakalat* of the Ottoman period reveal with few exceptions a greater concern for commercial efficiency than aesthetics. The structures in question are vast edifices (1,450 square meters for Qaytbay's *wakala* at Bab al-Nasr, and 1,500 square meters for the Wakala al-Ghuri), disposed in a traditional manner around a large interior court, with shops on the ground floor, living spaces on the second, and incorporating a multi-storied *rab*. They are remarkable for their attention to decoration, expressed particularly in the monumental doors, which are fit for palaces or mosques. The ornamentation of Qaytbay's caravanserais is particularly fine, with a great quantity and variety of sculpted motifs, some of which (the double moldings with little rounded curls) would reappear in a somewhat impoverished version on Ottoman monuments. Great decorative use is made of the windows and grilled balconies that punctuate the exterior and interior facades—this would also be one of the characteristics of the Ottoman caravanserais.[13]

Qahira's invasion by commercial activities left less room for residences, and the privileged classes were pushed far from the center: only 15 percent of known emirs' residences for the years 1496–1517 are situated in Qahira, as against 52 percent for 1341–1412 and 36 percent for 1412–1496. An old trend was now reaching its final stages: Qahira, monopolized by commercial and artisan activities, was being abandoned to those who pursued these activities, the common people.

Facade of the *wakala* of Qaytbay at Bab al-Nasr, 1480

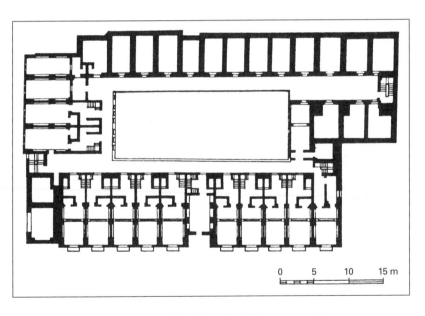

0    5    10    15 m

Plan of the *wakala* of Qaytbay (after N. Hanna)

The expansion of the city beyond Qahira continued, or resumed, after the period of shrinking it experienced in Maqrizi's time. Here as well as in Nasir's time we must distinguish between royal initiatives and urban development proper.

Sultans and emirs continued to found areas of settlement to the north. One instance is the Belvedere of the Five Faces (al-Khams Wuguh), built by Sultan Mu'ayyad near Kawm al-Rish as a substitute for Siriyaqus. The sultan asked the ruling elite to build houses nearby, an undertaking that failed and left only ruins in its wake by 1454. Another is the complex built by Emir Yashbak farther north near Matariyya in 1480, consisting of pleasure pavilions, a madrasa, and other buildings of which there remains only the *qubba,* or dome, which has given its name to a contemporary quarter of Cairo. And there are the building projects of Adil Tumanbay (who reigned for only one year, 1501) at Raydaniyya, where a maydan was built. Travelers, writing with their customary exaggeration (Beydenbach, 1483; Arnold von Harff; van Ghistele, 1482; Felix Fabri, 1483), claim that from Matariyya the road was lined with palaces that continued without a break as far as Cairo. But these structures do not signal that the city was truly expanding into that area, which remained an enclave of summer residences with many parks and gardens. Farther east were the religious and funerary monuments built in the City of the Dead under the Circassian Mamluks, along with the "houses" where many Cairenes congregated on Fridays and holidays, which may have given the appearance of urban development. The city truly started at Husayniyya, which seems to have recovered only with difficulty from the crisis it experienced in the late fourteenth century. The activity around the Pond of al-Ratli, which is so often mentioned by Ibn Iyas after 1510, stemmed from its role as a summer colony with abundant water and vegetation for prosperous Cairenes.[14]

Everything would indicate, on the other hand, that development resumed during the fifteenth century in Cairo's southern district. Restoration set to rights the damage suffered during the crisis. At the Mosque of Ibn Tulun, the structures that had been built inside the *ziyada,* or zone around the shrine, were swept away—a priest belonging to the mosque had rented a plot of land there on which he built a house after 1378, going so far as to breach the wall of the mosque to facilitate his comings and goings, and even added a stable. This house and others were demolished in 1439 and 1441 in the presence of the sultan himself. Construction proceeded apace: no fewer than 20 mosques and madrasas were built from 1412 to 1516 in the area between the southern tip of the Birkat al-Fil and the area of the Ramp (Suwwa, R 4) on either side of al-Saliba Street and around Rumayla Square, representing a quarter of the total number (81) built in Cairo during this period. Emirs continued to settle in the southern region at this time: 60 percent of the emirs' residences we have been able to locate are there, particularly in the area near the Citadel and around the Birkat al-Fil. The area apparently grew in population and developed nicely. In 1419 the sultan decided to displace a contingent of the Arab Ysar tribe that had settled south of the Citadel to make room for new constructions. To no avail, apparently, as the Arab al-Ysar were still there in 1510, when the heaps of garbage they made proved offensive to the sultan. In 1439 the sultan ordered the tombs at Rumayla and the Ramp to be transferred elsewhere, perhaps to make way for settlement in this area. This seems to be confirmed by the construction of markets and rental buildings during the reigns of Barsbay, Qaytbay, and Ghuri in the area near the Citadel. Sometime before the early sixteenth century, the Arms Market (Suq al-Silah) and the Tent Market (Suq al-Khiyam) took their place "under the Citadel" beside the Horse Market, whereas in Maqrizi's time they had still been in Qahira's central district.[15]

The Citadel was itself the stage for much activity, particularly under Sultan Qaytbay, who undertook various restoration projects to the mosque, the Great Iwan, and the Striped Palace. He built a pavilion in the Royal Courtyard (al-Hawsh), which was surrounded by the structures where the great ceremonies of state—reviews, presentations, and royal audiences—unfolded. But it was under Sultan Ghuri that the Citadel and its environs were given what has proved to be their more or less final aspect. According to Ibn Iyas, Ghuri restored a great part of the Citadel, Duhaysha, the Hall of Columns, and the Great Palace and built a pavilion facing onto the Hawsh. Starting in 1503, the great square extending outward from the foot of the Citadel (Maydan) was reconfigured by Ghuri, as our chronicler tells us at great length. The height of the encircling wall was raised, and a num-

Aqueduct of Ghuri (*Description de l'Egypte,* Bibliothèque Nationale)

ber of structures were built: a palace, belvedere, pavilion (*maq'ad*), and platform (*dikka*). The Maydan could be closed off by means of two gates equipped with iron chains.

In 1507 the sultan had a garden planted there. Soil was imported, and from Syria there came "trees, transported in crates along with their soil: apple trees from Syria, pear trees, quince trees, cherry trees, and grape vines, as well as sweet-smelling flowers such as white rose, lily, iris, and other flora from Syria, even a coconut palm, also potted. This maydan, with its trees and streams of running water, could be compared with the Ghawta [oasis] of Damascus."[16]

To water his new plantings, Ghuri decided to demolish the ancient aqueduct of Old Cairo and build it anew. His engineers placed its point of departure at the Forage Wharf. A well that connected to the Nile was built there, and six waterwheels powered by oxen lifted water into the canal system. The aqueduct, built on arches supported by pillars, traveled east along the course of Nasir's aqueduct, reached Saladin's wall, then angled northeast to end at the Maydan and the Citadel. This structure, which had a total length of 3,405 meters (2,155 of which account for the section rebuilt by Ghuri), was erected between May 1507 and October 1508. Ibn Iyas was admiring but critical: it was "a true marvel, but the vast sums poured into its construction were collected through inequitable measures and con-fiscations." Thus supplied with water, the Maydan became a sumptu-ous garden. In 1509–10, the trees planted there began to bear "the most varied and wonderful blossoms." The sultan, on a great plat-form inlaid with ivory and ebony, sat there in majesty,

> shaded by a jasmine bush, while mamluks, always chosen for their beauty, cooled him with the motion of their fans. From the trees hung cages of songbirds . . . with a thousand melodious songs . . . while a great variety of birds ranged freely—Abyssinian hens, man-darin ducks, and partridges. The sultan sometimes settled beside the reflecting pool, which was forty cubits long and was filled daily with water from the Nile by machines that worked night and day lifting water into the aqueduct. On most Fridays a throne was erected for the sultan in this place.[17]

It was here that sumptuous feasts were given on various celebratory occasions, and here also that embassies were received—to which we owe descriptions by Western writers, whose admiration matches that of our native chronicler. Trevisano, the doge's ambassador, described the Maydan as follows:

> It is a square extending from the foot of the walls where magnificent games of horsemanship are held. This very large square is twice the size of St. Mark's Square and longer than it is large. The sultan's gar-den is as enormous as the square. In the center . . . rises an open pa-vilion resting on columns and covered in green plants . . . From each column hung a cage with a small songbird . . . The garden was full of pomegranate, pear, and fig trees, of vines, myrtle and other species of tree.

We may derive some idea of the brilliance of these festivities, and also of the prestige of the sovereign who ordered them, from the fact that in 1512 there were no fewer than fourteen ambassadors in Cairo at once, for whom sumptuous receptions were given at the Maydan:

> [The ambassadors] of the Safavid Shah Isma'il; of the king of Geor-gia; of the Ramadanid prince, the lord of the Turkomans; of the Ot-

toman sovereign, the ruler of Asia Minor; of the Turkoman lord
Yusuf ibn Sufi Khalil; of the prince of Tunis, king of the West; of the
sherif of Mecca; of Prince Mahmud; of the Turkoman lord Ibn
Durghul; of the delegates of the province of Aleppo and of General
Husayn, chief of the expeditionary corps to India; the ambassador of
the king of France; the Venetian ambassador; and an envoy from Ali
Dawlat . . . The polo tournaments at the Maydan ended on Tuesday
the 29th (14 July 1512) in the presence of all these ambassadors . . .
This was followed by a sumptuous feast . . . After the noon prayer,
the mamluks engaged in games of combat with the lance, astonishing the ambassadors with their skill . . . It was an unforgettable spectacle.[18]

The growth of Bulaq provoked a call for development westward
along the main roads leading to the Nile. But it was only in the last
quarter of the fifteenth century that spectacular progress started to
occur in this area. In the southern portion, Nasir's Maydan al-Kabir
al-Nasiri remained a focal center for the mamluks and emirs, and it
was several times restored and rebuilt, notably in 1420, 1440, and under Qaytbay, who organized a great review of the horse there in 1475
before setting out on campaign. Yet the presence of this enormous
empty space obviously hampered urban development.

It was therefore in the north, 500 meters beyond the Canal, in an
area that was more or less free of buildings, that the major urban undertaking of Qaytbay's reign was sited. One of the sultan's highest
officials, the Circassian emir Azbak min Tutukh, governor of Syria
and commander-in-chief *(atabek)*, undertook large-scale construction. The project had two aspects that were in fact linked: a real estate speculation intended to finance the religious foundation *(waqf)*
under whose auspices it was carried out; and an attempt at urban
development aimed at bringing settlement to the area. The work
started in 1476 and lasted until 1484. Azbak first built a stable for his
camels "for he lived far from there." Next, writes Ibn Iyas, "the fancy
took him to build there." He had the ground terraced, a lake dug, and
its banks built up. The palace was built on the southeast bank of
the pond. A rental building and shops were placed adjoining it.
On the other side of the street, a mosque was erected, as well as a

fountain with its endowed neighborhood school and a commercial and financial complex beside it: shops, two *urbu*, a *qaysariyya*, two public baths, and some houses intended to encourage Cairenes to come and settle there. Of this impressive complex, nothing survives (the mosque was razed in 1869) except the name, Azbakiyya, which remained the name of the *birkat* and the district. According to Ibn Iyas, Azbak invested 200,000 dinars in this undertaking, clearly an enormous sum, in keeping with his power and financial resources.[19]

Ibn Iyas writes that once the groundwork was completed, "the population started to build splendid residences and summer houses there. Construction continued until the year 901 [1495–96, the date of Qaytbay's death]: everybody wanted to live in Azbakiyya, which thus became an independent suburb." The chronicler also describes the festivities that accompanied the breaching of the dike across the lake at the time of the flood: "Superior officers attended from within the palace, and the populace came en masse to drink in the spectacle. The public ceremony was held every year, with a banquet and fireworks, and numerous craft plying the lake. These were wild celebrations, on which untold sums were lavished."

There is very little doubt that the great vogue enjoyed by the region was due to the sultan's interest in the undertaking and a general tendency to follow the fashion. The increase in emirs' residences in the western district between 1496 and 1517 (19 percent of the total number, as opposed to 3 percent for 1412–1496) is obviously linked to popular interest in Azbakiyya. But it is not certain that the favor Azbakiyya enjoyed with the emirs brought genuine urban development in the area, whose luster seems to have dimmed after the deaths of Qaytbay and Azbak (1498). The district was partly looted and burned in 1497. Azbak's buildings were stripped of their valuable elements (marble) in 1508, and these were used on Ghuri's constructions. The fact that prostitutes settled near Azbakiyya and in Azbak's developments is probably a sign that the district was declining. The area was in any case occupied and ravaged by the Turkomans during the Ottoman occupation in 1517. Azbakiyya's palmy days, already celebrated by travelers at the turn of the century, would recur a little later.

## THE RISE OF BULAQ

By contrast, Bulaq's rise was lasting, as it was not the product of a sultan's or an emir's whim but responded to deep changes acting on the Mamluk state. The recession of the Nile had long since made the port of Maqs unusable and necessitated the creation of a new port farther west—docks were built in Bulaq as early as the reign of Baybars (1260–1277). Nasir's public works, in particular the excavation of the Khalij, were insufficient to revive al-Maqs in a durable way. Bulaq began to play the crucial role of grain-supply center to Cairo. The subsequent wanderings of the Nile, with islands appearing and changing shape opposite Bulaq, did not unduly disrupt Bulaq's development, although they were certainly harmful to the functioning of Old Cairo.

It was the northward orientation of Mamluk policy in the fifteenth century and the growing importance of the Mediterranean that gave the port its lasting prosperity.[20] The raids of the Frankish corsairs and the consequent naval expeditions in the Mediterranean obliged the Mamluks to launch a policy of naval development, which benefited Bulaq. It was there that the shipyards were located and the Mediterranean fleets outfitted. Two corvettes sailed from Bulaq for Cyprus in 1424; in November, Barsbay ordered the Bulaq shipyards to build 4 corvettes; in June 1425, a fleet of 40 boats streamed north; between 11 May and 18 May 1426, a fleet of 180 sail set forth from Bulaq to conquer Cyprus in the midst of general rejoicing—it would return in triumph that August with King Janus in tow. Expeditions of this kind continued subsequently without interruption, and the demand for wood to supply the shipyards also obliged the Mamluks to send ships to the forested zones of southern Anatolia. The growth of trade with the Franks would also contribute to Bulaq's development: from the reign of Barsbay on, spices arriving from Jidda and Suez passed through there rather than on the old route through Aden, Aydhab, Qus, and Misr.

Starting in Barsbay's time, the town of Bulaq thus experienced phenomenal growth. Commercial structures were built there; artisan manufacture flourished (sugar refineries, grain mills, leather works); Sultan Jaqmaq (1438–1453) built docks there; and the roads to Cairo were improved. When a fire ravaged the town in 1458, Ibn

Taghribirdi made a list of the thirty apartment buildings destroyed by it, a comment on the size of the population of traders and artisans then resident. Mosques were built in Bulaq (two in 1400–1420, three in 1420–1440), as well as public baths (five before 1517). Growth brought an influx of the poor to Bulaq—it was their precarious huts and shanties that offended the sight of Sultan Inal in 1458. The bustle and prosperity of Bulaq, which was generally a traveler's first point of landing, have often been described. Joos van Ghistele, writing in 1482–83, gives the following account:

> [It is] much bigger than Babylon [Qasr al-Sham] . . . There are rich and beautiful houses filled with every possible and imaginable kind of merchandise. For here is the principle entrepôt for the merchandise reaching Cairo by boat from all the neighboring regions, such as Sayett [Sa'id, Upper Egypt], Upper Egypt, Alexandria, Damietta, and other regions both up and down the Nile, a sight so remarkable as to be beyond description.

The restoration of the bridges north of Cairo by Sultan Ghuri was clearly related to the growth of the port.

Bulaq's growth brought on the decline of Old Cairo. Commercial activity now largely occurred in Cairo's northern port, and Old Cairo retained only a small part of the traffic with the east, a portion of the grain trade (corresponding to the production of Upper Egypt), and a relatively modest quantity of artisan manufacture. The town would remain interesting to travelers because of its biblical connections and the presence of a sizable Christian community with venerable churches. But the Jewish traveler Meshullam ben R. Menahem, who visited the town in 1481, writes: "Old Cairo, which is called Babozinia, is all in ruins, and few people live there."[21]

## CAIRO IN 1517

Despite Egypt's decline, its demographic and economic falloff and its political enfeeblement, the Cairo of 1517 maintained its brilliance, which had been inherited from the past and reburnished by Qaytbay and Ghuri, both great builders. The business center still impressed visitors with its activity, and the consequences of the blow dealt Cairo by Europeans in 1498, with Vasco da Gama's discovery of a southern route around Africa, were not yet truly felt. Its sultans' power seemed undiminished in the eyes of travelers, who continued to be fascinated by the splendor of royal protocol.

Leo Africanus, who reached Cairo in 1517 on the heels of the Ottoman conquest, provides a description of Cairo that is valuable on two counts, first because it shows us the city as it appeared at the very end of the Mamluk period, and second because Hasan al-Wazzan al-Zayyati, who was born in Granada before 1492 and only later adopted the name Leo, had a perfect knowledge of the language and the local customs. Thanks to firsthand information, he was able to write an account whose accuracy and detail are unparalleled in the copious but uneven literature of travel, whether from East or West.

Leo Africanus describes Cairo, "one of the greatest and most admirable cities in the world," as distinctly separate from its two suburbs, Bulaq and Old Cairo. This confirms van Ghistele: "Although the streets leading from Cairo to Babylon, from Babylon to Bulaq, and from Bulaq to Cairo are partly lined with inhabited houses, there are nonetheless empty spaces between these three urban areas with numerous walks, orchards, and gardens." Leo distinguishes the intramural city, Qahira, from the "suburbs" of Bab Zuwayla (southern district) and Bab al-Luq (western district).

Africanus estimates Qahira's population at 8,000 hearths. He describes its walls and gates and shows the importance of its main avenue, on which are "several universities, admirable for their proportions and the beauty of their building and ornamentation." He gives such a vivid and detailed picture of the central district ("Bein el Casrein") that it has justly remained a classic alongside the descriptions of Maqrizi and the French Expedition. Citing suburbs named "Beb Zueila" and "Gemeh Tulon," he describes the southern districts whose population he estimates at 12,000 hearths (an estimate that is probably a bit high, perhaps because of the size of the area). He identifies the districts as having a mixed character, both residential and commercial. In treating the suburb of "Beb el-Loch" (western district), he assigns it a population of only 3,000 hearths, which would be consistent with a patchy state of development. He mentions the great square that contained the palace and madrasa of "Iazbach" (Azbak) where the people gathered on Fridays, "because in this suburb one finds certain low distractions, such as taverns and women of easy virtue," and also boatmen. He estimates the population of Bulaq, two miles from the intramural city, at 4,000 hearths and dwells on its commercial and manufacturing activities, its port, where one sometimes saw "a thousand boats," and its beautiful buildings, both religious and private. He describes the "suburb of Sharafa," the south cemetery, as an urban area, attributing to it 2,000 hearths. And he briefly describes the Old City (presumably Misr al-Qadima), called "Misruletish," as being "endowed with a fair number of artisans and merchants." He cites the island of "El Mishias" (Rawdah), across from Old Cairo, as "densely settled" and "[containing] approximately 1,500 hearths"—a figure that is probably closer to the combined total for Old Cairo and Rawdah.[22]

Nothing could give a more forceful idea of the power of the Mamluk state on the eve of its collapse than the passage in which Ibn Iyas describes what was to be the last royal progress of a Mamluk sultan, Ghuri's departure for his campaign in Syria against Selim on 18 May 1516: "On that Saturday, early in the morning, all the commanders of one thousand gathered on the Maydan around the sultan in parade dress . . . The battalions of the emirs accompanying the royal procession began to file by." There follows a long list of the contingents and their leaders.

> The sultan emerged by the Gate of the Stables . . . preceded by the royal trumpet corps. He thus took his place at the head of a cortège of great beauty—rarely had there been so sumptuous a procession. In the lead were three elephants, decorated with pennants, followed by the army in parade dress, then the officers of the guard with their switches, driving back the onlookers, then the emirs of the drum, the emirs of ten in full complement, the high civilian officials . . . They preceded the commanders of one thousand, who rode by all together . . . Then came the four lord judges and shaykhs of Islam . . . the emir of the faithful, Mutawakkil the Abbassid . . . Then came the sultan's hand-led horses, preceded by two rows of plumed and saddled horses with yellow silk blankets and kettledrums, and two rows of horses with saddlecloths and saddles decorated with gold and gold-brocaded saddle cushions. Some had saddles of crystal inlaid with gold and carnelians applied with enamel.

Finally, after the baggage train (containing, most notably, a sum of one million dinars, plus the value of the ingots brought for the campaign), there came

> [the sultan] Malik Ashraf Abul-Nasr Qansuh Ghawri—may his victory be glorious . . . The sultan rode a tall bay steed with a gold saddle and saddle cloth. He wore a bonnet and a white tunic from Baalbek with wide golden embroideries on black silk. There were reported to be 500 mithqals of Venice gold in the braid alone . . . Then came the sultan's standard waving over the sovereign's head.

The procession entered Cairo by the Zuwayla Gate and crossed the city with its extraordinary pomp, to the great emotion of the masses: "From all sides came the good wishes of the populace, and the women sent forth ululations of joy from the high windows. The procession continued on and out through Bab al-Nasr—it was a solemn day."[23] On 24 August 1516, the Ottoman sultan Selim I crushed the Mamluk army at Marj Dabiq in northern Syria, and Ghuri was killed in combat.

# III
# THE TRADITIONAL CITY
# (1517–1798)

*The Ottoman period began with the defeat of the Mamluk army un-
der Sultan Tumanbay (1516–1517), Ghuri's fleeting successor, in a
battle against the forces of the Ottoman Sultan Selim in Raydaniyya,
at the gates of Cairo, on 23 January 1517. On the following day, a
Friday, detachments from the Ottoman army entered the city, and
the Friday prayer was performed in the name of Selim Shah from all
the pulpits of Old Cairo and Cairo: "O God, give succor to the sultan,
the son of a sultan, the sovereign of both continents and both seas, the
destroyer of both armies, the sultan of both Iraqs, and the servant of
both sacred shrines, Malik Muzaffar Selim Shah! O God, lend him
powerful succor, grant him brilliant success, King of this world and
the next, Lord of Worlds!"[1]*

*Two hundred eighty-one years later, not far from the pyramids,
Napoleon Bonaparte's army won a victory over the Mamluks on 21
July 1798. The following day, Bonaparte was visited by a delegation
of clerics, to whom he announced: "People of Cairo, I am pleased with
your behavior. You did well not to take sides against me. I came to destroy the mamluk race . . . Let prayers be held today as on every day
. . . Fear not for your families, your houses, your lands, and especially
for the religion of the Prophet, which I like."[2] During the evening,
French troops began to penetrate Cairo.*

*Between these two decisive battles there devolved nearly three
centuries of Ottoman rule. It has long been spoken of as a foreign
rule, tyrannical and obscurantist, responsible for the decline of Egypt
and Cairo. We will have occasion to nuance that picture somewhat*

*here. In fact, Ottoman Cairo represented the pinnacle of an 800-year history—the realization of an urban program launched in 969, reoriented southward by Saladin in 1176, and extended by Muhammad al-Nasir with his attempt to settle the western district. The city, whose growth began with the Ayyubids and the Mamluks, had fully developed in 1798 when the scientists of the French Expedition drew up the map of Cairo for the* Description de l'Egypte, *with the urbanization of the southern portion of the city completed and that of its western portion nearly so.*

*It was also during the Ottoman period that the organization of the "traditional" city occurred, before the great changes of the nineteenth and twentieth centuries. From this point of view as well, the continuity between the Mamluk and Ottoman periods is evident. This is due to the relative stability of the socioeconomic conditions underlying Cairo's urban development, the maintenance of many of its institutional structures, and the endurance of its aesthetics. But while the Ottoman city borrowed much from the Mamluk period, it was inarguably an original entity.*

# 9

# A New Political System

BEFORE THE OTTOMAN CONQUEST Egypt constituted the center of an empire that included Palestine, Syria, and the Hijaz. Afterward it was reduced to a simple province, one of thirty-two (thirteen of them within the Arab world). Cairo retained an eminent position as the second city of the Ottoman Empire after Istanbul and as the center of the richest, most populous, and most culturally prestigious province in the Arab territories under the sultan's rule, but Egypt was henceforth governed from Istanbul as were all the other provinces in the empire.

The new political order had a difficult start. The Ottoman regime in Egypt faced revolts from the Mamluk emirs Janim and Inal in 1522 and a more troublesome one from Ahmad Pasha in 1524, which forced the grand vizir of Suleyman the Magnificent, Ibrahim Pasha, practically to reconquer the country. Ibrahim Pasha remained in Cairo for three months organizing the governmental entities that would rule Egypt all through the next century.[1] The edict (kanun-name) promulgated by him in 1525 established the military organization of the province and its civil administration. He determined the prerogatives of the governor (beylerbey), who lived in the Citadel, and the workings of the council (diwan). He listed the provinces whose administration was to be in the hands of a governor (kashif) or a shaykh in the case of the Arabs of Upper Egypt. He also settled problems relating to taxes in cash and in kind, to the assessment of taxes on land, and to religious foundations. As in other Ottoman provinces, the general blueprint for the administration of Egypt combined typically Ottoman institutions with elements borrowed from the old (Mamluk) order.

### THE ADMINISTRATION OF EGYPT

In keeping with Ottoman tradition, Egypt's administrative system henceforth rested on three basic elements: the governor, the judge, and the janissary militia. Because of Egypt's importance, which it owed to its large population, the size of its economy (and hence its tax revenues), and its cultural preeminence, governors received the title of pasha and held ministerial rank. Many of the pashas appointed to Egypt had previously held the post of grand vizir: Rami Muhammad Pasha negotiated the Treaty of Karlowitz (1699) on behalf of the sultan, then served as grand vizir before becoming governor of Egypt from 1704 to 1706. Conversely, former pashas of Egypt were sometimes called to high function afterward: Yahya Pasha left Cairo in 1743 after two years in office to assume the duties of grand admiral *(kapudan pasha)* in Istanbul.

The jurisdiction of the pashas was very broad. As the sovereign's local representatives, they exercised supreme authority in civil and military affairs. The pashas established residence in the Citadel, succeeding the Mamluk sultans. They oversaw the general administration of the province, maintained public order and safety, saw to the collection of taxes and the preparation of the tribute *(khazina)* that went annually to Istanbul. But though their authority was considerable, it was limited by the precariousness of their office. A few pashas in the first century kept their position for long periods, such as Sulayman Pasha (1525–1538) and Dawud Pasha (1538–1549), but it became the rule subsequently to replace pashas frequently. In all, 110 pashas governed Egypt from 1517 to 1798.

This "statutory" instability was exacerbated by local political upheavals that sometimes accelerated the turnover of governors. Between 1760 and 1765, Cairo had eight pashas: Ahmad Pasha, who arrived in October 1760, was deposed in August 1761 by the emirs, who reinstated his predecessor, Mustafa Pasha; Bakir Pasha, who was then sent by the Porte, died two months after his arrival in 1762; he was replaced by Muhammad Pasha, who arrived in October 1762 and

The Citadel in the Ottoman period from the side
of Rumayla (drawing by Pascal Coste,
Bibliothèque Municipale de Marseilles)

was replaced in September 1764 by Hajji Muhammad Pasha, who in
turn died shortly after his arrival; Hajji Hasan Pasha, who made his
appearance in January 1765, was swiftly cashiered; Mustafa Pasha
kept his office only a short time and was replaced in September 1765
by Hamza Pasha: he held good until March 1767, at which point he
was deposed by the emirs.

The authority of the pashas was also limited by the checks and
balances set in place by the Ottomans: the *daftardar*, for instance,
who was appointed from Istanbul to administer the treasury; the *qadi*
(judge), at the apex of the judicial system, who saw to it that the pasha's activities remained in conformity with Islam and whose direct
links to Istanbul allowed him to alert the imperial authorities to any
local deviations; the agha, also appointed from Istanbul, who commanded the janissary militia *(odjaq)*. Two councils, the High Council
and the Ordinary Council, manned by the principal dignitaries—officers, *ulama*, and prominent men—advised the pasha but could also
raise obstacles to arbitrary or tyrannical actions.

The judges sent by Istanbul to Cairo had the rank of "great mullah." Locally they were called *qadi al-qudah* (judge of judges) or *qadi askar* (military judge). At first appointed for life, the judges of Egypt were subsequently assigned on a yearly basis like their colleagues from other provinces.[2] During the seventeenth century there were eighty judges, almost always in office for a single year, more rarely for two or three years, and in exceptional circumstances for four. It happened, though, that two or even three judges might succeed each other in a single year, as in 1031/1622. All the military judges were Turks. They were assisted by deputies (*nuwwab;* sing. *na'ib*), who were generally chosen from among the local *ulama*. The city of Cairo had fifteen courts of justice. Some were specialized, such as the "military" division (*qisma askariyya*), which settled cases concerning military personnel and their dependents, and the "Arab" division (*qisma arabiyya*), which adjudicated over matters concerning the natives, including the various minorities. There were twelve local courts: two for Cairo's suburbs (Bulaq and Misr al-Qadima/Old Cairo), and ten for the various districts of Cairo. These were normally located in a mosque or madrasa from which they received their name. There were no courts on the west bank of the Khalij because of the sparse development of this area.

The jurisdiction of the judges was almost boundless. The surviving registers record the matters addressed in these courts of justice: personal law (inheritance, divorce); religion and morals; matters of law proper (civil and criminal justice); questions concerning professional and commercial activity, and real estate transactions; problems relating to the administration of the city and urban planning (nuisances of all kinds); the administration of religious endowments; and so on. The influence of the judges was felt even in the "political" realm, since they sat on the councils that advised the governor: in the High Council (Diwan al-Ali) there were four muftis and the *qadi*, who also participated in the Ordinary Council. The judges saw to it that orders from Istanbul were duly executed and that the authorities acted within the framework of the religious law they were bound to uphold. The backing of the *ulama* was sought in cases of internal dissension, and they were therefore called on to intervene in many struggles in which the power factions came into conflict with each other or with the people. When a dispute erupted in 1709 between the janissaries and the six other militias in Cairo, the religious and legal authorities (the *qadi*, the representative of the descendants of the Prophet, and the *ulama*) came to an agreement and issued a ruling (*fatwa*) directing the janissaries to submit; a messenger from the *qadi*'s staff brought the text to the janissaries, who obeyed.

The power of the Ottoman sultan also rested on the janissary militia. The janissaries took part in the conquest of Egypt, and a detachment stayed on to help the governor administer the country. Known in Cairo as *mustahfizan* (guardians), the janissaries were assisted by six other militias created in the sixteenth century, the most numerous being the *azab*. In 1674 the number of military men on the rolls in Cairo was 15,916, of whom 6,461 were janissaries and 2,205 *azab*, who were foot soldiers. The janissaries were not the highest paid, but they had the advantage of numbers and influence and earned substantial income through tax-farms and their ties with the urban population. Their commander was an agha appointed from Istanbul, but in practical terms they took their orders from a "lieutenant" (*katkhuda*). The military role of the agha was subsequently reduced, but he retained his prestige and his place on the *diwan*. He was responsible for maintaining order in the city during the day and also had an important jurisdiction in the administration of the city.

The Ottomans kept a portion of the administrative organization they found in Egypt at the time of the conquest, in accordance with their custom of preserving local customs and institutions when these did not conflict with their authority. Selim entrusted the government of Damascus and Cairo to officials of the former regime. While the revolts of the first years of the new regime led the sultans to "Ottomanize" the administration, they retained a certain number of Mamluk institutions. In particular, they allowed the old ruling elite to keep a part of the authority they had held in Egypt—after all, the recruitment of mamluks by buying and co-opting slaves who were then freed differed little from the practice of *devşirme* governing the recruitment of janissaries (the levy of slaves of Christian origin, who were converted to Islam and ultimately freed), and the Mamluk system was therefore familiar to the Ottomans.

The mamluks thus kept control of administration in the provinces, and this allowed them to preserve their bases of material power and to organize themselves into a political order that would soon compete with that of the pashas. Furthermore, they were called on to take part in forming the militias of the Shawushiyya (1524), the Sharakisa (Circassians, 1524), and the Mutafarriqa (1554). The highest offices in the Egyptian province were filled from their ranks: the *amir al-hajj,* or commander of the pilgrimage; the *sirdar,* or commander of military expeditions; the *qa'im maqam,* or viceroy, who assumed power if anything happened to the pasha. Thus invited to share political power, the old aristocracy was able to rebuild its strength and authority. Somewhat more than a century after the Ottoman conquest, the most powerful Mamluk emir, Ridwan Bey, managed to impose a quasi-monarchical authority over Egypt (1631–1656).

The fiscal organization of Egypt illustrates the Ottomans' policy of compromise. Financial resources were provided by the tax-farming of agricultural lands *(iltizamat)* and the farming of taxes and duties in the cities, Cairo in particular. Controlling provincial administration as they did, the Mamluks apportioned to themselves the greater share of rural *iltizamat,* which gave them the resources to perpetuate themselves as an elite caste (purchasing slaves, maintaining large households). The janissaries took for themselves a large portion of the urban tax-farms, from which they drew their political power. The pashas collected in passing the sums needed to administer the country, and the surplus went to Istanbul in the form of Egypt's annual tribute *(khazina).* At the end of the eighteenth century, the levy on peasants totaled 412 million paras, of which 49 million were paid to the governors and 274 million to the *multazim,* which is to say to the mamluks and the military. The rest went to the treasury to pay the expenses of the government, with the remainder being sent to Istanbul. The *khazina* rose from 16 to 35 million paras, a relatively modest levy if we consider the devaluation of the currency and the fact that the money officially received from the *fellahin* represented only a portion of total receipts.[3] The greater part of the tax revenues therefore stayed in Egypt. From having been the hub of an empire Egypt became a simple province, but with only limited effects on the financial resources of the local ruling caste and on their ability to be patrons of architecture.

## THE COMPETITION FOR POWER

The history of the Egyptian province from the sixteenth to the eighteenth century is one long struggle for political power and its attendant profits. In the sixteenth century, the pashas were clearly in authority, but as early as 1586 the soldiery rebelled in response to the devaluation of their wages through inflation. The beys who governed the provinces soon joined sides with the soldiers. The rebellion of 1609 was so serious that a military campaign was needed to quell it; one chronicler described the victory of the sultan's forces as "the second conquest of Egypt." In the end, the Mamluks' rise to power proved irresistible—from 1631 to 1656, the Egyptian political scene was dominated by Ridwan Bey. The prestige of this emir was reinforced by a flattering genealogy that linked him to the great Mamluk sultans Barquq (1382–1399) and Barsbay (1422–1438), and even to the Quraysh tribe of the Prophet, a claim that Barsbay had also made.

Toward 1660, power shifted to the janissaries, who claimed such eminent personalities as Küchük Muhammad (d. 1694) and Ifran Ahmad (d. 1711). The Mamluks were weakened by factional rivalries, and the janissaries, who controlled urban tax-farms and customs duties in Suez and had woven ties of protection with the economically active population of Cairo, were on the ascendant. But power struggles within the militia itself, causing a series of crises, the most severe in 1711, weakened the janissaries. The balance of power then shifted back to the mamluks and beys. In the first decades of the eighteenth century, the structure of the ruling class was changing little by little: the mamluk system (the purchase of slaves from the Caucasus who were then educated and enlisted into military and administrative roles) was obligatory for all the ruling caste, but the dynamic element in this caste was no longer the old "parties" but "houses" (*buyut;* sing. *bayt*), which included both soldiers and mamluks. A few years after the French Expedition of 1798, the great emir Ibrahim Bey, describing "the good old days," listed the elements of this caste without making distinctions: "Know, my son, that we were ten thousand in number in Egypt, either generals [*muqaddamu uluf*], emirs [*umara*], *kushshaf* [governors of provinces], officers of the *odjaq*, mamluks, simple soldiers [*ajnad*], agents [*khuddam*], or followers

Mosque of Muhammad Bey Abu Dhahab, 1774

[*atba*]. Each emir lived in retirement in his own territory, and all of us lived very well."[4]

Among these houses *(buyut)*, the house of the Qazdaghliyya became preeminent from the time of Ibrahim al-Qazdaghli, lieutenant of the janissaries *(katkhuda)*, who exercised uncontested authority over Egypt, in cooperation with Ridwan (1743–1754), *katkhuda* of the once-rival *azab* militia. After Ibrahim, the Qazdaghli emirs established almost total control over Egypt, and Ali Bey al-Kabir (1760–1773) even tried to assert his independence from the Porte and build a state that would recreate the Mamluk Empire. His failure no doubt discouraged his successor, Muhammad Bey Abu Dhahab (1773–1775), from entertaining the same ambition. Finally, Ibrahim Bey and Murad Bey would share power during the last quarter of the eighteenth century, exploiting Egypt in accordance with their own best interest while the Porte was unable to impose on them more than the appearance of submission. They even stopped paying the yearly tribute. In retribution, the imperial government sent an expedition in 1786 led by Ghazi Hasan Pasha, hoping to reestablish the Porte's authority in Egypt, but to little avail. By 1791 the duumvirate had returned to power, and it was on them that Bonaparte's army fell in 1798.

### THE SULTAN'S PRESTIGE

The growth of these local powers and the weakening of the sultan's authority in Cairo reduced the pasha to a figurehead, under constant threat of being deposed if he departed from his assigned role. Ali Pasha, a person of very high rank (he had been grand vizir), arriving in Cairo in 1740 after the deposition and internment of Sulayman Pasha, characterized his program of government modestly: "'I did not come to Egypt to sow discord between the emirs, nor dissension among its inhabitants. My mission is to safeguard the rights of each. The sultan, our master, has ceded the territory of the country to me, and I in turn give it to you,' he said to the emirs in the course of a solemn assembly. 'Only do not make difficulties for me in the collection of taxes.'"[5]

Nonetheless, the proper shows of submission were observed. There were public rituals and demonstrations that bespoke the subjects' unshakable loyalty to Ottoman and Islamic power, which were indissolubly linked. Loyalty to the Ottomans was shown in particular by the decoration and lighting of the town *(zina)*. This was a very ancient tradition, often honored during the Mamluk period. Under the Ottomans, this was the manner used to celebrate the sultan's great victories and other important events (accession of a new sultan, birth of a son to the reigning sovereign), as well as more local events (a pasha's recovery from illness, the circumcision of a pasha's son, a victorious expedition). There were six such celebrations between 1600 and 1649, fifteen between 1650 and 1699, but only five during the next half-century and two during the half-century after that, occasions to rejoice in the dynasty's success having clearly grown fewer. During the *zina*, which might last three to ten days, houses were decorated with lamps, streets were lit, shops in the great suqs were hung with beautiful cloths, lit, and the ground covered with carpets. These celebrations sometimes occurred in rapid succession. There were three in 1696: one in January that lasted three days to celebrate the sultan's capture of eight citadels; one in August for the birth of the sultan's son Mahmud; and one in November for the circumcision of the sons of Isma'il Pasha. These festivities provided the opportunity for a sincere expression of loyalty to the dynasty, even if they were often ordered by the authorities and even if, in some circumstances, they could be fairly burdensome to the residents of Cairo, particularly the shopkeepers, who paid for the greater share of them: "I do not know who introduced the *zina* to Islam," wrote a chronicler about the *zina* of 1620 that coincided with an epidemic of plague. "In truth it is a scourge on the shopkeepers: it costs them money and interrupts their business."[6]

In 1624 Shaykh Mar'i, a well-known Egyptian historian, wrote a panegyric in twenty-two sections to celebrate the virtues of the Ottoman dynasty, with each section devoted to one of its merits. He concluded that the Ottoman sultans were popular, and that there was not one of their subjects "who did not love them and wish them victory." While this is undoubtedly the official view of a man of letters, a popular feeling of loyalty does seem to have been expressed toward the dynasty in periods of crisis, sometimes quite a fervent one. When Hasan Pasha, commander of the Porte's expedition against the Egyptian Mamluks, entered Cairo in 1786, he was greeted with wild en-

thusiasm: "Cannons were fired to celebrate his arrival, the people re-
joiced and placed great hope in him. He was considered the mahdi of
the period." During the French occupation in 1798–1801, the people
turned toward the Ottoman government for protection and gave vent
to fervid demonstrations of loyalty to the Ottomans. When the Turkish troops entered Cairo after the final departure of the French on 2
July 1801, writes Jabarti, the people

> rejoiced at the arrival of the newcomers. They welcomed them
> warmly and greeted their arrival with much joy and happiness.
> When they saw the Turks, men and children of all ages cheered:
> "May God grant the sultan victory!" The women, too, shouted from
> the windows and, according to their custom, moved their tongues in
> their mouths to make piercing cries of joy.[7]

# 10

# Urban Society

UNDER THE OTTOMANS, urban society was particularly diverse, but as during the Mamluk period it was based on the separation between the Egyptian population and the ruling caste—whose ethnic origins, functions, and activities differed from those of the ruled (ra'iya). This commonality between the two periods explains in part why the transition from one society to the other was quite easy. In many respects, Ottoman Cairo was similar to the Cairo of before 1517; the city would change much more between 1798 and the rule of Muhammad Ali. That the ruling class's organizational structures and relations with the subject population remained relatively constant, as is so evident in retrospect, must have helped the Egyptians accept the new rule, its general traits being familiar to them.

## THE RULING CLASS

The ruling class was composed of two elements.[1] The mamluks, from whose ranks came the main emirs and high officials of the state, were recruited according to a system of co-optation similar to the system that produced the military and political elite before the Ottomans' accession. Specialized traders sold young slaves, most of them Circassians or Georgians, to the heads of the great mamluk houses. One of the most famous emirs of the eighteenth century, Muhammad Bey, received the sobriquet "al-Alfi" because he was bought by Murad Bey from his previous owner for 1,000 irdabbs (alf) of grain.

The slaves were then raised in their masters' houses and prepared for their future military and political duties. Their education completed, they were freed and given a variety of responsibilities. Often they were bound to their masters by family ties, marrying their daughters or slaves. The ablest rose in the mamluk career ranks. They received rural tax-farms and succeeded their masters, often marrying the master's widow and living in his house. The greater number became members of the private armies that the principal emirs maintained, which sometimes numbered several hundred men.

The title "bey" (*bak* or *bayk*), which originally denoted a rank and not a specific function, was equivalent to the Mamluk title "emir of one hundred" (*amir mi'a*). There were in principle twenty-four beys, just as there had been twenty-four first-class emirs. The title *kashif* for the governors of the provinces was also an inheritance from the Mamluk sultanate. The members of the elite circle of beys were not, however, always former slaves—many were born as free Muslims. Certain historians have suggested that for physiological (or even climatological!) reasons, the mamluks were incapable of having offspring. In fact there are numerous instances of hereditary succession, and one of the chief figures in the history of the early eighteenth century, Isma'il Bey (d. 1724), was the son (and successor) of the powerful Iwaz Bey (d. 1711).[2] The Mamluk emirs derived their power from exploiting the peasantry (*fallahin*) through rural tax-farms, but most of them lived in Cairo, in residences that were often sumptuous and large enough to hold their numerous retinues.

The members of the militias (*odjaq*) formed the other element of the ruling class. The janissaries, the most numerous and influential of these, quickly ceased being recruited according to the traditional system of *devşirme*, which provided the sultan in Istanbul with a totally devoted army and created a reservoir from which administrators and leaders could be recruited. The "imperial" janissaries (*qabi quli*, the Arabic transliteration of the Turkish *kapi kulu*, "slaves of the Porte") who arrived in Cairo in the last decades of the seventeenth century to reinforce the local militia were for the most part Turks (of free Muslim origin) from eastern Anatolia, a great source of recruitment. Local recruitment supplied a large proportion of the janissaries as well. A *firman* (imperial decree) written to the governor of Damascus in 1577 complained of the vacant places in the janissary corps being given not to "brave and capable young men from Rum [Anatolia]" but to local youngsters. The same applied to Cairo. To round out their salaries, these soldiers took up other trades, sometimes modest ones, or followed the professions they had held before entering the militia. Volney, writing at the end of the eighteenth century, described the janissaries, the *azab*, and the other militia corps as "a collection of tinkers, boors, and vagabonds." Furthermore, many artisans and shopkeepers in Cairo affiliated themselves with the militias to receive their protection (and profit from the attendant privileges), which tightened the bonds of the militias, and the janissaries in particular, with the people of the city.

The janissaries and the *azab* drew a large part of their income (and hence of their political influence) from urban tax-farms (*muqata'at*) and from the payment they received for the protection of artisans and shopkeepers in the city. Closely bound to the city in which they lived, they were active patrons of architecture. These soldiers melded with the Egyptian population, marrying native women. This made them hard to mobilize. When a crisis occurred, their officers had to make repeated mobilization proclamations and visit the markets and caravanserais to rout out recalcitrants. When the Ottoman troops of Hasan Pasha arrived in Cairo in 1786, the janissaries of the city refused to take part in the procession marking the departure of the pilgrimage "for fear of coming into contact with the Ottomans," observes Jabarti, who was himself related through his family to the soldiery. Commenting on a time in 1807 when there was friction between Cairenes and the soldiery, Jabarti remarks that many of the Egyptianized soldiers feared an uprising of the people, for whom they had affection because they had "mingled with them, [lived in] their houses and quarters and married the women of the country."[3]

The ruling class siphoned off a considerable part of the country's revenues. The Mamluks, as we have seen, took their share from agricultural revenues. Emirs also participated in commercial ventures. The military caste, the janissaries in particular, controlled the urban tax-farms. The most profitable of these, the customs at Suez, through which port transited the main products of Egypt's long-distance trade—spices and coffee—brought in 36 million paras in 1798. And the soldiery levied a ten percent share on the estates of deceased artisans and shopkeepers whom they had protected.

The members of the ruling caste benefited from these privileges as a whole. But there was a great inequality of wealth and status between the rank-and-file mamluks or soldiery, who supplemented their meager income with commercial or artisan activities, and the great emirs, whose fortunes could be truly princely. The wealth and prodigality of Muhammad Bey Abu Dhahab (d. 1775) were proverbial. He built a particularly splendid religious foundation (*waqf*) for a very beautiful mosque in the center of Cairo across from al-Azhar Mosque. Uthman Katkhuda al-Qazdaghli, a prominent janissary emir, died in 1736 leaving an estate valued at more than 21 million paras, of which considerable sums were invested in luxury amenities, agricultural products, cattle, ships sailing the Nile and the Red Sea, and commercial goods (including 2.4 million paras worth of coffee). Such fortunes allowed the emirs to indulge their taste for luxury, to maintain their households, whose size was an important element of their success (a retinue of 150–200 was no rarity), but also to endow religious and charitable foundations. The most remarkable example is Abd al-Rahman Katkhuda al-Qazdaghli, whose vast fortune—inherited to begin with and supplemented by his office in the janissary *odjaq*—allowed him to build religious monuments all across Cairo (twenty-one, either built or restored) as well as public works (seven fountains, two bridges).[4]

It is easy to understand the melancholy of the emirs who, as parties to a losing faction, found themselves forced in 1711 to leave Cairo, "where they had lived in the greatest luxury and had had good times." They had enjoyed "every kind of choice food, magnificent clothes, blooded horses, beautiful slave women, running watercourses, large gardens and orchards with every kind of flower and fruit, and a host of servants." The chronicler al-Shadhili describes them (not unironically, perhaps) as making a halt at Tura, some distance from Cairo: "Each of them cried and was filled with grief at the thought of being separated from his attendants, his children, his house, his slaves, and his troops."[5]

## THE *Ulama*

The scholars of Islamic law and religion (*ulama*) occupied an intermediate position in Cairo between the ruling class, whom they served

A shaykh (*Description de l'Egypte,* Bibliothèque Nationale)

and looked to for patronage, and the native population, from whom they arose. The al-Azhar Mosque and its attached university formed the nucleus of this group. Its hierarchic world, from the shaykh al-Azhar to the teachers at the university (around one hundred) to the students (around three thousand), was organized into communities (*arwiqa*) that brought together people belonging to the same school of law (*madhhab*) or sharing the same geographic origin (Egyptian province or foreign country). Counting the staff and students of the madrasas, the convents (*zawaya*), which also had a teaching function, the staff of neighborhood schools (*makatib*), of which there were several hundred in Cairo, the heads of communities, the religious personnel of the mosques (imams, preachers), and the personnel of judicial institutions, one arrives at a figure of some 4,000 or 5,000 individuals, almost all of them Egyptians.

Despite their common origin and shared education, the *ulama* did not form a social class. The students, many of whom came from the countryside, lived a precarious existence. They depended largely on the subsidies they received from religious endowments and on various gratuities: regular distributions of food or clothing, and gifts on feast days. The professors at al-Azhar received no salary, and some were therefore very poor, while others engaged in professional activities related to their teaching—as copyists, calligraphers, or booksellers operating in the shops near the mosque. Many received revenue from religious endowments in which they served as administrators, or enjoyed the liberal patronage of an emir. Others, finally, grew rich from commercial ventures and even from the operation of urban or rural tax-farms. Shaykh Murtada al-Zabidi, the author of a famous Arabic dictionary, the *Taj al-arus*, received patronage from the great emirs, including 100,000 dirhams from Muhammad Bey Abu Dhahab as the price of his work, which the emir wanted to make the cynosure of a mosque library he had just built near al-Azhar (1774).

Jabarti, who shows unlimited indulgence toward his venerated master Zabidi, is less forbearing to Shaykh Muhammad al-Mahdi (d. 1815), who assembled a vast fortune through shrewd speculation and the judicious use of his contacts with the powers-that-were (including the French during their occupation of Egypt): "In conclusion," the chronicler writes, "Shaykh El Mahdy was one of the greatest scholars." Had he continued to teach "and not allowed himself to be drawn into the affairs of this world, he might have been the most extraordinary man of his century. But his search for earthly possessions so preoccupied him that he gave only one or two lectures . . . per week."[6]

Linked to the local population by their origin and activities, the *ulama* were indispensable adjuncts to the rulers, as their various competencies gave them a monopoly over religious, judiciary, and teaching positions. They sometimes played the part of intercessors between ruler and ruled in the crises that beset Cairo under the Ottomans. But they were too tied to the governing class by the stipends they received from them to be entirely resolute. We might add that for an Egyptian to become a "man of knowledge" (*alem*, pl. *ulama*) was one of the rare ways to rise in a society that was hierarchical and compartmentalized. The scholar's career also promoted geographic integration, as it provided an avenue for people of rural origin to settle in Cairo. The very success of the *ulama* tended to distance them from the society that had spawned them and whose diversity they reflected.

### THE NATIVE POPULATION (*Ra'iya*)

The native population was composed of what in Ottoman terminology were called "the subjects" (*ra'iya*). While the mamluks monopolized governmental, administrative, and military offices, and the *ulama* religious, judiciary, and cultural ones, the subjects constituted the economically active population of Cairo, whose number the *Description de l'Egypte* estimated at around 80,000. This native society was highly inegalitarian. Research into the archives of the Ottoman period shows that between the smallest estate recorded (that of the vegetable seller Ahmad al-Sa'idi, 145 paras, in 1703) and the largest (belonging to a coffee merchant, Qasim al-Sharaybi, 8,849,660 paras, in 1735) there was a ratio of one to sixty thousand. The disparity was equally sharp in the average size of estates: for the period 1776–1798 in a sample of 567 estates, 17 (3 percent of the total) account for 50.15 percent of the total value; at the other end of the spectrum, the 283 smallest estates (49.91 percent of the total) represent only 4.3 percent of the total value.[7] Inequality on so impressive a scale obviously reflected deep differences in material well-being and ways of life.

At the bottom of the heap there existed a true proletariat. The chroniclers called it "the populace" (al-amma) and placed this mass of humanity on the fringes of Egyptian society, outside history itself except in times of crisis or unrest. It consisted of people in the ambulatory trades (donkey drivers, porters, water carriers, peddlers), wage earners for artisans' corporations, and day laborers numbering in the aggregate—according to the Description de l'Egypte, some 60,000. The poorest, the day laborers, made do with salaries of from five to thirty paras per day. The Description de l'Egypte provides a picture of their precarious existence: these workers, according to M. de Chabrol, "wear a simple shirt of blue wool . . . Their lodging consists of a sort of hut that costs them ten paras a month in rent . . . All their furniture consists of a section of rush matting, where they sleep with their wives and children." They lived in the poor dwellings on the outskirts of the city, particularly in the awhash (shantytowns).[8]

In the next stratum of the population were the tradesmen, the small and medium artisans and shopkeepers, and the members of trade corporations, numbering some 15,000 in Cairo according to the Description de l'Egypte. The texts we have refer to them as "people of the trades" (ahl al-hiraf), "shopkeepers" (ahl al-aswaq), "retailers" (mutasabbibin). Their wealth varied greatly (from 1,000 to 30,000 or 40,000 paras), implying a great range in their material circumstances. Aided by companions, they generally worked in a store, which they might rent or own.

At the top of the Egyptian social ladder was the wealthy bourgeoisie. It was composed mostly of merchants as the artisan professions rarely brought their practitioners wealth, and numbered some 4,000 or 5,000. Here again, the range of fortunes varied widely: from 30,000 or 40,000 paras to upward of 10 million paras. The members of this bourgeoisie, however, had certain traits in common: the ownership of mamluks (a privilege reserved in principle for the ruling class), and the farming of tax lands, which raised them closer to the ruling caste, with whom they had many ties in common. The most prosperous stratum consisted of wealthy traders in coffee and yard goods, the two main products of Egypt's international trade, numbering in all some 500 or 600 people who, in the seventeenth and eighteenth centuries, dominated the country's economy. Of the 468 estates recorded between 1679 and 1700, those of 80 coffee traders (17 percent of the total number) add up to a value of 41.7 million paras (64 percent of the total value of 64.7 million paras). The fortunes of certain of these great traders compare favorably with the fortunes of the powerful emirs: in 1734 Qasim al-Sharaybi left an estate of 8.8 million constant paras, and in 1795 Mahmud Muharram one of 5.7 million paras.

Their houses indicated the opulence these merchants had at their command. Some were veritable little palaces, such as that of Jamal al-Din al-Dhahabi (1637) and of Mahmud Muharram (1779), which Muhammad Ali made into a residence for distinguished visitors to Egypt at the beginning of the nineteenth century. The relations established between these important traders and the ruling caste tell much about their power and authority: at the funeral of Qasim al-Sharaybi, all the greatest emirs were present, and the foremost emir of the time, Uthman Katkhuda al-Qazdaghli, went so far in expressing his respect as to walk on foot in front of the body from the mortuary to the cemetery.[9] When Napoleon went to Suez in December 1798, he was accompanied by merchants of whom the lowliest had in his suite "at least eight servants: one carried his pipe, another made coffee, a third was responsible for the tent." Observing the simplicity of the general's retinue, one of the merchants expressed surprise: "I have eleven people to serve me, when I am only a simple trader, while here is a man who may help himself to anything in this country and who makes do with three servants." And the author of the "Mémoire de la ville du Caire," speaking of the "households" in the city, remarked that whereas a "great lord" might have 150 or 200 people in his service, the house of a "good merchant" would have fewer than 20 or 30 retainers, while artisans generally made do with 2 or 3 slaves.[10]

## MINORITIES AND FOREIGNERS

Cairo still had sizable groups of minorities and foreigners of greatly varied origin. Of the city's 263,000 residents, as estimated by the authors of the *Description de l'Egypte,* some 25,000 belonged to minority groups (Copts, Jews, and Christians from the Ottoman Empire), and about the same number were "foreign" Muslims (Turks, Maghribis, and Syrians). The native Muslim population would thus have numbered around 200,000, and the ruling caste another 10,000.[11]

A Coptic scribe
(*Description de l'Egypte,*
Bibliothèque Nationale)

There were only 10,000 Copts in Cairo. This number seems small, since in the country as a whole the Christian minority represented 10 to 15 percent of the population. The Copts played an important part in certain artisan activities: as goldsmiths and silversmiths, as woodworkers, and as builders. Their average fortune seems to have been relatively low, but they drew prestige and influence from their activities as secretaries and intendants in the great Mamluk households. There were probably never more than 3,000 Jews in the city, all of them gathered in the Jewish quarter (Harat al-Yahud) near the center of Qahira. They traditionally played an important role in the trades that dealt with precious metals. Because of the capital they controlled, they also helped the ruling elite manage their tax-farms. As bankers to the janissaries, they long shared their prosperity, and they shared their decline as well when the janissaries were broken as a political and financial power by Ali Bey al-Kabir around 1760–1770 and replaced by the Syrian Christians.

The size of Cairo's "foreign" communities of Muslims and eastern Christians (some 40,000 individuals) was obviously a function of the large international trade centered in Egypt, but also of Cairo's position as a starting point and way-station for the pilgrimage *(hajj)* to the Muslim holy places. Between 1776 and 1798 the trade in textiles and coffee occupied 142 traders, of whom 63 (44 percent) were "foreign"

Muslims, owning 44 percent of the combined wealth. The creation of the Ottoman Empire rather reinforced Cairo's role as an entrepôt in the trade with the Orient (with coffee having replaced spices in the seventeenth century) and as a center of domestic trade within the empire. By facilitating movement from one end of the Mediterranean to the other, from Morocco to Iran, and from the shores of the Black Sea to Central Africa, the Ottoman Empire was also favorable to an increase in the pilgrimage, which the sultans took pains to encourage, considering it a facet of imperial policy. Thirty to forty thousand people gathered in Cairo annually to discharge their religious obligations and, in passing, to conclude business based on the exchange of Mediterranean goods for the products of the Orient. The movement of this mass of humanity through Cairo was also an occasion for intellectual and cultural exchange and increased the prestige of al-Azhar and its scholars.

The Turks were probably the most numerous group of "foreigners" in Cairo, with Ottoman rule favoring their settlement there. Numbering about 10,000, they lived in the area of the Khan al-Khalili as a homogeneous and turbulent community, their shared foreign language reinforcing their esprit de corps. A large number of Maghribis had always lived in Cairo—for historical reasons (notably the ties forged between Egypt and the Maghrib during the Fatimid period) as well as commercial and religious ones—and annual reinforcements came with the Maghribi pilgrim caravan. The Maghribis assimilated quickly and integrated easily into Egyptian society while not forgetting their ethnic origins: two eighteenth-century superintendents of the spice and coffee merchants were of Maghribi origin; and the Sharaybi, who arrived from Morocco in the seventeenth century, still considered themselves Maghribis a century later. The fact that there was a powerful group of Maghribis at al-Azhar promoted their maintenance of identity. Syrians and Palestinians were fewer in number (about 5,000), probably because their countries of origin were close enough that they had less need to settle in Cairo. They traded cloth and soap for other textiles and coffee. Their activity centered on the Khan al-Hamzawi and the Jamaliyya quarter, where the Wakala al-Sabun, or Caravanserai of Soap, was occupied largely by Palestinians.

Among the Eastern Christian communities living in Cairo, the

Greeks and Armenians played a minor role, pursuing their traditional trades as tailors, jewelers, and clockmakers. On the other hand, the Syrian Catholics (Melchite Greeks), who appeared in Syria in 1724 after a schism in the Greek Orthodox community, gradually increased in numbers during the eighteenth century, as Syrian emigrants continued to arrive chiefly from Aleppo and Damascus. The Syrian Catholics skillfully made use of the protection the French consuls gave them, becoming intermediaries between local and European traders. The fact that in 1769 Ali Bey withdrew the traditional customs revenues from the janissaries and their Jewish partners to bestow them on the Syrian Catholics is a reflection of the growing commercial and financial power of the Syrians and of the emir's ambitions toward Syria. The economic importance and influence of the Syrian Catholics continued to develop to the point where they displaced their Muslim compatriots in the Khan al-Hamzawi, the center of Syrian trade. The advent and growth of this new Christian community is one of the remarkable occurrences of the eighteenth century and reveals the increasing penetration of Frankish trade in the Egyptian economy.

## ORDERS AND CLASSES

Cairene society was thus very much divided into "orders," with an important vertical division between the ruling elite, who were of foreign origin, and the Egyptian "subjects," while the *ulama* filled an intermediary position. This assessment corresponds closely to the Egyptians' contemporary view of their society. They distinguished the following groups by ethnic origin and social function: the "people of the sword" *(ahl al-sayf)*, who were foreigners and held governmental and military office; the "people of the pen" *(ahl al-qalam)*, who held religious or scholarly office and participated in administration; and finally "the subjects" *(ra'iya)*, who were relegated to commercially productive activities and as such ensured the functioning of the system.

Egyptians were all the readier to accept a ruling class of foreign origin because a comparable system had been in place under the Mamluks and had brought Egypt glory and a high level of civilization. When Hasan Pasha arrived in Egypt in 1786, sent by the sultan to bring the Egyptian emirs back into line, he suggested to the *ulama* that they take the country's affairs into their own hands: "How can you bear to be ruled by two impious slaves [Ibrahim and Murad]? Why do you not league together to oust them from your midst?" His questions provoked only embarrassed replies from Shaykh al-Arusi ("The Egyptian people is poor and weak") and Isma'il Efendi ("The emirs form a strong and powerful party"). When Bonaparte made similar overtures, the shaykhs he questioned gave him a blunter answer, saying that "the lower orders fear only the Turks, who alone can govern them."[12]

Yet neither the subjects nor the "scholars" formed a truly homogeneous group. Also, there were points of contact between the "foreign" ruling elite and the subjects, a fact that helps explain why the society harbored a relatively low level of antagonism. The soldiery practiced other trades on the side, counter to the regulations governing the militias, while the militias also recruited locally and on a large scale from the poorest strata of the urban population. It was therefore quite difficult to distinguish this soldiery from the native population in whose midst they worked and lived, all the more so as they had often started families with Egyptian women. Inversely, those who practiced trades had early on begun to enter the militias in order to obtain their protection *(himaya)* in return for money. Of the estates left by 198 artisans and merchants in the last decade of the seventeenth century, 139 (70 percent) fell to the "military" division of the inheritance court, which reviewed estates belonging to members of the *odjaq*. The situation had progressed to the point that, in 1709, the sultan tried to forbid master tradesmen from affiliating with the militias on the grounds that they were "subjects"; the tradesmen replied that they were all "soldiers and sons of soldiers."[13] The motivations for affiliations between tradesmen and the soldiery are easy enough to understand: for the civilians, they provided protection against violence and injustice, and for the militias, a source of earnings through the duties charged the "protectees" on their entry into the affiliation and at their death, which provided the militia financial security and political power.

This trend toward affiliations developed in the mid-seventeenth century, when the janissaries were asserting their political dominance in Egypt. Ties were thus created at diverse levels of society. Ibrahim

Loggia (*maq'ad*) of Jabarti's house (watercolor by Pascal Coste,
Bibliothèque Municipale de Marseille)

Katkhuda, the leader of the janissaries, who governed Egypt from 1743 to 1754, married Lady Shuaykar, the daughter of a rich merchant named Muhammad al-Barudi, and it was this marriage that lay at the origin of his brilliant career, since his wife's fortune gave him the means to establish his political authority. The family of the shaykh and historian Jabarti also illustrates this intertwining of castes: a family of scholars from al-Azhar, they found themselves tied to representatives of the military "establishment" and to Red Sea traders through marriage and remarriage, through the purchase of mamluks, and through speculation in commercial ventures. The historian himself, a professor and man of letters, lived off the comfortable revenue afforded him by real estate and the leasing of a rural property.[14]

The ruling caste did not, therefore, constitute a totally closed world, and links were developed at different levels with the subject population. The horizontal stratification by socioeconomic criteria finds a distinctly privileged class at the top, in which members of the military oligarchy mingled with bourgeois merchants and scholars. At the bottom were the common people, a class strongly penetrated by the military. This quite original system came to an end in the last decades of the eighteenth century, when recruitment for the Mamluk oligarchy (culminating in beydom) and the militias was consolidated. At that time the houses *(buyut)* were formed that brought together mamluks and members of the military. When Ali Bey destroyed the janissary militia as an autonomous political force toward 1770, a new system of government crystallized in Egypt. Power came to be concentrated in the hands of one or several beys: Ali Bey himself, then Muhammad Bey Abu Dhahab, and finally Murad and Ibrahim Bey. Thus the gulf between the ruling elite and the indigenous population grew. Contemporary observers were not entirely conscious of it, as certain appearances were preserved that obscured the extent of the changes. But this political and social development largely explains the altered character of the history of Cairo and Egypt during the last decades of the century. The country witnessed harsh measures and government brutality, followed by popular unrest, so that the terms of Napoleon's famous proclamation were not unjustified: "For too long, this pack of slaves purchased in the Caucasus and Georgia has tyrannized the better part of the world . . . If Egypt is theirs to farm, then let them show the lease God gave them for it. A curse on the mamluks and happiness to the people of Egypt."[15]

# 11
# Expansion under the Ottomans

Historians have traditionally had few kind words for the Ottomans or the effects of their rule on Cairo:

> Cairo returned [under the Ottomans] to the dispersed patterns of settlement that had been favored by the earliest Arabs. The growing disorder of the city plan and the difficulty of communications . . . reflect the political and economic anarchy of the times . . . Details at every level confirm the precipitous decline of Cairo . . . It came to be no more than an aged city ruined by anarchy, devastated by epidemics, and preyed on by a band of brigands.[1]

From our present knowledge of the city's development under the Ottomans, it appears that Cairo, far from meeting such utter disaster, was in fact experiencing a period of genuine growth. This growth is apparent from the earliest scientific map of the city in our possession, prepared by the scholars of the *Description de l'Egypte* during their short stay in Egypt, when we compare it to a more realistic assessment of the glorious Mamluk period.

The fact that Cairo experienced three centuries of urban growth although it was no longer the capital of the vast Mamluk Empire but the administrative center of an Ottoman province is more paradoxical in appearance than in reality. The Ottoman Empire represented the largest political structure to take shape around the Mediterranean since the Roman Empire. The conditions were favorable for trade,

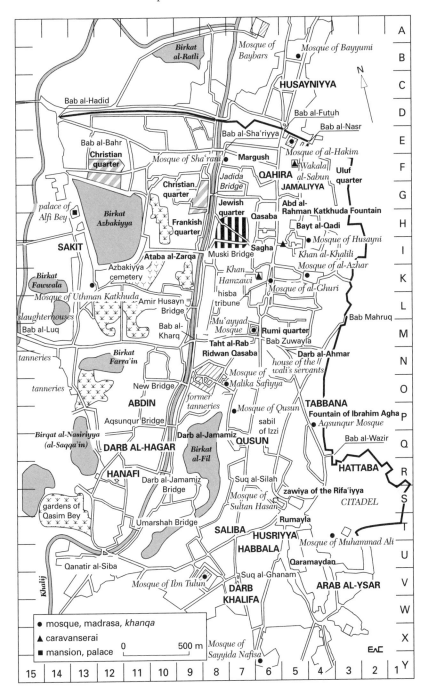

Map 8. Cairo in the Ottoman period (after *Description de l'Egypte*)

and Cairo, at the juncture of two continents with access to the Mediterranean and Europe, was uniquely placed to reap the benefits. Cairo remained the primary link for trade to the east, though it was gradually, but never more than partially, affected by the European discovery of a sea route to India. The city also occupied a central position with respect to internal trade within the Ottoman Empire, now eased by the absence of national borders and by the free circulation of goods and people. Finally, the expansion of the Ottoman Empire to include all the Arab world (with the exception of Morocco) and the encouragement of its ruling dynasty and their local representatives contributed to an increase in the annual pilgrimage to the holy sites, which greatly benefited Cairo and Damascus where the caravans gathered for the *hajj*. Evidence of the phenomenal boom that Cairo experienced can be seen in the development of the central commercial zones around the Qasaba, which increased in area from 38 to 55 hectares, and in the growing number of caravanserais (Maqrizi mentions 58, in contrast to 360 in the Ottoman period).

The economic boom obviously had an impact on Cairo's urban structure. But because we have no accurate maps earlier than the one published in the French Expedition's *Description de l'Egypte*, we are obliged to assess the growth on the basis of Cairo's architectural history and municipal events (though they are all too rarely reported in the chronicles).[2]

The Qahira district, already densely settled during the Mamluk period, underwent few transformations. Expanding economic activity in the central sector undoubtedly had an effect on its more residential zones. But the area it actually occupied, and the population within it, probably changed relatively little. This was not the case with the districts surrounding the Qahira, which functioned as suburbs, as is shown by the great number of domestic structures, the reduced specialization in economic activities, the lesser population densities, and the lower average wealth—except in the south, in the "chic" residential neighborhoods around the Pond of the Elephant (Birkat al-Fil), and in the west, around the Nasiriyya and Azbakiyya ponds.

Toward the end of the Mamluk period, the southern outskirts had become substantially urbanized, as we saw earlier. Because of the already high population density in the Qahira district and the space given there to economic activities, the population influx that Cairo was receiving (as were Aleppo and Damascus at the same period) was directed toward the southern neighborhoods. The first important indication of growth in the area beyond Bab Zuwayla is the great architectural project undertaken by Iskandar Pasha around Bab al-Kharj. Around 1556–1559 he built a large mosque, a monastery (*takiyya*), and a public drinking fountain (*sabil*). In addition, he either bought or built a number of commercial structures to finance the building of his religious edifices, including twenty-seven shops, two rental buildings, and a sugar refinery. These projects made it possible to overhaul the plan of the neighborhood, which is some 500 meters from Bab Zuwayla.[3] But the fact that there were tanneries nearby posed a significant obstacle to any large-scale urban expansion on this side.

The problem was solved in 1600 by a decision handed down from Istanbul. Wanting to name a great mosque after his mother, Sultan Muhammad III ordered the governor, Khidr Pasha, to buy the tanneries and build a monument in its place. This was to become the Malika Safiyya mosque. The tanneries were then moved outside Cairo, near Bab al-Luq. Four mosques were built nearby between 1610 and 1625, as the city expanded into the area: the Mosque of Malika Safiyya (wife of Murad III and mother of Muhammad III), a building whose Ottoman character is explained by the ruling family's role in its construction (1610); the Mosque of Ali al-Amri (1616?); the Mosque of Burdayni, built in a style very suggestive of the Mamluk period (1616–1629); and the Mosque of Yusuf Agha al-Hin (1625). The removal of the tanneries also allowed a large number of emirs to settle along the shores of the Birkat al-Fil, reinforcing the tendency we noted in the Mamluk period for the establishment of mansions and villas there. In the seventeenth century this area became the residential district par excellence of the ruling class: for the period 1650–1755, 40 percent of the emirs whose place of residence is known had palaces along the pond, which was surrounded by a continuous belt of houses.[4]

Cairo's southern expansion in the mid-seventeenth century was marked by large-scale urban works.[5] The construction undertaken by Ridwan Bey, the most powerful emir in Cairo, directly south of Bab Zuwayla, occurred between 1629 and 1647 and was certainly linked to the departure of the tanneries and the space thus freed up. An

Bridge over the Khalij (*Description de l'Egypte,* Bibliothèque Nationale)

area some 150 meters in length was renovated. The second project, which was also undertaken in the context of a religious foundation, concerns an area slightly to the southwest along the main thoroughfare that, passing by Darb al-Ahmar and Tabbana, leads from Bab Zuwayla to the Citadel. Ibrahim Agha, the dominant emir of the janissaries in about 1650, renovated the district around the Aq Sunqur Mosque at that time. He built or restored religious, public, and commercial monuments—whether fountains, watering troughs, rental buildings, or houses—along both sides of the street for almost 250 meters.

The fact that fountains were built in the southern part of Cairo is also a sign of urban expansion, since they were a necessary source of water for the local population. Their builders' religious aims and desire for self-glorification could be achieved only if people actually used the fountains. Of 111 public fountains whose date of construction during the three centuries of Ottoman rule is known, 46, or almost half, were erected between 1626 and 1775 in Cairo's southern districts. This is many more than in the central district of Qahira (30 fountains). During the same period, fourteen mosques were built in the southern portions of Cairo, as against twelve in Qahira. It was

Houses on the Khalij (drawing by Pascal Coste)

therefore in the south that the main architectural effort was under way during that century and a half.

The zone to the west of the Canal, or Khalij, was only patchily inhabited. Until the beginning of the eighteenth century, urbanization occurred only along the Khalij and along the main thoroughfares linking the center of Cairo with the suburbs of Bulaq and Old Cairo. The situation therefore had not changed much since the end of the Mamluk period. The western fringe of the city was still quite a rural area, dotted with ponds, gardens, and cemeteries; the middle-class homes beside areas that flooded at high water were often inhabited only during the hot season. That such a large proportion of the inhabitants there belonged to minorities (five of the seven Coptic districts mentioned in the *Description de l'Egypte* are west of the Canal) is also explained by the weak Muslim presence there. The Azbakiyya area, after the emir Azbak's unsuccessful attempts at urbanization, remained a somewhat marginalized area, as indicated by its fleshpots, bordellos, and hashish dens. These areas were also relatively unsafe: in 1723 the chronicler Ahmad Shalabi described this sector, to which women went in the spring to breathe in the fresh air, as a non-urban area (*al-khala*) where one ran the risk of meeting shady characters. And Jabarti reports on the disdain with which an officer of the janissaries responded to some shopkeepers from Azbakiyya who complained of the extortion they suffered from an emir's men: "O so and so [*ya fulan*], [do you think] we would beat our servants for the sake of the peasants [*fallahin*] in Azbakiyya?"[6] Though not an actual boundary, the Canal separated the city proper from a district that was still largely an area for walking. Jabarti describes some "Robinson Crusoes" who settled toward 1750 around the Azbakiyya and near the Nasiriyya pond, in the gardens of Qasim Bey, where the Cairenes came to stroll and take the air in summer.

Toward the end of the seventeenth and the beginning of the eighteenth century, this area started to become more urban, as indicated by two architectural projects. The first dates to 1732, when the great spice merchant, Qasim al-Sharaybi, built a mosque and a fountain on the east bank of the Azbakiyya at Ataba al-Zarqa; the modest scale of these monuments reflected the builder's status as a "subject" rather than his true power. But building a mosque for communal Friday prayer was an act of some consequence: none had been built in the area since 1661. The second, a much more ambitious architectural and city planning project, was sited on the southwest corner of the Azbakiyya. It was commissioned in 1734 by an emir belonging to Egypt's ruling coterie, Uthman Katkhuda Qazdaghli, who certainly was aware of the great projects undertaken two and a half centuries earlier by the emir Azbak. Uthman's mosque, one of the most remarkable monuments of the period, was built in a typically neo-Mamluk style with an Ottoman minaret. The building complex surrounding it included a fountain, a public bath, shops, and an apartment building *(rab)*, its range of functions presumably intended to serve the needs of an already sizable population. The mosque site was in fact known as the "al-Bakri market," and so great was the crowd at its inaugural prayer service that Uthman Bey Dhulfiqar, one of the foremost emirs of the day, was unable to gain entry to the new mosque.[7]

After this spectacular launching, settlement of the land around the Azbakiyya pond proceeded apace. While middle-class settlers occupied the eastern shore, the more agreeable southern shore with its villas facing the pond to receive the cool breeze from the north started to attract a number of emirs, who gradually spread also to the western shore. One of the most striking developments during the eighteenth century was in fact the migration of emirs from around Birkat al-Fil, long the most desirable residential neighborhood, to the western portion of the city. The growing urbanization of the southern sector of the city possibly hampered the wealthy, who felt the need for space and uncongested streets. From this point of view, the western district provided great facilities and advantages, which may explain why nearly half of all emirs' residences in 1798 were on the west side of the Canal, with fully 15 percent on the shores of the Azbakiyya.

Other indications of the general westward expansion, of which the migration of the elite was only one aspect, can be read in the city's architectural history. The crossing points over the Khalij, which obstructed movement between the center and the newly urbanized zones, were gradually improved. Three interventions are known to us from textual sources, the actual structures having been destroyed in the nineteenth century when the Khalij was filled in to make an avenue: the so-called New Bridge (al-Jadida), possibly restored in 1725 by the emir Ali Katkhuda al-Qaysarli, who was responsible for a number of edifices in the area, including a mosque; the Muski Bridge, restored by Abd al-Rahman Katkhuda al-Qazdaghli, probably in about 1754, at the time he built the very original al-Shawazliyya Mosque; and the "New Bridge," also the work of this tireless builder, probably dating to about 1761, when the nearby mosque and fountain of Sheikh Ramadan were built. The building or renovation of these structures undoubtedly improved access to the western neighborhoods; in fact Jabarti states this explicitly in writing of the bridge that led to the Abdin quarter.[8]

The accelerating urbanization of the western area during the eighteenth century is confirmed by the pace of construction there: between 1726 and 1798, the area saw fifteen new mosques and twelve new fountains, while the two previous centuries (1517–1725) had seen the building of only six mosques and two fountains. Architectural construction during the final three-quarters of a century of Ottoman rule was decidedly greater in the sectors of the city beyond the Khalij than in the Qahira district (eleven mosques and sixteen fountains) or in the southern sector (seven mosques and two fountains). The figures for public baths, whose demographic implications are obvious, indicate the same trend: four were built in the western district, as against three in Qahira and none in the south. After an initial trend to the southern sector, the main stream of settlement was now directed toward the areas west of the Khalij. The long process that had started in the Mamluk period with the first urban projects under al-Nasir and with Azbak's attempt at a settlement was just coming to its term when the French scientists arrived to document it for the map in the *Description de l'Egypte*.

In 1798, according to the French Expedition map, the city covered a total area of 730 hectares. However, if we take into account all the open spaces (ponds, gardens, cemeteries, public squares), the developed area including streets comes to 660 hectares, as follows: Husayniyya, 26 hectares; Qahira, 153 hectares; southern sector, 266 hectares; western sector, 215 hectares. The developed area had therefore increased greatly since the Mamluk period: 660 hectares versus 450, with the expansion having occurred in the southern sector, from less than 200 to 266 hectares, and especially in the western sector, from 100 to 215 hectares, whereas Qahira had attained its equilibrial size in medieval times.[9]

As to the city's population at the end of the Ottoman period, the French Expedition's *Description de l'Egypte* estimated it at 263,000 in 1798.[10] Looking at the distribution of structures on which urban populations are strongly dependent such as public fountains and baths, a distribution that is approximately identical for large sectors of the city and is most likely correlated to the number of people reliant on them, I have suggested the following repartition of Cairo's inhabitants: Husayniyya, 8,000 inhabitants; Qahira, 90,000; southern sector, 100,000; western sector, 65,000. This translates to an overall average density of 39,800 persons per square kilometer, with the following breakdown of densities by district: Husayniyya, 30,700 persons per square kilometer; Qahira, 58,800; southern sector, 37,500; western sector, 30,200. The overall density is virtually identical with the average figure of 40,000 persons per square kilometer arrived at by L. Torrès Balbas for the cities of Muslim Spain and by A. Lézine for the cities of the Maghrib.[11] The very high density of Qahira is explained by the relative overpopulation of Cairo's historical central district, and the marked increase in building height, with many buildings for communal residence having three, four, or even five stories. The density of the southern district was average, as was only logical for a more recently urbanized area with less vertical housing. The low density of the western district can be explained by its more recent and still partial settlement, and by the wide-scale development of residential zones for the rich and the middle class, and of lower-class rural dwellings.

In all, Cairo's population (estimated at between 150,000 and 200,000 in 1517) increased by about 50 percent during the Ottoman period. This increase seems excessive only if we accept the stereotype of Cairo's decline under the Ottomans. It corresponds to what we know about the cities of Damascus and Aleppo, where the developed area and the population increased by the same proportions between the sixteenth and nineteenth centuries.[12] In all probability, the city's rate of growth was anything but regular. The demographic conditions there were still "medieval," with high birth and death rates, and the rate of natural increase must have been less than five per thousand. During this period Cairo was not spared great natural disasters and the consequent famines, epidemics, and grave political crises. The overall growth of the population must often have been interrupted by calamities, and in particular the great epidemics of plague that followed one after another during the seventeenth and eighteenth centuries at an average interval of twenty years. The Ottoman period ended with a series of disasters (plague and famine in 1784–1785, epidemic in 1791, political crisis from 1786 to 1798) that left Egypt and Cairo in a state of exhaustion that was noticed by some observers.[13] Yet these crises did no more than slow down and sometimes interrupt the city's expansion and the growth of its population between 1517 and 1798. Despite this succession of misfortunes, Cairo was a larger city in 1798 than in the golden age of al-Nasir.

# City Administration and Daily Life

IT HAS OFTEN BEEN SAID that Cairo, like the other major Arab cities, was slackly administered, even neglected, during the Ottoman period. This claim overlooks the activities of the central and provincial authorities in this realm and the role of local institutions, which, though different from the municipal institutions of Western cities, played an active part in managing the city.[1]

## THE GOVERNING BODIES

We have only an imperfect idea of the orders handed down from Istanbul to Cairo. Yet the central government received a flood of information from its provincial governors and religious judges, being required to make decisions whenever problems arose. The influence of the imperial government no doubt made itself felt on city administration as long as local potentates did not impose themselves at the expense of the central authorities. But right up to the eighteenth century, the imperial government's interest in Cairo's architecture can be seen in the buildings created for the Ottoman sultan, such as the edifices built by Sultan Mahmud (1730–1754)—a monastery and a fountain in 1750; and by Sultan Mustafa (1757–1777)—two fountains in 1757 and 1759.

The Sublime Porte no doubt intervened when important municipal questions cropped up. Cairo's tanneries provide a good example. The problem was discussed from the mid-sixteenth century on, and a final decision taken only in 1600. On 23 July 1552 the imperial government wrote the vizir Ali Pasha and the high judge of Cairo to discuss the nuisance created by the tanneries for the surrounding neighborhoods: "It would be advisable to move the tanneries to a corner of the city . . . where it will not be noxious to the city within the walls." The grand vizir Rustum Pasha had stated his intention of establishing a religious foundation that would contain slaughterhouses and tanneries. He was ordered to remove them if they were inside the city, where they might provide a nuisance to the people of the quarter, and to replace them by building "tanneries and slaughterhouses outside the city in a suitable place . . . so that they will be noxious to no one." The matter was settled once and for all only at a much later date, when (as we saw earlier) Sultan Muhammad III ordered Khidr Pasha (1598–1601) to buy up the tanneries.[2]

The administration of Cairo itself and the resolution of a number of municipal problems came under the responsibility of the national authorities, who were sent by the Sublime Porte to govern Egypt. One of their main concerns was to ensure order, and they naturally intervened in the affairs of Cairo as the seat of the provincial government. Charged with seeing to Egypt's safety, the pasha intervened with the forces at his disposal to maintain order until his authority to do so was abrogated by local potentates. In the seventeenth century, during the troubles caused by the high price of goods, several riots reached the walls of the Citadel, where the government had its offices. The pasha was then obliged to use his power to reestablish order. When, in 1678, the cost of wheat rose to 180 paras per irdabb, there was a riot in Rumayla; when the price rose even higher, the mob destroyed the grain market and the neighboring shops; the pasha Abd al-Rahman sent in his troops to disperse the crowd, and thirteen people were killed. Until the beginning of the eighteenth century, the pashas showed an interest in urban matters, and their administrative measures were remarkable enough to arouse the interest of the chroniclers. Muhammad Pasha (1607–1611) ordered the removal of "a pickax-breadth of earth from all the streets of Cairo," because the accumulation of dust and refuse along with insufficient street cleaning was regularly causing problems. Maqsud Pasha (1642–43) ordered the dredging of two canals, the Khalij al-Hakimi and the Khalij al-Nasiri, which were threatened with silting. Muhammad Pasha (1652–1656) ordered the administrators of mosques to whiten these monuments, for which he came to be known as Muhammad "Abu l-Nur" (Father of Light). Finally, Muhammad Pasha (1699–1704) had the coverings of streets and shops in the markets torn down to widen the streets, then dug and leveled the ground. Thereafter the pashas' authority declined, and with it their intervention in the city's affairs.[3]

It was to the janissaries that Sultan Selim entrusted the task of guarding the city and Cairo's Citadel. This responsibility helped to strengthen the various links that developed between the militia and Cairo's subject population (entry into the trades by the military, requests for protection by the subjects) and to make the janissaries more effective agents. Even when replaced by the lieutenant (*katkhuda*) as the militia's actual leader, the agha of the janissaries continued to be responsible for police functions in Cairo. At the end of the eighteenth century, the historian J.-J. Marcel observed that the janissaries' main function was "to ensure the public peace" and that their agha was in charge of "policing the city" during the day. These broad powers caused the aghas to take a particularly active role during times of crisis and, specifically, to intervene in problems concerning the supply and pricing of goods, which provoked a good deal of public unrest in the seventeenth and eighteenth centuries. The inspection rounds made by Ali Agha were long remembered: on 20 February 1703, writes Jabarti,

> Ali Agha made his rounds wearing his turban of command. In front of him walked the officers and lieutenants, the *wali* [governor], the chief accountant, and the *oda basha* [noncommissioned officer] of his bodyguard with his men. Behind him walked the seven shawishes. The *qadi's* deputy headed the procession with a *kawas* beside him carrying a sack full of truncheons . . . Anyone found in violation of the law . . . was beaten senseless, often dying from the punishment . . . Thus did Ali Agha inspire great terror. Passersby drew aside as soon as they saw him. No woman dared look out the window while his procession was patrolling the streets.[4]

Being responsible for police functions in the city, the agha might intervene in municipal affairs. This same Ali Agha took an interest in traffic problems: he had one and sometimes two cubits of earth removed from the streets where the soil had built up and ordered the demolition of the benches (*masatib;* sing. *mastaba*) built in front of shops because they obstructed passage and could serve as barricades in times of public disturbance. Somewhat later, in 1711, during a political crisis, he again ordered the streets to be cleaned, the debris removed, the destroyed buildings rebuilt, and the facades of public monuments whitewashed (mosques and their minarets, fountains, and schools).

The decline of the janissaries in the eighteenth century, however, relegated the agha to a lesser role in urban affairs. Toward 1770, in the time of Ali Bey, Jabarti complains about the dumping of refuse into the Nile and the poor maintenance of the roads to Bulaq. He observes with regret that the last person to have taken responsibility for these problems was Abd al-Rahman Agha, who "always saw to it that the roads were clean and well maintained." After him, "vigilance decreased until it vanished altogether, to the point where some of the roads leading to Bulaq were obstructed by the garbage thrown there by the residents." Yet in 1786 Salim Agha would order that the door of the Mosque of Sultan Hasan be reopened (it had been closed in the wake of disturbances in 1736) and that the parasitic structures and shops obstructing the passage of the faithful be destroyed.[5]

Only a few relatively low-level officials were delegated to oversee urban affairs. The governor of Cairo *(wali),* who was also called the *subaşi* (a Turkish title), replaced the officer of this title from the Mamluk period, preserving most of his functions. Appointed by the pasha, his main responsibility was policing Cairo (he had counterparts in Bulaq and Old Cairo), particularly at night, as the agha oversaw police functions during the day. The *wali* had janissaries under his orders, who lived in barracks south of Bab Zuwayla (where the *Description de l'Egypte* locates "the house of the Oualy's [Wali's] men") and in stations distributed though the city's quarters. The *wali* made nocturnal rounds and could administer fines or even harsher punishments to scofflaws, but not the death penalty. Oversight of the city's morals was to some extent his province: he supervised taverns and prostitutes, of which he kept a list, but the taxes he levied in connection with these functions gave his office an unsavory reputation. He also took part in operations relating to the urban upkeep of Cairo:

he was responsible for cleaning the Khalij, using taxes collected from local residents for the purpose. He also organized fire fighting in Cairo, and a watch was kept at night from his "barracks" in the center of town. In case of need, he would go to the fire with his men and some assigned members of relevant trades—water carriers, fullers, and demolition men.

Just as traditional was the *hisba,* which functioned as a supervisory board for markets. Originally vested with a much broader mandate, this city magistrature was eventually reduced to supervising trades and commercial practices. The *muhtasib,* who was drawn from the Shawushiyya corps under the control of the janissaries, was a fairly modest functionary. He supervised a number of trade organizations having to do with food, which gave him a certain importance in times of crisis, as he was concerned with supply and prices; but he was often supplanted at those times by the agha. He was also responsible for inspecting weights and measures in the markets. His inspection tours were attended with a pomp that often elicited the excited notice of travelers: wearing a black robe and a special turban (a flat hat rising into a sort of cone and covered in white muslin), the *muhtasib* rode on horseback preceded by one of his agents carrying a large scale with standardized weights. With him came a numerous retinue that included janissaries, executioners, and servants carrying long poles and switches. The vigor and picturesqueness of the punishments he sometimes meted out made an impression on the Cairenes: dishonest shopkeepers were nailed to their shops by the ear, so that unscrupulous individuals were commonly said to be "large-eared"; a butcher who sold meat at short weight would have a compensating amount removed from his backside; a fraudulent pastrymaker would be made to sit on his burning pans . . . These brutal measures were only partly efficacious, and the shopkeepers went back to their cheating ways once the storm was past. The *muhtasib* presided at the *ru'iya* ceremony (sighting of the Ramadan moon), which provided an opportunity for the trade corporations of Cairo to pass in review. But the *muhtasib* was no longer in charge of morals and religious observance. He also had no further jurisdiction over minority groups *(dhimmi),* nor any say in matters of city management (street cleanliness, freedom of passage within the city)—all of which were matters that had once given his office importance. When much later, in 1818, under Muhammad Ali, a particularly energetic *muhtasib* tried to revive some of the former responsibilities of the *hisba* for city affairs, he provoked such a general hue and cry that the pasha had to recall him.

Judges had no specific mandate to regulate the affairs of the city, but their jurisdiction was so broad that they inevitably ventured into this domain. Surviving registers from the courts of law show that the range of judicial decisionmaking was limitless. Although this was nothing new, it seems that a judge's area of competence was defined more broadly in the Ottoman period than in medieval times. There are numerous examples: when a new building went up, the *qadi* verified that it did not obstruct the public way ("a mounted soldier or a loaded camel may pass without difficulty"), that it created no nuisance for the neighbors or infringement on their right to light and a view; when a structure was in bad repair, the *qadi* saw to it that it was not a hazard to neighboring houses or to passersby; he would have someone inspect a new door or window to be sure that it did not bother the neighbors; he responded to the complaints of residents over the noise a workshop was expected to bring into a neighborhood; he saw to the observance of morals. In all these cases, the judges called on expert witnesses to investigate on-site and make reports from which judicial decisions could be made.

In the absence of stated urban regulations and general principles governing building in the city, the jurists and judges of the modern era created, day by day, an empirical but clear doctrine concerning the main issues of city life and urban development. It is largely thanks to the work of the judges that the city maintained itself and even grew without falling into the anarchy that has sometimes been described.[6]

## THE ROLE OF COMMUNITIES

Since Cairo had no status as a legal entity and no autonomy, there were no statutory "municipal" institutions. Yet there were highly diverse groups *(tawa'if)* that dealt with every aspect of its residents' lives: groupings by profession (trade corporations), national origin (non-Egyptian groups), religion (the *dhimmi*), and geography (neighborhood communities). These groupings were of long standing, but the Ottomans, with little commitment to centralization, probably allowed them considerable independence. This system had the twofold advantage of absolving the rulers from forming a true administrative framework while providing them at least minimal control over the population through the shaykhs who headed the various communal groups. These communities therefore contributed, in various capacities, to the running of the city.[7]

The main non-Egyptian Muslim communities (Maghribis, Turks, and Syrians) were organized under the authority of shaykhs. These communities sometimes melded with the corresponding groups (*arwiqa*) at al-Azhar Mosque, which brought together shaykhs and foreign students: this was the case with the Maghribis, whose community shaykh (*shaykh ta'ifat al-Magharibα*) could be a scholar at al-Azhar. As with certain trades or certain commercial sites that were identified with a specific national group, it sometimes happened that the community had a strong geographic base. The Palestinians, for example, specialized in the sale of soap and in consequence the Wakala of Soap (Wakala al-Sabun) functioned as their center of activity; this caravanserai was, to an extent, the gathering place of the community. Around 1798 Ahmad al-Zaru, a soap merchant from Khalil (Hebron), was at the same time shaykh of the soap sellers' corporation, shaykh of their caravanserai, and the Palestinians' spokesman. A good portion of the Turks worked at the Khan al-Khalili or nearby and lived at no great distance from this caravanserai. As a result, the quarter had a strongly pronounced Turkish character, and Turkish was the dominant language there. The strong esprit de corps of its residents and their combativeness were often in evidence during Cairo's turbulent moments.

The minority religious groups (the *dhimmi*, or "protected," meaning the Christians and Jews) were organized in the same way. Their geographic distribution provides evidence that they were strongly segregated: the Jews inhabited the center of Cairo; the Copts lived in seven quarters, mainly to the west, their dispersion perhaps indicating a greater degree of integration. These minority religious communities remained under the authority of their traditional leaders, who had a fairly free hand in administering them—the authorities showed little propensity to intervene as long as order was maintained and the taxes levied against the *dhimmi* were duly collected. In the minority quarters, urban affairs were the province of the community shaykh.

The trade corporations, which were also called "communities" *(tawa'if)*, dealt primarily with professional matters, settling problems that arose within the corporation and attending to relations between the members of the trade and the public.[8] But it was through the shaykhs of these corporations that the authorities controlled and administered the economically active population of the city (virtually all the Egyptians proper) and levied taxes on the members of a trade. Because the corporations were usually geographically concentrated, they also had a local effect. They thus contributed to the maintenance of order. When the first revolt against the French in Cairo ended, the shaykhs and merchants of the great Ghuriyya Market (the main cloth market in Cairo) gathered before Napoleon on 26 October 1798 and agreed in writing as follows: "Henceforth we will maintain the streets of our quarters free from all . . . disturbance . . . we will take every care to restrain wrongdoers." The merchants agreed further to arrest anyone in the quarter who wanted to "disrupt order," and to signal the presence of any foreigners who settled in the neighborhood to the authorities. In addition to the simple policing of their quarters, the corporations inevitably assumed town planning functions: street cleaning, lighting, and no doubt participation in decisions affecting the management of the city, such as the relocation of the tanneries in 1600, or the removal of the gunpowder merchants from the center of town in 1671 and 1703 because of the public nuisance and safety hazards these activities represented.

More important still was the role played by the neighborhood communities of the *harat*, which were also under the authority of shaykhs. From the map of Cairo, it is clear that the geography of the *harat* (of which there were certainly close to a hundred) complemented that of the corporations: the business zone, which held most of the markets and commercial structures, was in the center, while the residential neighborhoods were mostly on the periphery. The *hara* constituted another "meta-administrative" framework through which the authorities might exercise control over the population. A number of taxes were levied on the quarters, with their apportionment within the *hara* determined by the shaykh. Being relatively closed structures, the quarters played a role in the internal policing of the city. It was also within the *hara* that the conflicts of communal life were resolved, sometimes in court before a judge, and there as well that problems relating to the maintenance of the city were often raised: a bath that needed renovation; complaints about the bad repair of a mosque, whose restoration should be performed by the religious endowment concerned; or complaints about obstructions of the public way—in short, the life of the city, in every detail, day by day.[9]

THESE DIFFERENT GROUPINGS of ethnic and religious communities as well as professional and geographic ones, which adjoined and overlapped, provided a structure around the population of Cairo. Although the city had no municipal administration, its inhabitants were held within a web of loyalties, dependencies, and controls that addressed every aspect of their social lives and extended over the city as a whole. These communities certainly played a primary role in the functioning of the city.

## THE *Waqf*

One typically Muslim institution that played an important part in shaping the city was the religious foundation, or *waqf* (pl. *awqaf*), equivalent to what is called *habu* in North Africa. The general principles of the *waqf* are well known: in fulfillment of religious obligations, property (in the form of money, land, or a building) is deeded in perpetuity to a religious or charitable foundation, in order that the proceeds from that property may benefit the foundation in question. The deeding of property may be total and immediate, as in a public-interest *waqf* (*waqf khayri*), or it may be partial and deferred, as in a family *waqf* (*waqf ahli*), in which the founder designates a private beneficiary of the endowment's income; full title to the endowment reverts to the foundation only when the family line of the original beneficiary dies out. *Awqaf* benefiting religious or charitable foundations, often endowments to maintain a monument such as a mosque or fountain in perpetuity, provided the wherewithal for running many religious, charitable, and educational institutions: places of prayer and their officiants, hospitals, and schools.

A *waqf* allowed its founder to provide income for his descendants and to avoid the rather strict constraints of Muslim inheritance law, so that he might favor some heirs over others. It was otherwise difficult to keep an estate from being frittered into small pieces under the rules of succession and, apparently, by the exactions of the powerful in troubled times. This was one reason the *waqf* system flourished in the Ottoman period. Cairo had thousands of *awqaf*. In 1920 it was estimated that one-eighth of the cultivated land of Egypt and 18,500 of its city buildings were tied up in these foundations.[10]

As it was important to provide the foundation with a substantial and regular flow of income, if possible one that was easy to collect, the founders of *awqaf* bought or built commercial structures—houses, shops, apartment houses, public baths, or establishments of artisan production—whose rental was intended to support the foundation. To ease the task of management, administrators had an interest in seeing that the property whose revenues they would be collecting and whose condition they would be monitoring was nearby. The buildings were thus often grouped close to the monument that the *waqf* was intended to benefit, and a foundation's prestige was tied to the number and size of the properties in its endowment. A large urban *waqf* could thus become a veritable urban planning project and even call for the remodeling or restructuring of a whole quarter. Such undertakings were most likely to occur in expanding sections of the city, in zones where more space was available and the density of buildings was lower. This explains why a certain number of Cairo's great *awqaf* were located in pioneer territory, in areas where they contributed to (or at least witnessed) the city's development. In the sixteenth and seventeenth centuries, three great *waqf* enterprises took shape in the southern sector of Cairo, which was then in full course of expansion. These are only samples, however, of a kind of undertaking that was very common in the Ottoman period.

Iskandar Pasha, who governed Egypt from 1556 to 1559, undertook extensive construction in the area between Bab Zuwayla and Bab al-Kharq.[11] This region was entirely transformed when it was modernized in the last decades of the nineteenth century, however,

Ridwan Bey Suq

and the pasha's buildings have all disappeared. Our only knowledge of them comes from the work of chroniclers, the plan of Cairo in the *Description de l'Egypte*, and the fine sketch of a minaret made by Pascal Coste around 1820.

The construction undertaken south of Bab Zuwayla by Ridwan Bey was part of the urban development of the southern sector. The greatness of Ridwan Bey, a powerful emir of the second quarter of the seventeenth century, shines forth in the sheer scale of his realizations. Around the magnificent residence he built for himself in 1650 on a site where there had been a succession of palaces, there arose structures that are listed in a series of *waqf* documents (*waqfiyyat*), the oldest of which dates to 1629 and the latest to 1647. The central element was a large suq for shoemakers: 125 meters long, Ridwan's avenue (*qasaba*) contains a covered section that constitutes, along with certain *wakalat*, the most impressive commercial structure preserved from Cairo's millenary past. Along a 50-meter section, the street is covered by a wooden ceiling pierced by skylights. On either side of the street, which is 6 meters wide, the stone facades of the ground floor are divided into bays containing shops. Strong corbels support a projecting second floor. The upper part is occupied by a *rab* of imposing dimensions. North of the palace was a *wakala*. There were also a dyehouse, a mill, thirty-one shops, several houses, two convents, and a public fountain, all in immediate proximity to the *qasaba*, spanning a length of 150 meters and an area of more than one hectare. How this complex was inserted into the street system of the quarter we do not know. Ridwan Bey preserved the main street (Shari al-Azam) that joined Bab Zuwayla to Saliba in the Mamluk era, but a map of Ridwan Bey's structures shows that the street was most likely enlarged and made regular at that time. The west side of the street is approximately straight along its entire length (130 meters); on the east side, Ridwan's structures are aligned, correcting the irregularities stemming from the older monuments. One of the *waqf* documents indicates that the street was narrow and needed improvement. This was clearly a case of urban development on the scale of the quarter as a whole.

A third example relates to an officer of the janissary corps, Ibrahim Agha, whom we know to have been active between 1651 and 1657. He was responsible for a great deal of construction in the

Tabbana quarter, on the street leading from Bab Zuwayla to the Citadel. The works attributable to him are enumerated in a long series of *waqf* documents. As early as 1632, these documents mention two houses in this area. A deed dating from 1641 mentions the tomb that the emir built for himself and the fountain beside it. One building project then followed another, among them the restoration of the Aq Sunqur Mosque, a Mamluk monument (1346) that Ibrahim Agha rebuilt completely in 1650–51, adding Ottoman-style ceramic decorations that gave it its popular name of "Blue Mosque." The latest *waqf* document, dated 1659, concerns a watering trough. Of the complex, which once extended for 250 meters and seems to have developed from north to south, apparently regularizing the street plan along the way, only a few structures survive.

Although not every aspect of the processes described above is entirely clear, one begins to get a sense of how the combined action of officials, communities, and the *waqf* institution contributed toward the running of a city that had no specialized municipal administration or public institutions, yet whose safety and essential functioning were nonetheless provided for.

## LAW AND ORDER

During the three centuries of Ottoman rule, Cairo was not a placid city. The conflicts that arose quite frequently within the ruling elite affected the city and its people. One example is the crisis of 1711, which pitted two powerful factions of emirs against each other for sixty-eight days. There were battles and bombardments. At the height of the conflict, a hundred cannon shots illuminated the night "like lightning," the chronicler records, and threatened to swallow up the earth itself. But while the emirs went at it outside the city, the markets were apparently open and people continued about their business almost normally. Much more damaging to Cairo's residents, if we are to believe the poet-songwriter Hasan al-Hijazi, was the interruption in the supply of water from the Nile: "[They] starved us by depriving us of everything. Instead of water from the Nile, we had to drink salty water [raised from wells] that made the burning in our guts all the stronger."[12] These political convulsions occurred near the Citadel, or in the southern section of the city where many emirs lived, but usually they were relatively short and caused only minor damages. To protect themselves, the residents often employed their most efficient means of defense: they closed the shops and markets, putting pressure on the emirs to restore peace. This took the form of a public proclamation of "safety and security" (al-amm wa l-aman), after which normal activities were resumed.

Riots provoked by economic hardship (scarcity and high prices) were frequent at the end of the seventeenth century (for example, in 1678, 1687, 1695), as were protests against arbitrary actions by the authorities toward the end of the eighteenth century (1777, 1786, 1787, 1790, 1795), but they troubled the settled order for only a short time and in a limited area near the Citadel, the seat of government, and in the neighborhood of al-Azhar Mosque, whose shaykhs were the designated spokesmen for the exasperated people. In September 1790, in the wake of violent and brutal acts by an emir in the suburb of Husayniyya, the people of that quarter rebelled. Markets and shops were closed. The protesters marched on al-Azhar Mosque, closing its doors and disrupting its classes. They climbed the minarets beating drums and making a general call for resistance. Shaykh al-Arusi had to promise to intervene. There were several confrontations in the city, leaving two killed and a number wounded. After ten days of tension and negotiations, a compromise was found, and the gatherings were dispersed.

The population of Cairo undoubtedly suffered more from the everyday oppression of those who held a small degree of power and whose excesses went unchecked. Examples of such depravity are easily cited. In 1725 the men (sarrajin) of the foremost emir, Cherkes Bey, entered merchants' houses at night and demanded cloth and money; a rich trader was murdered in his own home. At the end of the year, the sarrajin spread terror in the markets, three or four of them entering a shop together and taking what they wanted without paying. It took a "revolution" to force the bey into exile and stop these proceedings. It was equally commonplace for troops to inflict violence on individuals. In 1786, for example, when Hasan Pasha's troops arrived in Cairo, soldiers would enter a shop, hang a sign from the entry with the emblem (renk) of their unit, or simply write on the door "I am your partner." Having thus established his "protection" of the shopkeeper, the soldier would spend the day sitting quietly in the shop smoking his pipe and sipping coffee, then split the till with his supposed partner. There was nothing surprising in this behavior: in another incident from 1786, the brutal and extortionate followers of a certain emir were having their way with the residents of Husayniyya; when that emir was confronted by the foremost emir of the day, Ibrahim Bey "the Great," he answered him insolently: "We are all thieves. You steal. Murad Bey steals. And I steal as you do."[13]

Aside from explosions of violence and the "usual" extortions, Cairo enjoyed a remarkable degree of law and order. The reason, in all probability, other than the very close social control, was the expedited severity of the penalties inflicted on wrongdoers. The Ottomans seem to have harshened punishments and enriched their variety, to the point of making them popular spectacles. These were also fascinating to strangers, though from all reports they had punishments in their own countries that were just as fierce and picturesque. This description of an impalement, with all its gruesome detail, was written by Jean Coppin around 1640:

> In cases of death, the ordinary torture for common people . . . is impalement. I once saw two criminals pass by who had been sentenced to impalement, and curiosity impelled me to witness their end, which I would not have believed as horrible as it was. Each carried a round stake about the thickness of an arm, pointed on the end and coated at the top with soap, apparently to penetrate more readily . . . When they arrived at the designated place, the hands of one of the criminals were tied behind his back and he was made to lie down on his stomach . . . A [man] . . . started to make the stake penetrate him as far as possible through the anus, then finished making it pass with great blows from a wooden mallet until it emerged above the shoulders. Next the stake was set into a hole already dug for the purpose, and the subject was left upright . . . While the torture was under way, several of the Serjis [agents] reproached the prisoner for his misdeeds . . . Then they left to execute the second criminal in another place . . . Some remain alive for almost two days in this state before finally expiring.

The authors of the *Description de l'Egypte* note that domestic theft was rare in Cairo, and that the greatest probity was observed in the markets. The burglary of forty-eight shops in the Market of Ibn Tulun, committed in 1642, is recounted in great detail by the historian Ibn Abi l-Surur—proof that this kind of incident was extremely rare.[14]

The various institutions that provided structure to the population, in particular the trade corporations and the neighborhood organizations, paved the way for the authorities to control the people. Jabarti tells us the story of an investigation conducted toward 1740 into the disappearance of a woman who went to the public bath and never returned home. Emir Uthman Bey Dhulfiqar asked the husband to search his wife's clothes for anything unusual. The husband found a man's vest. The emir summoned the head of the tailors' corporation and ordered him to find its maker. "The head of the corporation made the rounds of all the tailors and eventually discovered the one . . . who had made the garment." Questioned by the emir, the tailor "recited the name of the person at whose request he had made the garment." A search uncovered the woman's body, and her murderer was beheaded.[15]

In another case, it was the *hara* that offered a framework for the investigation. A rumor circulated in 1724 that some fugitive emirs had returned to Cairo clandestinely and had entered the Darb al-Mahruq quarter. The authorities went to the place, questioned the doorkeeper, and closed the *hara* in order to conduct a proper search, to the great consternation of its residents, who could neither return home nor go about their business while the investigation continued.[16] The same chronicler who related the exploits of bands of thieves in Cairo cited as one of the city's features "the great safety that reigns there at night." The closing of markets and residential quarters at nightfall, and the prohibition against walking at night without lanterns or torches, contributed as much to the public peace (which most of the great cities of our time might well envy) as the patrols of the governor and his men.

### PUBLIC SERVICES

When problems arose relating to the management of the city, there were therefore authorities, communities, and institutions on hand to intervene, but mostly in a punitive role. The lack of specialized decisionmakers or administrative bodies inevitably had a negative effect on the city's functioning. This was certainly the case with the street system. There is much evidence of powerful individuals encroaching on the public domain. Jabarti tells the story of Emir Yusuf Bey, who, having just built himself a residence on the Birkat al-Fil and wanting to provide an access road for it worthy of his station, bought and tore down the houses that stood in his way. He even planned to demolish a mosque and was dissuaded from it only by the historian's father. Shaykh Ahmad al-Nafrawi (d. 1792), who owed his great power to the esteem in which he was held by Ali Bey al-Kabir, built his house in Giza by taking a parcel of land that belonged to the public way. When his protector died, the house was demolished. Shaykh Hasan al-Hawwari (d. 1795) built himself a house near al-Azhar Mosque by encroaching on neighboring properties and did not hesitate to destroy the Sinaniya madrasa to use its materials.[17]

Cairo thus kept, for the most part, the network of streets it had inherited from the Mamluks. The narrow, crooked street plan outside the city center corresponded to the needs of a city divided between central districts with ready access to the city gates and residential neighborhoods where no through-passage was necessary—this explains the apparent anarchy of the streets in most of the city. Furthermore, there was no wheeled transport in Cairo, and goods were carried on the backs of animals. Thoroughfares had to be wide enough, according to the law, for two laden camels to pass abreast.

Travelers were often perplexed at this irregularity. In 1658 Jean de Thévenot wrote: "There is not one fine street in Cairo, but a great number of small ones that twist and turn, showing that the houses in Cairo were all built without benefit of a city plan. An individual could build on whatever spot he chose, with no concern for whether or not he was blocking a street." When in 1814 Muhammad Ali decided to celebrate the marriage of his daughter with a particularly resplendent procession (in which 106 corporations would enter floats), the precaution was taken of sending a team of deputies along the route beforehand with their measuring instruments to make sure that it was passable and to destroy any structures that stood in the way. And this procession's route lay along some of the largest streets in the city. Here is a description of Cairo's congestion as written by J.-J. Ampère toward 1840: "Nothing has more animation than the streets of Cairo.

Imagine 30,000 people trotting or galloping on donkeys through narrow, winding streets. One is soon swept away by this whirlwind"—a passage echoing the one written four centuries earlier by Maqrizi on the crowds filling the Qasaba. That Cairo should have remained backward in this way at a time when cities in the West were experiencing vigorous growth constitutes a disturbing sign of the economy's stagnation.[18]

A city as large as Cairo in area (nearly 800 hectares), in length (5 kilometers), and in population (250,000) could not continue in existence without solving certain material problems. While to talk of "public services" in this context would be an anachronism, the needs of the population for street maintenance, fire fighting, transportation, and water supply were met, partly through a system of patronage and partly through specialized corporations, with only minimal oversight from the authorities.

The upkeep of the streets presented two problems: their day-to-day cleaning and the removal of the wastes and soil that encumbered them. The sweeping and watering of streets were normally in the hands of local residents, who might hire professional sweepers (*zabbalin*) for pay. Cleaning of this kind was probably performed with a certain regularity. Jabarti records that when the French arrived in 1798 and the population of Cairo fled to Bulaq, leaving only women, children, and helpless old men in the city, the streets remained "deserted and unclean, because they were no longer swept or watered." The task may have been neglected at times, whence the repeated intervention of the competent authorities (the agha, *wali*, and *muhtasib*) and the often critical appraisals of travelers and local observers too. According to Shaykh Hasan al-Hijazi, Arab streets contained "seven evils: urine, wastes, mud, dust, rudeness, noise, and the inhabitants of the streets themselves, who resemble ghosts in a cemetery."[19]

A corporation of donkeyback soil carriers (*tarrabin*) were charged with removing this detritus toward the mounds that had formed over the centuries around Cairo, especially on the city's northeast border, and that have survived to the present day. But this work does not appear to have been carried out with the necessary care, as the accumulation of wastes, dust, and soil had the effect of raising the street level, making passage difficult and gradually burying the public monuments and houses lining the streets. The sight of buildings even to-day buried sometimes up to window level or accessible only by a downward flight of stairs reminds us of the seriousness of the problem. The authorities sought to remedy it by organizing cleaning operations at distant intervals. Muhammad Pasha (1607–1611) ordered a cubit of earth removed from in front of every house and shop. The order was so unusual that he justified it by saying he wanted to remove even the soil trodden by the mutineers of a recently quelled rebellion, and Shaykh Abdallah al-Danushari wrote four verses on the incident. Similar undertakings were initiated by Qara Muhammad Pasha (1699–1704) and by Ali Agha in 1711 after the end of the "revolution." The upkeep of the Khalij that crossed Cairo and that served, according to the season, as a watercourse (during the Nile's annual flood) or as a sewer, was accomplished under the governor's supervision using public funds and assessments on local residents. Apparently it was attended to with some irregularity, as the canal had a tendency to silt up. Around 1643 Maqsud Pasha had 1.5 cubits (close to one yard) of earth removed from it.

The lighting of Cairo's streets went back to the Mamluk period, as we are reminded by Ibn Abi l-Surur toward 1650.[20] Lamps (*qanadil*) were lit in the suqs and streets. During the French occupation, it was ordered that lamps be lit at night, one for each house or for every three shops, probably in accordance with a well-established rule, as this same prescription was revived in 1814 and 1817. The *waqf* of the fountain of Abd al-Rahman Katkhuda (1744) provided for the cost of a lamp to light the fountain's door, increased to three lamps during the nights of Ramadan. One Turkish traveler mentions a corporation of lamplighters numbering 240, one of their specific tasks being to decorate shops with lamps on feast nights and during Ramadan. In times of unrest, the authorities reinstated the obligation to light shops and houses so as to reassure the population and prevent crime.

The city's size made a system for transporting people and goods necessary. The service was provided by a number of trade corporations that primarily relied on donkeys. One of the scholars of the *Description de l'Egypte,* Chabrol, estimated the number of donkey drivers at 30,000, a high number but perhaps not an unreasonable one. Clients could find animals for hire at what amounted to stations, the

A donkey driver (*Description de l'Egypte,* Bibliothèque Nationale)

A water carrier in the street (*Description de l'Egypte,* Bibliothèque Nationale)

most important being near the entrances to the city and near the crossroads of the main roads and suqs. There were three corporations of donkey drivers specializing in the transportation of men and women. Thanks to Chabrol we know the rates they charged: 8–10 paras to go from one end of Cairo to the other, 30–40 paras to hire the animal for an entire day. There were also a corporation of donkey drivers for carrying goods and a corporation of camel drivers for transporting merchandise and baggage. The system was based entirely on free enterprise, and the authorities did not intervene, except negatively when, in preparation for a military campaign, they requisitioned animals from donkey and camel drivers and from water carriers.[21]

The most essential "public service" in the daily life of Cairenes was the supplying of the city with water. For the satisfaction of their water requirements, the residents of Cairo could count neither on rain, which was very scarce and irregular (only 1.2 inches, or 30 millimeters per year), nor on wells, which supplied only a brackish water unfit for human consumption and used only in times of crisis. The sole source of drinking water was the Nile, which lay at a distance of between 800 meters (at the height of Bab al-Luq) and 1,300 meters from the western edge of the city. Water therefore came to the city from the Nile and was either distributed by specialized corporations or collected in public fountains. The Khalij gave water only during the three months following the summer floods.[22]

The water carriers *(saqqa'un)* drew water from the river at particular locations and loaded their filled skins (the *rawiya* of cowhide, and the *qirba* of goatskin) onto camels and donkeys, shuttling back and forth between the Nile and the city. They were organized into five corporations along the western edge of the city: one corporation of camelback water carriers at the centrally located Bab al-Luq, and four corporations of donkeyback water carriers, located along a north–south line at Bab al-Bahr, Bab al-Luq, Hara al-Saqqa'in, and Qanatir al-Siba. The distribution in town was performed by a corporation of street-based retail water sellers, another of carriers of cistern water (located at Bab Zuwayla, in the center of Cairo), and one of carriers of "salt" water, no doubt used for cleaning—an entirely rational distribution across the geographic and technical spectrum. The water was sold to passersby or delivered directly to homes, where it was often paid for according to an ingenious subscription system. The water carrier inscribed lines on his client's door corresponding to the quantity delivered, or he used a necklace of blue pearls, removing one per waterskin. The number of water carriers is naturally impossible to estimate. The numbers suggested by travelers—30,000 to 50,000—are purely imaginary. There were still 3,876 of them in around 1870. Probably there were about 10,000 water carriers, based on the water needs of the population (30 liters, or 8 gallons, of water per person per day on average) and the quantities that could be carried (a camel could carry about 200 liters of water per trip).

This system also made use of public fountains where water was stored. These fountains, of which a considerable number were built in the Ottoman period (the *Description de l'Egypte* sets their number at around 300), were distributed quite evenly throughout the built-up area as a function of the distribution of people, with the greatest concentration in the most active streets of the city. There were 12 in Husayniyya, 101 in Qahira, 131 in the southern sector, and 64 in the western, most recently urbanized, sector. As supplying water had strong religious connotations, one of the favorite ways for rich patrons to perform good works during the Ottoman period, particularly among the military caste, was to build fountains. The officers of the militia corps could thus show their piety and their concern for the

Fountain of Sultan Mahmud, 1750 (drawing by Pascal Coste)

city and its people, at the same time ensuring that their memory would stay evergreen, and all for a relatively modest cost. While size and decoration varied considerably, the fountains all had the same structure: an underground cistern *(sahrij)* of up to 200 cubic meters into which water from the Nile (or the Khalij in flood season) could be poured through openings on the street. At street level there was a room lit by one or several windows covered by grillwork and through which the water was distributed. A copper mouthpiece mounted on the outside allowed passersby to slake their thirst. Most of the fountains had a second floor where a class *(maktab)* was held at which an instructor taught the Qur'an, reading, and writing to the children of the quarter, often orphans, whose upkeep was provided for in the terms of the *waqf.*

Most of these fountains were kept functioning by a religious foundation. *Waqf* documents establish in minute detail the revenues assigned to the fountains by their founders and the expected apportionment of costs. The expense of maintaining the fountain built by Abd al-Rahman Katkhuda in 1744 in the center of Cairo, one of the largest and most sumptuous built under the Ottomans, was particularly high: 12,645 paras per year, of which 7,500 were earmarked for buying water, 120 for emptying and cleaning the cistern, 360 for the purchase of miscellaneous materials, 120 for incense to perfume the water jars, 180 to keep a lamp lit at the door, 45 for three lamps to

Grill of the fountain of Ruqayya Dudu, 1761

Facade of the fountain of Abd al-Rahman Katkhuda, 1744

burn in the water-distribution room during the nights of Ramadan, and 4,320 paras as payment to three distributors of water working during the day (and at night during Ramadan). In addition there were the operating costs of the school, amounting to 13,370 paras per year for the salary (and clothing) of the teachers and for the upkeep of twenty orphans, Muslims, minors, and paupers (one para per day and clothes during Ramadan).

This system ensured that the population of Cairo would have water, except during periods of unrest, when the free passage of water carriers between the Nile and the city was interrupted (as in 1711), or when the emirs decided to requisition the water carriers' donkeys and camels and the water carriers reacted by hiding their animals, as happened in 1629 before a military expedition to Yemen. But in ordinary times, though it may strike us as surprising, this "public service" functioned in a generally satisfactory way without any intervention by the authorities. The supply of water to Cairo gives a significant example of the way private enterprise (within the framework of trade corporations) could combine with patronage (the building and maintenance of fountains by dignitaries within the framework of religious foundations) to satisfy the essential needs of Cairo's population.

# 13

# Spheres of Activity

THE DOCUMENTS OF THE RELIGIOUS COURT (Mahkama) and the *Description de l'Egypte* allow us to form a fairly detailed idea of the structure of Ottoman Cairo. It undoubtedly differed little from the structure of the Mamluk city. On the other hand, the spatial organization of Cairo conformed closely to our concept of the "traditional" Arab city.[1]

The importance of economic functions in organizing the city is remarkably highlighted in Cairo by the Qasaba's enduring role as a central artery. Lying between the two palaces, the Great Avenue was conceived by the Fatimids as having a primarily political function but over the centuries became the center of Cairo's economic life. In the Ottoman period, the growth of economic activities devoured a portion of Qahira, as it were. The zone of religious and cultural activities, centered around the Mosque of al-Azhar but also around the great religious foundations of the Qasaba, was deeply embedded in the vast complex of commercial and artisan activities. The city's heavy concentration was only partially countered by the political and military center established by the Ayyubids outside Qahira. In fact the gradual expansion of the city southward was drawing the Citadel more and more closely into the city's web. This process, well on its way in Mamluk times, was completed under the Ottomans.

The vigorous "centrality" of the city on either side of the Qasaba and around al-Azhar Mosque divided the city into two sectors, one

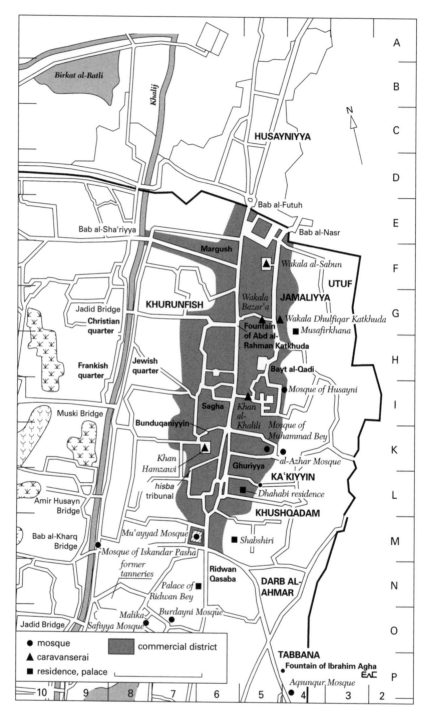

Map 9. The Ottoman city: the central district

public and one private, with distinctly separate functions: economic and religious activities in the center, and residences around the periphery. The network of more regular and open streets in the center, more tortuous and often closed ones in the residential areas, reflects this division of the city. The gradual expansion of Cairo in the Mamluk and Ottoman periods had created suburbs around Qahira to the south and west. Until the end of the eighteenth century, the distinction between the center, a city enclosed within its girding walls, and the exterior zones remained perfectly defined: "inside Qahira" and "outside Qahira" are routinely specified in court documents. Working outward from the central zones, Cairo developed according to a doubly concentric structure. The most important and most profitable activities, especially those relating to international trade, were established near the center, while secondary and noisome activities were pushed toward the periphery. The same went for residences: the fine houses of the wealthy merchant class occupied the more central zones, while "popular" and poor housing tended to be at a distance. This structure can be found in most of the large cities of the Islamic world during the Ottoman period, Tunis and Aleppo in particular.

This is only a schema, naturally. There were constraints and impetuses acting on the developing city that explain why, at the end of the eighteenth century, the actual Cairo illustrated only imperfectly our model of a city organized in successive rings around a center. But the asymmetry of Cairo's structure can be explained by the characteristics of its site and by the human interventions that occurred from the foundation of the city on. The city's very site—a terrace bordered on the east by the buttress of the Muqattam Hills, widening toward the south in the direction of Upper Egypt and toward the north in the direction of the Nile delta, the Mediterranean, and Asia Minor, limited on the west by the Nile, and then, as the river gradually withdrew, by the two canals—imposed constraints until the end of the Ottoman period.

A geographic obstacle, the high escarpments of the Muqattam Hills (which contemporary Cairo has only now surmounted), prevented the city from developing eastward. The vast zone of cemeteries implanted to the northeast, which urban expansion has also recently absorbed, blocked the city from expanding to that side. The eastern border of the city on the north, used for dumping the wastes and earth that accumulated in the town, saw the formation of "mounds" that are still problematic for city planners today. Lying only a few hundred meters east of al-Azhar Mosque, they represented an additional obstacle to any eastward expansion of the city.

No obstacle stood in the way of development to the south toward Fustat, then toward the Citadel, except to the southeast in the form of the Great Qarafa cemeteries and the debris that accumulated on the site of destroyed Fustat. The expansion, which had begun vigorously under the Mamluks, continued under the Ottomans, forming a vast suburb.

To the west, despite the attractive presence of Bulaq, development of the lands freed up by the retreat of the Nile was hindered under the Mamluks by the canal. It was during the Ottoman period that this sector was finally urbanized almost completely, forming another suburb.

Toward the north, the Mamluks made attempts at development because of the traditional attraction of important religious and commercial routes—the beginning of the pilgrimage route and the road to Syria and Asia Minor. The fact that the center of the empire was in Istanbul should have conferred an advantage on the roads leading toward that city and sparked the growth of a suburb sited similarly to the Maydan Quarter in Damascus. This was not to be, however. Al-Husayniyya remained a dumpish suburb without much independent economic activity and a population that was notably poor, perhaps because of the predominance of the river and maritime routes, which was already evident in Mamluk times and favored the development of Bulaq. Because of the city's unequal expansion, the "central" district of historical Cairo found itself occupying an off-center position in the northeast quadrant.

The strong expansion of the city southward and westward and the size of the suburbs and their distance from the main center of town (Bayn al-Qasrayn was 2 kilometers from the Citadel and the Mosque of Ibn Tulun, as well as from Bab al-Bahr and Bab al-Luq) also explain the development of secondary economic centers and the displacement of certain specialized economic activities to districts near the city's periphery.

ECONOMIC ACTIVITIES

The central core of the city, formed on either side of the Qasaba, retained the preeminence it had had since the time of Maqrizi.[2] Under
the Ottomans, the markets and caravanserais occupied a zone of approximately 55 hectares within which most of the business activity of
the city was concentrated: 228 caravanserais were there (of the 348
located), and 57 suqs (of 144). The impressive commercial growth of
Cairo becomes apparent if we compare these figures with those cited
earlier for the beginning of the fifteenth century: 44 caravanserais
and 48 suqs, grouped on 38 hectares. The increase occurred particularly in the Jamaliyya area along the pilgrimage route and the road
to Syria, where 36 *wakalat* were located (Maqrizi cited only 5 caravanserais), and the quarter of Amir al-Juyush, commonly called
Margush, on the road to Bulaq, which had 30 *wakalat* (Maqrizi recorded none).

The spine of this complex was still situated in the vicinity of
the great commercial centers of Khan al-Khalili, Bunduqaniyyin,
Ghuriyya, and al-Azhar Mosque, where there were 116 caravanserais
and 40 markets in the space of 18 hectares. The economic weight of
the center seems even more preponderant if we take into account the
agents, merchants, and artisans of Cairo, nine-tenths of whose activity was centered there: of the 391 estates of artisans and merchants
studied during the last two decades of the eighteenth century, 256
(65 percent) belonged to individuals working within this central region of Qahira (Margush, Jamaliyya, Sagha, Khan al-Khalili, al-Azhar,
Ghuriyya/Hamzawi, Mu'ayyad). The total value of their estates allows
us to gauge even more clearly their relative importance within Cairo
generally: 30.1 million paras out of a total of 34 million for all of
Cairo (88.3 percent).

It was in this district that most of Egypt's foreign trade activity
was concentrated. The great foreign trade in coffee, which took the
place of the spice trade in the seventeenth century, was distributed
throughout 62 caravanserais in the center, the main ones being
Wakala Dhulfiqar, Khan Ja'far, Khan Zarakisha, Khan al-Basha, and
Khan al-Masbagha. One of the most prominent coffee traders in the
eighteenth century, Muhammad al-Dada al-Sharaybi (d. 1725), built

Shop in Cairo (E. W. Lane)

himself a *wakala* near the Khan al-Hamzawi: a great gate opened onto a courtyard around which were 14 shops on the ground floor and living quarters on the second floor; what was once the third floor has disappeared. This monument, which was obviously designed to serve the commercial activities of its builder, speaks volumes about that personage's power.[3] The great cloth trade was also concentrated between the al-Ghuri suq and the Fahhamin: from 1776 to 1798, 33 cloth traders (out of 78 studied) exercised their trade in this district, with fortunes representing 62 percent of the total. The same went for the trade in soap, tobacco, and sugar (a luxury trade, attached to an

The Khan al-Khalili (after R. Hay)

active export market). These business activities left little room for artisan activities. The most notable exceptions were the coppersmiths (*nahhasin*), whose atelier-stores were in Bayn al-Qasrayn Street, and the turners *(kharratin)* and boxmakers *(sanadiqiyyin)*, located near the al-Ashrafiyya and at the start of the road leading to al-Azhar. The exception is perhaps due to the high quality of these artisans' products and their important place in the life of Cairenes.

The center was organized around several important points. The

Great Mosque, built a bit to the east of the Qasaba, was integrated into the center by the expansion of the markets and caravanserais. The Sagha, where precious metals were worked and sold, occupied an even more central position, because it was there that money was changed. A picturesque trace of these activities comes down to us in the names of the streets: a small street directly south of Sagha, the Street of Cut Coins (al-Maqasis), evokes the illegal practice to which moneychangers resorted in times of economic stress. Immediately to the west was the neighborhood where Cairo's Jews lived, the Hara al-Yahud; its residents played an important role in gold- and silversmithing and in banking activities. The most precious goods were traded in a covered market, the Khan al-Khalili, erected in the center of the district: its complex of caravanserais and suqs, built in part at the end of the Mamluk period (1511), has been described repeatedly by foreign merchants impressed by its richness and activity. Here, for example, is what Gabriel Brémond wrote in 1643–1645:

> The "Can ël Kalil" . . . is in the form of a sumptuous palace, well proportioned, and built of handsomely dressed stone, three stories high. At the bottom are fine stores, arrayed in a square around a lovely open space in the middle, and all around, before them, vaults resting on fine pillars, where merchants assemble and engage in trade. The square in the middle serves for the sale of goods at auction, and for the trade or exchange of bulk merchandise. Only good merchants may remain here, and there are many exquisite jewels, spices, and other items of value. The principal lords and Sanjaks resort to this place on market days to buy at auction all that is most beautiful, as is very much the custom. Above, on the upper floors of this building, live the most honorable foreign merchants, who come with caravans and bring an abundance of precious merchandise: from the Indies, Persia, etc. Beside it are streets where the most exquisite perfumes are sold, rugs of various fashions, and the gold-smiths and cutters of precious stones, who are Jewish.[4]

Shops had remained unchanged since earlier times and resembled those in the other great Arab cities of the period, as well as in the "medinas" of our own time. The shop (*dukkan, hanut*), of which Edward Lane has given us a classic description in his *Manners and*

*Customs of the Modern Egyptians*, was a small space some five or six feet high and three or four wide, sometimes extended by a room that served as a storeroom. The floor was raised two or three feet above the ground and extended by a bench of stone and brick *(mastaba)* encroaching on the street. This is where the shopkeeper and clients sat to hold their discussions and drink coffee. As these benches impeded traffic and could serve as barricades in times of unrest, it is not surprising that there was periodic talk of getting rid of them. Shops were so simple and primitive that it was easy to build them in series at a moderate cost (2,000 to 3,000 paras). The suq (market) was an open structure; a double row of shops along a street or at a crossing sufficed to make a market. Generally a market was occupied by a group of shopkeepers who all practiced the same trade and belonged to the same corporation. The name of a trade by itself, such as *nahhasin*, could thus refer to an occupation, a market, or a place, albeit one where the commercial activity was liable to change—in the Suq of the Fahhamin, right in the middle of Cairo, the modest "coal merchants" had long since given way to the more opulent cloth merchants. While most suqs sprang up spontaneously, there also existed certain monumental suqs, the most remarkable being the "qasaba" built by Emir Ridwan Bey between 1629 and 1647 just south of Bab Zuwayla, which largely survives to this day.[5]

The function and the architectural structure of caravanserais had altered little since Mamluk times. The word *wakala* henceforth came to be used to designate Cairo's caravanserais—*khan* was reserved for a small number of instances, *qaysariyya* practically lost all currency, and *funduq* has totally disappeared. But *wakalat*—storehouses for merchandise before its distribution, lodgings for merchants with stores on the first floor and living quarters above—would retain the same function. The extraordinary increase in the number of caravanserais (360 are known for this period, in contrast to the 58 cited by Maqrizi) explains why most were strictly utilitarian buildings with no architectural pretensions. A few of the surviving caravanserais are nonetheless worthy of their predecessors. The Wakala Dhulfiqar Katkhuda, built in 1673, was an enormous monument (2,625 square meters) whose entrance still impresses us with its power. With its 32 stores and 35 apartments around a courtyard, it has a rather horizontal layout, reminiscent of the architecture of Aleppo's *khanat*, which

*Wakala* of Dhulfiqar Katkhuda, 1673 (drawing by Pascal Coste)

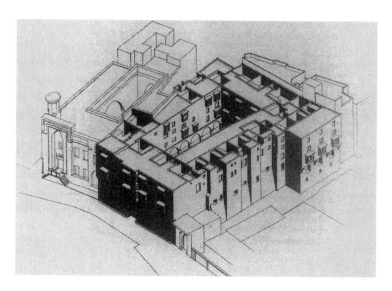

Wakala Bazarʿa, late seventeenth century (after F. Aalund)

may explain the important role Syrians played in this caravanserai and in the whole Jamaliyya quarter where it is situated. The Wakala Bazar'a, which neighbors the Wakala Dhulfiqar Katkhuda and was also built at the end of the seventeenth century, is by contrast typically Cairene in its verticality and reminiscent of the Wakala al-Ghuri, though with lesser decorations. It has a ground surface of 1,125 square meters and comprises four stories, marked on the facade by handsome windows with *mashrabiyya*. The inner facades facing the courtyard are also enlivened by *mashrabiyya* at the height of the two-story *rab* crowning the edifice.[6]

Although commercial activities predominated there, the central district was also marked by the presence of the mosque and Islamic university. A number of shaykhs were also engaged in business activities, sometimes related to their positions at al-Azhar: as booksellers (Suq al-Kutubiyyin), copyists, or calligraphers. The world of al-Azhar was characterized by the strong solidarity of its members in protecting their particular interests (the various revenues and donations earmarked for them, particularly within the framework of *awqaf*) and in defending subjects who appealed to the *ulama* as their natural intercessors in cases of governmental extortion or brutality. The mosque and the neighborhood around it were sometimes acknowledged as a place of refuge. With its 3,000 professors and students, the mosque was the center of a religious and judiciary activity that brought it great prestige and considerable political influence.

The center of the city still had a number of important administrative sites: the Hall of the Judge (Bayt al-Qadi), established in a fine residence from the Mamluk period (Bayt Mamay al-Sayfi, built in 1496), along with several courts; the office of the overseer of the markets (*muhtasib*), presumably at the stall (*dikkat*) of the *hisba;* the *wali's* station, located just south of Bab Zuwayla. But the center of political and military power was in the Citadel, where the pasha lived and where the janissary and *azab* militia corps were housed.

Because of Cairo's great size, there were other economic centers, near the gates and along the major arteries; around Bab al-Sha'riyya (8 markets and 14 caravanserais), Bab Zuwayla (5 markets and 16 caravanserais), along the Suq al-Silah and at Rumayla, at the foot of the Citadel (11 markets and 17 caravanserais), and around the Mosque of Ibn Tulun (9 markets and 14 caravanserais). Some of

| | 1679–1700 | | | | 1776–1798 | | | |
|---|---|---|---|---|---|---|---|---|
| | NUMBER OF ESTATES | % OF TOTAL | VALUE OF ESTATES (IN CONSTANT MILLIONS OF PARAS) | % | NUMBER OF ESTATES | % OF TOTAL | VALUE OF ESTATES (IN CONSTANT MILLIONS OF PARAS) | % |
| Qahira | 225 | 74.7 | 27.11 | 93.2 | 264 | 67.5 | 30.45 | 89.3 |
| Husayniyya | — | — | — | — | 7 | 1.8 | .17 | .5 |
| South suburb | 62 | 20.6 | 1.69 | 5.8 | 83 | 21.2 | 2 | 5.9 |
| West suburb | 14 | 4.6 | .28 | 1 | 37 | 9.5 | 1.46 | 4.3 |
| All of Cairo | 301 | 99.9 | 29.08 | 100 | 391 | 100 | 34.08 | 100 |

Source: André Raymond, *Artisans et commerçants au Caire au XVIIIe siècle*, 2 vols. (Damascus: Institut Français de Damas, 1973, 1974).

these noncentral markets were highly specialized, sometimes for historical reasons: the weapons and caravan supply markets at Suq al-Silah (Arms Market) and at Rumayla were naturally related to the presence of soldiers in the Citadel and its environs. It was in these markets that the troops bought the equipment they needed for campaigns. The size of the textile business around the Mosque of Ibn Tulun, and especially the sale of cloth from the Maghrib, had a great deal to do with the large North African population in the area—a very old phenomenon, since the mosque had been a gathering site for pilgrims from western North Africa even in medieval times.

Generally speaking, the least specialized activities, and the most noxious, were established far from the center—the economic importance of the southern and western suburbs was very much secondary to Qahira's. The table summarizes comparisons made a century apart between the Qahira district and the suburbs to the south and west on the basis of the fortunes of artisans and merchants (estimated from the estates recorded in the court registers). Despite the remarkable growth of the western suburb, the predominance of Qahira remains overwhelming.

In the two suburbs, the average fortune of an artisan or a merchant during the last two decades of the eighteenth century was only 24,130 paras (south) and 39,436 paras (west), or about one-fifth and one-third respectively of the average fortune in Qahira (115,328 paras). The disparity was due to the kinds of business activities usually pursued in the suburbs: specialized commercial activities of marginal importance; less profitable artisan activities, such as the processing of food products (grain milling, vinegarmaking); spin-ning, weaving and dyeing, leatherworking, woodworking, and metal-working.

Some activities were pushed back to the edges of Cairo into areas that contained at the same time residential zones for the poor, elite residential neighborhoods, and unbuilt areas. The large markets for goods from the countryside were thus situated near the city gates on huge empty lots, which were called *rahabat, arasat,* or *ruqa:* those protesting scarcity or high prices in the late seventeenth and eigh-teenth centuries often made the covered markets of Rumayla their goal. The big vegetable markets were located far south of the city—a shaykh of the vegetable sellers' corporation, Hajjaj al-Rumaylati, played an important political role in bringing Muhammad Ali to power in 1805. The sheep markets and the slaughterhouses were also near the edge of the city because they were a public nuisance. Butchers were the dominant presence in Husayniyya, and they were particularly active in the eighteenth century because of their links with the religious brotherhood of the Bayyumiyya. Other activities, either unpleasant or polluting (emitting smells or smoke), were es-tablished at a distance from the center: tanneries, oil presses, ovens of all sorts (especially pottery manufactories). In some instances an activity was removed to the periphery because of its requirements for space: such was the case with the making of rush mats in the south-east of Cairo (al-Husriyya quarter) and with ropemaking, which is the source of the place-name "Ropemakers" (Habbala), one of Cairo's poorest quarters. The displacement of these activities was sometimes a sign that the city was expanding. The Suq al-Ghanam (Sheep Mar-ket) moved from the entrance of Darb al-Ahmar, just southeast of Bab Zuwayla (which kept its name of "Old Sheep Market"), and was relocated even before the end of the Mamluk period to the south of the city. Similarly, the tanners left the central district to establish themselves in the Bab al-Luq district, while their original neighbor-hood kept the name "Old Tanneries."

The geography of Cairo's economic activities, though logical, was never purely functional. Rather, it moved in uneven phases of expan-sion and retreat. Some activities stayed put and found themselves ab-sorbed from the periphery into the interior of the city. In other cases, as we have seen, the activity was removed to the outskirts. The location of government activities in the Citadel also influenced the city's commercial geography: the Arms Market, which Maqrizi located right in the center, took up residence "under the Citadel" in Ottoman times. And the growth of Bulaq explains the development of economic activities in the Bab al-Sha'riyya region. Cairo was a living organism, and each of its elements to a degree reflected the entirety of its history.

## THE RESIDENTIAL QUARTERS AND TYPES OF HOUSES

The dwellings of this period are known to us only through the surviving houses of the rich and well-to-do, since only the best built and maintained have survived. Even the archives yield only a skewed view, as generally only the largest houses were mentioned in records of court transactions or estate inventories.

Our understanding of Cairo's housing has also been somewhat obscured by stereotypes. One of these is that Islamic society was actually as egalitarian as the society envisioned by the Islamic religion. Another is that there existed a single type of "Islamic" housing—an individual house, closed on the outside and opening onto an inner court, within whose precincts differences in social condition were erased. Still another stereotype is that in Arab cities those of different socioeconomic levels were not segregated, the poor living side by side with the rich in basically mixed quarters.[7] Recent research by Nelly Hanna has allowed us to correct these views, both as to the general data on residential geography and as to the nature of Cairene houses, which were in fact highly diverse.[8]

The residential geography of Cairo was organized more or less concentrically, with the houses of the rich and well-to-do in the center and those of the poor at the edges. This phenomenon appears clearly in the map of residential zones for the years 1738–1744, though there are inevitable anomalies: Cairo's asymmetrical development; the existence of "middle-income" multifamily housing in the center, the *urbu* (sing. *rab*); the tendency of the ruling elite to live in "aristocratic" quarters on the outskirts of town; and the development of minority quarters. Thus the residences of the rich were concentrated in Qahira around the central business district and in parts of the southern and western districts; the average price of these

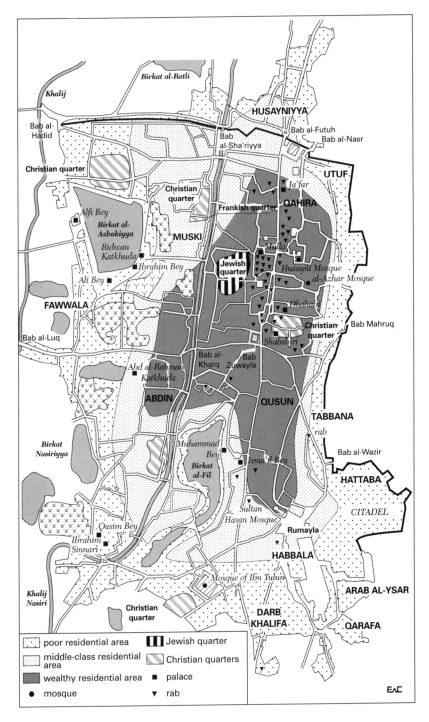

Map 10. Distribution of residential areas (1738–1744) (after Hanna)

| RESIDENTIAL ZONE | PALACES | MID-LEVEL HOUSING | MODEST HOUSING | TOTAL | AVERAGE PRICE (PARAS) | RAB | HAWSH | COST OF RENTING LAND (IN PARAS PER 100 CUBITS) |
|---|---|---|---|---|---|---|---|---|
| High-income (central zone) | 23 | 56 | 49 | 128 | 20,684 | 76 | 1 | 171 |
| Middle-income (intermediary zone) | 16 | 121 | 199 | 336 | 8,931 | 7 | 10 | 76 |
| Low-income (outskirts) | — | 25 | 109 | 134 | 4,825 | — | 19 | 17 |
| Total | 39 | 202 | 357 | 598 | — | 83 | 30 | — |

*Source:* Based on Nelly Hanna, *Habiter au Caire aux XVIIe et XVIIIe siècles* (Cairo: IFAO, 1991), table 23, p. 185.

*Note:* Does not include minority quarters or elite residential quarters, where the distribution of houses follows a different pattern.

houses was 20,684 paras. In the intermediary zone, which started largely outside Qahira, the average price of a house was 8,931 paras. Finally, in the "popular" quarters on the city's fringes the price of a house averaged 4,825 paras. This distribution holds only in a general sense, since there were houses of each type (palatial, middle-income, and modest) in almost every area. The *urbu* were centrally distributed, while the *ahwash* (enclosed shantytowns) were logically enough in the outlying areas. The table summarizes the types of housing in the three zones (high-, middle-, and low-income) for the years 1738–1744.

This pattern of residence is perfectly understandable. The artisans and merchants of Cairo wanted to live as close as possible to the central business district, where the markets and caravanserais in which they worked were located. But the crowding of the central district removed it from their reach as the density of the buildings coincided with high prices. Only the wealthiest segment of the population could establish somewhat large residences there. The one exception, however, was the apartment buildings, where the density of the residents allowed the laws of the marketplace to be overruled. The outskirts, where rural and usually indigent immigrants settled on first arrival in the city, primarily hosted an underprivileged population, yet interspersed in these areas were elite residential neighborhoods. The comparisons made by Nelly Hanna on the rental cost of land in the seventeenth century appear to confirm this hypothesis.[9]

Residence of Dhahabi, courtyard entrance

The neighborhoods near the business centers on either side of the Qasaba were a customary place of residence for the merchant bourgeoisie. Shaykhs from al-Azhar were also drawn to them by their proximity to the mosque and university. There still exist a few of these residences, whose discreet luxury we may admire: the houses of Jamal al-Din, provost of merchants (1634), and of Mustafa Ja'far, a coffee trader (around 1713); the al-Mulla (1654) and Shabshiri (late seventeenth century) houses, which perhaps belonged to families of the *ulama*.

These were costly residences. The one bought by Isma'il Abu Taqiyya, provost of the great traders, was valued at 46,628 paras. They varied considerably in size: 360 square meters for the Shabshiri house, 700 for the Dhahabi house. Characteristic of these houses is their resolutely vertical architecture, the high cost of the land prompting its dense occupation—but it was also a way of ensuring an interior division into public spaces, devoted to social interchange, and private spaces, where family life unfolded, with the superposition of several reception rooms varying in form and function. In plan, these houses were quite similar. A bent passageway led to an inner courtyard, a place where people came and went, which opened onto the service areas and an unenclosed reception hall *(takhtabush)* for the more modest class of visitors. A stairway and a door, usually decorated, ascended to a loggia overlooking the courtyard through two or three arcades; this was the *maq'ad*, a sitting room used especially in the warm season and always facing north to catch the cooling breezes, furnished with carpets and divans, and often agreeably decorated with painted woodwork. A large interior room on the second or third floor, the *qa'a*, luxuriously appointed and decorated (polychrome marble, coffered ceilings), and sometimes of imposing size— it might even include a pool and water fountain in the sunken central area *(durqa'a)*—served as the setting for receptions, for parties, and for family life. The house also typically had a fine variety of balconied windows with turned-wood *mashrabiyya* distributed across both the outer and inner facades. They provided the rooms with light and ventilation, at the same time allowing the residents to look out without being seen—this greater extroversion appears to have been a development of the Ottoman period. All in all, the architecture of these houses stayed remarkably faithful to local traditions and changed relatively little.[10] Until the eighteenth century, Ottoman influence was limited to the addition of quite minor decorative elements.

Next to this prosperous bourgeois housing, which corresponds to what we call "traditional" housing, there was also a form of group dwelling without a courtyard, the *rab*, which offered an ingenious compromise to the merchants and artisans who wanted to settle near the central district where they worked but lacked the means to build

Facade of the Tabbana *rab*

themselves individual houses in that part of the city.[11] The chroniclers have often described the occupants of these apartment houses, who belonged to the middle class. The known residents of *urbu* at the end of the eighteenth century had fortunes on the order of 20,000 paras, designating them as small merchants or artisans. And the value of the apartments, at around 4,000 paras, seems to correspond to the means available to this middle-income class, most of whom only rented their apartments at the moderate cost of 100–300 paras per year. Almost all these apartment buildings were located in the central district and along the large commercial streets. This form of lodging was apparently resorted to by one-tenth of the native population, some 20,000 people.

The *rab* took one of two forms. It could be an independent building of three or four stories whose ground floor was given over to shops and storehouses: the Tabbana *rab*, which is 64 by 13 meters, contains fifteen residential units. When the *rab* was built above a *wakala*, a common occurrence, it consisted of two or three stories looking onto a courtyard, but it remained entirely separate from the caravanserai whose upper stories it occupied and had one or several entries of its own. In both kinds of *rab*, the apartments had the same general plan: they were either duplexes or triplexes, equipped with an interior staircase, and having service areas, a main reception hall on two levels, and a private terrace on the roof. The surface area of an apartment floor might range from 30 to 35 square meters, giving the apartments a total area of 60 to 105 meters, depending on the footprint of the unit and the number of its floors. This layout provided a fair compromise between the concessions due to communal living and the traditional desire to isolate one's private life.

The rental buildings varied widely in size. Some had twenty apartments or more, with a total number of residents easily surpassing one hundred. The cost of building or buying a *rab* was quite substantial, but the prospect of receiving regular rent made the *rab* an attractive speculation for a private "investor." It was equally attractive to the founder of a *waqf*, since the rental money, managed by the *waqf* administrator, could be earmarked for the upkeep of a religious or charitable building or foundation. A *rab* situated in the Waziriyya quarter and containing nineteen apartments was purported to bring in 4,932 paras per year, or 259 paras per apartment.

Another kind of group housing, quite different in nature, was also located in the central district: the caravanserais (*khanat* and *wakalat*), which housed an extremely varied population of merchants (often foreign), as well as of Egyptians and military men. Some 10,000 Cairenes undoubtedly resided in caravanserais (5 percent of the total population of artisans and merchants in the years 1776–1798). Many soldiers lived in these establishments, and their immoral behavior, consumption of illicit drink, and patronage of prostitutes often caused the caravanserais to be shut down by the authorities.

Beyond the residential zone for the wealthy bourgeois, one found houses that were sometimes just reduced versions of the well-to-do residences described above. Their surface area was smaller, they had fewer rooms (which were therefore less specialized), and the separation between public and private spaces was less distinct. These "mid-level" houses can be identified by their somewhat lower cost (7,000–27,000 paras) and by the occupations of their residents (more modest artisans and merchants).[12] A few rare examples still exist in Cairo and

Bulaq. Intended to house an extended family or several unrelated families in separate residential units, these houses varied greatly in surface area (from 31 to 285 square meters) and generally had no courtyard, which goes against the idea of a single "Islamic" dwelling type. The reason for these atypical houses was essentially economic—the wish to make the best possible use of the space available. Their organization greatly reduced the isolation of the family unit, another traditional stereotype concerning the Islamic dwelling. These houses already existed in the fifteenth century and were therefore not an Ottoman invention.

At some distance from the center were the residential quarters (*harat*). As in all Arab cities, these constituted the basic urban unit. It was in these that the greater part of the population lived. In Cairo, their location on the periphery corresponded to the "popular" residential zone, and it is certainly in this belt, which is continuous in the north, east, and south of the city, that the sixty-three *harat* recorded in the *Description de l'Egypte* were situated. Each of these quarters, covering an average area of 2.5 hectares, housed slightly more than 1,000 people, or around 200 families. Quasi-familial relations generally obtained between the inhabitants, and the shaykh could easily handle the quarter's administration. Everything would seem to indicate that the *hara* residents belonged to a rather modest socioeconomic level. The traveler Carsten Niebuhr wrote: "The quarters serve as a communal dwelling for artisans and other poor inhabitants who . . . work . . . not in their own houses but in small shops in the suq or along the commercial streets." The homogeneous nature of the quarters was, however, only relative, for there existed "rich" *harat*, which were more centrally located, such as those of Mabiyida (G 5) and Ja'idiya (H 4), and within the quarters themselves there were wealthier residents, who sometimes played the part of patrons to the *hara* residents, whom they represented and defended almost in an official capacity. But the poverty of the *hara* residents on average is apparent: their net worth (29,054 paras in the *harat* of Qahira, 11,566 in those of the southern sector, 23,755 in those of the western sector) was much lower than the average for the area as a whole.

The *harat* were relatively closed units. They had very few openings to the outside, often a single one that could be closed (generally at night) by a door or gate. The main street, *darb*, which often gave

Entrance to the residential quarter Hara al-Mahiyad (after A. Rhoné)

the quarter its name, gave access to a network of increasingly smaller passages and, finally, blind alleys. Usually the *harat* hosted no commercial activities, but they did have a market (of the *suwayya* type) with a few shops that sold food, and possibly a flour mill and a public oven. The public facilities of the *hara* might be rounded out by a small place of prayer for daily observances—the Friday prayer generally being celebrated in the large mosques in the central districts.[13]

The *hara* was the basic social unit of the city and the setting of an active communal life. Researching a *hara* in contemporary Cairo, the sociologist Nawal al-Messiri has made observations that are just as applicable to the past: "Living in a *hara,* especially a closed *hara* [such as the Sukkariyya (M 6)], is like living in one's own kingdom. The area is supervised, and no person from the outside may enter it. The very moment such a person crosses the threshold of the quarter, he is noticed . . . All the children know each other, and the parents too. It is like a village."

One aspect of this solidarity was the control that inhabitants had over each other. In one instance, the residents of a *hara* complained to the *wali* that one of their neighbors had received a suspicious-looking individual, and they petitioned that he not be allowed to return. In another case, the people complained about three women who were in the habit of swearing, uttering curses, and beating their neighbors, and asked that the women be evicted. People who were in the habit of drinking wine and carousing were disapproved of. Bachelors, because they threatened the stability of families, were generally received with suspicion. The English Orientalist Edward Lane experienced this around 1830, when the inhabitants of the *hara* where he had rented a house suggested to him that he buy a female slave, "which would exempt [him] from the opprobrium cast upon [him] by the want of a wife." Lane held firm, but Gérard de Nerval reports that when the shaykh of his *hara* put him on notice either to give up his house or choose a wife, he resolved finally to spend 625 francs to buy a Javanese slave woman, Zeynab, his "yellow wife."

Neighborhood solidarity was also expressed in local celebrations, which might be either private (weddings, circumcisions) or public (mainly religious), and which called for parades with torchbearers, musicians (drums and "oboes"), and singers. On a less peaceful plane, there were the gangs of youths who roamed the *hara* to defend it, and whom the chroniclers never mention without obvious antipathy, using terms that have all taken on a pejorative sense: *zuʿars* (ruffians) and *shuttars* (hoodlums). Neighborhood solidarity could take an aggressive turn and lead to rivalries between the *harat.* Some *harat* to the east of the city (Husayniyya, Utuf, Hattaba) settled their scores in the uninhabited zones of the "desert" well into the nine-teenth century. The combativeness of these gangs was sometimes put to good use by the authorities, who used them as ancillary militia units—in 1613, the pasha of Cairo sent the corporation (*ta'ifa*) of the Fawwala quarter against rebellious soldiers, and in 1777, Isma'il Bey mobilized "the people of the *harat* and the gangs."[14]

Even modest houses remained beyond the means of Cairo's "pro-letariat," who often lived in *ahwash*. According to E.-F. Jomard in the *Description de l'Egypte,* these were "large courtyards or enclosures filled with shanties four feet high, where a host of poor people live, crowded in pell-mell with their animals . . . vast closed courtyards . . . empty lots . . . Wastes are brought there . . . and the poorest inhabit-ants live there in shanties." This, in all likelihood, was where the poorest workers lived, those whom Chabrol was talking about: "A sort of hut that costs them ten paras per month in rent . . . Their entire furnishing consists of a section of rush matting, where they sleep with their wives and children." A *hawsh* might contain several dozen living quarters. The courtyard, used communally by all the residents of the *hawsh*, sometimes contained a well and a public toilet. This type of lodging existed in Syria at the same period and in the Hijaz, at Medina; it was therefore a perfectly traditional form of housing. It was clearly the poorest segment of the population, the 30,000 ser-vants and workers mentioned by Chabrol and Jomard, who lived in these sorts of accommodations. In a document of the Court in 1763, the monthly rent of each unit in a *hawsh* was estimated at a derisory three paras. The *ahwash* were situated at the outskirts of the city (like the *harat*), in the zone inhabited by the poorest population, which often comprised those who had recently immigrated from the countryside—explaining the fairly "rural" character of their ac-commodations.[15]

### THE FASHIONABLE NEIGHBORHOODS

The ruling elite needed vast residences that allowed them to house their large households and surround themselves with gardens. For reasons of safety, and also from social exclusivism, they often wanted to isolate themselves from the local population. Muhammad Ali Bey al-Alfi, who had several residences outside Cairo, the most luxurious

Palaces on the Birkat al-Fil (*Description de l'Egypte,* Bibliothèque Nationale)

of which was completed on the Azbakiyya in 1798, avoided crossing Cairo when he traveled from one house to another because he had a horror of passing through the suqs and "offering himself as a spectacle" to the shopkeepers and passersby. Also, the summer season in Cairo was painfully hot, and Cairenes who had the means to do so followed the ancient tradition of removing themselves to a breezy spot where there were water and vegetation. The banks of the Khalij (site of the houses drawn by Pascal Coste in 1820–1830) and the ponds, low areas left behind by the Nile as it retreated westward, were in all periods attractive sites for building summer houses, which sometimes turned into year-round residences.[16] Fashionable houses were thus often to be found outside the city.

Emirs began settling around Birkat al-Fil as early as the Mamluk period. The trend strengthened in the sixteenth and seventeenth centuries as the emirs abandoned Qahira more or less completely, driven away by the increasing economic activity there. The removal of the tanneries in 1600 opened up the Birkat al-Fil area to "aristocratic" settlement, particularly in the northern part (Dawudiyya). Between 1650 and 1755, three-quarters of all emirs' residences were in the southern section of Cairo, and 40 percent of these were on the

Birkat al-Fil, which was surrounded at the time by a belt of hand-some residences. Here is a description by Fulgence, a European living in Cairo around 1700:

> The most beautiful houses in Cairo are situated around this *birka*. It is flooded for eight months of the year, and it is a perpetual garden during the other four. During the flood, one sees a great number of gilded brigantines on which persons of consequence and their wives take the air at nightfall. There is not a day when fireworks are not set off and music is not heard. The latticed windows are filled with innumerable women of quality, whom one may constantly glimpse thanks to the illumination of these houses during festivities. It is one of the most beautiful spectacles the night has to offer.[17]

The emirs next moved to western Cairo, probably because the gradual peopling of the southern district made them want a quieter and safer place of residence. Beyond the Khalij lay watered and verdant zones where one could build agreeable houses with gardens and outbuildings for the servants and mamluks. The wealthy class of Cairo, the great merchants and shaykhs, had already settled in large numbers on the banks of the Azbakiyya. The Sharaybi had an enormous residence there, which, according to Jabarti, had twelve apartments, each forming a large separate dwelling. Important members of the *ulama* lived on the Azbakiyya as well. A few emirs had houses there, but they started to settle in the area only in the mid-eighteenth century. We may take as a symbolic date for the start of this trend the purchase by the great emir Ridwan Katkhuda of the Sharaybi residence before 1744. He made it, says Jabarti, into "a masterpiece of architecture, magnificence, and beauty." Settlement in the Azbakiyya area was subsequently very rapid: in 1798, twenty of the 130 emirs' residences mentioned in the *Description de l'Egypte* were on the banks of the pond, whose east, south, and west shores they had literally colonized. At this time, almost half of all emirs lived in the Cairo's western district. The charms of night in the Azbakiyya quarter were celebrated toward the end of the century in equally enthusiastic terms by Savary and by Hasan al-Attar. The European traveler writes: "This square, the largest in the city . . . forms an immense pool surrounded by the palaces of the beys, which are lit by lamps of dif-

Courtyard of the palace of Qasim Bey (*Description de l'Egypte,*
Bibliothèque Nationale)

Courtyard of the palace of Uthman Bey (*Description de l'Egypte,*
Bibliothèque Nationale)

ferent colors. Several thousand boats with lights hanging from their masts produce an ever-shifting pattern of illumination." To which the shaykh and poet answers: "I sing the fair days of my life that were passed at [Azbakiyya] . . . There one sees boats floating on the waters like stars on the celestial vault. Magnificent dwellings form a circle around the pool and serve as frames around so many beautiful moons. Palaces shaded by green trees, where the tender dove sings her song."[18]

These sumptuous palaces of the elite are now gone, following the modernization of the Birkat al-Fil and Azbakiyya areas in the nineteenth century, the only exception being the residence (1794) of Ibrahim al-Sinnari, an obscure mamluk, whose house is one of the most modest and not representative of their true magnificence. The illustrations in the *Description de l'Egypte,* contemporary descriptions, and above all the documents of the Mahkama give us a more accurate idea of these gigantic and luxurious abodes. The palace built by the pomp-loving Abd al-Rahman Katkhuda near Bulaq covered 10,550 square meters and cost 1.6 million paras. These palaces might have dozens of rooms, vast courtyards, large service areas to lodge the civilian and military households of the emirs (sometimes numbering in the hundreds) and to stockpile all the necessary stores (food, tools, arms . . .). The plates in the *Description de l'Egypte* show the luxury and ampleness of the garden court at the palace of Qasim Bey, and the five-tiered arcade of the *maq'ad* in the palace of Uthman Bey. These palaces, which the residences of the wealthy bourgeois copied in small, typically had numerous reception rooms and annexes. Jabarti gives us an idea of the scale on which the great emirs of the mid-eighteenth century lived:

> Consider in the first place that the house of any great personage would have two kitchens. One, on the lower story, was used to prepare food for the men, while the other, which was in the harem, was reserved for the residents of that part of the house. The table of each of these great lords and dignitaries was set twice a day, at noon and at night, in a spacious setting, open to all comers. The master of the house took his place at this table along with his guests and, at a slight remove, the persons of his retinue and his mamluks . . . Anyone had the right to take a seat at this table.

The same author gives us a detailed account of the construction of the last and among the most beautiful of these great residences, built by Muhammad Bey al-Alfi on the west shore of the Azbakiyya and completed in 1798. Kilns for plaster and lime were built on the site itself; slabs of stone were quarried from the mountain and transported there; old houses were bought for the marble that could be salvaged from them; two baths were installed, one on the ground floor and one on the second; and, remarkably, all the windows were glazed with glass panes, an innovation that obliged the chronicler, bereft of adequate terminology, to use the circumlocution "boards of glass." The inscription over the door of the great drawing room (qa'a), composed by Hasan al-Attar, summed up the splendor of an entire caste on the very eve of its disappearance:

> The sun of congratulations has illuminated a drawing room whose beauties are increased by thousands.
> On the door, joy has declared that al-Alfi has renewed the heaven of his happiness.[19]

Al-Alfi inaugurated his new palace on 27 February 1798. On 14 February the Directory in revolutionary France had approved Talleyrand's report and would soon send Napoleon to Egypt, where the great man would make himself at home amidst the emir's furniture.

### THE MINORITY NEIGHBORHOODS

The location of the minority neighborhoods was also atypical. Several reasons can be cited for the segregation of the minorities: on the one hand, the authorities sometimes wanted to maintain surveillance of the minorities and therefore keep them close by or, conversely, keep them as far as possible from the Muslim majority. On the other hand, the *dhimmi* wanted to group together for reasons of community, in order to engage more freely in their religion and make it easier for their own leaders to govern them, but also from concern for their safety.[20]

The *Description de l'Egypte* mentions seven separate areas where Christians lived. Their dispersal can be explained by the relative tolerance shown toward Copts in Cairo. The total area of these districts comes to 16.7 hectares, and the figure of 10,000 Copts proposed by the *Description* (for an average density of 400 residents per hectare) therefore seems reasonable. Aside from the Harat al-Rum, which was inside Qahira and the seat of the Coptic patriarch, most of the

Christian quarters (Harat al-Nasara) were located in the western section of the city, beyond the Khalij. They remained fairly isolated until Cairo's expansion folded them into an area with a strong Muslim majority. The largest and most important was on the north shore of the Birkat al-Azbakiyya. After 1600 it seems to have grown considerably in size. The population was strongly Coptic. The quality of their housing seems on average to have been a bit higher than that of Cairo's population as a whole.

In the very center of town, the Harat al-Yahud gathered the 3,000 Jews of Cairo on 6 hectares. The proximity of the goldsmiths' quarter (Sagha) undoubtedly explains the location, one that also allowed the authorities to keep watch over the Jews and, if need be, protect them. The quarter had the shape typical of a *hara*, with an arborescent structure branching from its main street, which gave onto the Suq al-Samak (the three openings to the outside other than its main entrance, clearly featured on the *Description* map, could have been later additions). But the quarter also had a mosque where Friday prayer was celebrated, the Jami Barakat Ibn Quraymit, built in 1499 and probably restored in 1579–80, indicating that the quarter was not totally homogeneous. Its population spanned quite a range of socioeconomic levels, since segregating the community outweighed any other possible organizing principle. All the different sects of Judaism (Rabbinites, Karaites, Samaritans) were represented.

The same communitarian logic can be found among the Syrian Catholic immigrants. Their community began forming in 1730, when the Melchites, principally from Damascus and Aleppo, began to settle in Cairo. The newcomers shared the lot of neither their compatriots the Muslim Syrians, since the authorities inevitably considered them as *dhimmi*, nor the Copts or Greeks, whom they did not accept as orthodox. The Syrian Catholics settled along the Khalij in the Sudun and Junayna quarters. They thus found themselves immediately next to the Franks, with whom they had ties through their commercial dealings. The Frankish consuls, the French in particular, gave them protection and helped them emancipate themselves from the Orthodox Church and be recognized by the Ottomans as forming a community in their own right. This actively forming community demonstrated the strength of community factors, which here outweighed socioeconomic ones.

### THE SUBURBS

There were several towns and villages near Cairo. Bulaq and Old Cairo, two distinct satellite towns, were only a short distance from the city. Bulaq was a little more than a kilometer to the northwest and Old Cairo the same distance to the southwest, with both serving the capital as outer ports on the Nile. Hence the importance in both these ports of customs duties, their revenues being higher than in the ports of Alexandria and Damietta: at the end of the eighteenth century, the sum sent to the imperial treasury was 2.8 million paras, but the duties collected by those who farmed customs came to 15.4 million paras. Customs duties were an important pawn in Egyptian politics: they passed into the hands of the janissaries around 1671 but were, like many other privileges, seized around 1770 by Emir Ali Bey, who transferred their management from the Jews to the Syrian Christians. After his death, the dominant emirs (Murad and Ibrahim Bey) took control of customs for themselves.

There was a degree of osmosis between the two satellite towns and Cairo. We know of several trade corporations that operated simultaneously in Cairo and one or another, if not both, of these towns. The linkage of economic interests and activities was very strong between Cairo and Bulaq, weaker between Cairo and Old Cairo. There is no question but that these were distinct towns, however. Shaykh al-Dardir, planning to lead the masses against the emirs in 1786, speaks of bringing together the people of Cairo's residential quarters (*harat*) and of its suburbs (*atrafs*) of Bulaq and Old Cairo.[21] The two towns were also independent "administrative" entities: each had its own *wali*, its own *muhtasib*, and its own *qadi*, assisted by a deputy (*na'ib*) who represented the *qadi askar* of Cairo.

Bulaq and Old Cairo evolved in opposite directions during the Ottoman period. Bulaq continued to experience the growth that had begun under the Mamluks and was reported by Leo Africanus in 1517. The establishment of the Ottoman Empire and Egypt's improved ties of every kind, commercial in particular, with the Ottoman centers (Istanbul and Anatolia) and provinces added to Bulaq's importance as Cairo's doorway to the Mediterranean. The developing relations with European countries had the same effect. Whereas Egypt in the Mamluk period had been a transit point for luxury goods from the Orient, the discovery of a direct sea route to Europe would deflect this trade. Luxury items were gradually replaced by more ordinary commodities—linen, rice, grain, leather, and sugar—whose volume would require the construction of more and larger caravanserais starting in the first decades of the sixteenth century. Somewhat later, on a scale that grew increasingly massive from 1600 on, coffee began to arrive from Yemen, and Cairo became the great center of coffee distribution. This new commodity would ensure the prosperity of Cairo and its port.

The sixteenth century was a period of active growth for Bulaq, during which time the pashas of Cairo constructed a series of caravanserais there. Foremost on their minds were clearly the profits to be made from creating religious foundations: for instance the *wakalat* built by Sulayman Pasha (1525–1538) for linen; the caravanserais of Dawud Pasha (around 1564) and Sinan Pasha (around 1571) for grain; the constructions of Hasan Pasha al-Khadim (1583) and of Ahmad Pasha (between 1591 and 1595); and the two *wakalat* by Bayram Pasha (around 1626). Some of these caravanserais are among the most enormous ever built in the Islamic world, such as the Wakala Hasan Pasha, which measures 112 by 67.5 meters, equivalent to 7,560 square meters; or the Wakala al-Kharnub, 78 by 48 meters, equivalent to 3,840 square meters, with forty shops. These are far bigger than even the largest caravanserais built in Cairo during the Ottoman period, the Wakala Dhulfiqar in Jamaliyya, for instance. This gigantism reflects the commercial activity in Bulaq during the first Ottoman century, but also the financial might of the governors who commissioned them.

Later, local magnates would take over this role from the pashas, whose authority and means were diminishing. The boom in the coffee trade in the late seventeenth century no doubt contributed to the renewed flurry of architectural activity: six *wakalat* were built by Mustafa Mirza (around 1699) and Yusuf Sa'id (around 1702), plus a remarkable number of commercial structures and public baths. Part of the projected profits was to be used to maintain the mosques and public fountains that were also built at this time. The first decades of the eighteenth century may well have seen a slowdown, but shortly before 1770 Alfi Bey built a complex in Bulaq that included a mosque, a *khan,* and a *qaysariyya* with two gates, described by the traveler Carsten Niebuhr as "a great bazaar or covered market." At the end of three centuries of Ottoman rule, Bulaq had sixty-five *wakalat*, or proportionately more than Cairo.

Commercial activities naturally provided the main element of this growth: the trade in coffee, which was reexported to Istanbul and the provinces of the Ottoman Empire, and thence to Europe; the commerce in raw textile materials (linen and cotton), which arrived from Upper and Lower Egypt, a part of which was reexported, the linen merchants being often in partnership with merchants from Istanbul; the trade in the grain that circulated on the Nile, which played an essential role in provisioning Cairo, bringing the authorities to intervene in Bulaq whenever there was a food shortage; the importation of wood for heating and construction, a commodity that Egypt lacked and that came from other countries around the Mediterranean; the trade in oil, imported from Tunis by Maghribis living at the Wakala al-Zayt (Caravanserai of Oil). Bulaq was also a center of artisan manufacture, in some cases connected with its trade: boat-building for the watercraft that plied the Nile, thus explaining the corporations of caulkers, framers, carpenters, and sawyers in Bulaq. The list of corporations drawn up by the French in 1801 enumerates 34 corporations belonging to Bulaq itself and another 50 that it shared primarily with Cairo and Old Cairo. They speak to the bustling commercial activity of this town and the variety of trades practiced there. By contrast, a provincial capital like Algiers, which was a more populous town than Bulaq, had only 57 trade corporations in the seventeenth century.

At the end of the eighteenth century, E.-F. Jomard estimated Bulaq's population at 24,000. The town unquestionably experienced great growth during the three centuries of Ottoman rule, as evidenced by the increase in commercial structures and public monuments. Nelly Hanna, who counts twenty-five mosques, twelve fountains, and seven public baths that were primarily built in the Ottoman period, reports strong urban expansion to the north and west. She also notes the appearance of the large north–south artery parallel to the Nile on lands that the river's westward retreat was gradually uncovering. A major portion of the new commercial structures were built near this thoroughfare and some of the town's important mosques as well: from north to south, the Mosques of Sulayman Pa-

Mosque of Sinan Pasha in Bulaq, 1571

sha (c. 1532), of Alaya (seventeenth century), of Sinan Pasha (1571), and of Mustafa Mirza (1698). It was in this area that the wealthiest residents lived. Farther east were the zones where artisan manufacture was developing, and where a more modest population lived in a network of irregular and often dead-end streets. This division and

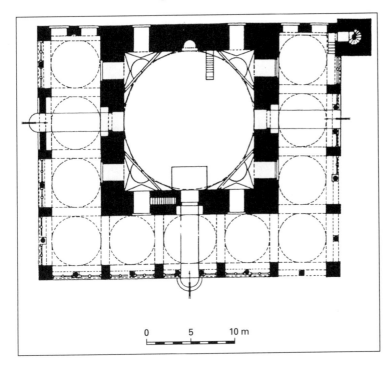

Plan of the Mosque of Sinan Pasha (Antiquités du Caire)

contrasting use of space suggest a classic urban organization, though modified by the presence of the river: the grouping of business activities along the port and their gradual extension northward, while the poor residential and artisan manufacture sector expanded in a direction away from the river.

All this activity and dynamism no doubt justified the traveler Savary's reaction, even accounting for his usual overenthusiasm and his tendency to use the accounts of earlier travelers, in this case that of Leo Africanus: "Boulak . . . is the port where all the merchandise coming from Damietta and Alexandria lands . . . The town is two miles long but of little width. It contains superb public baths and vast *okals* . . . Alongside the houses of Boulak, one sees thousands of boats of all shapes and sizes riding at anchor."[22]

Old Cairo gives a completely different impression. Western travelers, attracted by the real or imaginary biblical remnants there, bemoan its all-too-apparent degradation. Savary finds little to say about the former Fustat: "Masr el Atik is now only one-half league in ex-

Old Cairo (*Description de l'Egypte,* Bibliothèque Nationale)

tent, but it is still heavily populated and a considerable business center. It is the port where boats from Upper Egypt land." In fact Old Cairo was completing a decline that had already been under way in Mamluk times and that reflected the dominance of the Mediterranean sea routes over the route to Upper Egypt. Toward 1798 the city had only 10,000 inhabitants, a large fraction of whom were Christian (some Greek Orthodox Christians, but mostly Copts who worshiped at the Churches of Saint George and Saint Sergius), living in the midst of a majority Muslim population. The *Description de l'Egypte* mentions no fewer than eight mosques, including of course the Mosque of Amr, whose dilapidation would cause Murad Bey to rebuild it in 1797.

Business in Old Cairo was centered on trade with Upper Egypt, for which it remained the natural port. The grain trade in particular was centered there, the grain being stored in vast warehouses. Travelers gave the name "Joseph's granary" to the warehouses where wheat was set aside as part of the annual tribute. These were described as square courtyards surrounded by brick walls and filled with grain, which was covered with rush mats. Old Cairo also received dates, sugar, and livestock, but the trade in these items, though once the monopoly of Old Cairo, passed largely to Bulaq. Artisan activities in Old Cairo were therefore modest. The most remarkable was the manufacture of clay vases. Old Cairo had only thirteen trade corporations of its own, plus thirty-two that it shared with other locations, Cairo in particular; and the *Description de l'Egypte* mentions only one *wakala* there. The description by Jean Coppin, dating from 1638–1640, seems conscious of the decline of a town whose foundation, exactly 1,000 years earlier, had opened the first chapter in a brilliant history: Old Cairo, he writes, is "more filled with ruins than with houses . . . There is a fairly long stretch of houses along the bank [of the branch of the Nile] . . . behind these houses one finds a few others scattered without any order . . . But it is all dispersed confusedly between a number of shacks and ruins."[23]

It would hardly be worth mentioning the little villages on the west shore of the Nile, Imbaba and Giza, were they not destined to become centers of bustling growth in the outward explosion of contemporary Cairo. Savary records: "Across from Bulaq, we see the small village of [Imbaba]. It is no more than some miserable rounded earth huts in the shade of sycamores . . . A few houses of mud-baked brick and a small mosque can just be seen in the distance amidst the foliage of date palms and tamarinds. In winter, the residents of Cairo go there to buy excellent butter, and in summer, delicious melons."

This small rural village had once known a certain animation as a silk weaving center, as had Giza. When the traveler R. Pockocke passed through, coarse cloth for bed linen was still being made there. Giza was a true small town, the capital of a rich agricultural province, the endpoint of caravans arriving from Tripolitania with cattle for the butchers of Cairo, and a market for agricultural products. It was also an active center of artisan manufacture: in 1801 there were fifteen trade corporations there, plus thirteen corporations that it shared with the towns on the east bank of the Nile. Aside from a corporation of boat captains and another of Nile fishermen, Giza boasted makers of green jars (reputed to cure "stomach flux"), weavers, and indigo dyers.

For the rural beauty of its landscape, its quiet, and its isolation, Giza was a sought-after summer resort. Savary, off on the traditional excursion to the Pyramids, spent the night in a "pretty country house" rented in Giza by the French merchants. Isma'il Bey built a pavilion for himself at Giza to which Murad Bey repaired in 1791, making it his primary residence, so that an entire court came to take its place around him.[24]

In 1798 Cairo was larger and more populated than at any other moment in its history until then. The number and density of the commercial structures in Qahira testify to the liveliness of a city that had remained, despite the great changes in international trade routes, one of the main centers of Mediterranean and Eastern commerce. Even in the realm of urban architecture, the contributions of the Ottoman period are not negligible in quantity or quality. In particular, it is to this period that we owe the creation of an urban setting that appears intact in nineteenth-century engravings, although Cairo's modernization in the last century and a half has erased all but a few fragments. What is called "traditional" or "medieval" Cairo is certainly the city inherited from the three centuries between the arrival of the Ottomans and the Napoleonic expedition.

The prospect of the city visible from the Citadel fixed itself at this time, and it would long remain just as J. A. de Gobineau described it in 1855 on his passage through Egypt, the image of the city of the *Thousand and One Nights*:

> One has to climb to the Citadel . . . One sees . . . to left and right the expanse of the city incised with thousands of streets, strewn with squares, encumbered with mosques and great buildings, and in a hundred places flowering with bouquets of trees and gardens. It is not gay, it is not bizarre, it is not majestic as one normally understands the word, which is to say that it lacks all symmetry; but it is large, vast, full of air, life, heat, freedom, and in consequence beauty . . . Power breathes there. It was not Antiquity but epochs already old that created this, epochs that lacked neither belief nor thought, courage nor wealth, nor energy either.[25]

# IV
# CONTEMPORARY CAIRO
# (1798–1992)

It is traditional to date Egypt's entry into the modern world from 1798, the date of the French Expedition, and the transition to a new phase of the country's history is confirmed by the accession in 1805 of the reforming pasha Muhammad Ali (1805–1848). Naturally there is something artificial in establishing such exact milestones for a process that in fact developed slowly and with many hesitations through-out the nineteenth century. The French occupation unquestionably sounded Ottoman Egypt's death knell. For Cairo it marked the end of slightly more than eight centuries of evolution, with remarkable con-tinuity from Mamluk to Ottoman times. Even if it was not an entirely new world that dawned in 1798 and in 1805, the arrival of the French wiped clean the historical slate and allowed Muhammad Ali to organize a new government, a new society, and a new economy. To a certain extent, the seed of contemporary Egypt was contained in the Egypt that took shape in the first half of the nineteenth century.

# 14

# A Slow Awakening
# (1798–1863)

IN CAIRO ITSELF, little change occurred during the period from Napoleon's arrival in 1798 to the accession of Isma'il Pasha in 1863. Even the outline of Cairo hardly altered, certainly less than between the Ayyubids and the Mamluks or between the Mamluks and the Ottomans. The map drawn up by Pierre Grand in 1874 is no more than an adaptation of the map in the *Description de l'Egypte*. In the areas to the west of the city, one can just start to see the effects of Isma'il's policy of urban development. The stagnation reflected in the maps is evident in our demographic data: the population of Cairo, estimated at 263,000 by the scholars of the French Expedition, had probably increased little at the death of Muhammad Ali in 1849 and had barely surpassed 300,000 in 1863. If an awakening occurred, its effects were still barely felt in Cairo.[1]

### THE FRENCH OCCUPATION (JULY 1798–AUGUST 1801)

The wake-up effect for which the brief French occupation is credited, in an Egypt that had been slumbering since the Ottoman conquest in 1517, has been somewhat exaggerated. The reality is quite different with respect both to the supposed decadence of the Ottoman era and to the lasting changes brought on by the French presence. If Muhammad Ali had not come to power in 1805, the impact of the French Expedition would no doubt be recognized as very limited. But by destroying the system set in place by the Ottomans, the

Canal-opening celebration during the French occupation
(*Description de l'Egypte*, Bibliothèque Nationale)

French allowed the genuinely new enterprise of Muhammad Ali to get underway. Even if negative, the consequences of the French Expedition were therefore still decisive for Egypt.[2]

The Egyptians of the time naturally manifested no gratitude for the supposed "beneficial effects" of an occupation that they vigorously opposed, specifically with two violent insurrections, which met with the usual retribution for violence, namely, repression and destruction. The presence of the French, who were doubly foreign as Europeans and as Christians, provoked unrelenting hostility among the population. The administrator, Poussielgue, wrote to General Desaix on 19 March 1799: "The people are inflammable. They suffer the rule of a Christian nation so impatiently that it would take only a spark to touch off a general revolt."

Among the elite there were inevitably those who opted for collaboration with the occupier, though more from resignation than from conviction. And there were aspects of French civilization that aroused curiosity and even interest among the local population—as evidenced in the half-admiring, half-skeptical comments of Jabarti on the new inventions brought by the French. Some seemed to him no more than gadgets, such as the hot-air balloon demonstrated rather unconvincingly by the soldiers at the Azbakiyya: "What they promised did not come true. They claimed a sort of ship would travel through the air thanks to the marvels of technology . . . In fact it was no more than a kite such as menservants make on holidays and at public festivities." The French could expect no more from the Egyptians than their acquiescence in what was in any case unavoidable, while they bided their time until the will of God and the protection of the Ottomans should drive out these invaders from another world.

The governing bodies that the French managed with great difficulty to set in place represented a compromise between the modern principles they favored and the local customs they could not but take into account if they wanted a minimal cooperation from the natives. Napoleon landed in Egypt on 2 July 1798 and arrived in Cairo on 22 July. On 25 July he formed a *diwan* (council) comprising nine members drawn from the foremost shaykhs. He appointed an agha of the janissaries, who was in charge of the police, a *wali* (night agha), a *muhtasib* (supervisor of weights and measures), chosen on the *diwan*'s recommendation from among the mamluks because "the people of Cairo fear only the Turks . . . who alone can produce an effect on them."

With some adjustments and changes in its organization, the system of councils recruited from prominent Egyptians (Jabarti served in 1800) subsisted under the direction of a Frenchman until the departure of the expeditionary forces: Fourier, then Girard, were commissioners to the *diwan* of 1800. The council's members received a monthly stipend of 14,000 paras, plus 400 paras for each day of actual attendance. The councils participated in governing Cairo and provided an intermediary between the French and the local population, whose suffering they managed to mitigate somewhat. To the three aghas, who also received a fixed stipend, the French added a number of other officials, among them the "director of trades," who supervised the occupational corporations with the twin purpose of seeing to public order and ensuring the collection of the taxes levied on the corporations. The creation of a half-Muslim and half-Coptic court of commerce and an office of property records (September 1798) affected not only the material interests of the Egyptians but also their civil status.[3]

From the start of the French occupation, Cairo was divided into

Map of Cairo from the *Description de l'Egypte:* the Qahira district

eight administrative districts. Their outlines, known to us from the *Description de l'Egypte* map, only partly take into account the "natural" boundaries that might have guided this division.[4] The districts were known in Arabic as *khitat,* a name charged with meaning since it was the term used for the concessions demarcated in Fustat at the time of the Arab conquest, then in Qahira at the time of its founding. Expedition documents mention "district commanders," who were beyond any doubt French officers. They may have been assisted by natives—this would explain the reference to the "house of the Turkish commander of the [eighth] district." Our texts refer elsewhere to an emir living in the *khitat* and to a *"khitta* dignitary" *(kabir al-khitta).*

These districts were useful for the administration of the city and also for the levy of taxes. For the *firda* levied in September 1800, the tax on each of the eight districts was assessed at 25,000 riyals. Within this new framework, the French kept the traditional organization by quarters *(harat).* A document in the Expedition's archives, dated 31 October 1798, gives a list of the shaykhs of fifty-six quarters, accompanied by a preamble: "The shaykhs whose names appear below stand as guarantors for the residents of their respective quarters. They will be held responsible for any disorder that might occur there, and if they are unable to remedy it they promise to inform immediately the agha of the janissaries." One of the main responsibilities was in fact to see to the maintenance of law and order. But the shaykhs, like their predecessors in Ottoman times, also had fiscal responsibilities: the shaykhs of the quarters were in charge of collecting taxes under the supervision of the "amirs of the district." On 23 January 1801, when General Menou decided to inaugurate a census of births and deaths, the *diwan* proposed that the watchmen of the quarters and streets be assigned the operation and asked the shaykhs to gather the relevant information from the undertakers and midwives.

The French used Cairo's existing corporative organization to provide a solid base for administration and finances. A document signed by d'Allonvilly, "director of corporations," and dated 17 January 1801, drew up a list—apparently complete—of the trade corporations in Cairo and the neighboring communities and of their shaykhs: 278 corporations, 193 of them in Cairo. The document was presumably designed to allow the levy of a recently created tax on "the arts and trades." But the French also used the corporations to maintain law and order, as shown by the promise given by the shaykh and merchants of Ghuriyya on 26 October 1798 in Bonaparte's presence: "Henceforth we will maintain all the streets of our quarter free of any trouble."[5]

In certain areas the French were simply reaffirming traditional concerns that went back to Mamluk times. Matters of hygiene and public order account for French ordinances concerning the thoroughfares. As early as 27 September 1798, Jabarti reports that "the order has been given to light the streets and suqs at night with lamps, at the rate of one lamp per house or one for every three shops. There are also instructions to sweep and water the streets, and to maintain the cleanliness of the public way in the matter of garbage and refuse." This order would often be reiterated. The archives of the French Expedition record that sanctions were issued with almost military severity, possibly to encourage compliance. On 30 July 1800 the order appears with a tariff of the fines for noncompliance: one "pataque" (the local name for a thaler) for a first offense, four for a second, ten for a third, and finally a month in prison for a fourth infraction. These were not empty threats. The register of prisons cites, in December 1800, January 1801, and May 1801, the names of Cairenes who were sent to prison "for having failed to comply with the order concerning lamps."[6]

More novel, but also clearly related to questions of public order, were the directives to demolish the gates closing off the alleys that provided access to the quarters. Detroye's journal notes, on 4 August 1798: "The streets are obstructed by a prodigious number of gates that separate the different quarters. The general-in-chief, fearing that these doors might be used in a riot to stop the progress of the troops, has ordered that they be demolished." In his chronicle, Jabarti mentions on several occasions the removal of the wooden gates (31 July, 22 September, and 6 November 1798). Transported to the Azbakiyya and broken up, the wood was used to supply the army with firewood. After the second revolt in Cairo (1800), the order was given to destroy the benches in front of the shops to allow freer passage through the streets, but more particularly to keep the Cairenes from using them to make barricades as they had done during the first revolt (1798). Although the removal of the benches was probably not complete, the order did cause serious inconvenience to shopkeepers, whom one now saw "sitting in their narrow shops like mice in their holes," Jabarti noted with some malice.[7]

The sanitary measures taken to avoid the onset (or exacerbation) of any epidemics were at best only partially successful, as the city of Cairo and the occupying army suffered several accesses of the plague, notably in February–March 1801. The orders given—airing of clothes and bed linen on terraces, fumigation, quarantine, cleaning—and the publication of morbidity statistics belong to the classic prophylactic arsenal of the day. The prohibition issued in September 1798 against burying the dead in cemeteries within Cairo's precincts, especially those of Azbakiyya and Ruway'i, and to use only the Qarafa Cemetery was intended to make the city more sanitary, as was the effort at demolishing the tombs in the Azbakiyya cemetery (29 September). These measures also tended to improve the environment in an area heavily occupied and inhabited by the French, whose headquarters were in the palace of Alfi Bey. So strong was the popular sentiment stirred up by the first swings of the pick-ax against the tombs in

Palace of Alfi Bey: Bonaparte's headquarters on the Azbakiyya
(*Description de l'Egypte,* Bibliothèque Nationale)

The destruction at Azbakiyya Pond
(*Description de l'Egypte,* Bibliothèque Nationale)

Azbakiyya, however, that the project was called off and would be successfully resumed only under Muhammad Ali.[8]

The works of actual urbanism are few. We will not include, naturally, the destruction carried out, sometimes quite extensively, in conjunction with the effort to quell the revolts of 1798 and 1800 within the city. The 1798 revolt was fairly brief and restricted in area. Although the Husayniyya district was involved through the incitements of the dignitary Badr al-Din, the main neighborhood caught in the revolt was the al-Azhar quarter, which was strongly held by the insurgents. The quarter was violently bombarded on 22 October, and on 23 October French soldiers profaned and pillaged the mosque. Jabarti, horrified and scandalized, recorded the depredations, vandalism, and acts of sacrilege systematically committed there.

More devastating yet were the effects of the revolt of March–April 1800, which spread to the entire city, but especially to the tanneries, Azbakiyya, the northeast districts, the Butcher Quarter (Husayniyya), and Bulaq. The Cairenes offered a determined resistance to the reconquest of Cairo by the French army, now led by General Kléber. The rebellion lasted thirty-seven days. Heavy shelling landed on Jamaliyya, and the Butcher Quarter was burned. Jabarti describes several instances of the damage caused by the battle, particularly in the Maqs area, Birkat al-Ratli, and Husayniyya, which was apparently subjected to systematic destruction in September 1800, as well as in Azbakiyya: "All turned to sparkling fire and ruins, as though there had never been enchanting villas here, or gatherings of friends, or promenades . . . Time and adversity have so ravaged these places that their beauty has dissolved, their dwellings have emptied." We might dismiss this as the sort of rhetorical flight to which the chroniclers were prone were there not an engraving from the period that provides a truly saddening picture of the ruins surrounding the famous pond.[9]

A good part of the work done by the French inevitably had a military purpose: the building of small forts around Cairo, the clearing away of great lengths of the north and northeast walls, the fortification of the Coptic quarter north of Azbakiyya, and demolition in strategic sectors. The Citadel was particularly affected—in the area of Suwwa, in the Qarafa, and on the side of the Muqattam Hills, part of which was destroyed for fear that it would be used for shelling the fortress, a consideration that obviously never suggested itself to Saladin in selecting the site.

The only urban improvement to speak of was the work carried out around Birkat al-Azbakiyya. Raised-earth levies were built along the north and west shores of the pond, and trees were planted, indicating an effort made to render the quarter agreeable. It was of course the center of the French military organization, and many officers resided in the neighborhood; on this point Jabarti confirms the indications in the *Description de l'Egypte* map. It seems, still according to Jabarti, that the French planned to put a road through the city from the southwest corner of the Birkat al-Azbakiyya to the Muski Bridge, the Khan al-Khalili, and Bab al-Barqiyya (Bab al-Ghurayib): "A large road with shops and caravanserais on either side, colonnades, trellises, arbors, and gardens" that would link up with the road to Bulaq. But this undertaking, foreshadowing the "New Street" built by Muhammad Ali, was never realized for lack of time and means, except for work completed around the Muski Bridge. By contrast, the French laid out the road between Azbakiyya and Bulaq, from the pond itself to the Maghribi Bridge (Qantara al-Maghribi), which was rebuilt, and from the bridge to Bulaq. This was done for strategic reasons, as was the repair of the bridges over the Khalij, both inside and outside the city.[10]

Thus in the realm of urban works the French had no lasting influence on Cairo's development. But a few of their plans and certain of the projects they actually carried out may have helped prepare the way for the organizing measures taken by Muhammad Ali and his successors.

### MUHAMMAD ALI AND CAIRO (1805–1848)

A soldier of fortune, Muhammad Ali arrived in Egypt in 1801 during the last days of the French Expedition and, though only an officer in an Albanian corps of the Ottoman army, managed to seize power in Cairo and obtain his elevation to pasha from the Porte (1805). His long reign then enabled him to eliminate the old Mamluk aristocracy (1811) and to conquer the Hijaz, Palestine, and Syria (1831). Finally, the sultan and the great powers recognized him as hereditary pasha of Egypt and ruler of the Sudan (1841).

Under the rod of Muhammad Ali, Egypt leapt into the modern world to take its place on the international political and economic stage. The social structure of the country was thrown into upheaval, its political and administrative system was reformed, a modern army was established, and a new economy developed. Whatever our judgment on the success of the attempts at industrialization and on the reasons for their failure (whether domestic dysfunctions or external pressures, crowned by the treaty of 1841), we must acknowledge that a new Egypt was born. Its commercial expansion and orientation toward Europe brought about the extraordinary growth of Alexandria. Within a half-century, this modest and somnolent outer port of Cairo (10,000 inhabitants) was transformed into a buzzing Mediterranean metropolis: 105,000 inhabitants in 1848 (including 5,000 foreigners) and 232,000 in 1882 (including 49,000 foreigners).

The upheaval, the whirlwind that shook Egypt, seems largely to have bypassed Cairo. From 1805 to 1849 the city changed little. There is nothing to indicate a development even slightly responsive to the great changes sweeping Egypt, either in Grand's 1874 map or in the population figures, which became more reliable around the time that demographic problems started to come to the fore. The (fairly unreliable) census of 1846 assigns Cairo a population of 256,000, somewhat below the figure arrived at by the *Description* in 1798.[11]

Cairo's stagnation and Muhammad Ali's apparent lack of interest in the city are problematic. All during his reign, Egypt's population remained largely stable. From the 4 million persons in Egypt in 1800 (a figure considered more accurate by the experts than the 2.6 million estimated in the *Description*), the population rose to 4.7 million in 1849. This very low rate of increase, a quasi-stagnation, can be explained first by demographic catastrophes: outbreaks of plague (the 1835 epidemic killed 500,000 people) and especially cholera (180,000 deaths in 1831). Egypt was also paying for Muhammad Ali's grand politics. There were the conscription and military campaigns occasioned by Egypt's active foreign policy, and further losses from the corvée and forced labor employed in the construction and maintenance of the great irrigation and drainage canals. Mortality was quite high on work sites and among the masses of humanity (up to 400,000 peasants) called up each year to take part in public works.

It was Alexandria, in fact, that became the magnet for demographic growth. Alexandria replaced Cairo as the center of international trade in Egypt, and the capital looked on passively while a town that had been its outer port expanded rapidly to become its rival. Muhammad Ali introduced no policies in Cairo to stem the economic tide turning in Alexandria's favor. Rather, in his desire to make Egypt a great power he sought to benefit the new city, which was oriented toward the Mediterranean, the main theater of his diplomatic interests. The new economy and the new Egyptian commerce were based on heavy goods (such as cotton), and only a seaport would serve to market them. Finally, Alexandria with its varied and dynamic new population reflected the pasha's politics, whereas Cairo provoked his distrust: its society was linked to a past he was actively abolishing, and its people were capable of fomenting serious unrest. These circumstances could explain the pasha's predilection for residences outside and at a certain distance from the city.

The administrative organization of Cairo was changed in minor aspects only. The police function passed into the hands of the Zabtiyya (founded in 1834–35), which was responsible for the trial of lesser crimes, and police posts were established in every quarter of the city. A Department of Buildings and a Civil Engineering Office were instituted in 1829 and 1837 respectively. The *wali* was reduced to an honorific post, and the *qadi's* role in urban affairs was greatly reduced. The greatest innovation was to divide the city into precincts (*athman,* or "eighths"), apparently a borrowing from French civil administration. The shaykhs of the *athman* composed reports and dealt with all the more important business, which brought them into direct relations with the police and authorities. At the lowest level, the shaykhs of the quarters continued to play a decisive role in urban affairs. The trade corporations remained an organ of communication between the members of an occupational group, the public, and the authorities on a wide range of issues. Aside from a few modifications, then, the city administration retained its traditional form.

The manner in which urban problems were resolved (or neglected) on a day-to-day basis also remained traditional. Contemporary accounts, particularly those of the innumerable travelers from Europe, exhibit broad contrasts according to the quality of the writer's information and his momentary humor. Progress was certainly made in street maintenance, both as to cleanliness and flow of traffic. The English traveler J. A. St. John remarks in 1832: "The streets, formerly disgustingly filthy, are now remarkable for their cleanliness, being all swept three times a day . . . Refuse is collected in piles, and four hundred carts, pulled by young oxen, are employed in removing it beyond the city."

The Orientalist Edward Lane, writing in 1835, describes how an old urban problem, the obstruction of streets by the benches in front of shops, was solved:

> Muhammad Ali has lately caused the benches in most thoroughfare streets to be pulled down, and allowed them to be rebuilt only in the wider parts, generally to the width of about two spans. At the same time, he has obliged the tradesmen to paint their shops and to remove the unsightly coverings of matting that shaded many of the suqs, prohibiting the replacing of them except by coverings of wood. Not long afterward the viceroy ordered the inhabitants of Cairo to whitewash the fronts of their houses.

For all that these are judicious rulings, they still indicate a somewhat erratic attention to the day-to-day problems of the city. Only in 1845 was a plan *(tanzim)* drawn up that envisioned widening and opening the streets. Cairo's Council of Tanzim enjoyed a brief but promising period of activity.[12]

The city thus changed little in appearance during this innovative and event-filled half-century. Many of the projects undertaken and much of the progress accomplished after 1830 may in any case be attributed to Ibrahim Pasha, Muhammad Ali's son, who died in 1848. A number of public works were undertaken to prepare the way for future developments. The mounds of debris surrounding Cairo were leveled along the north and west borders. And the grading and planting carried out under Ibrahim Pasha of some 160 hectares in the zone between the city and the Nile behind the flood dike facilitated the urban development projects ultimately undertaken by Isma'il Pasha. The same went for the work of filling in the lowlands (flooded when the Nile was in spate) that were so numerous in Cairo: Birkat al-Fil (partially), Birkat al-Ratli, Birkat of Qasim Bey, and especially Azbakiyya Pond. The drainage of this pond by means of a circular canal (around 1837) and its filling in made it possible to create a European-style garden, overlooked by palaces and, most remarkable innovation, by hotels: the Orient Hotel (in the northeast) and Shepheard's Hotel, in 1849 (on the western shore, on the site of the al-Alfi palace). For reasons of health and also to facilitate projected improvements to the street system, several cemeteries within the city were closed (such as the one at Azbakiyya).

The irregular network of streets remained one of the major obstacles to modernizing the city. The first carriages appeared at this time, at first simply as curiosities reserved for the royal family—one such being the landau sent to the pasha by the French government in 1824 accompanied by a letter from Chateaubriand, in recognition for a stay in Cairo he had made sixteen years before: "It is to give Your Excellency a most brilliant demonstration of His Majesty's satisfaction in this regard that I have been ordered to send you a carriage and harness." But these equipages, which were to multiply until there were some thirty carriages in 1840, could scarcely circulate except outside the city, mostly along the avenue leading to Shubra: "All the passersby stopped before the Pasha's carriage in mute admiration, its appearance more surprising to them than the pyramids," wrote d'Estournel in 1833.

With the nature of traffic altered by economic and technological developments, the authorities were already considering how to open the city to circulation. Two new streets were proposed by the Tanzim. The first, perhaps a reprise of the French plan, was to lead from the Muski Bridge to the al-Azhar quarter, cutting through the old city from west to east and opening the business district to European merchants: this was the future New Street (Sikkat al-Jadida). The roadway was to be 8 meters wide, a generous size at the time. The process of acquiring lots and demolishing the buildings that stood in the way began in 1845, but only a portion of the road had opened to traffic by 1849. A more ambitious project was the street intended to pierce the city diagonally from Azbakiyya to the Citadel (the future Muhammad Ali Boulevard). This project started in 1845 with the razing of the cemeteries near Azbakiyya and the purchase and destruction of a number of houses, but it was finished only under Isma'il.

Slowly the old city assumed a new physiognomy as its buildings were constructed in a style foreign to local traditions. A new style appeared with the prohibition against building *mashrabiyya* (nominally for safety reasons, but probably also to legislate "modernism") and the use of glass windowpanes, a style that was half European and half Turkish, accompanied by a new organization of interior spaces that would become widespread in the second half of the century. In 1847, under the supervision of four artillery officers, the houses on Cairo's streets received numbers.[13]

One doesn't know whether to credit Muhammad Ali with a complete renovation of the Citadel, but he destroyed a good number of the monuments of the preceding centuries and replaced them with buildings that are painfully banal and in some cases aggressively ugly. Security reasons probably led Muhammad Ali to abandon his Azbakiyya residence in 1807 and move to the Citadel. In March 1811 a massacre of the mamluks rid him of the old elite, when twenty-four beys and an undetermined number of lesser dignitaries lost their lives in a passageway leading from the Citadel, where they had been invited for a ceremony. Shortly afterward, in 1812, he had almost all the Citadel's Mamluk buildings destroyed, the ground leveled, and the walls rebuilt: "A palace . . . vast quarters for the army, a large terrace, an arsenal, a powder-house, and a hall of currency were constructed." The Citadel bustled as of old, once more crowded with officers and government functionaries.

The new constructions at the Citadel formed two building complexes, neither very remarkable: a palace at the very south, known as the Jewel Palace, and the harem to the north, consisting of three buildings. At least, as Edmond Pauty remarks, there was a good view from the Jewel Palace: "The view from there, which extends over the city to beyond the Nile and the Pyramids, is delightful. Toward the mosque, through a well-planted garden, the slender silhouettes of minarets invite the soul to soar through the sky."

The Citadel's principal ornament was the great mosque, for which the pasha had requested a design in 1820 from the French architect Pascal Coste. Originally from Marseilles, Coste worked in the pasha's service, and we owe many admirable sketches to his stay in Cairo. Coste accordingly made a study of Cairo's mosques, from which he produced a monumental project in the neo-Mamluk style, considering it rightly to be the national style. His premature departure in 1830 prevented the realization of this project, and a mosque closely inspired by the Mosque of Sultan Ahmad I in Istanbul was finally erected by an anonymous Armenian architect. Inaugurated in 1833, it was completed only in 1857. Little can decently be said of a monument whose elements and details are heavy or in bad taste but

Mosque of Muhammad Ali in the Citadel, 1833

whose silhouette has become as inalienable a feature of Cairo's skyline as the Eiffel Tower of Paris'. At the beginning of the century, Arthur Rhoné, a great connoisseur and lover of Cairo, wrote very discerningly on this subject: "From afar, [the mosque] produces a considerable effect by virtue of its mass, its large domes, its slender minarets rising like ships' masts. As one approaches, the effect changes, and one is affected painfully by this enormous Turkishism, so heavy, and so null after the lovely creations of early Arab architecture."[14]

Muhammad Ali, who favored more rural residences, built himself country palaces. These sometimes sparked later urban development and were transformed into suburbs destined for brilliant futures. Such was the case with the palace and garden established north of Cairo in Shubra. Work began in 1809, and the pasha moved there the next year, making it his primary residence. The palace was built on the edge of the Nile, and one reached it by a handsome alley planted on either side with acacias and sycamores, an avenue Gérard de Nerval characterized as "the most beautiful in the world," and which would be called "the Champs-Elysées of Cairo, the meeting-place of Cairo's native and European high society." An English engineer, Galloway, installed gaslights there in 1829. The residence was abandoned after the pasha's death, but urban development followed, and in 1909 a double row of rental houses stood along the old alley, now provided with a tramline. Other palaces built for members of the royal family were also absorbed into the expanding city at the end of the nineteenth century: Qasr al-Dubara, Qasr al-Ayni, and Rawdah, which was built by Ibrahim Pasha on the island and is today a Club Méditerranée hotel.[15]

Muhammad Ali's industrial enterprises had an important effect on the development of Bulaq. Damaged by the French in the wake of the rebellion of 1800, the city resumed its bustling commercial activity toward 1814, thanks to the presence of the pasha's arsenal and warehouses. In the years following, a number of industrial installations were located there: textile factories starting in 1818, a foundry in 1820, and a printing works in 1822, from which the first great texts printed in Egypt emerged (editions of Maqrizi and Jabarti among them) and of which the modern facilities of the newspaper *al-Ahram* are distant successors. Several of the schools of higher education founded by the pasha were also established in Bulaq; one was the civil engineering school founded in 1821, which became a polytechnic institute in 1834. Bulaq's destiny as a commercial and manufacturing center began to overshadow its function as a pleasant suburb on the banks of the Nile. The town developed as a center of industrial activity with a poor working-class population. While Cairo itself was stricken with immobility, the city's future was taking shape outside the city limits.

### FROM MUHAMMAD ALI TO ISMAʿIL (1848–1863)

Following years of frenetic change, no large-scale projects were undertaken during the reigns of Muhammad Ali's successors, Abbas I (1848–1854) and Saʿid (1854–1863). They did have a certain influence on the history of the city, however. Abbas Pasha laid the groundwork for the future Abbasiyya district by deciding to build barracks for his troops on the edge of the desert on the road leading to the two villages of Matariyya and Heliopolis, and by encouraging the peopling of this area by granting lands there and establishing a hospital, a school, and a palace.[16]

It was during his reign as well, in 1851, that an agreement was signed with the English to build a railroad between Alexandria and Cairo. Another section was to unite Cairo and Suez, thus establishing a link between the Mediterranean and the Red Sea on the road to the Indies. The first section was completed in 1854, just before the death of Abbas, and the second in 1858. Cairo became an easily accessible city and, before long, a railroad junction. A railway station was built in 1856 near the northwest corner of the city not far from the old Bab al-Hadid (Iron Gate)—supporting the popular belief that the gate was so named because of the "iron road" (Sikkat al-Hadid). From there, modernization would enter the old city. While urbanization was occurring on both sides of the railway, the construction of barracks by Saʿid Pasha at Qasr al-Nil (on the site of today's Hilton Hotel) renewed interest in the area on Cairo's western edge. These two points of development to the north and west framed the zone in which Ismaʿil would concentrate his efforts at urban development.

No less consequential for Cairo was the signing of an agreement in 1854 between Saʿid and Ferdinand de Lesseps for the building of the Suez Canal. Though the realization of the canal was delayed somewhat because of British obstruction, the ongoing project and then its completion repositioned Egypt and its capital on the great route to the Orient and made it an essential link in the developing network of global transportation. Egypt took its place once and for all on the great field of world politics and the world economy. Modernization, which had been launched on a voluntary basis by Muhammad Ali and had consequently remained incomplete, now became a necessity for Egypt and Cairo. And modernization, given the material and cultural state of the world in 1860, could only mean Westernization.

# 15

# The Dream of Westernization
# (1863–1936)

THE YEAR 1863 was an important one for Cairo, for it marked the accession of Isma'il Pasha (1863–1879), the first ruler in nine centuries to make an overall plan for the city's development. Inevitably his plan echoed Western models, as Europe's ascendancy in political and economic matters seems to have extended to urban ones as well.

Whether Haussmannian or not (it had been foreshadowed in Muhammad Ali's plans for Cairo and embodied in Alexandria), the new urbanism was predicated on an organization of space in which the street system had primacy, an urban geometry based on the grid and a prior knowledge of the structures to be built. The new concept of urban development henceforth privileged perspective and alignment, and therefore imposed a new architecture based on buildings with standard apartments, again organized on a Western model, though the local tradition of the *rab* might well have supplied a native form of group housing.[1] Such developments could occur, of course, only in new spaces. In any event, the population increase that started in the mid-nineteenth century required Cairo to expand beyond the limits of the traditional city. Limited in space, relatively overcrowded, and structured according to a different principle of urban life, the old city offered neither a suitable ground for the new urbanism nor accommodations for a fresh influx of residents.

The adoption of the new urban plan and its near-immediate consequences for the city (which became a "double" city) proceeded with no real break from the time of Isma'il to the period of English

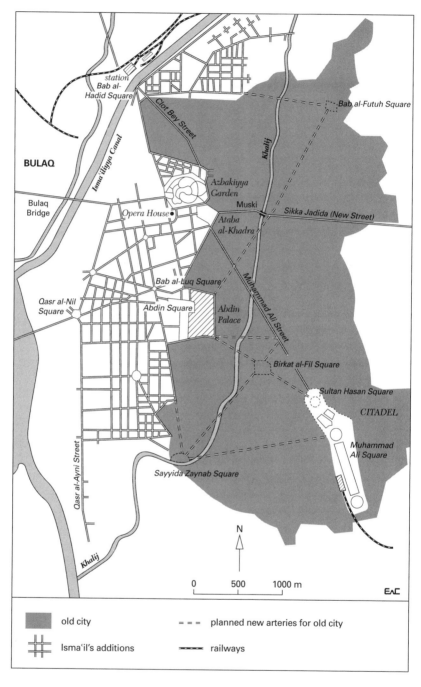

Map 11. Isma'il's Cairo (1869–1870) (after Abu-Lughod)

colonization. Under Isma'il, the city planning process was internalized and, to a certain degree, mastered by the Egyptians; under British rule, it was more or less imposed and inevitably wore a colonial aspect. The "British" city of the years 1882–1936 was merely a development of the changes sketched out during the few years of Isma'il's reign.

Until the 1930s, Cairo's urban development coincided with a moderate level of demographic growth. First evident around 1860, the population increase did not begin to accelerate dangerously for urbanists and city planners until 1936. The population reached one million around 1930; at this level Cairo's housing and material needs could still be predicted and organized.[2]

## ISMA'IL AND THE TEMPTATION OF THE WEST (1863–1879)

From the time of his accession to power, Isma'il launched a campaign to modernize Egypt not unlike the one led by his ancestor Muhammad Ali. Conditions were favorable. With the excavation of the Suez Canal now proceeding vigorously (its inauguration would occur on 17 August 1869) and a temporary cotton boom boosting the country's economic power, Isma'il was able to reap the political benefits of Egypt's strong position and obtain his elevation to the rank of khedive (8 June 1867), thus increasing his autonomy. In Isma'il's plan, an enlarged and embellished Cairo was to be the symbol and showpiece of Egypt's progress, and it naturally became a priority for him.

Isma'il's desire to transform his capital resulted in several initiatives. In 1864–65 he organized a Ministry of Public Works to coordinate his urban policies. The pasha was not without competence in technical fields: in 1846 he had accompanied a group of Egyptian students to Paris, where, in addition to French, he had studied modern science and some aspects of engineering. At that time he met Ali Mubarak, who would stay in France until 1849 and eventually become his righthand man in the fields of education and public works.

Spectacular technical innovations were introduced in Cairo. In February 1865 the Lebon company, already active in Alexandria, was granted the concession to supply gas to Cairo and the suburbs of Bulaq and Old Cairo. The following year the company established a plant in Bulaq, and in April 1867 the train station at Bab al-Hadid was lit to celebrate the inauguration of the new public utility. The Azbakiyya district, the new quarter of Isma'iliyya, the major thoroughfares, and the khedive's palaces were the first to benefit from public lighting. Thereafter the network spread rapidly: in 1882, 70 kilometers of streets were lit by close to 2,500 gas lamps. In May 1865 the concession to supply Cairo with municipal water was granted to Cordier. A pumping station was installed near Qasr al-Ayni at the mouth of the Khalij, and in 1867 a conduit to the Citadel was laid. Difficulties slowed the progress of the undertaking: by 1891 only 4,200 customers received home delivery of water, and for a considerable time Cairenes had to make do with a network of hydrants that replaced the traditional fountains. During the same years, excavation was completed on the Isma'iliyya Canal, which brought fresh water to the construction site of the Suez Canal (1864–1866) while preparing the areas bordering it for the city's expansion to the north and northwest between Qasr al-Nil, Bab al-Hadid, and Abbasiyya.[3]

But Isma'il's projects soon assumed a more grandiose cast. The pasha had considered modernizing his capital long before his trip to Paris, but it was unquestionably at the Universal Exposition of 1867 with its triumphant display of contemporary urban planning in the Haussmannian mode that prompted Isma'il to execute his plans and transform Cairo into a worthy rival of the great European capitals. During his visit he declared: "Over the past thirty years Europe's influence has transformed Cairo. Now . . . we are civilized." In Paris the khedive met Haussmann, toured his finished projects and work sites, and made contact with Pierre Grand, a civil engineer who was to direct Cairo's street service for many years, and also with Barillet-Deschamps, who created the Bois de Boulogne in Paris and would design the Azbakiyya Garden. At the inauguration of the Suez Canal in 1869, an event of international importance, representatives from all over the world would be congregating in Egypt and would find a modern country and a modern capital there. Time was therefore very short. Transforming the old city was out of the question; neither the time nor the means were available. A European-style facade would instead be tacked onto the western edge of the old city to impress the expected influx of European dignitaries. Thus were the nature and limits of Isma'il's enterprise defined.

In undertaking such an ambitious program Isma'il was fortunate to have the services of one of the most remarkable figures in modern Egyptian history. Born in 1824 in Lower Egypt into a family of modest means, raised as a traditional Islamic scholar, then admitted to the polytechnic institute and sent to Paris to study engineering, and finally recalled to Egypt in 1849, Ali Pasha Mubarak embarked on a career as an engineer, civil servant, and officer in the engineering corps. Isma'il first appointed him undersecretary of state, then minister of education and minister of public works (in 1868), two posts he would hold simultaneously until 1870. His work as an educational reformer was considerable. He was also a remarkable historian. But we are concerned with him here as the man entrusted by Isma'il with carrying out Cairo's program of modernization and also with making preparations for the celebrations hosted by the khedive on the occasion of the inauguration of the Suez Canal.[4]

The text of a law drafted by Ali Mubarak, though never officially promulgated, supplies the general outline of Isma'il's urban projects—it was discovered and studied by Ghislaine Alleaume. The law of 8 July 1868 reorganized municipal government and divided the city into new administrative units. Paying closer attention to Cairo's historic and natural boundaries, Ali Mubarak divided the city into four administrative districts (aqsam; sing. qism), each of which included two of the eight athman created by Muhammad Ali (Bab al-Sha'riyya and Azbakiyya, Darb al-Ahmar and Jamaliyya, Khalifa and Qusun, Abdin and Darb al-Jamamiz). The suburbs were assigned to four administrative districts: Old Cairo, Bulaq, Shubra, and Wayli. The importance thus given to the suburbs—the northern suburbs in particular—is significant, since it was in these "extramural" areas that most of the city's expansion would occur under Isma'il.

The redistricting also officially underscored Cairo's unification with Old Cairo and Bulaq, which until then had been separate entities. A department of urban planning was created in each qism under the direction of a head engineer for the district. Its function was to oversee construction, mapping projects, and compliance with the rules of the Tanzim, "given that the urban projects expected to be realized in Cairo are numerous and extensive and that the three persons presently assigned to this duty are inadequate to it" (article 2). An appendix to the draft law drew up a chart of the personnel needed to execute and direct the anticipated projects: thirty-nine people, including an inspector for the Tanzim, a chief engineer, eight engineers, and ten designers. The law made provisions to begin the mapping of the city: the engineers of each *qism* would draw "maps of all the streets and alleys in their districts, so that the Ministry of Public Works can then redraw street alignment appropriately, according to the size of each street and the amount of traffic it bears" (article 4).

This project was a necessary preamble to the map of Cairo that Pierre Grand would draw up in 1874. It also would allow the Tanzim to prepare the great street cuts being planned throughout the city. Construction standards would be maintained by the corporation of builders acting in a supervisory role to ensure "a respect of technical considerations, solidity, comfort, and beauty." Every contract relating to street construction would have to be registered with the Ministry of Public Works, which would henceforth have full responsibility in matters of urban planning, while the municipal police (Zabtiyya) was relegated to a minor role. As article 6 stipulated: "In order for the operations of the Tanzim to proceed smoothly and effectively according to a single model throughout the country, it is necessary for all personnel associated with it to come under the authority of the Ministry of Public Works." Ali Pasha Mubarak thus defined a coherent policy to centralize the administration on behalf of the reformist government, a policy that also gave technicians (engineers such as himself) control over the process of urban renovation.[5]

The new plan was directly inspired by the Haussmannian model: a network of straightened, widened thoroughfares would connect a dozen squares (maydans), and New Street would be extended to the desert east of Cairo. But owing to lack of time and money, construction was limited chiefly to a vacant zone northwest of the old city between the road to Bulaq, Bab al-Luq, the road to Old Cairo (present-day Qasr al-Ayni Street), and the bank of the Nile, comprising an area of some 250 hectares. This sector would give the city a facade of urban respectability, while the old city remained largely unaltered.[6] The Isma'iliyya quarter was established rapidly because the land had been prepared by Ibrahim and no lengthy process of acquiring and demolishing existing structures was necessary. Once the streets and sidewalks had been demarcated, the khedive offered the land free of charge to anyone who would build a structure worth at least 2,000 Egyptian pounds. The area actually developed in the Isma'iliyya quarter in 1874 measured 104 hectares, with streets accounting for 30 percent of that area, and buildings for 13 percent. The vast gardens that composed the remainder provided a reserve of land for subsequent development. By the end of Isma'il's reign, only a few hundred buildings had yet been erected, but the structure of the district had been laid out, and the maps of the day (Pierre Grand's in particular) show the location of the great arteries of the future: Qasr al-Nil, Sulayman Pasha, and Qasr al-Ayni Streets.[7]

Just as spectacular was the transformation of the Azbakiyya into a garden, in a district where the urban tissue of the old city and the modern street system met. Perhaps it was intended as the new center of the city—the placement of the opera house in that district (it was built hastily on the model of La Scala in Milan for the inaugural celebration of the Suez Canal, in time for a performance of *Rigoletto* on 1 November 1869) tends to confirm it. Barillet-Deschamps arrived from France to transform Azbakiyya Square into an English-style garden on the model of the Parc Monceau, with small lakes, grottoes, and bridges. Inaugurated in 1872 with the khedive in attendance, the Azbakiyya Garden offered the public various amenities: shops, a photographer's studio, a tobacco stand, a shooting gallery, restaurants and cafés (European, Oriental, and Greek), a Chinese pavilion, and pedal boats. According to Doris Behrens-Abouseif, "Every day a khedival orchestra of Turkish and European musicians played military music. In various settings, native or European music was played, as appropriate. The Egyptian public had no taste for European music performed in European-style cafés, preferring Eastern cafés where Arab music played all night." To facilitate access to Jazira and the west bank of the Nile, an iron bridge was built in 1869 between the river's eastern shore at Qasr al-Nil and the southern tip of Jazira, though not in time for the Empress Eugénie to use it in reaching her Cairo quarters, the riverside palace on Jazira, today's Hotel Umar Khayyam. Barillet-Deschamps drew up plans for a great park on Jazira, the subsequent site of the Gezira Sporting Club, and planted shade trees along the good road that now led from Giza to the pyramids.[8]

The year 1869 marked the apogee of Isma'il's reign. Thereafter the pace of his urban projects declined as Egypt started to experience financial difficulties due, on the one hand, to reversals in the economic climate and, on the other, to the khedive's profligate spending,

Muhammad Ali Boulevard

exacerbated by the unscrupulousness of European financiers and entrepreneurs. Large-scale public works were nonetheless undertaken. Work began in 1872 on Clot Bey Street, which connected the railway station and Azbakiyya. Work on its extension, Muhammad Ali Boulevard, connecting Azbakiyya and the Citadel, started after 1873. This incision into the old city ran a straight course for 2 kilometers and entailed the demolition of 700 dwellings and a variety of other buildings, including historical monuments such as the Qusun Mosque, which suffered irreparable damage. The wide roadway was bordered by sidewalks and shaded in some parts by trees and in others by arcades. Gaslights were installed along the entire length of the road, which was swept three times a day. But behind the avenue's handsome facades, the old city remained unchanged, with its increasingly leprous houses and poorly maintained streets. To the west, the modern city was growing. Abdin Palace was completed in 1874, an enormous horseshoe-shaped structure in the European style, whose presence encouraged the major administrative bodies to establish quarters in this part of town.

Isma'il's great public works were coming to an end. Egypt's insolvency and its progressive subordination to foreign powers first slowed their pace, then put an end to them altogether. Ruinous loans contracted in Europe (starting in 1862) forced Egypt into bankruptcy. When Isma'il sold his shares of the Suez Canal to the British government in 1875, Britain realized a splendid financial coup and a good political investment besides. In 1876, an international commission of financial control was appointed. In 1878 a British minister of finances and a French minister of public works were named to the Egyptian cabinet. A last attempt at resistance proved fatal to the khedive: in 1879 Great Britain and France pressured the sultan to depose him. It was his son Tawfiq (1879–1892) who was in power at the time of Colonel Urabi's nationalist rebellion and the entry of British troops into Cairo. The "temporary" British occupation of Egypt was to last until 1954.

Despite this final disaster and the incomplete state in which Isma'il left his urban undertakings, the khedive's public schemes had shaken up Cairo's development and anticipated many of the changes that English colonization would no doubt have brought. A new Cairo was born during this fertile decade and a half. After a long period of demographic stagnation, Cairo's population began to grow rapidly; according to Justin McCarthy's estimates, the population increased from 305,000 in 1863 to 374,000 in 1882, 19,000 of whom were foreigners. The area of the city, which had hardly changed from 1798 to 1863, more than doubled, reaching 1,260 hectares in 1882. The combined length of its streets quadrupled, from 58 to 208 kilometers. Essential elements of modernization, municipal water and street-lighting, had been introduced. The development of the northern suburbs (Shubra, Wayli) prepared the way for the future, but the expansion westward was particularly impressive—the new quarter of Isma'iliyya, the future center of Cairo, had been sketched out as well as its streets, which remain in active use to this day: Qasr al-Nil (1,250 meters), Imad al-Din (1,720 meters), Falaki (1,260 meters), Sulayman Pasha, and Qasr al-Ayni Streets.

As important as the quantitative progress was the deep qualitative change that occurred when Isma'il laid out his new districts, a change reinforced during the colonial period. Henceforth there would be two Cairos side by side. Cairo's old city had undergone great transformations. Its former open spaces had been put to new uses, either subdivided (Birkat al-Fil) or transformed (Azbakiyya), and thoroughfares had been built through its ancient quarters. But these changes had not profoundly altered the physical structure of the old city. A new city, however, organized along European lines and marked by a massive foreign presence, had sprung to life on the west. Profound inequalities appeared between the old and new quarters: in 1872 Azbakiyya paid 33 percent of the city's taxes, and Darb al-Ahmar 2.7 percent. This pattern was common in colonial cities of the nineteenth and twentieth centuries. In Cairo, though, colonialism made its appearance within the city's urban structures even before Egypt succumbed to colonial rule. Divided into old and new even before 1882, the city aptly fitted the description applied to it when Muhammad Ali Boulevard was first built: "Cairo is like a cracked vase whose two halves can never be put back together."[9]

## THE COLONIAL CITY (1882–1936)

Britain's occupation of Egypt in 1882 was initially intended to be temporary but developed into a durable arrangement. It officially ended in 1936, the date of a treaty recognizing Egypt's independence and its entry into the League of Nations. Yet because of the agreements signed and, not long after, because of the war Britain maintained a military presence there. It was only in 1954, when an agreement to evacuate British troops was reached, that Egypt's independence truly came into effect.

During this half-century Egypt, now virtually independent from Turkey (its increasingly tenuous links to the Ottoman Empire were finally severed in 1914), was implicitly subject to colonial rule. This reality became official with the declaration of a British protectorate over Egypt at the start of World War I. From 1882 on, however, all power was effectively in the hands of the British consul-general, Lord Cromer, who was omnipotent in the exercise of his functions from 1883 to 1907. Even after 1918, when the political landscape was altered by the birth of the nationalist movement, it was generally the British representative whose will prevailed in the three-cornered contest between himself, the king, and the Wafd nationalist movement. It was also British advisers and technicians who governed the country, especially after 1904, when, in the context of the global game of imperialism, France left Britain a free hand in Egypt. In his

*Cairo Memories,* Magdi Wahba remembers the displays of British pomp:

> First there was the changing of the guard outside the British Resi-
> dence; then, through the cast-iron doors pricked in gold with the
> monogram of Victoria Regina, the high commissioner's black Rolls
> Royce slowly emerged. On either side of the car as it slowly ad-
> vanced rode a detachment of the King's Horse . . . The procession,
> led by officers of the Egyptian mounted police, continued as far as
> the small cathedral of Saint Mary . . . where Bishop Gwynne of
> Cairo and Khartoum . . . waited in a chasuble and alb to receive the
> high commissioner . . . It was a world of ceremony complete unto it-
> self, and the patriotic convictions served up in Bishop Gwynne's ser-
> mons inspired the congregation with a feeling of the everlastingness
> and certainty of fate.[10]

The most striking phenomenon during this half-century, and the most consequential for the future, was naturally the rapid growth of Cairo's population, which increased from 374,000 in 1882 to 1,312,000 in 1937, an increase of 250 percent over fifty years, when the increase during the previous eighty-four years had been only 26 percent. This still represented a relatively moderate rate of popula-tion growth. As the country had until then been underpopulated, growth undoubtedly contributed to its development—the increase in Egypt's population boosted the country's power in the region (Egypt played a dominant role in the Arab League, created in 1945) and added to its prestige. It was after 1936 that demographic growth would become a burden, and one increasingly difficult to handle.

From 1882 to 1917 the population of Cairo increased at about the same rate as Egypt's as a whole. Throughout this period Cairo's popu-lation stayed at about 6 percent of the country's total: 5.5 percent in 1882, 5.9 percent in 1897, 5.8 percent in 1907, 6.2 percent in 1917 (791,000 Cairenes, of a total 12.7 million Egyptians). During these years Egypt's agricultural production increased at an average rate of 1.6 percent per year, faster than the population growth. Among the factors that favored an increase in average agricultural revenues (30 Egyptian pounds per year around 1914) were the large-scale public works undertaken in the Nile Valley (repair of the delta dams, construction of the first Aswan dam in 1902), the spread of perennial irrigation, and the growth of cotton farming. The relative agricultural prosperity explains why emigration from the country to the city remained fairly light. During World War I, however, Cairo's population began to increase at a rate faster than that of the country as a whole. With 1,060,000 residents in 1927 and 1,312,000 in 1937, Cairo represented 7.5 percent and 8.2 percent, respectively, of the Egyptian population (totaling 14.2 million, then 15.9 million inhabitants).

This accelerated trend toward urbanization affected all of Egypt. It was clearly linked to the slowing down of agricultural production, whose annual increase (0.4 percent per year in 1914–1947) was significantly below the annual increase in population. Consequently, average agricultural revenues declined—in 1947 they stood at only 26 Egyptian pounds. Rural overpopulation became more marked, causing a powerful tide of emigration to urban areas. Egypt's urban population represented 17 percent of its total population in 1897, 19 percent in 1907, 20.9 percent in 1917, and 26.1 percent in 1927. The upsurge in the population of Cairo accounted for more than half of this immigration: in 1927, of slightly more than one million Cairenes, only 614,000 had actually been born in Cairo. At the same time, improvements in Cairo's sanitary conditions brought about a rapid decline in the mortality rate and a corresponding rise in the rate of natural increase (from 0.7 percent to 1.2 percent per year in 1917–1927, according to Janet Abu-Lughod). The swelling population of Cairo was due less to the attraction of the city, where industrialization was proceeding at a relatively slow pace (despite the great progress made during the war), than to the overpopulation of the countryside, of which Cairo more than any other urban area absorbed the overflow. All the elements of the crisis we are witnessing today were beginning to come into play.[11]

In the midst of this overall increase there were also a large number of foreigners living in the country, Europeans in particular, whose influx into Egypt, encouraged by the presence of British rule, was spectacular: 68,653 foreigners in 1878, 151,414 in 1907. In 1927 there were 76,173 foreigners in Cairo, of whom 59,460 belonged to the four main foreign colonies (18,289 in 1882). In the years 1882–1927 the British presence had increased tenfold (to 11,221 in 1927) and now surpassed the French (9,549). But the largest colonies belonged to the Greeks (20,115) and the Italians (18,575). The various colonies were quite diverse. The Italians, Magdi Wahba observed, experienced their golden age in 1930, "with a class structure that extended from a quasi-proletariat of garage mechanics and chambermaids to an intellectual aristocracy centered around the Mixed Tribunals, Vittorio Emmanuele Hospital, and the very rich architects, builders, and bankers."[12] In the 1930s the Fascists tried to organize the community through sports clubs, retirement homes, and vacation camps in Italy. The politicization of the Italian colony brought about its downfall in 1940. The Greeks, like the Italians, formed a stratified community, but one that had neither the brilliance nor the opulence of the Greek community in Alexandria. It was an introverted enclave: "The Greek newspapers of Cairo were like parish bulletins, full of local news and obituaries." The French-speaking community extended well beyond the bounds of the French colony: the circle of the Mixed Tribunals, the banks, the Catholic missions, Fouad University, the royal family ("with the exception of King Fouad himself, who preferred Italian"), the Egyptian plutocrats, the department stores, the Suez Canal, the press, "young girls . . who wished to make a brilliant match, those who frequented tea rooms and restaurants, the nascent movie industry, the legal profession, first-class bordellos, hotels, tramline and subway conductors, scientific societies, the department of antiquities, and naturally the French community itself were all francophone." The British also formed a self-contained community, one that was largely professional and middle-class:

> Cultural centers, fashionable lecture series, touring reviews of brash French music-hall artistes were not for them. Their pleasures were simpler: gardening in Maadi and Zamalek, flower shows, traveling libraries, antiquities, amateur theater (crowned every year by a production of Gilbert and Sullivan at the opera), and polo at the Gezira Sporting Club, in which officers of the cavalry regiments quartered at the Qasr al-Nil barracks participated.

The foreigners formed a whole exotic world with more or less durable ties to Egypt (more in the case of the Greeks, less in the case of the British), ties that fell away during a series of crises: in 1936 (independence), 1939 (World War II), 1948 (Palestinian war), 1952 (Cairo fire and revolution), 1956 (nationalization of the Suez Canal and Suez crisis).[13]

Such rapid demographic growth implied construction on a considerable scale, and in fact the building trades in Cairo between 1897 and 1907 experienced a boom comparable to the one Isma'il had provoked earlier. During that decade "the value of the cotton crop doubled, Europeans invested as much money in Egyptian companies as they had once lent to Isma'il, while the number of foreigners living in Cairo rose from 35,385 to 55,987." The demand for land was so great that land values soared to astronomical levels. The *Egyptian Gazette* reported on 7 March 1906 that "a property of 7,000 square meters in the Isma'iliyya neighborhood . . . bought by Mrs. Fink from Abd al-Qadir Pasha seven years ago for 14,000 pounds was sold by her to Osman Bey Sharif for 42,000 pounds." Several weeks later the *Gazette* reported that the property had been sold again, this time for 103,000 pounds. The peak was reached in 1907 and 1908, when, respectively, 3,164 and 3,444 building permits were issued, as compared to 1,071 in 1879 and 1,834 in 1882. In 1907 there were 21,744 construction workers in Cairo (of 94,898 in all of Egypt), triple the number in Alexandria.[14]

Urban projects executed within and around Cairo (the filling of the last ponds, the leveling of hills) increased the absorption capacity of the old city, whose quarters were able to take in an important number of the new arrivals. The population of the Jamaliyya quarter increased by 44,788 between 1882 and 1927, and Darb al-Ahmar's by 52,544 in the same period. But the old quarters were approaching their saturation limit, and hundreds of thousands of new Cairenes turned to the western and northern districts for open space to settle on.

Cairo's built-up area thus increased from some 1,000 hectares in 1882 to 16,331 in 1937. The search for new land encountered a variety of obstacles. To the west, the river posed a barrier that could be surmounted only with difficulty, and the size of its annual flood made riverine land inhospitable. Open areas to the north and northeast were too far from the center of the city, and the lack of water hindered urban development. These various problems were resolved, however, during the years 1897–1917, and a "second city of Cairo," to

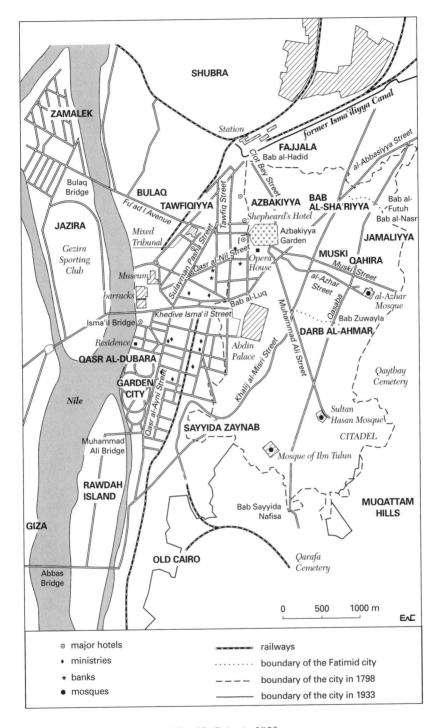

Map 12. Cairo in 1933

323

use the expression of the geographer Pierre Marthelot, saw the light of day.

A modern mass transit system was established between 1894 and 1917. In December 1894 Baron Empain (who later achieved fame as the founder of the modern suburb of Heliopolis) obtained the concession to provide Cairo with a tramway system. The necessary capital was raised in Europe, where the Egyptian market was considered attractive. The original agreement called for the building of eight lines, six of which were to start from Ataba al-Khadra Square at the southeast corner of the Azbakiyya Garden. Within two years, 22 kilometers of tramlines had been laid. The center of Cairo was thus linked to Muhammad Ali Square (the former Qaramaydan), to Qasr al-Ayni and Old Cairo, to Bab al-Luq and Nasiriyya, to Bab al-Hadid, to Bulaq, to Fajjala and Abbasiyya. This first network was overlaid onto Isma'il's planned city, and the old city remained outside the network except along the opening made into it by Muhammad Ali Boulevard. The company's concession was then extended to new lines, and in 1917 Cairo had thirty tramlines connecting to points within the city (in 1900, Line No. 10 was inaugurated, joining Maydan Zahir to Sayyida Zaynab along the course of the old Khalij, which had by then been filled) as well as to distant points (Rawd al-Faraj, Athar al-Nabi, Heliopolis), with extensions across the Nile (Imbaba, Giza, the pyramids). These 65 kilometers of tramlines, which constituted Cairo's quasi-definitive tram system (only two more lines were added in 1931), put the city's center a mere hour away from its furthest extremities and, in 1917, carried 75 million passengers per year.

The arrival of automobiles in 1903 accelerated the transformation of the city's street system. Some streets were macadamized even before 1882. The surface area of hard-topped streets went from 30,600 square meters in 1882 to 1,354,000 in 1900 and to 3,408,000 in 1927. But this modernization benefited mostly the new city, where modern wheeled traffic was in any case most common. The number of automobiles grew from 656 in 1914 to 24,136 in 1931. In the old city, the street system remained generally archaic, and only a few large arteries (Khalij and al-Azhar Streets) were introduced to improve what was obviously a deficient network and one unsuited to modern transport.

The Aswan Dam, built in 1902, answered a desire to increase

Early twentieth-century building at Sayyida Zaynab

Egyptian agricultural production by adding to its perennial cropland. In Cairo, control of the Nile's flood also meant the ability to stabilize the banks of the Nile on both shores and on the islands of Jazira and Rawdah so that new residential quarters could be built there. It also meant that bridges could now be constructed, allowing Cairo to extend westward. Three bridges, begun in 1902 and finished in 1907, now supplemented the bridge built by Isma'il in 1872 between Qasr al-Nil and Jazira; the Malik al-Salih Bridge between Old Cairo and Rawdah, the Muhammad Ali Bridge between Qasr al-Ayni and the north end of Rawdah, and the Abbas Bridge between Rawdah and Giza, which opened a southern route to the west shore. With the construction of the bridge between Bulaq and northern Jazira (1908–1912) and its extension toward Imbaba, there were now three routes to the west bank, two via Jazira and one via Rawdah. This system would stand unchanged until 1952, when the University Bridge was built between northern Rawdah and Giza. The filling of the Isma'iliyya canal in 1912 finally allowed expansion to proceed northward (Bulaq, Shubra, Rawd al-Faraj) and provided a main transportation axis to the northeast (Heliopolis).[15]

With the city growing rapidly, the needs of an ever-larger population had to be met. Streetlighting progressed rather slowly between 1882 and 1902, by which time only a quarter of Cairo's 400 kilometers of streets were lit. Starting in 1905, a push was made both to improve the quality of lighting (by adopting the Auer system) and to extend the area lit. In 1927 there were 9,986 gas lamps and 330 electric streetlights, three times as many as in 1902. But the network was still inadequate, and glaring inequalities remained between the "European" and "native" areas. Improvements were made to the municipal water system, which relied primarily on an intake point at Rawd al-Faraj, upstream from the city. Around 1927 some 50 million cubic meters of water were supplied to the city and its suburbs (compared to 7.8 million in 1882). Here again the old city received short shrift: only 225 hydrants in contrast to the 360 fountains that had existed during the Ottoman period. The problem of a drainage system, which was to pose such severe difficulties to the metropolis, was studied in 1882, but successive plans (notably by Ali Pasha Mubarak in 1882, Latham in 1890, and from an international competition in 1892) failed one after another, either for lack of funds or for want of endorsement by the Capitulatory Powers. Only in 1907 was a workable plan developed by the British sanitary engineer James Carkeet, who had previously worked in Bombay. He proposed to drain 281 hectares (the new districts to the northeast) by gravity and 2,321 hectares by means of compressed air generated by a plant near Qasr al-Nil. This efficient and relatively inexpensive plan was based on a study of Cairo's population and its water consumption. Despite some flaws, the system was installed and functioned in a relatively satisfactory manner. The first tier of the sewer system, inaugurated in 1915, consisted of more than 100 kilometers of collectors and ten ejection stations. Difficulties started to crop up in the 1960s, when the system, designed to cover the city's needs until 1932 (when its population reached one million), was required to serve more than 3 million inhabitants.[16]

Surprisingly, the city of Cairo lacked municipal status, something that Alexandria had been granted as early as 1890 because of the successful lobbying of its foreign communities, and that forty-three other Egyptian cities could claim by 1912. The capital received a municipal charter only in 1949. It was the Tanzim created under Muhammad Ali, a simple subsection of the Ministry of Public Works, strongly anglicized after 1882 and headed by Undersecretary of State Sir Scott-Moncrieff, that managed the affairs of the capital. The city's public services fell under five separate jurisdictions, coordinated by a High Council created in 1929. But the Tanzim had no discrete budget, and Cairo's maintenance depended on the generally slender allocations set aside for it in the national budget.

The absence of any coordination among the entities involved (Tanzim, ministers, and concessionaires) explains why it was not until the municipality *(baladiyya)* was created that an overall development plan could emerge, the first since Ali Pasha Mubarak. The fact that public utilities had been granted as concessions to foreign companies, usually for a very long duration (up to ninety-nine years), is undoubtedly one of the reasons for this situation, as well as the various favors and privileges granted to foreigners by the system of the Capitulations, both in the realm of law (the Mixed Tribunals) and in the realm of taxation. The Capitulations were abolished only in 1937 and the Mixed Tribunals in 1949. Under the circumstances, it is easy to understand deficiencies in legislation. Mercédès Volait describes one instance in which a proposal for a law was drawn up in 1907 on standard widths and clearances for streets,

> but it was not even submitted to the legislating authorities, so conscious was the administration that final approval depended on the

agreement of the Capitulatory Powers, in fact if not in law. And their agreement was highly unlikely, as it was common knowledge that the Powers were always slow to ratify any new laws that might affect their own nationals . . . Thus British officials on the Tanzim more than once found themselves in open conflict with the British occupying authorities over what, for their part, the authorities felt committed to guarantee: the preservation of the capitulatory privileges.

Politics outweighed practical considerations, and it was not until 1940 that standards on housing lots and construction practices could be passed into law. The difficulty was the same in obtaining legislation relating to the fabric of the old city, and here the *awqaf* presented an added obstacle. "Work could proceed only very slowly. An engineer on the Tanzim Council once calculated that given the level of allocations, 'Haussmannization' in Cairo would take 145 years."[17]

Technological improvements and the modern mass transit system gradually opened new areas to urban expansion. Until 1900, the city changed only slowly and largely conformed to the plans drawn up in Isma'il's time for the area bordering the old city. The zone to the west of Azbakiyya filled with commercial and financial buildings built on the sites not occupied by villas, with the consequence that the city's business center shifted to this area. Slightly to the south, government buildings and ministries were established east of Qasr al-Ayni Street, and this development was followed by the construction of residential buildings for the government functionaries employed there.

Development began in the districts of Fajjala and Tawfiqiyya, located between the old city and the Isma'iliyya Canal. The lands along the Nile, until then the site of princely residences, were opened to urban development. The establishment of the British Residence in the Qasr al-Dubara area was followed by the subdivision of the strip along the Nile into lots, and in 1906 the Garden City area came under construction, with its handsome residences set in the midst of gardens and its curved, English-style streets. The Baehler company bought the northern section of Jazira and divided it into parcels in 1905–1907—it was to become Cairo's other "chic" neighborhood, Zamalek, with beautiful villas (some of which survive to this day) built on a checkerboard plan. To the south, Rawdah was becoming populated, while settlement began to spread to the west shore of the Nile at Imbaba and Giza.

To Cairo's northeast, on the semidesert plateau extending beyond the Abbasiyya quarter, a large-scale enterprise resulted in the creation of a new town. Baron Empain, a Belgian businessman whose work we have noted in the context of public transportation, wanted to create a residential complex 10 kilometers north of Cairo, on a site that offered indisputable climatic advantages (perfect dryness, strong daily variation) but was totally without water and would need to be linked to the city center by modern rapid transit. The new town received the name of Heliopolis, though the ancient site of this name was in fact closer to the valley (Empain searched for traces of it unsuccessfully).[18] Given the shortage of living space in Cairo and the high price of land, the future oasis, "where rents would be cheap and the air pure," would attract "those who experience difficulty today in finding lodging in the capital."

The Heliopolis Oasis Company was formally founded on 14 February 1906, but already by 20 May 1905 Edouard Empain and Boghos Pasha had bought the lands and obtained the railway concession. The Egyptian government sold all rights to 5,952 feddans of desert (1 feddan = 4,000 square meters) at the very low price of one Egyptian pound per feddan. The terms of the agreement were quite strict, however: streets, buildings, and plantations could cover only one-sixth of the area sold (amended to one-quarter in 1907), and many conditions were imposed. But the buyers obtained for free, and for a period of sixty years, the concession to run an electric railway connecting the subcity to Cairo and two tramway lines. To the company's original 2,500 hectares a further 5,000 were added in 1910.

Baron Empain's initial plan was not to build a town but to subdivide and sell the land once improvements had been made. By 1909 the tramlines were in operation, and nearly 30 kilometers of streets, 10 kilometers of sewers, and 50 kilometers of water lines had been laid out. But the undertaking encountered a number of difficulties, including technological ones, and was battered by the crisis that struck Egypt in 1907. The company therefore found itself obliged to construct houses and buildings in order to rent them out. The operation started slowly: in 1910 there were only 1,000 residents in Heliopolis. Then the momentum picked up: 2,000 housing units

Street in Heliopolis

were built in fifteen years (1921), 2,000 more in seven years (1928), and another 2,300 in three years (1931).

By this time Baron Empain had won his bet. The number of residents in 1930 was 28,544 (on 3 million square meters of built-up land); in 1947 they numbered 50,000. In the meantime, the necessary infrastructure had been installed and was functioning in good order. The electric train, or "metro," and the tramways were carrying more than 10 million passengers per year by 1925. The company provided both public and private lighting. The water utility supplied 5,000–20,000 cubic meters of water per day, which also allowed for watering plantings. The company provided street cleaning and garbage removal; it even had a corps of five men assigned to combat mosquitoes. The company also helped establish places of worship (a cathedral, then mosques) and installed a hotel complex that, it was hoped, would make Heliopolis a center of rest and recreation. A racetrack was opened in 1910, and a sporting club with a golf course designed by a British specialist.

The design of Heliopolis derived from the European "garden city" of the late nineteenth and early twentieth centuries. The design called for two "oases" separated by an area of desert. One, more or less circular in plan, was to be a zone of villas, luxury apartments, and tourism and would also include the cathedral; the other was to contain the working-class city, including industrial installations and the mosque—a highly symbolic distribution of elements. Only the first oasis was executed, with middle-class quarters and a "popular" section. The network of streets evolved in a geometric fashion, but within a generally concentric overall plan. The idea of a "green city" was abandoned to answer the need for residential units, and the plan for a luxury oasis was scrapped as a popular quarter took shape. The circulation system centering on the cathedral square comprised streets that varied in width (from 10 or 11 meters for the streets between the housing clusters to 30 or 40 meters for the major arteries bordering the development and the grand avenues), a system that was clearly oversized to begin with, but one that proved able to absorb the increase in traffic.

The attention given to the plantings (silt was arriving from the Nile by donkeyback, then by truck, as early as 1906 and was spread over the sand so the company could have its nursery) and their maintenance gave Heliopolis an impressive covering of greenery. Regulations concerning buildings were very strict (unbuilt areas had to be maintained, height limits respected), and buildings had to conform to a hierarchy in keeping with the districts they were in. The company had defined four major types of construction: "garden cities" (small working-class apartment houses), bungalows, apartment buildings, and villas—all designed according to European standards and organization, although an effort was made on the more elaborate structures (palaces in particular) to create an exotic atmosphere. "It seems to have been successful," writes Robert Ilbert, the historian of Heliopolis. "Despite the mix of styles and the doubtful taste of some of the constructions, Heliopolis presents a unity that is deeper than what might derive from the rules of urban development. The recurrence in the decoration of pseudo-Muslim motifs (often borrowed from mosques) gives the city a certain charm . . . Heliopolis definitely has a style of its own."

Heliopolis had been designed for Europeans, the second oasis being intended for natives. But as new objectives developed, a less privileged class was targeted. In 1925 "Levantines"—a label that included Syrians, Lebanese, Palestinians, and Turks—outnumbered

Europeans by 5,000 to 3,000 (of a total 16,000 inhabitants), with Muslims in the majority. Ethnic and religious differences could be plotted on the map: "Each ethnic group tended to collect either around its place of worship . . . or around residential buildings corresponding to the social level of the group as a whole." Differentiation along social lines coincided with differentiation along ethnic and religious ones, and geographic distribution was governed by the economic resources of the various groups, which coincided with their origins. Ilbert notes: "It was because the Muslim workers were the least well-paid that they were obliged to live in a designated area of the city." Overall, the inhabitants of Heliopolis seem to have belonged to a well-to-do bourgeoisie of Europeans and Egyptians, midlevel functionaries, but there was also a poor population—in 1919 the company counted 3,600 illiterates among its 8,600 residents.

Heliopolis was of great interest as an experiment aimed at solving the problems Cairo was starting to face in housing its rapidly increasing population. It represents a prototype of the satellite city in the desert, of which Cairo would produce many examples (Nasr City and other New Cities). It also has a great deal to teach us about resolving the problems of a population that is highly diverse in religion, nationality, and socioeconomic level. Though a stronghold of minority groups, the town never experienced religious tensions.

Heliopolis also provides a case study of the problems that arose during the period of colonial rule. The venture does not seem to have yielded high returns for the European promoters, even though in the long run it proved a very marketable proposition; it seems to have succeeded largely because of the favorable terms of the original grant (extremely low land prices, cheap services). "The Heliopolis Company," writes Robert Ilbert, "though typically capitalist was not an exploitative operation. It found its capital largely abroad, and profits certainly returned there. But no scandalous draining of Egyptian funds seems to have occurred." In any case, the extent of housing for the poor illustrates a genuine philanthropic concern. The urban and architectural forms adopted and the preeminently social form of life suggest, finally, a spectrum of cultural models that it would be reductive to designate as manifestations of alienated colonialism. Heliopolis was obviously a colonial urban development, but Egypt profited from it: "Between 1920 and 1930, more than 20,000 people chose to live in this suburb of Cairo . . . The urban enterprise had succeeded. The capitalist enterprise as well."

Long a detached offshoot of Cairo, Heliopolis oriented the growth of the city toward the northeast until, around the middle of the century, the expanding urban fabric had filled in the enormous empty space originally separating them.

### THE TWO CITIES

In the colonial period the trend first manifest in Isma'il's urban projects of creating two cities side by side intensified. Before 1882, the dividing line separated a "traditional" sector from a "modern" one, but after Egypt's colonization the line marked a boundary between different nationalities, a harsher and more intolerable division. One could now speak of a "native" city and a "European" one, as in the large colonial towns of North Africa.

Two worlds that differed in every respect—even to the layout of their streets, which were anarchic to the east and regular to the west—faced each other across an invisible frontier running north and south from Bab al-Hadid to Azbakiyya, and from Abdin to Sayyida Zaynab. Foreigners turned modern Cairo into "the center of a capital from which Egyptians were excluded," wrote Ibrahim Farhi. "There was no visible limit between the Egyptian quarters and the others. We passed through the odor of deep-frying as you might pass through barbed wire to reach the smell of Greek bakeries and Swiss pastry shops."[19] The process of fusion that might still have been hoped for in Isma'il's time never occurred. On the contrary, the differences deepened, while the city's center moved inexorably west, where power, business activity, and wealth were accumulating, and where the urban signs of foreign rule were ostentatiously apparent.

Cairo's old city now covered only part of Ottoman Cairo, whose rectangle west of the broad avenue along the ancient bed of the Khalij had been somewhat encroached on by advancing modernism. Bulaq and Old Cairo belonged to this older sector. Pockets of modernity had been introduced into the old city: a few wide, straight thoroughfares cut into it; its open spaces (such as the Birkat al-Fil) had been subdivided, and modern buildings had been built there. Even today one finds traces of these constructions dating to the end of the nineteenth century and the beginning of the twentieth, and their Levantine-Baroque aspect is not without charm. But behind the alignments of European facades, the old fabric subsisted, growing ever more dilapidated.

While the "European" city developed, the old city, sacrificed to the modern city from the reign of Isma'il on, was more or less abandoned: its streets were neglected, cleaning was haphazard, water supply was only partial, and the sewers were poor or insufficient. The deterioration of these quarters was exacerbated by the rapid increase in population, whose density weighed heavily on the crumbling infrastructure and inadequate public services. Between 1882 and 1927 the population of the four districts that constituted the old city (Jamaliyya, Bab al-Sha'riyya, Muski, and Darb al-Ahmar) grew from 122,411 to 259,535, an increase of 112 percent. Bulaq had grown during the same period from 64,784 to 144,465 (an increase of 123 percent) and Old Cairo from 22,518 to 49,495 (an increase of 120 percent). But given the even more rapid growth of other parts of Cairo, in relative terms the eastern city declined markedly, and its resident population represented an ever-smaller share of Cairo's total population: 54.3 percent in 1897, 47 percent in 1917, and 34 percent in 1937.

This population was particularly poor. The more well-to-do had abandoned the old city, preferring to live in modern neighborhoods that had more amenities of every kind, and the old quarters were tending to become a refuge for the most downtrodden and recently arrived segments of the population. As the old city became more proletarian, its decline accelerated, as was evident in its increasingly shabby appearance and reduced business activity. Jacques Bercque and Mustafa al-Shakaa have described this process for Jamaliyya, a district that maintained its handicraft and business activities until around 1914, yet was progressively abandoned by its leading citizens and its merchants after the war: "Such was the case with the merchants from the Hadramaut, who . . . were obliged, one after another . . . to emigrate to more modern places." Coincident with the degradation of its economic functions the area grew increasingly overcrowded (2.8 persons per room), resulting in chronic unemployment: in 1947 there were 18,000 employed persons in a population of 100,000.

Municipal water supply was still precarious. A house often had to make do with no more than a well, which in some cases gave only brackish water. This tended to drive those who were concerned with their comforts to seek neighborhoods where the water and lighting utilities offered better service. There was still no electricity in the streets, which were lit by gaslights. The Water Company . . . had long ago placed a hydrant on the esplanade of Bayt al-Qadi . . . The water had to be purchased. From there . . . the water carrier went off to deliver the precious liquid to the ends of the blind alleys.[20]

Modern business activities had moved to the west and north. It was there, obviously, that the present and the future of the city were to be found. The western city seemed to converge on the two showiest symbols of foreign occupation, the barracks of the British army at Qasr al-Nil and the British Residence. Business was still centered in the city laid out by Isma'il: the villas had disappeared, replaced by large European-style buildings. The shops and department stores were there, along with the banks and main hotels (the famous Shepheard's Hotel among them, which was several times rebuilt but would disappear along with many other signs of Western influence during the great fire of 1952).

Inside a triangle bounded on one side by Qasr al-Nil Street, on another by Sulayman Pasha Street (a French officer in the service of Muhammad Ali, his statue was replaced after 1952 by a statue of Tal'at Harb, an Egyptian nationalist), and on a third by Fouad Street, one found

department stores, guarded by mustachioed Albanian porters with their "fustanellas" and high boots . . . Here French and English bookstores, tearooms and Parisian-style cafés (of which only Groppi's achieved international repute), were interspersed with clothing stores, milliners, art galleries, clubs for the rich, banks . . . Here Europeans, rich Egyptians, and Levantines of every class did their shopping, conducted business in their offices, and sipped coffee.[21]

It was there as well that the European population who controlled the levers of politics and economic power were concentrated. In sev-

Sulayman Pasha Square, renamed Talʿat Harb

eral neighborhoods the foreign (and particularly European) population was in the majority. In 1927, for instance, foreigners made up 62.3 percent of the Tawfiqiyya district. In the area as a whole, there were 23,524 foreigners from a total of 64,001 residents (37 percent). The governmental center was somewhat farther south, on Qasr al-Ayni Street, in a district where the streets were laid out along a grid, where most of the ministries and administrative buildings were sited, and behind which was Abdin Palace, the king's residence. To the west, between the Bridge of Ismaʿil and the northern tip of Rawdah, was the wealthy residential quarter of Garden City. The fashionable neighborhoods had crossed the Nile and become established in Zamalek, north of the parks, the racetrack, and the sports fields of the Gezira Sporting Club, which the English built to provide themselves physical pleasure as well as moral reassurance—ordinary Egyptians were accepted there only after a lengthy battle, which the British lost definitively only after World War II. After the 1952 revolution, those who remembered the Gezira Sporting Club of an earlier era still experienced a sharp pang of regret for the days when they had had it "all to themselves." Rawdah, farther to the south, and Giza, farther to the west, had residences of a distinctly upper-middle-class character. Imbaba still had the "popular" and rural aspect that it would keep for a long time to come, after having been caught in the trap of urban expansion. The western city, a business and residential district, in 1937 had a population of only 350,000, despite the importance of its role, equivalent to 26.7 percent of Cairo's total population, a proportion that had hardly changed since the beginning of the century.

Around Cairo, the city was beginning to develop in every direction, initiating the expansion that was to follow:

> To the south, Maadi offered a simulacrum of the suburbs of London or of an Indian hill-station, somewhat flattened. To the north, at the edge of Shubra, where Mohammad Aly had built a palace, the tentacles of a shantytown were spreading—hideously filthy, devoid of sanitary installations, with little electricity, fewer drains, and few distractions except the annual visit of an Algerian circus, sponsored by Farouk, ruler of Upper Egypt, and his four young and beautiful sisters. To the east extended the City of the Dead, silent and desolate.[22]

Within this poorly organized expansion, a new city was all the same taking shape north of Cairo, one that was strongly influenced to the west by the industrial development occurring in Bulaq and Shubra, while to the east Heliopolis was establishing itself as a residential city for the well-to-do bourgeoisie and the middle class, with a strong component of Egyptian minority groups. The two districts of Shubra and Wayli, which counted 30,731 residents in 1882, had increased to 272,626 in 1927. The northern sector's share in Cairo's total population had been growing with impressive regularity: 12.9 percent in 1897, 21.5 percent in 1917, 34 percent in 1937. In 1937 the northern sector had a population of 450,000, greater than that of the eastern city and much greater than that of the western city. Advances in transportation had made it possible for urbanized areas still at a distance from Cairo (the southern suburbs of Ma'adi and Hilwan) to grow considerably, though they as yet had only a relatively limited population.

This "exploded" city reflected a divided society, a colonized nation. Wherever one looked there was evidence of the primacy of foreigners—ensconced in their business districts from where they controlled the country's economy, sheltered in their residential neighborhoods where the Egyptian elite also lived. The dilemma facing Egyptians was clear: either to resign themselves to the slow asphyxiation of the old quarters or to accept assimilation into a way of life brought to them from outside, symbolized by the increasing dominance of Western-style buildings, whose spread coincided with the new form of urban development.

The use of Arab decorative motifs and the construction of buildings in the neo-Moorish style represented, between 1870 and 1930, a final effort to preserve a certain authenticity, readily apparent in Heliopolis. But the "Arab style" tended to retreat quickly to decoration. Attempts to design apartment houses with *mashrabiyya* windows failed:

> The reason for this is clear. The building model was so absolutely dominant that there was no possibility for accommodation: these designs introduced a further and intolerable segregation, despite the undoubted good faith of their promoters. Moreover, they inevitably suggested a veneer, as the building was identical on the outside with all the others, except for the balconies, which were crowned with turned wood.

Interior layout itself, beginning in the second half of the nineteenth century, was organized along Western lines, with the accent on entertaining: bedrooms, kitchens, bathrooms, and living rooms. Cairo had become, for better or worse, an outpost of Western architecture.[23]

# 16

# The Nightmares of Growth
# (1936–1992)

THE YEAR 1936 marks a political event that had only limited significance in the history of Egypt: the signing of the Anglo-Egyptian treaty failed to put an end either to British dominance, which lasted until the officers' revolution of 1952, or to British military occupation, whose final vestiges were swept away only in 1956.

For Cairo, however, the period that began in 1936 was truly a new era. The capital's existence and fate would henceforth be governed by a suddenly changed demographic evolution. Until 1937, Cairo's population grew at an annual rate of 1.5–2 percent (1897–1907: 1.4 percent; 1927–1937: 2.2 percent). In the decades following 1937, the annual rate of growth increased to almost 4 percent, after spiking at 4.8 percent in 1937–1947. The population of Cairo, which had doubled in 1882–1914 (thirty-two years) and again in 1917–1942 (twenty-five years), more than doubled in 1947–1966 (only nineteen years). As a consequence of this forward demographic leap, which far exceeded the growth rate of Egypt as a whole, Cairo's share of Egypt's population, which had risen slowly from 6 percent to 8.2 percent (in 1937), reached 12.2 percent in 1947 and 18.2 percent in 1976, declining to 17.1 percent in 1986. The subsequent decline in the rate of increase only slightly reduces a very rapid scale of growth, the effects of which will be acutely felt in the long term. This formidable population surge is giving birth to a "third city of Cairo," a metropolis that is the first city of Africa and one of the largest in the world, but with specifically Egyptian characteristics.[1]

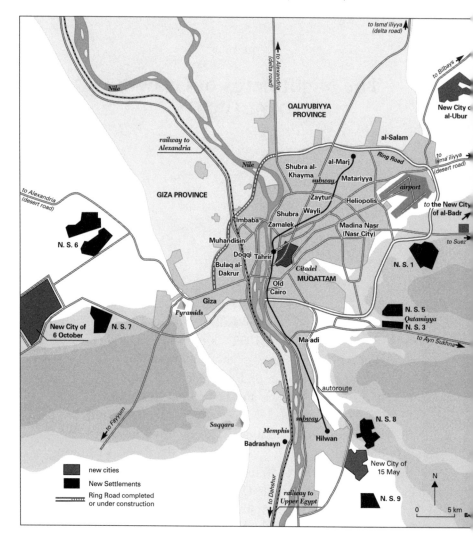

Map 13. Greater Cairo (1991) (after Berthet and Belliot) [may not be included]

## GALLOPING POPULATION GROWTH AND EXPANSION

All of Egypt was affected by what Simonne and Jean Lacouture have aptly described as "galloping population growth." Egypt's population went from 15.9 million in 1937 to 30.07 million in 1966, virtually doubling in twenty-nine years, then reached an estimated 57 million in 1990, doubling again. Egypt's population grew at a rate of 1.8 percent for the period 1937–1947 (1.2 percent in 1927–1937), subsequently rising to 2.3 percent, and then to 2.5 percent in 1976–1986. But the urban population, and Cairo's in particular, increased even faster, reaching almost 4 percent between 1937 and 1966.

This accelerated rate of growth is the result of two factors, whose effects have combined and reinforced each other: natural increase and rural-to-urban migration. The natural rate of increase of Cairo's population was for a long time moderate, but it has caught up with the national rate and remained very high because the lower birth rate common in urban areas was offset by a decline in death rates as a result of improvements in the city's sanitary conditions. The figures for birth and death rates in Cairo are, respectively, 4.31 and 1.59 percent in 1960–1965 (a growth rate of 2.72 percent) and 3.25 and 0.88 percent in 1980–1985 (a growth rate of 2.37 percent). The fact that Cairo's population is therefore getting younger indicates that the rate of natural increase will remain high, and a concerted effort will be needed to meet enormous future needs in education, jobs, and housing. Cairo's growth cannot be stopped by putting limits on internal migration; the phenomenon must be accepted as a long-term given, even if the rate of growth slows in the years to come, as trends appear to indicate.[2]

The second factor is a powerful current of urban migration, which has carried an ever-growing stream of rural residents into Egypt's cities, and to Cairo in particular. The phenomenon is a result of Egypt's strong demographic growth, which has far outstripped the increase in available resources and has created an almost explosive pressure in rural areas, where joblessness is rampant. Urbanization is a nationwide phenomenon: the urban population accounted for 27.4 percent of the overall population in 1937, 38 percent in 1960, and 43.9 percent in 1986. Cairo has been most affected by this trend; during the years when urban migration was at its most intense, 1960–

1966, it absorbed 80 percent of all migration within Egypt. It was estimated at the time that more than one-third of the capital's residents had been born elsewhere. Other reasons for the immigration were the attraction of the capital, the expectation of better living conditions there, and, especially during Nasser's tenure, a vigorous policy of industrialization, which created new jobs. Most of these immigrants to the city had little education (45.6 percent were illiterate), few professional qualifications (42.6 percent were unskilled laborers), and earned a meager income. Their arrival in Cairo thus exacerbated the city's problems.

THE SIZE OF THE PROBLEM explains the fantasies to which this "invasion" of Cairo gave rise. In 1985 the governor of Cairo estimated the city's population at 11.5 million, on the basis of catastrophic estimates (the population was in fact "only" 8.6 million in 1986). In consequence he proposed banning all immigration to the city, issuing ration cards that would go only to "native" Cairenes, allowing only the children of "residents" to attend schools, and so on. These notions triggered a controversy in the press on the theme of Cairo as a "closed city." The establishment of a pass system, a Cairene nationality, a uniform (or armband) to identify "aboriginal" residents were among the prospects evoked with great hilarity by Cairo's journalists.[3]

Yet urban migration was already declining markedly. The annual number of internal migrants decreased from 40,000 to 23,000 in 1986, representing just 10 percent of Cairo's annual increase (in contrast to 22 percent for 1960–1975). According to the 1976 census, 73 percent of Cairo's residents had been born in the city, and only 10 percent came from rural areas. The trend of Egyptian emigration to other Arab countries (Libya, Saudi Arabia, the Gulf emirates, and Iraq), estimated at 2.5 million—a trend that is all the more remarkable given the reputation of Egyptians for abhorring expatriation in any form—has helped alleviate internal population pressures. Emigration has also brought a considerable influx of foreign currency, the sum of transfers by private entities reaching an estimated U.S. $3.7 billion in 1990, and this infusion has helped development, particularly in the areas of real estate and light industry. Furthermore, the signing of a peace agreement with Israel has allowed Egyptians to return to the cities along the Suez Canal. However, the Gulf crisis in 1991 caused massive numbers of Egyptian emigrants to return, threatening to create severe problems in the future. Internal migration to Cairo, though dramatically lower than twenty years before, has remained an important factor in the growth of the city's population.

It is easy to imagine that the departure of a few thousand foreigners in the wake of the 1952 revolution, the Suez Canal crisis of 1956, and the campaign of nationalization launched by the Nasser government after 1960 would have gone more or less unnoticed. Yet among these foreigners were an important number of high-level experts and specialists, as well as minor technicians, whose departure impoverished Egypt. On a social and political level, however, their departure helped restore Egypt's capital to the Egyptians, just as Nasser's policies, whatever their shortcomings, restored the nation as a whole to the Egyptians and brought about a social and economic shift that altered Cairo's physiognomy.

To absorb so much population growth (an added 200,000 residents a year on average in 1976–1986, and 270,000 in 1990 for greater Cairo), Cairo was obliged both to expand and to increase its density. Today the city extends 65 kilometers from the west (6 October City) to the east (Badr City) and 34 kilometers from the north (Shubra) to the south (Hilwan). Its built-up area covers 20,791 hectares—or even 32,000 hectares according to some assessments. At its leading edge, the city has pushed into areas previously devoted to agriculture, a fact of great concern to Cairo's urban planners during the 1970s and 1980s, who watched with alarm the rapid rate at which concrete was invading the productive land of the Nile delta and were anxious to direct the expansion toward desert lands. According to the urban planner Galila El Kadi, 8,900 hectares of farmland were lost to development between 1945 and 1982. The phenomenon seems to have slowed, and at its current rate of 150–200 hectares per year—rather than the 590 hectares sometimes reported—it seems to cause the planners less anguish. But the urban Moloch has devoured agricultural land in a different way: red brick, used particularly for unlicensed construction, is made by stripping the clay layer from the soil and also consumes agricultural land. From 1972 to 1982, 7,140 hectares of farmland were made infertile in this way. Recent measures have prohibited the manufacture of red brick, but the fact that brick factories still operate on the outskirts of Cairo seems to indicate that the problem has not really been solved.

The transformation of funerary complexes into permanent habitations is another facet of Cairo's unstoppable expansion. The phenomenon—not a recent one, as it happens (there were already 51,675 residents in these districts in 1937)—provoked lively interest in the 1960s, when occupation progressed to the tombs (traditionally complexes with several rooms and a courtyard), and clusters of dwellings sprang up on vacant lots. In a recent study, El Kadi estimated the 1986 population of Cairo's cemeteries at 179,000, a figure considerably lower than the one sometimes suggested. Most of the residents (87 percent) are individuals who have been pushed out of Cairo's old city because of overpopulation and the deplorable living conditions there. Generally they are poor and have little education (64 percent are illiterate), but 73 percent of residents sixteen and older (a higher number than in the city) pursue a wide variety of occupations: undertakers and *waqf* functionaries, of course (the *waqfs* control the cemeteries), but also artisans, small merchants, civil servants, and so on.

The capital has been able to grow only at the cost of near saturation, with density reaching extraordinary proportions in certain old quarters: 2,280 residents per hectare in the al-Utuf quarter. The same number of people in the Paris metropolitan area would occupy an area three times as great. Such a concentration is possible only because the living units are overcrowded: the average number of persons per room was 2.3 in 1960; 20 percent of households lived in a single room in 1976, and it was common for several families to share one living unit. Increased density has been made possible by the addition of extra floors to existing buildings and the profusion of precarious structures on rooftops. This time-honored practice accelerated so much in the 1970s that it came to the notice of the press. According to a report in *al-Ahram* in 1980, 290 new instances of added floors were counted in the eastern section of the city within the space of three months and 272 in Madinat Nasr (Nasr City). That same year, a colloquium was held to discuss a phenomenon that was cropping up more and more frequently in the news: in July 1980 a six-story building collapsed in Siufi (the building permit had been granted for only four floors, and the materials had not met specifications); in Sharabiyya, forty people were dug out from under a building that had been raised an extra three stories without a permit. "Housing authorities readily admit that they have to condone the raising of extra floors, since it is cheaper—and simpler—than building from the ground up." Few cases of illegal construction resulted in demolition; as G. Bianchi and R. Ilbert have noted, "When a catastrophe occurs, the landlord pretends to total innocence, as though there were nothing strange about adding floors of reinforced concrete on top of wooden ceilings. It is true that as a result the landlord may have to serve a prison sentence, but few of the many illegal extra floors constructed end up collapsing, and the added profits make the risk worthwhile." The deterioration of old buildings as a result of overcrowding and inadequate maintenance, the defects in new construction, and the practices just mentioned explain the devastating consequences of the earthquake of 12 October 1992.[4]

Cairo's growth in the last decades has profoundly upset the structure of the city. Until 1976 or so, it was possible to track Cairo's development by keeping tabs on three major sectors: the old city, the western city, and the northern city. The eastern, or old city, despite an absolute increase in numbers (from 574,000 to 773,053), declined continuously in size relative to the city as a whole, representing 34 percent of Cairo's population in 1937, 22.2 percent in 1960, and 14.3 percent in 1976. Despite ever-higher densities, this area (which continued to receive the city's poorest population, especially new migrants looking for a first urban home) at long last reached a point of demographic saturation, and even began to see a decline in population. The modern western city increased drastically in absolute numbers (from 350,000 to 617,480) while registering a gradual decline in its share of the city's overall population: 27 percent in 1937, 19.6 percent in 1960, and 12.1 percent in 1976.

The most spectacular changes during this period were taking place in the northern sector of the city. From 34 percent of the total population in 1937 (450,000 residents), this area grew to hold 46.5 percent of the population in 1960 and 55.8 percent in 1976 (2,837,014 residents), well over half of all the people in the city. Cairo expanded impetuously in this area, near the head of the Nile delta, as though Egypt's capital were resuming in the twentieth century its millennial displacement northward, the successive stages of which we have discussed in this book.

The combined percentage of these three areas (95 percent in 1937, 88.3 percent in 1960, and 82.2 percent in 1977) shows that Cairo's expansion was also occurring, with a delayed but comparable vigor, in the southern sector of the city, where old residential towns like Ma'adi and Hilwan were in turn caught up in frenetic growth: Ma'adi had 42,944 residents in 1947, and 267,056 in 1976; Hilwan had 24,028 residents in 1947, and 316,190 in 1976, a record growth of 1,200 percent in thirty years. A new urban configuration was starting to appear.

Three major zones are apparent today, trending in contrasting directions. The "central core" on the east bank includes the old Islamic city, the nineteenth-century city center, and Shubra, a rectangle of 5,000 hectares that counted 2.9 million residents in 1986. In this area, the population flow is reversed. The growth rate declined from 2.1 percent in 1960–1966 to 0.3 percent in 1966–1976, and became negative, at −0.7 percent, in 1976–1986, representing a loss of 200,000 residents. The central core boasted 53 percent of the total population in 1960 but now has only 27 percent. The "first ring," or first tier around the central core, includes the urban extensions built during the first three-quarters of the twentieth century: Shubra al-Khayma, Matariyya, Heliopolis, Madinat Nasr, Ma'adi, Basatin on the east bank, and Imbaba, Giza, Doqqi, and the pyramids on the west bank. This area has also seen a deceleration in growth, yet the growth rate remains very high (7.6 percent per year for 1960–1966, 5.3 percent for 1966–1976, and 4.7 percent for 1976–1986), in fact higher than the overall rate for greater Cairo. The population of this first concentric tier was 5.3 million in 1986, or 50 percent of the overall population (it was 27 percent in 1960). Finally, there is the "second ring" on the edge of the city, which encompasses former agricultural zones of the delta and the Giza region, the old center of Hilwan, and desert areas to the west and east, where organized efforts at settlement are now under way. Growth there was 3.8 percent in 1960–1966 (the period when the industrial center of Hilwan was under development), 2.9 percent in 1966–1976, and 5 percent in 1976–1986.

With 2.4 million residents, this zone represents 20 percent of the total population.

The general trend is toward a deconcentration of the population. Although this was a desired development, it has not had purely positive effects, given the encroachment on rural areas and the ever more extended municipal services (transportation, water, and so on) called for by urban sprawl. Recently the demographic trend in Cairo has been toward a redress of the population balance between the two shores of the Nile. While the city was born on the east bank, it has developed strongly on the west bank, where the population was 21 percent of Cairo's total in 1966, 24 percent in 1976, and 29 percent in 1986. This trend again poses serious problems, since providing circulation from one shore to the other requires ever more numerous and extensive bridges.[5]

### URBAN PROBLEMS

The numbers suggest the magnitude of the problems facing Cairo today, as much in terms of urban services and infrastructure as in the very life of the population. The day-to-day existence of so great a mass of humanity, spread over so extensive an area, is the source of innumerable difficulties, similar to the difficulties that make the engineers of Western cities blanch but in a more precarious social and economic environment. The average estimated individual income in 1990 was $550, which places Egypt in the ranks of poor countries. The country is not without resources: petroleum (43.9 million metric tons, of which 23.4 million are exported, bringing in $1.545 billion), tourism ($950 million), the Suez Canal ($1.770 billion), and the foreign currency sent to Egypt by its emigrants, all of which represent undoubted assets. But the country's economic growth (2.47 percent in 1990) lags behind its rate of population growth (2.55 percent in 1976–1986), leaving a substantial portion of the population in conditions of real poverty. Fifty percent of Cairenes are estimated to be living below the poverty line.

One indication of current problems is the vexed issue of vacant housing units, tallied in the 1986 census. Although the city is undergoing a severe housing shortage, the census revealed that 467,000 housing units, or 15.4 percent of all units in the greater Cairo area, remained unoccupied. This paradoxical situation reflects the refusal of landowners to rent their property under the rent-control laws that have been in force for the last forty years, as well as their inability to find rental prospects able to pay "normal" rents. The proportion of empty apartments in the poor districts of the central city is low (7.2 percent), but high (18 percent) in the first and second concentric rings, with Heliopolis and Madinat Nasr having a record vacancy level of 29.5 percent. The dysfunctional real estate market is the reflection of a dysfunctional society in which 5 percent of the population share 54 percent of the aggregate income, while at the other end of the social scale, 56 percent make do with only 12 percent of it.

Cairo's problems assumed a dramatic aspect in the 1940s and 1950s when the city's population growth took off and surpassed 4 percent (presaging a doubling of the population every eighteen years). The means used to address the problems varied widely. The period 1952–1973, the years of the Nasser revolution, was characterized by state intervention and an active social policy resulting in the nationalization of the concessionary companies (Heliopolis, Ma'adi) and of the public utilities (water, transportation), the construction of low-income housing, and the freezing of rents.

The net effect of these policies was negative. Lacking sufficient means, the government was unable to spend the requisite amount on housing, low-income housing in particular, and other priorities gradually pushed housing into the background. The spending curve fell regularly, by 18.2 percent in 1959–1960, and by 8.4 percent in 1970–1976. Between 1965 and 1975, 75,000 housing units were built, whereas the demand for that period had been estimated in 1966 at 264,000 units. Undertakings aimed at helping the neediest often ended up profiting more fortunate strata of the population. The new city planned on the Muqattam Hills was a failure, but the other large construction project of the Nasser regime, the City of Victory (Madinat Nasr, or Nasr City, whose name, of course, echoes Nasser's own), designed in 1959 for insertion on the edge of the desert between Cairo and Heliopolis, was a success. In the long run, it will house 500,000 residents. But low-income housing accounts for only part of the project, which is addressed primarily to the middle classes. The development of the Muhandisin area on the west bank benefited the middle class of civil servants and technical specialists. The perverse effect of the rent laws has already been mentioned.

The Nasser government must nonetheless be credited with a serious campaign of public spending to reduce overcrowding in the city. In some instances there was clearly a political agenda, as with the renovation of the large public square of the Maydan al-Tahrir, which, rid of its cumbersome British barracks in 1946, was graced with the hideous state office tower, the famous Mugama'a, a concrete hymn to the inefficient and harassing bureaucracy of Nasser-style socialism; or as with the building of the Nile Corniche, thanks to the removal of the last obstacle, the garden of the British Residence, which had extended to the Nile, causing all traffic to detour around it and providing a daily reminder of the British presence. Beltways were designed, such as the Salah Salem highway, which in its present extended form links Old Cairo to the Cairo airport. Bridges were built and others begun to improve communications with the expanding western city: the University Bridge (1958), and another built between the Bulaq and Isma'il Bridges.

The new policy of "openness" *(infitah)* inaugurated in 1974 by Nasser's successor, Anwar Sadat (1970–1981), brought an end to Nasser's socialism and introduced liberal ideas. These took the form of government withdrawal from active construction, with the slack to be taken up by private initiative, stimulated by global economic development. The result, however, was a surge in speculation that raised the price of land sharply (by a factor of ten to fifteen). The five-year plan for 1981 projected that the government would finance 6 percent of construction and the private sector 94 percent. State aid tended to go to those with the very lowest income. A large number of housing units were in fact built (463,000 in 1976–1981), the majority without building permits (64 percent) in what might be called unofficial urban development, thanks to investments of the national capital and revenues resulting from emigration. The fact that a considerable stock of vacant housing was left in the wake of this boom also points to the emergence of a speculative and inflationary trend; the rates of inoccupancy are particularly high in areas of "spontaneous development," and the number of marginal residences (huts, tents, shanties, tombs) is on the rise. As Mercédès Volait has put it, "There is no lack of [housing] units, but they are often ill adapted to the financial means of needy households . . . While showing on the one hand how the savings of the middle class can be mobilized for investment in the housing sector, this excess reveals more than anything the inability of the public authorities to control the market and to establish a real policy of low-income housing." The five-year plan for 1987–1992 set a target of 170,000 housing units in the first year, of which 124,600 would be low-income.[6]

Although undoubted progress has been made since World War II, no one can claim that Cairo has the administrative structures in place to deal with the great challenges posed by development. The creation in 1949 of a municipality *(baladiyya)* in Cairo and a Ministry of Municipal and Rural Affairs was an important step, as were the abolition of special privileges for foreigners and the restoration of public services and utilities to Egyptian hands, including the nationalization of transportation companies in 1956. The abolition or close state control of *waqf* property has also led to better use of space and better management of part of Cairo's real estate. But uncertainty over the form that Cairo's administration should take and the tendency to manage the city bureaucratically from on high have certainly hampered efforts to plan the city's growth almost as much as the lack of resources or the division of greater Cairo in 1981 among three governorates: Cairo, with 5.87 million; Giza, with 2.39 million; and Qaliyubiyya, with 1.125 million.

Urban planning often failed to keep pace with reality, even when the reality was plainly foreseeable. The master plan of 1956 anticipated that Cairo's population would reach 5.5 million in the year 2000, a number it surpassed in 1965 (4.2 million in Cairo proper, 6.1 million in greater Cairo). Hence the succession of plans, each intended to correct the errors of the one before. Hence also, perhaps, a more recent tendency to foresee the future in dark terms: population forecasts for the 1980s were predicated on a population of 10–12 million residents in 1986, and the results of the census provided a "happy surprise" for demographers and urban planners.

Urban planning has gone through a number of stages. The first master plan, in 1956, called for six satellite cities, strongly industrial in nature, of which only one, Hilwan, was actually developed, and two suburban zones on desert land, of which only Madinat Nasr saw the light of day. The second master plan (1970), developed by the

High Commission of Greater Cairo, was established in a climate of catastrophe: the explosion of Cairo's infrastructures, in particular the sewers (1965), and the military disaster of the 1967 war. In order to deal with the population of 14.8 to 16 million residents of Greater Cairo projected for 1990, plans were made to create satellite cities and new cities, build what would become the 6 October Bridge between Ramses Street and the west bank of the Nile, and construct a belt parkway to contain the city's expansion. But the signing of a peace agreement with Israel, the priority given to reopening the Suez Canal and rebuilding its towns, and the new policy of economic liberalism hampered the execution of this plan.

A third master plan was prepared in 1983. Developed in collaboration with the French, it projected a population increase of 7.6 million residents by the year 2000, of whom 3 million would be housed within the urbanized perimeter, a million on agricultural lands, and 0.9 million in the ten "New Settlements." It envisaged the completion of the beltway, or "Ring Road," which would encircle the urban area along only three-fourths of its circumference (73 kilometers) so as not to encourage the urban development of agricultural zones. And it planned a division of the city into sixteen "uniform sectors," each of 500,000 to 2 million inhabitants, designed to form independent urban entities that would be relatively self-sufficient in terms of employment and public services. These efforts to give orderliness to Cairo's growth were partially successful, though the forecasts on which they were based have not been entirely borne out and the intended work was only partly completed. Even on the planning level there were breakdowns; according to a report by M. Belliot and J. Berthet, "In 1991, some local technical officers were still using as a reference urban development plans dating back to 1969, that is, predating by almost fifteen years the master plan approved in 1983."[7]

A large part of Cairo's expansion goes forward without the help of any planning in agricultural areas that one would wish to preserve. Except in the relatively rare cases in which expansion occurs on state lands, there would be nothing illegal about this development on the outskirts of Cairo if it were not in disregard of urban planning prescriptions: "Most zones of spontaneous [urban development] (thirteen of the fifteen studied) occurred on farmland around existing villages," writes Galila El Kadi. "The farmland . . . is private property,

Unplanned development in al-Marj

each parcel privately owned under clear title. These lands . . . are sold, bought, and subdivided. In these cases, the transaction is legal, but the situation is not." The old rural structure of the land becomes incorporated into the urban fabric: the canals become sewers, and the paths streets, whence the regular aspect of the parcels. The new buildings generally have three to five stories, the usual limit for structures without elevators, and all the elements are borrowed from modern architecture. The development of these areas has been helped by emigration, as the capital is often supplied by emigrés (who accounted for 30 percent of buyers, according to a study), and by the liberal economic policy that has encouraged private initiative.

These dwellings answer to the vast housing needs of the middle and lower classes. Zones of unplanned or "spontaneous" urban development, according to El Kadi, extended in 1981 over 2,921 hectares, representing 10.8 percent of the built-up area, and gave housing to 1.58 million people, or 20 percent of Cairo's population. They form a belt around the city to the north, west, and south, and their development hinges on how infrastructure develops, the direction that regulated districts take, and the presence of productive activities (which provide work): 50,000 workers in the Hilwan industrial zone (out of a population of 120,000) live in surrounding areas of unsanctioned urban development.

As these developments spring up without any regulation, they lack all the necessary public services (paved streets, running water, sewers, schools) until their legalization eventually comes through, as it usually does, after lengthy negotiations: an unregulated district on private lands such as Basatin receives municipal water in 94.2 percent of its units. The lack of infrastructure imparts to a development of this kind "the aspect of a large urban village," but as the unplanned developments evolve they begin "to resemble the popular quarters of the legal city, which makes it hard to distinguish between the two." They are neither shantytowns nor flimsy shelters, but "substandard cities . . . housing that has every appearance of decency but that is marginal, badly built, often crowded, and always poorly equipped." The rise in land and housing costs as a result of high demand and the consequent speculation has resulted in increased settlement on government lands, and although the location of these lands in the desert and the shaky legal basis of their occupation count against them (the intermediaries who parcel them out often have no proper title to them), their cost can be ten to fifteen times less than that of private land.

Force is rarely used to resolve these anomalies, though the Cairo authorities did bulldoze a 3,000-square-meter subdivision with 200 homes on government land at Matariyya. The mud-brick and palm huts, which had no amenities and looked "uncivilized," had been built at night and on weekends. They were rented out by unlicensed entrepreneurs for 25 Egyptian pounds (E£) per month and E£500 in key money. In reaching such an exceptional decision, the government probably gave less weight to the unsanitary conditions and the legal violations than to the fact that the development was in a "sensitive" zone (the Obelisk district) and especially that the land had been earmarked for a telephone exchange building. Unregulated dwellings accounted for 82 percent of the housing units produced in Egypt between 1976 and 1982. Such buildings will continue to be built, barring the unlikely event that the government will assume responsibility for or provide leadership on the problem of low-income housing.[8]

Some fifty years after the building of Heliopolis, and in an entirely changed political climate, the attempt was made to build a new city in the desert zone east of Cairo, Madinat Nasr. As originally planned, it was to include an official district (ministries, sports facilities, universities), a district for industry, offices, and entertainment, and a residential district in which the neighborhood for single-family homes was "protected" from the industrial district by low-income housing. Covering an area of 8,000 hectares and expected to house a population of 500,000, the city got off to a slow start—as might any project of this size and nature. The goal of attracting a diverse population was not truly achieved due to the size and cost of the parcels: at E£30,000 for a 150-square-meter lot, the cost was equivalent to fifty years of a worker's accumulated salary. Yet with many of the same problems as Heliopolis, the town did develop and can be accounted a success.

Given the extent of Cairo's housing needs and planners' desire to deconcentrate Cairo and protect its surrounding farmland, new axes of urban development have been sought. The master plan for 10 Ramadan City was developed as early as 1976. A public organization for new cities has assumed the responsibility for planning these new urban communities, of which thirteen are projected. Seven were to be readied by the year 2000 to absorb Cairo's estimated population growth of 2 million people. Four of these are independent cities at a fair distance from Cairo: 10 Ramadan (projected population 500,000), al-Sadat, al-Amal, and al-Badr. Three of them are satellite cities closer in: 6 October (projected population 500,000, to the southwest), 15 May (to the south), and al-Ubur (to the northeast). These cities are also planned to include industrial zones that can supply jobs on the spot (up to 80,000 jobs per city).

The gigantism of these projects, their complexity and cost, have provoked lively criticism. After difficult and slow beginnings, some of the cities have truly got off the ground: Sadat, 10 Ramadan, 6 October, 15 May, and al-Badr, where, at the end of 1989, 58,490 housing units had been completed or were under construction. Industrial development, always a delicate undertaking, is making encouraging progress: in 1989 there were an estimated 260 businesses with 21,595 employees operating in 10 Ramadan City, and 138 businesses with 7,764 employees in 6 October City. This "industrial development can be considered a successful example of industrial decentralization," writes G. Meyer, despite the difficulties relating to the great distances laborers must commute and the problem workers have in finding housing nearby (speculation drives up residential costs and creates high vacancy levels). A study of the residents of 10 Ramadan City (13,400 in 1989) indicates that their socioeconomic level is markedly above the national average: only 3.3 percent receive less than E£50 per month; nearly half (48 percent) have incomes of E£100–200 per month. The illiteracy rate is only 21 percent. Only 30 percent of the residents are native Cairenes, while 26.5 percent are from the province of Sharqiyya, indicating that the city functions less as a catchment for Cairo's overflowing population than as a focal point for internal migration. But this is one of the new cities that is particularly far from the capital.[9]

Given the heavy investment these new cities required, which was difficult to support in times of recession, and given the problem of providing satisfactory help under these conditions to the neediest element of the population, the planners (aware of the vigorous growth of unofficial housing) devised a new type of development: in return for limited government aid, private development could be guided along lines more in harmony with the general interest. The "New Settlements" would offer small building lots on improved sites at prices comparable to those found in zones of unregulated development, but in desert zones fairly close to Cairo. These New Settlements, expected to appeal to middle- and lower-income groups, would house one-third of the 7 million new residents anticipated in the greater Cairo area between 1982 and 2000. To this end, 300–500 hectares of land would be prepared per year. As starting up these settlements has proved difficult, the authorities have planned to build sets of 10,000 housing units in six of them as a first stage of development.

It is difficult to say what the outcome of this project will be. Attractive though its prospects are, many obstacles stand in the path of this undertaking, which has not truly got underway. Even the New Cities have only begun to come into being: Galila El Kadi and M. Rabi report that "according to the 1986 census, [they] provide housing for no more than 70,000 residents . . . This figure corresponds to the increase in the population of greater Cairo over a seventy-day period. In other words, it is in greater Cairo that urban growth is still strongest, and greater Cairo is constantly encroaching on the surrounding farmland." Given the cost of these projects and the difficulty of convincing people to live in desert areas in an offputting environment, one might wonder whether a realistic management of the developed spaces on agricultural land might not better serve Cairo's needs.[10]

Because of Cairo's growth, its population increase, the lengthening distance between the downtown center and the fringes of the city, a great effort has necessarily been made to improve the city's facilities. And if all the city's problems have not been solved, at least the general state of crisis of the 1960s has been overcome. The near-paralysis of traffic faced by private vehicles on the unavoidable stretches of road—the bridges across the Nile, the streets of Cairo (where parking was so difficult that "attendants" began to station themselves along the curb, and for a modest sum would push double- and triple-parked cars out of each other's way)—was equaled only by the overburdening of the public transportation system, from whose crowded and irregular buses passengers hung off in clusters. A 1985 study estimated the average occupancy of a municipal bus at 90 to 100 persons—not counting "clandestine" passengers! A considerable investment was made in the street system. More bridges were built over the Nile, with forty-five bridges and roads with viaducts and overpasses completed between 1982 and 1988. The Ring Road, launched in 1983, is nearly completed, with a bridge over the Nile planned at Fustat.

These public works, exorbitantly costly, have the drawback of favoring private vehicles and accelerating urbanization. Meanwhile, improvements to the public transportation system, which all the plans call indispensable, remain insufficient. The buses, each of which carried 2,000 passengers per day in 1972, carried only 1,600 per day in 1990. At least the first line of a future subway system has been completed (with engineering assistance from the rapid transit authority in Paris). This broad-gauge line runs north and south a distance of 42.5 kilometers and has thirty-three stations. Its underground tunnel, excavated at a cost of E£1.75 billion (U.S.$880 million) through the center of town, joins al-Marj to Hilwan, with a carrying capacity of 60,000 passengers per hour in either direction. A second line connecting Shubra al-Khayma to Giza (18 kilometers), intersecting with the first at Tahrir Square, is under construction. Although the subway may have unwanted effects (facilitating the city's expansion to the north into agricultural lands), it represents a consid-

Traffic problems in the old city, along the former Khalij

New bridge across the Nile at Imbaba

erable advance, since it should in time carry 18 percent of passengers using public transportation in greater Cairo.[11]

The sewers in the 1960s were in as dire condition as the traffic. The system, expected to serve a population of one million, was by then totally inadequate. In 1965 the collectors were overflowing, especially in the working-class quarters, whose facilities were the poorest. In the worst cases, and to prevent explosions and malodorous geysers, a number of sewerage manholes were capped with heavy plugs of cement. On one of these curious excrescences, shaped like a termite mound, an urchin from the lower-class district of Sayyida Zaynab had written a typically savage *nukta,* or sally of Cairene wit: *maqam sidi Baladiyya* ("tomb of Sir Municipality"). That year, emergency measures were taken to deal with the worst problems (the so-called "hundred days' plan"), but the city's low spots remained under threat of flood during the winter, owing to the rise in the water table after the building of the Nile dams.

The upgrades subsequently made to the sewer system proved inadequate given Cairo's population increase, and the outlying zones were still not connected to the system. Two large sewer systems were then readied under the direction of an Anglo-American consortium (AMBRIC). A huge project, the largest in the world, its cost was estimated at E£4 billion. The system, which handles sewage as well as runoff, is expected to increase from the present capacity of 1 million cubic meters per day to 5 million. The British, working on the east bank, have built an underground "megatunnel" 5 meters in diameter, which winds along for 17 kilometers at a depth of up to 30 meters, running from Maʿadi to the giant plant at Jabal al-Asfar, whose treatment capacity will be 3 million cubic meters per day (from 1 million at present). What is to be done with the 5,000 metric tons of sludge created each day has not yet been determined. On the west bank, the Americans are engaged in the open-air excavation of a collector that will extend for 21 kilometers and end at the Abu Ruwash treatment center (whose capacity is 500,000 cubic meters per day). Completion, projected for 1995, will call for a total rehabilitation of the system and an extension of its secondary lines. These few figures give some idea of the magnitude of the problems needing to be solved to ensure even the simple survival of a megalopolis such as Cairo. As Galila El Kadi has pointed out, the total expenditure for the eleven new cities and satellite cities during the period 1979–1987 came to just E£1.5 billion, one-third of the cost of the sewer system.

Other just as mind-boggling examples of municipal improvement could be given for other equally vital areas of life. In the delivery of drinking water there is a great disparity between the various districts of Cairo. Seventy-three percent of the population of Cairo receives home delivery of water, but only 29.1 percent at al-Marj and 26.1 percent at Manshiat al-Nasr. During the 1980s the drinking-water supply on the east bank rose from 2 million cubic meters per day to 3 million thanks to a new station recently brought on line at Fustat. A station built at Imbaba on the left bank allowed the supply there to be doubled to 600,000 cubic meters per day, an amount that is barely sufficient for the population in that area. A few figures demonstrate the progress made: for water, 48.4 percent of dwellings were connected to the municipal water system in 1976, and 73.8 percent in 1986; for electricity, 38.3 percent were on the grid in 1976, and 84 percent in 1986.

Then there is the problem of the wholesale food market. Built in 1947 on a 9-hectare lot at Rawd al-Faraj, on Cairo's northwest, to replace the old market on Ramses Street (now right in the middle of Cairo), the new market contributed to the development of the district, whose population grew from 165,000 in 1947 to more than 300,000 in 1986. In 1987 preparations were made to transfer the market to the satellite city of al-Ubur, 30 kilometers north of Cairo. The new wholesale market, designed on the model of Paris' Rungis market, will have the capacity to handle 2 million tons of food products per year and should open for business in 1992. Two other wholesale markets are planned: one in Giza, near the new city of 6 October (in New Settlement No. 7), and the other near Hilwan (15 May City). Cairo's international airport also merits mention—its current capacity is 10 million passengers per year, and there are two enlargements on the drawing boards for 5 million passengers each.[12]

The present and future of Cairo are naturally bound to the city's rate of growth. As internal immigration slackens, this will depend more and more on natural demographic factors. Rapid reduction in the birth rate has already lowered the rate of natural increase, despite a concomitant drop in the death rate. Experts forecast that the downward trend will become more pronounced, with the rate of natural increase (23.7 per 1,000 in 1980–1985) diminishing at five-year intervals to 20.8, 17.1, and 14.7 by the year 2000. This nonetheless represents an annual increase of 250,000 persons in 1986, to which an estimated 23,000 immigrants per year must be added. In this case, and excepting a renewed surge in internal migration, it is possible that Cairo's population in the year 2000 will be well below the often predicted 16 million mark, somewhere more in the neighborhood of 13 million.

Construction in the last fifteen years has been considerable: 162,000 dwellings per year between 1983 and 1987 (four-fifths of them in the private sector). Given the relative slackening in population growth, the relatively advanced development of the new cities, and the cushion of 523,000 vacant housing units in Cairo, the housing problem is less dire than it was some twenty-five years ago, which might justify a revision of the development policies of the last forty years. As El Kadi observes, "In the context of Egypt's present economic crisis, one of the urgent tasks at hand is to rationalize the mobilization and allocation of existing resources and means. This necessarily requires adopting a true strategy for the country's improvement, one that would allow a redeployment of the population, business activities, and investments." It would also require confronting a problem that neither a socialist planned economy nor a technological and free-market ethic has been able to solve, which is to provide housing for the majority of the population.

The problem is obviously related to employment. Urban development in Egypt has not been driven mainly by industrialization, as in Europe, but by a rural exodus caused by insurmountable agrarian problems. Consequently, unemployment is very high in Cairo (17.3 percent of the working population in 1986), but so is underemployment in the overstaffed government services (where 43 percent of jobs are located, while 20 percent are in the industrial sector). A considerable portion of the city has no stable employment and must therefore get by on a very low standard of living. But the number of young men and women entering the job market, after leveling off between 1975 and 1985, started rising again in the late 1980s and accelerated in the 1990s. It is obviously the fate of the young (who constitute more than half the population) that will determine Cairo's future.[13]

## THE SOCIAL DIVISION OF SPACE

Cairo's impetuous growth in the past half-century complicates any image one might try to form of it. The traditional city of the late Ottoman era and the two side-by-side cities of the colonial era have been absorbed into a whole so diverse as to prevent any simple conclusions. The faces of the city blur; its centers are many and mobile. But this "fragmented" Cairo can still be reconstituted into more or less coherent wholes, each clearly revealing deep social differences. A 1988 survey of Cairo residents shows how consciously Cairenes draw the distinction between *raqi* (fashionable) districts and *sha'bi* (popular) ones, and how very explicit the criteria are: density ("Here, at Madinat al-Tahrir, it is peaceful, a nice *raqi* area"); noise (*"sha'bi* is what you have here, at al-Husayn, a little *baladi,* full of people. In a *sha'bi* quarter there is always noise, bustling, lots of people, but a *raqi* quarter is peaceful"); the nature of the buildings ("Muhandisin is *raqi,* the height of the buildings is different . . . the construction is modern, the buildings are different, cleaner . . . each person lives apart in his own apartment"); cleanliness ("In Imbaba, the al-Munira district is very crowded, unclean. Al-Basrawi Street is not asphalted, there are no sewers even"); retail services ("Heliopolis is full of shops with expensive dresses and there is a supermarket. In Darrasa, there are *jam'iyyat* [cooperatives] and long lines").[14]

In this city, which its population feels is divided in two, Galila El Kadi distinguishes three types of social space, defined primarily by their density, education level, business activities, land costs, and quality of facilities.[15] The space belonging to the "lower strata," with its large share of laborers (50 percent) and high illiteracy rate (more than 40 percent), is the city's largest (6,354 of its 13,112 hectares) and most populous (4,054,497 residents). It is also the one where the facilities are the most marginal: more than 50 percent of the population has neither running water nor sewage drains, and more than a quarter has no electricity. This social space actually consists of two separate zones. The first comprises the central area of the old "Fatimid" city, its traditional outlying areas (Bulaq and Old Cairo), and its more recent accretions (the eastern districts, including the cemeteries); there densities are highest (more than 1,000 residents per hectare), dwellings are most overcrowded (an average of 3.1 persons per

Modern dwelling in Cairo's old city

room), and the buildings are extremely rundown (50–60 percent of dwellings are in a state of deterioration). The residents of this part of the city are the most homogeneous (entry-level workers, the unemployed, new immigrants). It is here also that the population decline since 1966 has been most marked. The second zone consists of the neighborhoods of unplanned and "spontaneous" dwellings that ring the city: Matariyya and Shubra al-Khayma to the north; Imbaba, Giza, and the pyramids (al-Ahram) to the west; Ma'adi and Hilwan to the south. More prosperous than those in the central zone, the residents of these outlying districts belong to the middle class but have

The transformation of Cairo's old city

only limited income. Population density is not as high here (400 residents per hectare). The inadequate infrastructure is especially marked because of the "illegal" nature of settlement in agricultural areas.

The second social space belongs to an intermediate and even prosperous level of the population. It occurs in the areas to the west of the Fatimid city (Zahir, Azbakiyya, Abdin, Sayyida Zaynab), where the first modern expansions were built at the end of the nineteenth century, and which remain one of the city's business and trade centers; also in the near north area (Shubra, Rawd al-Faraj, Wayli), whose development dates from the first decades of the twentieth century, and which has a strongly industrial character. This social space covers an area of 2,518 hectares and has a population of 2,086,490. Population density is generally high, but with significant differences between the two zones (717 residents per hectare to the west, 899 to the north). The population enjoys a higher level of education (illiteracy rates of one-quarter to one-third, depending on the area) and is more strongly represented in the liberal and service professions (approximately one-fifth) and less strongly in the worker category (less than one-third). The infrastructure is generally acceptable, especially in the older, central part of the city, while the area to the north is relatively underprivileged in this respect.

The space occupied by the upper strata is at once extensive (4,240 hectares), more sparsely inhabited (770,447 residents), and geographically scattered. It consists of a relatively old center (Qasr al-Nil, Rawdah, Zamalek), which extended westward in the 1960s to the left bank of the Nile (Doqqi and Ajuza), and of two residential suburbs that have been absorbed by the city's recent expansion, Heliopolis and Madinat Nasr in the north and Ma'adi in the south. Population density is low (on average fewer than 200 residents per hectare). The group is distinguished by the high proportion holding university degrees (30 percent) and its low illiteracy rate (12 percent), as well as by its occupational profile: around 40 percent are professionals or in the services; a small number (7 percent) engage in industrial work. Forming an enclave within the city, the fashionable districts on the west bank are blocked off by the railroad, which separates them from large zones of unplanned and irregular housing (Imbaba, Bulaq al-Dakrur) and impedes further expansion. With dwellings at the saturation point, detached single-family houses and small buildings are being replaced by high-rise buildings. The other two islands of fashionable living have the option of expanding out toward the desert. Real estate speculation has pushed land prices very high in these districts, to around E£1,000 per square meter (compared to a maximum of E£300 and E£600 respectively in the "popular" and intermediate quarters).

This social division of space, already profoundly evident before 1936, was reinforced in the Nasser period, when many of the constructions benefited the middle and upper-middle classes, while the neediest settled in the old central district and the "agricultural" areas of the urban fringe. The division has been accelerated by the adoption of a liberal free-market attitude, which tends to let the "laws of the market" play themselves out while government withdraws in part from the problem of housing the poor.

## THE FACES OF THE CITY

The history of Cairo and its discontinuities have thus brought together urban areas that differ widely in their concept, their economic role, and the social and cultural level of their residents. Such contrasts have always existed, and we encountered them before in the medieval city and the traditional city. They are also present in all great modern metropolises, but they are particularly distinct here. Thousands of Cairenes commute daily from the hovels of the central district, or from the housing of the distant fringe areas with its minimal facilities, to the modern buildings of the Nile Corniche or Doqqi. At the same time the mass media sharpen the general awareness of these differences, making them all the harder to bear. This probably accounts to a certain extent for the periodic eruptions that have occurred in Cairo—in 1952, in 1977, and in 1986. The looting of luxury stores and fashionable sites in wealthy neighborhoods is one way that the residents of the other Cairo take their revenge, directing their anger at symbols of an envied and reviled West. Cairo's expansion has only pushed back the place where "that broken giant [i.e., the people of Cairo] regroups and strikes."[16] In 1952 it was the hotels and department stores of the east bank; in 1986, the hotels, cabarets, and stores of Giza and the Avenue of the Pyramids.

Of the "Oriental" city whose history has occupied the greater part of this book, little remains but relics—in the old central district, in Bulaq (at the foot of Cairo's second Hilton Hotel), and in Old Cairo. A few assemblages of admirable monuments, of rare architectural complexes (in the Qasaba, the group of large Mamluk sanctuaries; around Bab Zuwayla, the large covered Ridwan Suq and the Darb al-Ahmar; the Saliba area; and the Citadel) still testify to Cairo's millennial splendor. But the dominant impression in the eastern city is one of poverty, exacerbated by the neglect of public services. Modern buildings, quick to deteriorate, replace the old structures, which have worn out prematurely from overcrowding and lack of maintenance. The traditional activities that kept the old city running (trade and handicrafts) are in decline or survive in the Khan al-Khalili neighborhood as though it were a reservation for tourists. The old section of Bulaq was severely damaged by the 1992 earthquake and is likely to disappear all the faster as a result.

These central districts are losing density as their residents move elsewhere, mainly to the northeast and south, in search of more comfortable conditions. In 1976–1986 the population density in Bab al-Sha'riyya fell from 1,003 residents per hectare to 723. The number of

Maydan al-Tahrir

occupants per room fell from 2.8 to 1.6 in the central *qism*. One of the most striking characteristics of recent development in the old central district is the proliferation of light industry in workshops employing four or five individuals and using inexpensive equipment to manufacture consumer products: shoes in Bab al-Sha'riyya, aluminum utensils in Jamaliyya. The light industry in this district is a new phenomenon; it developed after 1980, thanks in part to the income of emigrés. A district like Darb al-Asfar, traditionally a bastion of upper-middle-class residence, has been profoundly affected by this manufacturing trend. The change threatens to destabilize the old city because of its noxious side effects (noise, pollution) and the harm it will do to the buildings in the fragile historical zones. Indeed, the "revitalization" of these areas through industrialization may well spell their death warrant.

On the western edge of the old city, starting at Port Sa'id Street (the former course of the Khalij), a twin process of modernization (approaching from the west) and decay (spreading from the east) is creating a transition zone that fuses the old and new cities. These districts are often neighborhoods that were renovated at the end of the nineteenth or the beginning of the twentieth century and are becom-

Garden City, old and new

ing *baladi*. Rundown modern buildings predominate, and the ruins of the old city are growing scarcer. In the early 1990s the venerable mosque built in 1506 for Emir Qanibay al-Rammah collapsed, and it remains, encircled by scaffolding, as a testament to the irremediable decline of historic Cairo.[17]

The city that was modern during Isma'il's reign and in the early colonial period, west of Azbakiyya and the Abdin Palace, emerges gradually from the old quarters. Business still congregates there, just as administrative entities concentrate a little farther south, but there is a perceptible movement out of the area toward the western districts. The buildings sometimes show their age excessively, whether old or recent, falling prematurely into disrepair from lack of maintenance. But there is incessant activity on Tal'at Harb, Qasr al-Nil, and Sharif Pasha Streets, which are crippled by traffic during rush hour. There are many stores selling often quite ordinary goods—luxury outlets have all migrated to Zamalek and Doqqi. Liberation Square (Maydan al-Tahrir) is a funnel for automobile traffic, but westbound traffic now detours toward the highway that straddles Jazira, whose entrance a bit farther north is announced by a tangle of entry ramps. Maydan al-Tahrir is a bus station and an access point to the subway; it serves as the border between colonial Cairo and "metropolitan" Cairo, whose tall buildings block the view toward the Nile. A few buildings in this area symbolize Egypt's wider influence: the Arab League Building and the exceedingly quaint Egyptian Museum, a center of tourist pilgrimage. In Garden City, large modern buildings and banks rise among the palaces and mansions that sit with peeling facades in the midst of neglected gardens. More symbols: the outmoded palaces of the British Embassy and the Suez Canal Company (nationalized in 1956) are overshadowed in their gardens by the enormous bunker of the United States Embassy, whose high walls and windowless upper floors (a security measure) protect the foreign policy secrets of the United States, the successor to the power once vested in the British Residence and the Canal authority.

For dozens of kilometers the Nile now flows between a double wall of high-rise buildings, giving an indication of the changes Egypt has undergone in the last forty years. This concrete Nile frontage, which was the despair of the celebrated Egyptian architect Hasan Fathi, is nonetheless the most spectacular and the most impressive aspect of Cairo in our day, along a river that, hour after hour and season after season, preserves all its majesty and magic. Around this central zone stretch the fashionable districts of modern Cairo and the caravanserais of our time, the great palaces, the Hilton, the Semiramis, Shepheard's, the Meridian (whose facade unfortunately blocks the splendid view of the Nile to the south), and, on the other bank, the Sheratons. From here, there is no trace of human misery to

The east bank of the Nile

spoil the Nile's enchantment: the old city is only a sumptuous back-drop in the distance, a scroll of domes and spiky minarets that unfurls as far as the Citadel. The Sporting Club, once the center of British colonial life, can now be spied on brazenly from the highway heading west across the Nile and Jazira.

North on Jazira is the still handsome district of Zamalek, ravaged by the aerial crossing of a city highway. Here too the old palaces and beautiful mansions, often housing embassies, are giving way to high-rises and hotels. In the iron-framed central pavilion of the massive Umar Khayyam Hotel, the memory of Empress Eugénie's stay in 1869 still persists, and of the great millennial colloquium organized there a century later by Saroit Okasha and Magdi Wahba. Shops have proliferated in the once quiet streets of Zamalik—the service sector has taken hold in that district, which now has a part to play in the re-tailing of luxury goods in the capital. The modern stores, with their somewhat gaudy luxury and Western-style products, have not en-tirely evicted the old *baladi* shops—the laundries, for instance, where artisans follow the local custom of storing water in their cheeks and atomizing it in fine droplets over the laundry they iron for their wealthy customers.

The west bank of the Nile is becoming lined with ever more and taller buildings. Cairo's expansion in this area since the 1950s has been so rapid that it has sometimes swallowed whole villages. The rural neighborhoods of Imbaba, where a camel market was still held not so long ago, have been transformed into a modern district with fairly low-income housing projects. To the north, in a typical unregulated housing zone that is extending onto agricultural lands, urbanization is in process. From there one can see impressive high-rise buildings on the far side of the Nile, across which a giant bridge is being built. As one moves farther south, there is a gradual transition to the districts developed during the Nasser era: Muhandisin (The Engineers), a development designed for civil servants and the middle class; and Doqqi, which has become one of the main residential districts for the wealthy in Cairo. One reaches it from the west along a street whose sections are known to taxicab drivers by the brand names of American cigarettes because of the ads obsessively displayed from the street lamps.

Throughout the area the buildings are growing taller, and commerce is moving in, with luxury stores making it one of the fashionable centers of the contemporary city. The Avenue of the Arab States affords, along a stretch of a few hundred meters, a history of the city's past half-century. At its start, which abuts on poor and almost rural neighborhoods, there are somewhat rundown low-income buildings (*sha'biyya*) from the Nasser period, small shacks where food can be bought, and carts that sell sugarcane, the traditional delicacy of the old city. Then the street improves, the buildings become larger and more modern, giving way to a zone displaying the luxury and abundance of the consumer society. To the west, the Sa'id railway has formed an obstacle barring further urban expansion. For a long time, one looked out the windows of the city's last buildings to where, only a few yards beyond the tracks, the colorful spectacle of farm life in the delta unfolded as it had for a thousand years. But the city is extending with the irresistible urban expansion of Giza. Among the villas scattered along the road to the pyramids, multistoried buildings have proliferated, along with Western-style restaurants and nightclubs—the likely targets of popular riots. The rush of development that spread over the west bank of the Nile fifty years ago was aimed at the farmland of the governorate of Giza. In villages that are sometimes hard to reach because of bad roads, in the middle of fields,

Avenue of the Arab States in Muhandisin: the consumer society

along canals, one finds developing zones of unplanned and unregulated housing, whose spread the urban planners are trying to stop.

To the north, the city expanded first along the major arteries radiating outward from the Azbakiyya district. This process explains the
great variety of suburbs and outlying districts, and the unformed
character of these ill-structured, poorly linked neighborhoods. This
is the prime area for unplanned development. In 1950 Shubra al-
Khayma was farmland, with small villages scattered across it; then industrial facilities moved in. During the years that followed, Shubra
al-Khayma's population rose from 39,000 (1947) to 100,000 (1960), to
173,000 (1966), to 394,000 (1976), to 711,000 (1986), for an annual
growth rate in these periods of 7 percent, 8.1 percent, 7.7 percent,
and 5.5 percent, a Cairo record. Urban forms extend as far as al-
Marj, 13 kilometers as the crow flies from Tahrir Square. When you
get off the subway, whose ambience (down to the tickets) recalls the
metro serving greater Paris, you find yourself in a traditional, half-ru-
ral and half-urban environment, with small food stores and sidewalk
vendors like those in the old city and in rural villages. A few hundred
yards on, you reach the very edge of the city's pioneering front.
Groups of average-sized buildings continue to crop up, dispersed in
the typically Egyptian rural environment where people are omnipres-
ent and the vegetation perpetually green.

In marked contrast to these underprivileged districts, Cairo's northeastern zones contain two examples of modern, planned urban development: Heliopolis, dating from the colonial period at the beginning of the twentieth century, and Madinat Nasr, dating from the Nasser period at midcentury. Built on the edge of the desert but linked to the center of town, these two new cities rise impressively along the highway leading to the Cairo airport. In Heliopolis, buildings of five and six stories or more have sprung up on lots intended for single-family houses. Some of the original villas survive, such as the extravagant one belonging to the developer, which was modeled on the temple of Angkor Wat and is now decaying slowly in the midst of tall weeds, although it may be saved by a conservation effort. The housing here is denser than planned, but it has not greatly affected the suburb's airy feel, as the streets are often very wide and the plantings, though not luxuriant, soften the rather "mineral" aspect of Cairo's thoroughfares, noticeable in both the old city and the modern neighborhoods. Shopping centers shine brightly at night, spots of color betraying the consumerism of the area's middle- and upper-class residents.

To the south one traverses Old Cairo, a pendant to Bulaq, evoking an image of the thousand-year-old Cairo that is now vanishing. The expressways bypass Fustat altogether, which sleeps around its glorious relics (the Mosque of Amr and its Coptic churches), and speed along the river through once-rural zones where outsized buildings have now sprouted like mushrooms in the midst of a still fairly agrarian landscape. Ma'adi is no longer the quiet residential community it once was. Its colonial-style villas set back among gardens and trees are giving way to rapid urban expansion. Farther on, the urban fabric that once stretched thinly along the road has become more substantial, and one soon raises on the horizon the tall smoke-wreathed chimneys of the steelworks and factories of Hilwan, whose industrial zone was built in the 1960s. When the wind blows from the wrong quarter, the entire west bank of the Nile is covered in smog that clears only a dozen miles from Cairo, near the pyramids of Dahshur. Enormous settlements extend around the factories, set down in desolate desert country at a distance from the Nile, unrivaled in their ugliness except for the housing projects of the Nasser period a bit to the north between Old Cairo and the Citadel, though

The New City of 6 October

these are somewhat more tragic because of their enormous size and desert setting. One has to search in Hilwan to find the remains of its turn-of-the-century architecture and urban planning—the town was chosen by Khedive Tawfiq for his secondary residence, and in the first decades of this century its thermal springs made it a peaceful spa town a dozen miles south of Cairo.

A look at the New Cities, one readily persuades oneself, might provide a glimpse of the Cairo of the future. With some difficulty, along as-yet-unfinished autoroutes or worn and poorly laid-out roads, one manages to get from Hilwan to 15 May City, which it is easier to reach from Cairo via the highway. Approaching the new city, one sees clusters of tall buildings scattered among intersections and access roads. Development is to take place in three phases, in increments of twelve neighborhoods. The master plan calls for low-income, middle-income, and upper-income housing, all carefully separated, with the upper-income housing in the center near the amusement park and the commercial district—a general structure suggesting the structure of the "traditional" city described in these pages. But the reality is not as attractive as the plan. The big, housing-project-style buildings are numbingly banal, and the effect is somewhat sad. On this Friday, the residents are attending mosque, or else strolling in a small commercial area that, for its conviviality, resembles the shops of Cairo's old city more than the sophisticated shopping centers of the fashionable neighborhoods. The capital is far away—a two-hour commute in each direction, says a lower manager, who is happy to have resolved his housing problems. The city will no doubt become humanized when it manages to reinvent a form of communal life comparable to that of past centuries.

Also located to the south but on the west bank of the Nile, 25 kilometers in a straight line from Tahrir Square, 6 October City looks sprucer at first sight. One is surrounded by the desert, which is already crossed by the highways that will connect the new settlement to Cairo. In the central residential district, medium-sized buildings of five and six stories border neatly asphalted streets lined with street lamps, while areas of vegetation soften the landscape. There are community facilities (sports installations, a cultural center, schools, a mosque), and they seem poised to create the conditions for developing a community. The construction is of good quality in the central areas, a little hastier (and more crowded) in the outlying ones. At a distance and somewhat hidden is an industrial zone that will provide the residents with work. Businesses have been brought in from Cairo or created here with outside investment in what seems a promising fashion. Once clear of the hurdles raised by its distance from Cairo (where many of the residents will no doubt work) and the desert environment, this town should develop rapidly, on a site west of the pyramids of Giza, north of Saqqara and Memphis, and just about opposite the site of Fustat on the other side of the Nile. Cairo seems to have returned to its origins.

# Retrospective

TODAY ONE LEAVES CAIRO BY AIR. The streets and highways one takes to get to the international airport cross modern neighborhoods that could be those of any large Mediterranean metropolis. The statue of Ramses II on the square in front of the railway station (brought from Memphis in 1955) is as exotic in this context as the obelisk that stands in the Place de la Concorde in Paris. Metropolitan Cairo, in less than a half-century of expansion, has swallowed up the history-laden sites described at the beginning of this book, sites used for centuries as summer retreats, as places to walk or to hunt, and highly prized by the Mamluk sultans and their Ottoman successors: Gubb Pond, where crane and heron were hunted; Siriyaqus, a favorite retreat of Nasir's in the autumn; Matariyya, where tents were raised and banquets given; Habash Pond, where the sultan organized polo matches; Tura, where one went to stroll and spend the night. All these names are today the names of districts or suburbs of modern Cairo.

In this enormous city, measuring some 30,000 hectares in area, whose rapid expansion threatens to leave mapmakers behind, the historic city that developed over the twelve centuries from 642 to 1860 today forms only a minuscule core of 400 hectares, progressively devoured by the modernization of its western edge, while Old Cairo and Bulaq are living their last days. The transformation is a recent one, the change starting around 1936–1945. The problem facing Qahira is identical with the problem of preservation that faces the medinas of many large Arab cities. The temptation to stop evolution and create a museum-city has entered official discourse—in the 1970s and 1980s there was talk of protecting a "Fatimid city" that no longer exists. The survival of the residents of these old quarters depends on the maintenance of commercial activities that are corrosive to the urban fabric and the (Western-style) modernization of traditional housing that has reached extreme limits of dilapidation. Perhaps we should set our sights on preserving the most notable monuments and the few areas where coherent complexes survive, giving weight to architectural decoration as a precious witness to Egyptian authenticity, and as a tourist asset.

It is useless to try to hide the fact that, even with so limited an agenda, it will soon be too late. The archaeological legacy is being destroyed before our eyes—spectacularly, when a monument collapses or is abandoned to its all-too-certain fate, and insidiously, when a "contemporary" building insinuates itself into the ancient fabric and distorts it. From the Citadel, the French traveler Gobineau would today see more modern buildings than minarets and, in the background of the panorama he described, the high-rises of modern Cairo along the Nile.

The contemporary city is a changed city, one whose problems are little different from those of cities in the third world—problems that stem from seemingly limitless growth in a precarious social and economic environment. Progress was made in the 1980s, after Cairo nearly succumbed to apoplexy and paralysis. The years of concerted effort since then have brought about impressive results; the city has, in the broadest sense, returned to operation: its public services have been saved from the disaster that threatened, and new spaces in the surrounding deserts have been opened to expansion. Contributing to the improved situation are better-coordinated policies and a concerted effort to forecast and anticipate the future, but there has also been a respite in the inexorable population growth due to emigration, to the slowing of rural-to-urban migration, and to the flattening of the population's rate of natural increase.

Modern Cairo remains an admirable, even a fascinating, city. The life and animation pulsing through it, its countless crowds, are a fabulous spectacle. The contrast between its modern districts, often broadly laid out, and the old city, so harmonious when seen from a distance, leaves an unforgettable impression. The majestic beauty of the Nile is constantly renewed with a charm, a color, and a grandeur that reflect nuances in the time of day or night and the variations in the seasons. But Cairo risks becoming an ordinary city, another example of the vast conurbations proliferating throughout the world. It may find renewal in a better-controlled modernism or in a problematic return to a spent cultural tradition. The population threat is still present, poised to sweep away the fragile barriers that technicians and politicians have managed to erect to direct its flow. In the past, demographic growth has been an asset to Egypt, giving it power, prestige, and authority. Today it is a mortal danger. Cairo long played the part of safety valve for Egypt's population growth. Tomorrow it could be Egypt's detonator.

CHRONOLOGY

GLOSSARY

ABBREVIATIONS

NOTES

SELECT BIBLIOGRAPHY

INDEX

# CHRONOLOGY

| | |
|---|---|
| *1279–1290* | Reign of Sultan Qalawun. |
| *1291* | Capture of Acre by Sultan Khalil. |
| *1293–1340* | Reign of Muhammad al-Nasir. |
| *1325* | Excavation of the Nasiri Canal. |
| *1348* | The Black Death. |
| *1356–1362* | Construction of the Mosque of Sultan Hasan. |
| *1364–1442* | Ahmad al-Maqrizi. |
| *1382–1398* | Reign of Sultan Barquq. |
| *1399–1412* | Reign of Faraj ibn Barquq. |
| *1400* | Tamerlane's campaign in Syria. |
| *1422–1438* | Reign of Barsbay. |
| *1426* | Expedition against Cyprus. |
| *29 May 1453* | Capture of Constantinople by Mehmed II. |
| *1468–1496* | Reign of Qaytbay. |
| *1476–1484* | Emir Azbak's construction of the "Azbakiyya." |
| *16 August 1488* | Mamluk defeat of the Ottomans near Adana. |
| *1501–1516* | Reign of Sultan Qansuh al-Ghuri. |
| *1507–1508* | Construction of the aqueduct to the Citadel. |
| *1511* | Construction of the Khan al-Khalili. |
| *24 August 1516* | Selim I defeats Ghuri at Marj Dabiq. |
| *1516–1517* | Reign of Tumanbay, last Mamluk sultan. |
| *23 January 1517* | Selim I defeats Tumanbay at Raydaniyya. |

| | |
|---|---|
| *1520–1566* | Reign of Sultan Sulayman. |
| *1525* | Ibrahim Pasha proclaims the law *(kanunname)* governing the province of Egypt. |
| *1610* | Construction of the Mosque of Malika Safiyya. |
| *1656* | Death of the emir Ridwan Bey. |
| *1711* | "Revolution" in Cairo. Deaths of Ifranj Ahmad and Iwaz Bey. |
| *1734* | Construction of the Mosque of Uthman Katkhuda in Azbakiyya. |

| | |
|---|---|
| *1743–1754* | Duumvirate of Ibrahim and Ridwan Katkhuda. |
| *1753–1825* | Abdarrahman al-Jabarti, historian of Egypt. |
| *1760–1773* | Dominance of Ali Bey al-Kabir. |
| *1773–1775* | Muhammad Bey Abu Dhahab the dominant emir. |
| *1786* | Ottoman expedition into Egypt under Hasan Pasha. |
| *1791–1798* | Duumvirate of Murad and Ibrahim Bey. |

～)

| | |
|---|---|
| *1798–1801* | Napoleonic Expedition in Egypt. |
| *October 1798* | First Cairo rebellion. |
| *March–April 1800* | Second Cairo rebellion. |
| *1805–1848* | Reign of Muhammad Ali. |
| *1841* | Muhammad Ali is acclaimed hereditary pasha of Egypt. |
| *1848* | Reign of Ibrahim Pasha. |
| *1863–1879* | Reign of the Khedive Isma'il. |
| *17 November 1869* | Inauguration of the Suez Canal. |
| *July 1882* | British occupation of Egypt. |
| *1906* | Foundation of the Heliopolis Company. |
| *18 December 1914* | The British establish a protectorate over Egypt. |
| *1919* | Birth of the Wafd nationalist movement. |
| *26 August 1936* | Treaty establishing Egypt's independence. |
| *May 1948– February 1949* | First war in Palestine. |
| *23 July 1952* | Officers' revolution. |
| *November 1956* | Suez crisis. Second war with Israel. |
| *June 1967* | Six-Day War. |
| *September 1970* | Death of Gamal Abdel Nasser. |
| *October 1973* | Fourth war with Israel. |
| *September 1978* | Camp David agreements. |
| *1981* | Death of Anwar al-Sadat. |
| *1986* | general census: Cairo's population estimated at 8.63 million. |

# GLOSSARY

*agha:* chief of the janissary militia

*ahl al-qalam:* people of the pen

*ahl al-sayf:* people of the sword

*al-Ahram:* Cairo newspaper

*alim* (pl. *ulama*): scholar, doctor of law

*amir* (pl. *umara*): high dignitary

*amir al-hajj:* commander of the pilgrimage

*amma:* the populace

*ashraf* (sing. *sharif*): descendants of the Prophet

*askar:* soldier

*athman:* "eighths," administrative divisions

*awamm:* people from the populace

*awlad al-nas:* descendants of the Mamluks

*azab:* militia

*bab:* door, gate

*bahr:* sea, Nile

*bak, bayk:* bey, dignitary of Ottoman Egypt

*baladi:* "country" or local

*baladiyya:* municipality

*bayt* (pl. *buyut*): house, party of emirs

*bedestan:* covered market for precious goods

*beylerbey:* governor

*bimaristan:* hospital

*bir:* well

*birkat:* pond

*da'i:* Fatimid propagandist

*daftar:* register

*dar:* house, palace

*darb:* alley

*dhimmi:* "protected," member of Christian or Jewish minority

*dhira:* cubit

*diwan:* council

*dukkan:* shop

*faddan:* unit of area (0.4 hectare)

*fallah* (pl. *fallahin*): peasant

*faqih* (pl. *fuqaha*): doctor, jurisconsult

*fatwa:* religious ruling

*firman:* imperial decree

*funduq* (pl. *fanadiq*): caravanserai

*geniza:* storehouse for documents in Jewish communities

*hadith:* tradition in Islamic religion

*hajj:* pilgrimage

*hammam:* public bath

*hanut:* shop

*hara* (pl. *harat*): residential quarter

*hasil:* store in a caravanserai

*hawsh* (pl. *ahwash*): enclosure, courtyard

*hikr:* grant of land for building

*himaya:* protection

*hisba:* market authority (see *muhtasib*)

*iltizam:* rural tax-farming

*iqta* (pl. *iqta'at*): endowment of land

*irdabb:* unit of measure for grain

*iwan:* open hall or room

*jabal:* mountain

*jami:* Friday mosque

*kanunname:* ruling

*kapudan pasha:* chief admiral

*kashif:* provincial governor

*katkhuda:* lieutenant colonel

*kawm* (pl. *kiman*): butte, small hill

*khala:* undeveloped area

*khalij:* canal

*khan* (pl. *khanat*): caravanserai

*khandaq:* trench

*khanqa:* convent

*kharab:* ruins

*khatib:* prayer leader

*khazina:* annual tribute

*khitta* (pl. *khitat*): concession, block of land in a newly founded city

*khutba:* Friday sermon

*madhhab:* school of law

*madrasa:* school, college of Islamic law

*mahalla:* quarter

*maktab* (pl. *makatib*): neighborhood elementary school

*malik:* prince, ruler

*mamluk* (pl. *mamalik*): one who is "in the possession" of his master

*maq'ad:* loggia, open sitting room

*mashhad:* sanctuary, shrine

*mashrabiyya:* latticework balcony of turned wood

*masjid:* mosque

*mastaba* (pl. *masatib*): bench (in front of shops)

*maydan:* field for equestrian exercises, square

*mihrab:* niche indicating the direction of Mecca

*minbar:* pulpit

*miqyas:* Nilometer

*miri:* that which belongs to the imperial treasury

*mu'allim:* intendant, master of a trade

*mufti:* counselor who issues *fatwas*

*muhtasib:* overseer of the markets, chief of the market authority

*multazim:* titleholder of an *iltizam* (rural tax-farm)

*muqata'a:* tax farm

*musalla:* open-air prayer site

*mustahfizan:* name of the Cairo janissaries

*mutafarriqa:* Cairo militia

*na'ib:* deputy, viceroy

*nawba:* clique

*nazir:* administrator

*odjaq:* militia

*qa'a:* reception hall

*qabi quli* (Turkish: *kapi kulu*): imperial janissaries

*qadi* (pl. *qudah*): judge

*qantara* (pl. *qanatir*): bridge

*qasaba:* avenue

*qasr:* fort, palace

*qaysariyya* (pl. *qayasir*): covered market, caravanserai

*qibla:* direction of Mecca

*qism* (pl. *aqsam*): district

*qubba:* dome

*rab* (pl. *urbu*): apartment complex

*ra'i:* supervisor of a quarter/ community

*ra'iya:* "subjects," natives

*Ramadan:* month of fasting

*riwaq:* community at al-Azhar, reception room

*ru'iya:* sighting of the Ramadan moon

*Rumi:* Byzantines and Italians

*sabil:* fountain

*sahn:* courtyard

*saqqa* (pl. *saqqa'in*): water carrier

*shah bandar al-tuggar:* provost of the spice and coffee merchants

*shari:* large street

*sheikhat:* district

*sirdar:* military commander

*subashi:* prefect of police

*sufi:* mystic

*suq:* market

*suwayqa* (pl. *suwaqqat*): small, nonspecialized market

*tabaqa:* quarters, lodging

*taht al-qal'a:* under the Citadel

*ta'ifa* (pl. *tawa'if*): community

*tajir* (pl. *tujjar*): merchant of coffee and cloth

*takhtabush:* reception room

*takiyya:* convent

*tanzim:* plan

*tariq:* road

*tell:* hill

*turba:* tomb

*ulama* (sing. *alim*): scholars, doctors of law

*umara* (sing. *amir*): high dignitaries

*wakala* (pl. *wakalat*): caravanserai

*wali* (pl. *wulah*): governor, prefect of police

*waqf* (pl. *awqaf*): religious foundation or endowment

*waqfiyya: waqf* deed

*zakat:* legal alms

*zawiya:* convent

*zu'ar:* gangs of neighborhood youths

*zuqaq:* street

# ABBREVIATIONS

BEO     *Bulletin d'Etudes Orientales*

BIFAO     *Bulletin de l'Institut Français d'Archéologie Orientale*

BJMES     *British Journal of Middle Eastern Studies*

BSMES     British Society for Middle Eastern Studies

CIHC     *Colloque international sur l'histoire du Caire, 1969*, ed. André Raymond, Michael Rogers, and Magdi Wahba (Cairo: Ministry of Culture, 1972)

IFAO     Institut Français d'Archéologie Orientale

JARCE     *Journal of the American Research Center in Egypt*

JESHO     *Journal of the Economic and Social History of the Orient*

JRAS     *Journal of the Royal Asiatic Society*

MIFAO     *Mémoires de l'Institut Français d'Archéologie Orientale*

MMAFC     *Mémoires publiés par les Membres de la Mission Archéologique Française au Caire*

OUCC     Observatoire Urbain du Caire Contemporain

# NOTES

### PART I. FOUNDATIONS

1. Jean Yoyotte, Georges Posener, and Serge Sameron, *Dictionnaire de la civilisation égyptienne* (Paris: F. Hazan, 1959), p. 189.

#### 1. FUSTAT, THE FIRST CAPITAL

1. Quoted in Gaston Wiet, *L'Egypte arabe,* vol. 4 of *Histoire de la nation égyptienne* (Paris, 1937), p. 20.
2. Charles Diehl, *L'Egypte chrétienne et byzantine,* vol. 3 of *Histoire de la nation égyptienne* (Paris, 1933), pp. 535–544; T. W. Arnold, *The Preaching of Islam* (London: Luzac, 1935); Georges Anawati, "Factors and Effects of Arabization and Islamization," in *Islam and Cultural Change in the Middle Ages,* ed. Speros Vryonis (Wiesbaden: Harrassowitz, 1975), pp. 22–23.
3. J. Jarry, "L'Egypte et l'invasion musulmane," *Annales Islamologiques* 6 (1966). Jarry shows that one must look beyond the division between the Melchite Greeks and the Monophysite Copts to understand the Christian reaction to the Arab conquest—for instance, to the rifts between various sects and factions such as the "Blues" and the "Greens."
4. H. Zotenberg, "Mémoire sur la chronique byzantine de Jean, évêque de Nikiou," *Journal asiatique* 7 (1879), 363, 383.
5. On the problematic nature of our sources of information, see Wladyslaw Kubiak, *Al-Fustat: Its Foundation and Early Urban Development* (Cairo: American University in Cairo Press, 1987), to which I am principally indebted for my description of the history of Fustat; Sylvie Denoix, *Décrire le Caire: Fustat-Misr d'après Ibn Duqmaq et Maqrizi* (Cairo: IFAO, 1992)—the author was kind enough to show me her manuscript in preparation, for which I am very grateful; and idem, "La ville de Fustat" (Diss., Université de Provence, 1984). On the archaeological excavations: Ali Bahgat and Albert Gabriel, *Fouilles d'al-Foustat* (Cairo: Musée National de l'Art Arabe, 1921); George Scanlon and Wladyslaw Kubiak, "Preliminary Reports: Excavations at Fustat," *JARCE* 4–21 (1964–1978); Roland-Pierre Gayraud, "Istabl-Antar (Fostat), 1987–1989. Rapport de fouilles," *Annales Islamologiques* 25 (1991). Papyruses also provide valuable information, as shown in the works of Y. Ragib, especially *Marchands d'étoffes de Fayyoum au IIIe/IXe siècle,* 3 vols. (Cairo: IFAO).
6. On the founding of Fustat, see Wiet, *L'Egypte arabe;* Marcel Clerget, *Le Caire. Etude de géographie urbaine et d'histoire économique,* 2 vols. (Cairo: Imprimerie Schindler, 1934); Janet Abu-Lughod, *Cairo: 1001 Years of the City Victorious* (Princeton: Princeton University Press, 1971); Kubiak, *Al-Fustat;* Denoix, *Décrire le Caire;* also A. R. Guest, "The Foundation of Fustat," *JRAS,* January

1907; Paul Casanova, *Essai de reconstruction topographique de la ville d'al-Foustat ou Misr* (Cairo: IFAO, 1919); J.-C. Garcin, "Toponymie et topographie urbaines médiévales à Fustat et au Caire," *JESHO* 27 (1984).

7. Ahmad ibn Wadih Ya'qubi, *Livre des pays,* trans. Gaston Wiet (Cairo: IFAO, 1937), p. 184.

8. Kubiak believes that thirty or forty concessions of three to four hectares apiece, each with 300–350 inhabitants, were established over a very great area.

9. Clerget, *Le Caire,* 1: 112; J.-C. Garcin, "Habitat médiéval et histoire urbaine," in J.-C. Garcin, B. Maury, J. Revault, and M. Zakariya, *Palais et maisons du Caire,* vol. 1: *Epoque mamelouke (XIIIe au XVIe siècles)* (Paris, 1982); Gayraud, "Istabl-Antar," pp. 63–66.

10. Wiet, *L'Egypte arabe,* pp. 9–10, 22.

11. Kubiak, *Al-Fustat,* pp. 118–120.

12. Louis Hautecoeur and Gaston Wiet, *Les mosquées du Caire* (Paris, 1932), pp. 15–16; Wiet, *L'Egypte arabe,* pp. 32–60.

13. Abu Salih, *The Churches and Monasteries of Egypt,* ed. and trans. B. T. A. Evetts (London, 1895); Clerget, *Le Caire,* 1: 112; Wiet, *L'Egypte arabe,* pp. 39, 43, 57, quotation p. 58; De Lacy O'Leary, *The Saints of Egypt* (New York: Macmillan, 1937); Kubiak, *Al-Fustat,* pp. 80–83, 131; Gayraud, "Istabl-Antar," pp. 82–83.

14. Clerget, *Le Caire,* 1: 110; Kubiak, *Al-Fustat,* pp. 85–88; Gayraud, "Istabl-Antar," pp. 60, 83–84.

15. Taqi al-Din Ahmad ibn Ali al-Maqrizi (hereafter Maqrizi), *Al-mawa'iz wa al-l'tibar fi dhikr al-khitat wa al-athar* (hereafter *Khitat*), 2 vols. (Cairo: Bulaq Press Edition, 1853), 1: 296; Garcin, "Toponymie," pp. 117–118; Kubiak, *Al-Fustat,* pp. 88–93, 97–99.

16. On the Mosque of Amr, see Kubiak, *Al-Fustat,* pp. 95–96, 106–107, 111–116; idem, "The Circulation Tracks of al-Fustat," *African Bulletin* 28 (1979); K. A. C. Creswell, *Early Muslim Architecture,* 2 vols. (Oxford: Clarendon Press, 1932–1940), 2: 171 ff.; Doris Behrens-Abouseif, *Islamic Architecture in Cairo: An Introduction* (Leiden: E. J. Brill, 1989), pp. 47–49.

17. Zotenberg, "Chronique de Jean de Nikiou," pp. 356, 357, 385; Wiet, *L'Egypte Arabe,* pp. 44–54, 57–58; idem, "Kibt," in *Encyclopaedia of Islam,* 2d ed., 5 vols. to date (Leiden: E. J. Brill, 1960–), 2: 1048–61; Arnold, *The Preaching of Islam,* pp. 66–68; D. C. Dennett, *Conversion and the Poll Tax in Early Islam* (Cambridge, Mass.: Harvard University Press, 1950), pp. 87–88; I. M. Lapidus, "The Conversion of Egypt to Islam," *Israel Oriental Studies* 2 (1972), 249–254; Anawati, "Arabization and Islamization," pp. 27–28, 31–33, 38–39; idem, "The Christian Communities in Egypt," in *Conversion and Continuity: Indigenous Christian Communities in Islamic Lands, Eighth to Eighteenth Centuries,* ed. Michael Gervers and R. J. Bikhazi (Toronto: Pontifical Institute of Mediaeval Studies, 1990). On the Copts, see Pierre du Bourguet, *Les Coptes* (Paris: Presses Universitaires de France, 1988).

18. Maqrizi, *Khitat,* 1: 304–305.

19. Georges Salmon, "Etudes sur la topographie du Caire. La Kal'at al-Kabch et la Birkat al-Fil," *MIFAO* 7 (1902), 2–4; Wiet, *L'Egypte Arabe,* p. 61; Gayraud, "Istabl-Antar," pp. 70–72.

20. J.-J. Marcel, *Histoire de l'Egypte* (Paris, 1848), p. 84; Clerget, *Le Caire,* 1: 115,

118; Wiet, *L'Egypte Arabe*, pp. 75 (Maqrizi quotation), 76–80, 109–110; Salmon, "Etudes sur la topographie," pp. 1–9, 12, 28–29.

21. Hautecoeur and Wiet, *Les mosquées du Caire*, pp. 208–216; Creswell, *Early Muslim Architecture*, 2: 348 ff.; Behrens-Abouseif, *Islamic Architecture*, pp. 51–57.

22. Ibn Hauqal, *Configuration de la terre*, trans. J.-H. Kramers and Gaston Wiet, 2 vols. (Beirut and Paris, 1964), 1: 145. According to Maqrizi (*Khitat*, 1: 305; see Salmon, "Etudes sur la topographie," p. 9), al-Qata'i was finally destroyed during the crisis of Mustansir (eighth Fatimid caliph, 1035–1094), in 1058.

23. Ibn Hauqal, *Configuration de la terre*, pp. 144–145; R. Blachère, "L'agglomération du Caire, vue par quatre voyageurs arabes du Moyen Age," *Annales Islamologiques* 8 (1969), 4–12; al-Muqaddasi, *Ahsan al-taqasim fi Ma'rifat al-aqalim*, trans. A. Miquel (Damascus, 1963), p. 81; A. Miquel, "L'Egypte vue par un géographe arabe," *Annales Islamologiques* 11 (1972).

## 2. CAIRO, FATIMID CITY

1. On the Bahgat-Gabriel excavations, see Ali Bahgat and Albert Gabriel, *Fouilles d'al-Foustat* (Cairo and Paris: Musée National de l'Art Arabe, 1921); and Aly Bahgat Bey, "Les fouilles d'al-Foustat," *Syria*, 1923. On the question of dates, see George Scanlon and Wladyslaw Kubiak, "Re-dating Bahgat's Houses," *AARP* 4 (1973). Preliminary reports on the excavations of George Scanlon and Wladyslaw Kubiak are found in "Excavations at Fustat," *JARCE* 4–21 (1964–1978). See also Scanlon, "Fustat: Archaeological Reconsiderations," in *CIHC*. The results of the area C excavations are found in Kubiak and Scanlon, *Fustat Expedition Final Report*, vol. 2: *Fustat C* (Winona Lake, Ind.: Eisenbrauns, 1989).

2. S. D. Goitein, *A Mediterranean Society: The Jerusalem Communities of the Arab World as Portrayed in the Documents of the Cairo Geniza*, 5 vols. (Berkeley: University of California Press, 1967–1988). The Geniza documents are discussed in 1: 1–28 and idem, "Geniza," in *Encyclopaedia of Islam*, 2d ed., 5 vols. to date (Leiden: E. J. Brill, 1960–), 2: 1010–12.

3. On Cairo under the Fatimids, I have relied particularly on Ayman Fu'ad Sayyid, "La capitale de l'Egypte à l'époque fatimide. Al-Qahira et al-Fustat" (Thesis, Université de Paris I, 1986). I thank the author for his kindness in sending it to me.

4. K. A. C. Creswell, "The Foundation of Cairo," *Bulletin of the Faculty of Arts* (University of Egypt) 1 (1933); J. M. Bloom, "The Origins of Fatimid Art," *Muqarnas* 3 (1987).

5. Gaston Wiet, *L'Egypte arabe*, vol. 4 of *Histoire de la nation égyptienne* (Paris, 1937), quotation p. 153; Goitein, *A Mediterranean Society*, 1: 33–34; Thierry Bianquis, "La prise du pouvoir par les fatimides," *Annales Islamologiques* 11 (1972), 11; Yaacov Lev, "The Fatimid Imposition of Isma'ilism on Egypt," *ZDMG*, 1988, p. 138.

6. Creswell, "Foundation of Cairo," pp. 266–268; Fu'ad Sayyid, "La capitale," pp. 155 ff.

7. Nasir-i Khusraw, *Sefer Nameh, Relation du voyage de Nassiri Khosrau en Syrie,*

*en Palestine, en Egypte, en Arabie, et en Perse, 1035–42,* ed. and trans. Charles Schefer (Paris, 1881), p. 131.

8. The wall and gates having disappeared early on, their original course and location are the subject of continuing discussion among specialists. The northeast and southeast corners in particular have not been traced with any certainty. Furthermore, because the east and west walls were replaced in the following century by Badr al-Jamali's fortifications, it is difficult to reconstruct the original outline.

9. Paul Casanova, "Histoire et description de la Citadelle du Caire," *MMAFC* 6 (1891–92), 525; Creswell, "Foundation of Cairo," pp. 269–286.

10. J.-C. Garcin, "Toponymie et topographie urbaines médiévales," *JESHO* 27 (1984), 127. For a description of Qahira and the palaces, the key source is still Paul Ravaisse, "Essai sur l'histoire et sur la topographie du Caire d'après Makrizi," *MMAFC* 1.3 (1881–1884), 422. See also Yaacov Lev, "The Fatimid Army," *Asian and African Studies* 14 (1980), 167–169.

11. Ibn Hauqal, *Configuration de la terre,* trans. J.-H. Kramers and Gaston Wiet, 2 vols. (Beirut and Paris, 1964), 1: 144–145. *Trans.:* A congregational mosque, "a place of meeting and study as well as of prayer," is a great mosque where the Friday sermon is preached.

12. A. Miquel, "L'Egypte vue par un géographe arabe," *Annales Islamologiques* 11 (1972), 118–119 n. 64, 120.

13. Bianquis, "La prise du pouvoir," pp. 90–91.

14. Goitein, *A Mediterranean Society,* 1: 32–33; Thierry Bianquis, *Damas et la Syrie sous la domination fatimide,* 2 vols. (Damascus: Institut Français de Damas, 1986, 1989), 1: 157–161.

15. Goitein, *A Mediterranean Society,* 1: 44–45, 60–61, 66; 2: 402–403; Gustav E. von Grunebaum, "The Nature of the Fatimid Achievement," in *CIHC,* p. 206; Claude Cahen, "Les marchands étrangers au Caire," ibid., pp. 98–99; Bianquis, *Damas et la Syrie,* 1: 163–164; Yaacov Lev, *State and Society in Fatimid Egypt* (Leiden: E. J. Brill, 1991), p. 159.

16. Nasir-i Khusraw, *Relation de voyage,* pp. 149–150; Wiet, *L'Egypte arabe,* p. 306.

17. Bernard Lewis, "An Interpretation of Fatimid History," in *CIHC,* p. 289; Youssef Eche, *Les bibliothèques arabes publiques* (Damascus, 1967), p. 79. On the Shiite shrines, see the works of Y. Raghib, especially "Essai d'inventaire chronologique des Guides à l'usage des pèlerins du Caire," *Revue des études islamiques* 41–42 (1973).

18. Bianquis, *Damas et la Syrie,* 2: 683; Gary Leiser, "The *madrasa* and the Islamization of the Middle East," *JARCE* 22 (1985).

19. Abu Salih, *The Churches and Monasteries of Egypt,* ed. and trans. B. T. A. Evetts (London, 1895), p. 2; Wiet, *L'Egypte arabe,* pp. 194, 220, 268–273. The verse is from Rida ibn Thawb, trans. Max Rodenbeck in *Cairo: The City Victorious* (New York: Alfred A. Knopf, 1999), p. 79.

20. De Lacy O'Leary, *The Saints of Egypt* (New York: Macmillan, 1937), p. 11; von Grunebaum, "Fatimid Achievement," pp. 210–211.

21. Abd-Allatif, *Relation de l'Egypte,* trans. S. de Sacy (Paris, 1810), p. 466.

22. Julio Navarro Palazón, *Una casa islamica en Murcia* (Murcia, 1991).

23. Gaston Wiet, "Recherches sur les bibliothèques égyptiennes," *Cahiers de civilisation médiévale* 6 (1963); Eche, *Les bibliothèques arabes;* R. G. Khoury, "Une

description fantastique des fonds de la bibliothèque royale . . . au Caire," in *Proceedings of the 9th Congress of the UEAI* (Leiden: E. J. Brill, 1981).

24. Guillaume de Tyr, *Texte français du XIIIè siècle,* ed. M. Paulin (Paris, 1879–1880), pp. 279–280.

25. M. Canard, "Le cérémonial Fatimide," *Byzantion* 21 (1951); M. Espéronnier, "Les fêtes civiles et les cérémonies d'origine antique sous les Fatimides," *Der Islam* 65 (1988).

26. Marius Canard, "La procession du nouvel an chez les fatimides," *Annales* (Institut d'Etudes Orientales de l'Université d'Alger) 10 (1952).

27. Nasir-i Khusraw, *Relation de voyages,* p. 142.

28. The palaces are known only from the descriptions of generally later authors, Maqrizi's being the most detailed. Their boundaries and general structure were reconstrued only in the late nineteenth century, thanks to the work of Paul Ravaisse, who based his research on historical sources and on the place-names recorded at the end of the eighteenth century in the *Description de l'Egypte*. For the palaces, I have relied mainly on Ravaisse, *Essai sur l'histoire;* and Fu'ad Sayyid, "La capitale," pp. 240 ff. See also Nasir-i Khusraw, *Relation de voyage,* pp. 128–129, 158; G. Schlumberger, *Campagnes du roi Amaury Ier* (Paris, 1906), pp. 118–121; André Raymond and Gaston Wiet, *Les marchés du Caire. Traduction annotée du texte de Maqrizi* (Cairo: IFAO, 1979), pp. 144–145, 188; J.-C. Garcin, "Habitat médiéval et histoire urbaine," in J.-C. Garcin, B. Maury, J. Revault, and M. Zakariya, *Palais et maisons du Caire,* vol. 1: *Epoque mamelouke (XIIIe au XVIe siècles)* (Paris, 1982), pp. 165–166. The location index (a letter and a number) refers to the grid on the map of Cairo in the *Description de l'Egypte,* which is reproduced on most of the maps in this volume.

29. Raymond and Wiet, *Les marchés du Caire,* pp. 217–218.

30. Nasir-i Khusraw, *Relation de voyage,* pp. 127, 133; Raymond and Wiet, *Les marchés du Caire,* pp. 155, 163, 178, 212, 214–215; Fu'ad Sayyid, "La capitale," pp. 712–715.

31. Georges Salmon, "Etudes sur la topographie du Caire. La Kal'at al-Kabch et la Birkat al-Fil," *MIFAO* 7 (1902), 49–64; Doris Behrens-Abouseif, "The North-Eastern Extensions of Cairo under the Mamluks," *Annales Islamologiques* 17 (1981); idem, *Azbakiyya and Its Environs, from Azbak to Isma'il, 1476–1879* (Cairo: IFAO, 1985), pp. 2–5.

32. Louis Hautecoeur and Gaston Wiet, *Les mosquées du Caire* (Paris, 1932), pp. 232–239; Doris Behrens-Abouseif, *Islamic Architecture in Cairo: An Introduction* (Leiden: E. J. Brill, 1989), pp. 67–72. A recently found inscription has made it possible to locate and identify the Bab al-Barqiyya on the east wall (*Description de l'Egypte:* Bab al-Ghurayyib, K 3). Dated 1087, its text continues the text of the Bab al-Futuh inscription (Wiet, "Une nouvelle inscription fatimide," *Journal asiatique* 249 [1961]). Less grandiose than the three others, the gate has unfortunately not been the object of conservation measures (Fu'ad Sayyid, "La capitale," pp. 428–437).

33. See Behrens-Abouseif, *Islamic Architecture,* pp. 9–10, 58–77; also Hautecoeur and Wiet, *Les mosquées du Caire,* pp. 217–251; and K. A. C. Creswell et al., *The Mosques of Egypt,* 2 vols. (Giza, 1949).

34. A. Udovitch, "Time, the Sea and Society," *Settimane di Studio* (Spoleto) 25

(1978), 521–511; Goitein, *A Mediterranean Society*, 4: 7; idem, "Artisans en Méditerranée orientale," *Annales* 5 (1964), 848; idem, "Le commerce méditerranéen avant les Croisades," *Diogène* 59 (1967), 58. See also A. Udovitch, "A Tale of Two Cities: Commercial Relations between Cairo and Alexandria," in *The Medieval City* (New Haven: Yale University Press, 1977).

35. Nasir-i Khusraw, *Relation de voyage*, pp. 151–152; Abd-Allatif, *Relation*, p. 409; Goitein, "Artisans en Méditerranée," p. 850; idem, *A Mediterranean Society*, 1: 81, 367. See Paul Casanova, *Essai de reconstitution topographique de la ville d'al-Foustat ou Misr* (Cairo: IFAO, 1919); and Sylvie Denoix, *Décrire le Caire: Fustat-Misr d'après Ibn Duqmaq et Maqrizi* (Cairo: IFAO, 1992).

36. If we consider the area for which place-names have been recorded in the work of Paul Casanova and Sylvie Denoix, and if we grant that the wall later built by Saladin must roughly have marked the boundaries of urban development, we obtain an area some 1,500 meters from east to west and 2,000 meters from north to south, within which are the residential areas excavated by Bahgat and Scanlon.

37. Marcel Clerget, *Le Caire. Etude de géographie urbaine et d'histoire économique* (Cairo: Imprimerie Schindler, 1934), p. 239; Fu'ad Sayyid, "La capitale," pp. 649–650; Thierry Bianquis, "Une crise frumentaire dans l'Egypte fatimide," *JESHO* 23 (1980), 96; M. Reinhard, *Histoire générale de la population mondiale* (Paris, 1968), p. 84; J. Heers, *La ville au moyen âge* (Paris, 1990), pp. 341, 346–347; private communication on Venic from Daniele Pini.

38. Goitein, *A Mediterranean Society*, 5: 310; Miquel, "L'Egypte," p. 119; Raymond and Wiet, *Les marchés du Caire*, p. 181.

39. Goitein, *A Mediterranean Society*, 4: 15–16, 20; Fu'ad Sayyid, "La capitale," pp. 625–628.

40. Nasir-i Khusraw, *Relation de voyage*, p. 156; Goitein, *A Mediterranean Society*, 1: 83, 193, 238–239, 296 (quotation), 308, 317–318, 340–341, 349–350; 4: 14, 26–30.

41. Ibn Hauqal, *Configuration de la terre*, 1: 144; Miquel, "L'Egypte," p. 117; Nasir-i Khusraw, *Relation de voyage*, pp. 146–147.

42. A. Lézinem, "Persistance de traditions pré-islamiques dans l'architecture domestique de l'Egypte musulmane," *Annales Islamologiques* 11 (1972); Goitein, *A Mediterranean Society*, 4: 58, 81; Gamal Mehrez, "Les habitations d'al-Fustat," in *CIHC*, pp. 321–322; Pierre Grimal, *La civilisation romaine* (Paris, 1962), pp. 286–290.

43. Goitein, *A Mediterranean Society*, 2: 368–369; 4: 14, 19, 34–36, 40, 53; Lev, *State and Society*, pp. 153–160.

44. Goitein, *A Mediterranean Society*, 4: 369; M. Gil, *Documents of the Jewish Pious Foundations* (Leiden: E. J. Brill, 1976), pp. 88, 123, 165, 241, 363.

45. On this topic see the works of Bahgat cited in note 1 above, especially *Fouilles d'al-Foustat;* and Scanlon and Kubiak: "Excavations at Fustat," "Fustat: Archaeological Reconsiderations," and "Redating Bahgat's Houses." On the Geniza documents, see Goitein, *A Mediterranean Society*, 4: 59 ff.; idem, "A Mansion in Fustat," in *The Medieval City;* idem, "Urban Housing in Fatimid and Ayyubid Times," *Studia Islamica* 47 (1978); Garcin, "Habitat médiéval," pp. 155, 170.

46. Garcin, "Habitat médiéval," p. 173 (reference to Abd Allatif's *Relation*); Kubiak and Scanlon, *Final Report: Fustat C.* On housing during pharaonic times, see

Dominique Valbelle, "Eléments sur la démographie et le paysage urbain," *Cahiers de recherche de l'Institut de papyrologie et d'Egyptologie de Lille*, p. 7.

47. On the non-Muslim communities see Goitein, *A Mediterranean Society*, 1: 71; 2: 284–289; 4: 21, 193–199; Lev, *State and Society*, pp. 179 ff.

48. O'Leary, *Saints of Egypt*, p. 140; H. Munier, *Recueil des listes épiscopales de l'Eglise copte* (Cairo, 1943), p. 27; I. M. Lapidus, "The Conversion of Egypt to Islam," *Israel Oriental Studies* 2 (1972), 261; Doris Behrens-Abouseif, "Locations of Non-Muslim Quarters in Medieval Cairo," *Annales Islamologiques* 22 (1986).

49. Benjamin of Tudela, *The Itinerary of Benjamin of Tudela*, ed. M. N. Adler (London, 1907), p. 70; Norman A. Stillman, "The Eleventh-century Merchant House of Ibn Awkal," *JESHO* 16 (1973); Goitein, *A Mediterranean Society*, vol. 2 passim.

50. Wiet, *L'Egypte arabe*, pp. 219–254, quotation p. 242; Goitein, *A Mediterranean Society*, 4: 25, 241–242; 5: 440; Fu'ad Sayyid, "La capitale," pp. 508, 654–665, 671–674; R.-P. Gayraud, "Istabl Antar, 1987–1989," *Annales Islamologiques* 25 (1991), 86.

51. Fu'ad Sayyid, "La capitale," pp. 415 ff.; Raymond and Weil, *Les marchés du Caire*, p. 181.

52. Schlumberger, *Campagnes du roi Amaury Ier*, pp. 132 (quotation), 133, 172–177; Maqrizi, *Histoire des sultans mamelouks de l'Egypte*, trans. M. Quatremère, 2 vols. (Paris, 1845), 2: 135; idem, *Khitat*, 2: 69; Wiet, *L'Egypte arabe*, pp. 289–297; Fu'ad Sayyid, "La capitale," pp. 585–592; Bianquis, *Damas et la Syrie*, 2: 655.

53. Maqrizi, *Khitat*, 1: 338–339; Schlumberger, *Campagnes du roi Amaury Ier*, pp. 194–196; Andrew S. Ehrenkreutz, *Saladin* (Albany: SUNY Press, 1972), p. 48; Fu'ad Sayyid, "La capitale," p. 666.

54. Review of the data by Wladyslaw Kubiak, "The Burning of Misr al-Fustat in 1168," *Africana Bulletin* 25 (1976); Abu Salih, *Churches and Monasteries;* Benjamin of Tudela, *Itinerary*, pp. 69–73; Ibn Jubayr, *The Travels of Ibn Jubayr*, trans. R. J. C. Broadhurst (London: Jonathan Cape, 1952), pp. 31–58; Goitein, *A Mediterranean Society*, 1: 18; 4: 12, 103; Gil, *Documents*, pp. 309–311, 485–509; Fu'ad Sayyid, "La capitale," pp. 666–673, quotation p. 670.

55. Benjamin of Tudela, *Itinerary*, p. 71; Ibn Jubayr, *Travels*, pp. 42–49; Wiet, *L'Egypte arabe*, pp. 208–209; Goitein, *A Mediterranean Society*, 2: 242; 3: 364 ff.; 4: 254; Raymond and Weit, *Les marchés du Caire*, p. 181; Lev, "The Fatimid Army," p. 168; Behrens-Abouseif, "Locations," p. 122; idem, *Azbakiyya*, p. 4.

56. Clerget, *Le Caire*, 1: 141, 239.

## 3. CAIRO UNDER THE AYYUBIDS

1. Andrew S. Ehrenkreutz, "Saladin's Coup d'Etat in Egypt," in *Medieval and Middle Eastern Studies*, ed. S. Hanna (Leiden: E. J. Brill, 1972). See also idem, *Saladin* (Albany: SUNY Press, 1972), p. 187.

2. Thierry Bianquis, *Damas et la Syrie sous la domination fatimide*, 2 vols. (Damascus: Institut Français de Damas, 1986, 1989), 2: 690; Ehrenkreutz, *Saladin*, p. 187.

3. Maqrizi, *A History of the Ayyubid Sultans of Egypt,* trans. R. J. C. Broadhurst (Boston: G. K. Hall, 1980), p. 89.

4. Muhammad ibn Wasil, *Mufarrij al-kurub,* 5 vols., ed. G. al-Shayyal (vol. 1) and H. M. Rabi (vols. 2–5) (Cairo, 1957–1977), 5: 341; Gaston Wiet, *Cairo: City of Art and Commerce,* trans. Seymour Feiler (Norman: University of Oklahoma Press, 1964), p. 43 (Maqrizi quotation); Ehrenkreutz, *Saladin,* pp. 77–78; Stephen Humphreys, *From Saladin to the Mongols* (Albany: SUNY Press, 1977).

5. Paul Casanova, "Histoire et description de la Citadelle du Caire," *MMAFC* 6 (1891–92), 535; K. A. C. Creswell, *The Muslim Architecture of Egypt: Ayyubids and Early Bahrite Mamluks, A.D. 1171–1326,* 2 vols. (Oxford: Clarendon Press, 1952, 1960), 2: 55; Ehrenkreutz, *Saladin,* p. 84.

6. Ayman Fu'ad Sayyid, "La capitale de l'Egypte à l'époque fatimide: Al-Qahira et al-Fustat" (Thesis, Université de Paris I, 1986), quotation p. 677.

7. The architectural data on the Citadel and the wall are reviewed in Creswell, *Muslim Architecture,* 2: 1–63. See also Stanley Lane-Poole, *The Story of Cairo* (London: J. M. Dent, 1902), p. 175; Casanova, "Citadelle," pp. 354–355.

8. Abd-Allatif, *Relation de l'Egypte,* trans. S. de Sacy (Paris, 1810), pp. 171–172; Ibn Jubayr, *The Travels of Ibn Jubayr,* trans. R. J. C. Broadhurst (London: Jonathan Cape, 1952), pp. 43, 52; J. M. Rogers, "Kahira," in *The Encyclopaedia of Islam,* 2d ed., 5 vols. to date (Leiden: E. J. Brill, 1960–), 4: 448; Max van Berchem, *Matériaux pour un Corpus Inscriptionum Arabicarum, 1, Egypte* (Cairo, 1894–1903), 3: 465; G. Schlumberger, *Renaud de Châtillon* (Paris, 1923), pp. 219–220.

9. The text of the inscription is in *Répertoire chronologique d'épigraphie Arabe* 9 (1937), 124 (here with "was ordered" in place of "was founded"); Ibn Jubayr, *Travels,* p. 43; Ibn Wasil, *Mufarrij,* 2: 53; Casanova, "Citadelle," pp. 556–557; Creswell, *Muslim Architecture,* 2: 6.

10. Casanova, "Citadelle," pp. 568–588; see also Creswell, *Muslim Architecture,* 2: 1–40; Doris Behrens-Abouseif, *Islamic Architecture in Cairo* (Leiden: E. J. Brill, 1989), pp. 78–81.

11. Ibn Wasil, *Mufarrij,* 5: 60; E. Blochet, "Histoire d'Egypte de Maqrizi," *Revue de l'Orient latin* 8–11 (1900–1908), 344; Casanova, "Citadelle," pp. 588–598; Creswell, *Muslim Architecture,* 2: 5, 39; Behrens-Abouseif, *Islamic Architecture,* p. 81.

12. This according to Paul Casanova, who assigns the cubit a length of .656 meter, for a total of 19,220 meters. That length is broken down as follows: from the tower at al-Maqs to the Citadel, 5,504 meters; for the wall of the Citadel, 2,106 meters; from the Citadel to the tower of the Red Hill (Kawm al-Ahmar) at the southern extremity of Fustat, 4,723 meters; and from the tower of Maqsam to the tower of Kawm al-Ahmar along the bank of the Nile, 6,888 meters.

13. Ibn Jubayr, *Travels,* p. 43; Abu Shama, *Kitab al-rawdatayn* (Cairo, 1962), vol. 1, pt. 2, p. 687; Ibn Wasil, *Mufarrij,* 2: 52; Maqrizi, *History of Ayyubid Sultans,* pp. 80, 98, 133; Lane-Poole, *Story of Cairo,* pp. 174–175; Casanova, "Citadelle," pp. 535–542; Creswell, *Muslim Architecture,* 2: 41–62.

14. Abd-Allatif, *Relation,* p. 171; Ali Bahgat and Albert Gabriel, *Fouilles d'al-Foustat* (Cairo and Paris: Musée National de l'Art Arabe, 1921), p. 24.

15. Abd-Allatif, *Relation,* pp. 332, 350–376, 409–412, 420; Ibn Wasil, *Mufarrij,* 3: 127; S. D. Goitein, *A Mediterranean Society: The Jerusalem Communities of the Arab World as Portrayed in the Documents of the Cairo Geniza,* 5 vols. (Berke-

ley: University of California Press, 1967–1988), 4: 238–239; 5: 92; M. Gil, *Documents of the Jewish Pious Foundations* (Leiden: E J. Brill, 1976), pp. 378–379; Maqrizi, *History of Ayyubid Sultans*, pp. 139–141.

16. Ibn Wasil, *Mufarrij*, 3: 54; 4: 260; Maqrizi, *History of Ayyubid Sultans*, pp. 38–40; Creswell, *Muslim Architecture*, 2: 3; Fu'ad Sayyid, "La capitale," pp. 260–261.

17. Ibn Jubayr, *Travels*, pp. 43–44; Ibn Wasil, *Mufarrij*, 2: 55; Maqrizi, *History of Ayyubid Sultans*, pp. 55, 67.

18. Leonor Fernandes, *The Evolution of a Sufi Institution: The Khanqah* (Berlin, 1988), p. 22. On the Kamiliyya madrasa (listed as number 428), see Ibn Wasil, *Mufarrij*, 5: 162; Maqrizi, *History of Ayyubid Sultans*, p. 229; idem, *Khitat*, 2: 375. On the Salihiyya madrasa (and tomb number 38), see Maqrizi, *Histoire des sultans mamlouks de l'Egypte*, trans. M. Quatremère, 2 vols. (Paris, 1845), 1: 11; *Khitat*, 2: 374; Behrens-Abouseif, *Islamic Architecture*, pp. 87–90.

19. R. Blachère, "L'agglomération du Caire," *Annales Islamologiques* 8 (1969), 23; Maqrizi, *History of Ayyubid Sultans*, pp. 108, 285; André Raymond and Gaston Wiet, *Les marchés du Caire. Traduction annotée du texte de Maqrizi* (Cairo: IFAO, 1979), p. 219; Wiet, *Cairo*, pp. 49–53.

20. Maqrizi, *History*, pp. 58, 298; idem, *Khitat*, 2: 147; Doris Behrens-Abouseif, "The North-Eastern Extensions of Cairo under the Mamluks," *Annales Islamologique* 17 (1981), 162; idem, *Azbakiyya and Its Environs, from Azbak to Isma'il, 1476–1879* (Cairo: IFAO, 1985), p. 6; and idem, "Locations of Non-Muslim Quarters in Medieval Cairo," *Annales Islamologiques* 22 (1986), 123, 130. The sanguine projections of Marcel Clerget and Janet Abu-Lughod regarding Cairo's westward expansion seem excessive. See Marcel Clerget, *Le Caire. Etude de géographie urbaine et d'histoire économique*, 2 vols. (Cairo: Imprimerie Schindler, 1934), 1: 149; and Janet Abu-Lughod, *Cairo: 1001 Years of the City Victorious* (Princeton: Princeton University Press, 1971), p. 27.

21. Lane-Poole, *Story of Cairo*, p. 181; Ibn Jubayr, *Travels*, p. 44.

22. Maqrizi, *History*, p. 250; idem, *Khitat*, 2: 133 (quotation), 364, 413; Georges Salmon, "Etudes sur la topographie du Caire. La Kal'al al-Kabch et la Birkat al-Fil," *MIFAO* 7 (1902), 77–80. For a more sensible view of the development of the southern zone, one must give greater consideration than either Clerget (*Le Caire*, pp. 146–147) or Abu-Lughod (*Cairo*, p. 30) to the fact that the Ayyubids actually resided in the Citadel for quite a short time—thirty-three years, starting in the reign of Kamil.

23. Maqrizi, *History of Ayyubid Sultans*, pp. 63, 66, 215, 296.

24. Blachère, "L'agglomération du Caire," pp. 19–22; Goitein, *A Mediterranean Society*, 1: 18–19, 148; 4: 12.

25. Ibn Wasil, *Mufarrij*, 5: 278; Maqrizi, *History of Ayyubid Sultans*, pp. 260, 264, 294, 296, 298; idem, *Histoire des sultans mamelouks*, trans. M. Quatremère, 2 vols. (Paris, 1845), 1: 33; Gaston Wiet, *L'Egypte arabe*, vol. 4 of *Histoire de la nation égyptienne* (Paris, 1937), p. 370; Blachère, "L'agglomération du Caire," pp. 21–22.

26. Maqrizi, *History*, pp. 40, 68, 120, 161; Wiet, *L'Egypte arabe*, p. 299; T. W. Arnold, *The Preaching of Islam* (London: Luzac, 1935), pp. 107–109.

27. Mausoleum of al-Shafi'i, *Répertoire chronologique d'épigraphie Arabe* 9 (1937), no. 3339, pp. 95–96; Ibn Jubayr, *Travels*, p. 57; Gaston Wiet, *Précis d'histoire de*

*l'Egypte* (Cairo, 1932), pp. 230–232; idem, *Cairo*, p. 53; I. Lapidus, "Ayyubid Religious Policy and the Development of the Schools of Law in Cairo," in *CIHC*, pp. 283–284; Behrens-Abouseif, *Islamic Architecture*, pp. 11–12.

28. See Wiet, *Précis*, p. 234; Rogers, "Kahira"; and S. Ory, "Kitaba," in *The Encyclopaedia of Islam*, 5: 215; and, in general, Behrens-Abouseif, *Islamic Architecture*, pp. 11–14, 87–93, quotation p. 91.

## II. MEDIEVAL CAIRO

1. J.-C. Garcin, "Toponymie et topographie urbaines médiévales à Fustat et au Caire," *JESHO* 27 (1984), 155.

## 4. THE MAMLUKS

1. The major sources for the Mamluk period are Maqrizi, *Kitab al-suluk li ma'rifat duwal al-muluk* (Cairo: Lagnat al Ta'lif, 1936–1973) (hereafter *Kitab al-suluk*), parts 2, 3, and 4, covering the years 1304–1441; Abu al-Mahasin ibn Taghribirdi (hereafter Ibn Taghribirdi), *Al-nujum al-zahira fi muluk misr wa-al-qahira*, ed. William Popper, 7 vols. (Berkeley: University of California Press, 1926–1929), vol. 7, covering the period 1437–1468. This work has been translated into English as *History of Egypt, 1382–1469 A.D.*, trans. William Popper, 7 vols. (Berkeley: University of California Press, 1954–1963). See also extracts from Ibn Taghribirdi's *Hawadith al-duhur*, ed. William Popper, 4 vols. (Berkeley: University of California Press, 1930–1942), covering the period 1441–1469. Popper has published "systematic notes" on Ibn Taghribirdi under the title *Egypt and Syria under the Circassian Sultans (1382–1468)*, 2 vols. (Berkeley: University of California Press, 1955–1957). On Maqrizi see J.-C. Garcin, "al-Maqrizi," *Les Africains* 9 (1978); on Ibn Taghribirdi see Ahmad Darrag, "La vie d'Abu'l-Mahasin ibn Taghri-Birdi," *Annales Islamologiques* 11 (1972). The last great text on this period also covers the start of the Ottoman period: Muhammad ibn Iyas, *Bada'i al-zuhur fi waqa'i al-duhur*, ed. Mohamed Mustafa, 5 vols. (Cairo and Wiesbaden, 1961–1983). The last three volumes, covering the period 1468–1522, have been translated by Gaston Wiet as *Histoire des Mamlouks circassiens* (Cairo, 1945) and *Journal d'un bourgeois du Caire*, 2 vols. (Paris, 1950–1960). The bibliography for this period is abundant. Aside from Gaston Wiet, *L'Egypte arabe*, vol. 4 of *Histoire de la nation égyptienne* (Paris: 1937), I have particularly drawn on the works of David Ayalon and J.-C. Garcin (some of which appear in essay collections): David Ayalon, *Outsiders in the Lands of Islam: Mamluks, Mongols, and Eunuchs* (London: Variorum Reprints, 1988); J.-C. Garcin, *Espaces, pouvoirs et idéologies de l'Egypte médiévale* (London: Variorum Reprints, 1987); also Ira M. Lapidus, *Muslim Cities in the Later Middle Ages* (Cambridge, Mass.: Harvard University Press, 1967) and *A History of Muslim Societies* (Cambridge: Cambridge University Press, 1988).

2. Paul Veyne, *Le pain et le cirque* (Paris, 1976), p. 728; R. Brunschvig, "Abd," in *The Encyclopaedia of Islam*, 2d ed. (Leiden: E. J. Brill, 1960–), 1: 25–41.

3. Ibn Iyas, *Histoire des Mamlouks*, p. 19; Maqrizi, *Khitat*, 2; 213–214; R. S.

Humphreys, "The Emergence of the Mamluk Army," *Studia Islamica* 45–46 (1977); Barbara Flemming, "Literary Activities in Mamluk Halls and Barracks," in *Studies in Memory of Gaston Wiet*, ed. M. Rosen-Ayalon (Jerusalem, 1977); U. Haarmann, "Arabic in Speech, Turkish in Lineage," *Journal of Semitic Studies* 33 (1988); J.-C. Garcin, "Le système militaire mamelouk," *Annales Islamologiques* 24 (1988).

4. Ibn Taghribirdi, *History of Egypt*, 6: 11.

5. On the economy of Mamluk Egypt: Subhi Y. Labib, *Handelgeschichte Aegyptens* (Wiesbaden, 1965); Jacques Berque, "Les capitales de l'Islam méditerranéen," *Annales Islamologiques* 8 (1969), 83. On the Karimi merchants: Gaston Wiet, "Les marchands d'épices," *Cahiers d'histoire Egyptienne* (Cairo), 1955; E. Ashtor, "The Karimi Merchants," *JRAS*, 1956; W. Fischel, "The Spice Trade," *JESHO* 1 (1958); S. Y. Labib, "Les marchands Karimis," in *Colloque international d'histoire maritime*, ed. M. Mollat (Paris, 1970).

## 5. THE HIGH POINT OF MAMLUK CAIRO

1. Muhammad ibn Battuta, *Voyages*, French trans. C. Defremery and B. R. Sanguinetti, 4 vols. (1854; reprint, Paris, 1968), 1: 67–69; English trans. Sir Hamilton Gibb, *Travels* (London: Hakluyt Society, 1958); J. Russell, "The Population of Medieval Egypt," *JARCE* 5 (1966), 76; Michael Dols, *The Black Death in the Middle East* (Princeton: Princeton University Press, 1977), pp. 149, 176, 302.

2. Maqrizi, *Kitab al-suluk*, 2: 537, 644; idem, *Histoire des sultans mamlouks de l'Egypte*, trans. M. Quatremère (Paris, 1845), 2: 65; Gaston Wiet, *L'Egypte arabe*, vol. 4 of *Histoire de la nation égyptienne* (Paris, 1937), p. 482.

3. Ibn Battuta, *Voyages*, 1: 171; Maqrizi, *Kitab al-suluk*, 2: 230; Gaston Wiet, *Cairo: City of Art and Commerce*, trans. Seymour Feiler (Norman: University of Oklahoma Press, 1964), pp. 128–129; Doris Behrens-Abouseif, *Islamic Architecture in Cairo* (Leiden: E. J. Brill, 1989), p. 96.

4. Maqrizi, *Kitab al-suluk*, 2: 70, 501 (1339); 3: 251 (1375); idem, *Histoire des sultans mamlouks*, 2: 169 (1279); André Raymond and Gaston Wiet, *Les marchés du Caire. Traduction annotée du texte de Maqrizi* (Cairo: IFAO, 1979), pp. 140–141; J.-C. Garcin, "Toponymie et topographie urbaines médiévales à Fustat et au Caire," *JESHO* 27 (1984), 133. Ayman Fu'ad Sayyid, "La capitale de l'Egypte à l'époque fatimide: Al-Qahira et al-Fustat" (Thesis, Université de Paris I, 1986), pp. 262–263.

5. On the northward expansion see Doris Behrens-Abouseif, "The North-Eastern Extensions of Cairo under the Mamluks," *Annales Islamologique* 17 (1981), though the author overestimates the extent of urbanization; Maqrizi, *Kitab al-suluk*, 2: 240, 251, 260–262; Raymond and Wiet, *Les marchés du Caire*, p. 210; J. Bloom, "The Mosque of Baybars," *Annales Islamologiques* 18 (1982); Leonor Fernandes, *The Evolution of a Sufi Institution: The Khanqah* (Berlin, 1988).

6. Maqrizi, *Khitat*, 2: 146–148; idem, *Kitab al-suluk*, 2: 261, 539; idem, *Histoire des sultans mamlouks*, 4: 269 (quotation); Doris Behrens-Abouseif, *Azbakiyya and Its Environs, from Azbak to Isma'il, 1476–1879* (Cairo: IFAO, 1985), pp. 9–10.

7. Maqrizi, *Khitat*, 2: 116, 309; idem, *Kitab al-suluk*, 2: 543; J.-C. Garcin, "Habitat médiéval et histoire urbaine," in J.-C. Garcin et al., *Palais et maisons du Caire*,

vol. 1: *Epoque mamelouke (XIIIe au XVIe siècles)* (Paris, 1982), pp. 163–164; Galila El Kadi, *L'urbanisation spontanée au Caire* (Tours, 1987), p. 194.

8. Maqrizi, *Khitat*, 2: 151; idem, *Kitab al-suluk*, 2: 130–131, 251, 423, 449, 761, 769; idem, *Histoire des sultans mamlouks*, 1: 181, 221–222, 241; 3: 51; Behrens-Abouseif, *Azbakiyya*, pp. 6, 12.

9. Maqrizi, *Kitab al-suluk*, 2: 131, 419; idem, *Khitat*, 2: 151; Behrens-Abouseif, *Azbakiyya*, p. 12; Nelly Hanna, *An Urban History of Bulaq in the Mamluk and Ottoman Periods* (Cairo: IFAO, 1983).

10. *Index to Mohammedan Monuments in Cairo* (Giza: Survey of Egypt, 1951). See also Doris Behrens Abouseif, "The Citadel of Cairo," *Annales Islamologiques* 24 (1988); Paul Casanova, "Histoire et description de la Citadelle du Caire." *MMAFC* 6 (1891–92), 602–610, 619 ff.; and Wiet, *Cairo*, pp. 150–152.

11. Creswell has identified the central portion of this aqueduct, the segments on either side of where it bends northeast on meeting Saladin's wall (no. 78), as well as the waterwheel located south of the Citadel (no. 369).

12. There is some confusion about the course of this aqueduct. The authors of a study of the map published in Venice by Mathio Pagano in 1549 suggest that it followed the encircling wall around Old Cairo on the east and south (Saladin's wall); B. Blanc, S. Denoix, J.-C. Garcin, and R. Gordiani, "A propos de la carte du Caire de Mathio Pagano," *Annales Islamologiques* 17 (1981). But Creswell indicates a partial route identical with what would become Ghuri's aqueduct in 1508. It seems simpler to suppose that the aqueduct on the map is in fact Ghuri's, but that it is misplaced with respect to Old Cairo. On this question, see Victoria Meinecke-Berg, "Eine Stadtansicht des Mamlukischen Kairo," *Mitteilungen des Deutschen Archäologischen Instituts Kairo*, 1976, p. 32. On Nasir's construction, see Maqrizi, *Kitab al-suluk*, 2: 124, 302, 514, 549; Casanova, "Citadelle," p. 659; K. A. C. Creswell, *The Muslim Architecture of Egypt*, 2 vols. (Oxford: Clarendon Press, 1952, 1960), 2: 56.

13. Georges Salmon, "Etudes sur la topographie du Caire. La Kal'at al-Kabch et la Birkat al-Fil," *MIFAO* 7 (1902), 16–17; Raymond and Wiet, *Les marchés du Caire*, p. 210.

14. Maqrizi, *Kitab al-suluk*, 2: 540, 541, 543; Salmon, "Etudes sur la topographie," pp. 38, 82–85, 110 (quotation from Maqrizi), 117; Garcin et al., *Palais et maisons du Caire*, 1: 51–67; J. A. Williams, "Urbanization and Monument Construction in Mamluk Cairo," *Muqarnas* 2 (1984), 35–36.

15. Maqrizi, *Kitab al-suluk*, 2: 131, 543, 807; Raymond and Wiet, *Les marchés du Caire*, pp. 131, 141, 183.

16. Stanley Lane-Poole, *The Story of Cairo* (London: J. M. Dent, 1902), p. 259; Marcel Clerget, *Le Caire. Etude de géographie urbaine et d'histoire économique*, 2 vols. (Cairo: Imprimerie Schindler, 1934), 1: 159, 239–240; Janet Abu-Lughod, *Cairo: 1001 Years of the City Victorious* (Princeton: Princeton University Press, 1971), p. 37 n. 5; Dols, *Black Death in Middle East*, pp. 201–202.

17. This is the conclusion of Viktoria Meinecke-Berg, which seems more realistic than most of the traditional estimates; "Eine Stadtansicht des Mamlukischen Kairo."

18. I have developed this idea at greater length in "Cairo's Area and Population in the Early Fifteenth Century," *Muqarnas* 2 (1984). See also Viktoria Meinecke-

Berg, "Quellen zu topographie und baugeschichte in Kairo unter Sultan an-Nasir," *ZDMG* (Wiesbaden), 3.1 (1977), 539. J.-C. Garcin's suggestions for the area of Mamluk Cairo (Garcin et al., *Palais et maisons du Caire,* 1: 164; Garcin, "Toponymie et topographie," p. 136) seem inflated. See Maps 4–7 in this book.

19. Ibn Battuta, *Voyages,* 1: 67–68.

## 6. THE GREAT CRISIS

1. Gaston Wiet, *L'Egypte arabe,* vol. 4 of *Histoire de la nation égyptienne* (Paris, 1937), pp. 538–539.

2. On the Black Death in Egypt, see Gaston Wiet, "La grande peste noire en Syrie et en Egypte," in *Etudes d'Orientalisme dédiées à la mémoire de Lévi-Provençal* (Paris, 1962), especially pp. 376–377; Michael W. Dols, *The Black Death in the Middle East* (Princeton: Princeton University Press, 1977), especially pp. 57–60, 175, 182, 215. See also Daniel Panzac, *La peste dans l'empire ottoman* (Louvain, 1985), whose analysis of the plague is generally valid for an earlier period as well; Maqrizi, *Kitab al-suluk,* 2: 770–782; Ibn Battuta, *Voyages,* trans. C. Defremery and B. R. Sanguinetti, 4 vols. (1854; reprint, Paris, 1968), 1: 229.

3. Maqrizi, *Kitab al-suluk,* 2: 782; Wiet, "La grande peste noire," p. 376; Dols, *The Black Death,* pp. 166–167, 172–173, 183–185, 188–189, 255–277.

4. Dols estimates that there were twenty-eight outbreaks in the 169 years between the Black Death and the Ottoman conquest, with an average cycle of five years.

5. Maqrizi, *Kitab al-suluk,* 3: 12, 235, 1016, 1115; Dols, *The Black Death,* pp. 224, 230. See also J.-C. Garcin, "Le système militaire mamluk et le blocage de la société musulmane médiévale," *Annales Islamologiques* 24 (1988), maintaining that demographic events largely brought about the Mamluk "blockage."

6. Maqrizi, *Kitab al-suluk,* 3: 60, 251; 4: 175; idem, *Khitat,* 2: 316; Abd Allatif, *Relation de l'Egypte,* trans. S. de Sacy (Paris, 1810), p. 595; Dols, *The Black Death,* pp. 269–270.

7. André Raymond and Gaston Wiet, *Les marchés du Caire. Traduction annotée du texte de Maqrizi* (Cairo: IFAO, 1979), p. 221.

8. Maqrizi, *Kitab al-suluk,* 2: 897; idem, *Khitat,* 2: 73; Wiet, *L'Egypte arabe,* pp. 505–506. See also Jacques Revault, "L'architecture domestique au Caire à l'époque mamelouke," in J.-C. Garcin, B. Maury, J. Revault, and M. Zakariya, *Palais et maisons du Caire,* vol. 1: *Epoque mamelouke (XIIIe au XVIe siècles)* (Paris, 1982), pp. 59–61.

9. Quoted in Jacques Berque, "Les capitales de l'Islam méditerranéen," *Annales Islamologiques* 8 (1969), 81–82; W. Fischel, "Ibn Khaldun's Activities in Mamluk Egypt," *Semitic and Oriental Studies* (University of California) 11 (1951).

10. Maqrizi, *Kitab al-suluk,* 3: 1127, 1134; 4: 227.

11. Ibid., 4: 909; Raymond and Wiet, *Les marchés du Caire,* pp. 133–136, 148–149, 150–160, 168–169, 203–205.

12. Maqrizi, *Kitab al-suluk,* 4: 645; idem, *Khitat,* 2: 150, 314, 324, 328; Raymond and Wiet, *Les marchés du Caire,* p. 222.

13. André Raymond, "La localisation des bains publics au Caire au XVè siècle," *BEO* 30 (1978); idem, "Cairo's Area and Population."

## 7. MAQRIZI'S CAIRO

1. J.-C. Garcin, "Habitat médiéval et histoire urbaine," in J.-C. Garcin, B. Maury, J. Revault, and M. Zakariya, *Palais et maisons du Caire*, vol. 1: *Epoque mamelouke (XIIIe au XVIe siècles)* (Paris, 1982), p. 110. On Maqrizi (whose biography can be found in J.-C. Garcin, "Al-Maqrizi," *Les Africains* 9), see the remarks of his emulator and follower, Ibn Taghribirdi, *History of Egypt, 1382–1469*, trans. William Popper, 7 vols. (Berkeley: University of California Press, 1954–1960), 3: 87, 146. On Mamluk Cairo, I have often drawn on Stanley Lane-Poole, *The Story of Cairo* (London: J. M. Dent, 1902); William Popper, *Egypt and Syria under the Circassian Sultans (1382–1468)*, 2 vols. (Berkeley: University of California Press, 1955–1957); Gaston Wiet, *Cairo: City of Art and Commerce*, trans. Seymour Feiler (Norman: University of Oklahoma Press, 1964); Garcin, "Habitat médiéval"; Marcel Clerget, *Le Caire. Etude de géographie urbaine et d'histoire économique*, 2 vols. (Cairo: Imprimerie Schindler, 1934); and Janet Abu-Lughod, *Cairo: 1001 Years of the City Victorious* (Princeton: Princeton University Press, 1971).

2. These hypotheses are supported by W. Popper's maps in *Egypt and Syria*. Though based on later data (1382–1468), they confirm that settlement in the west was sparse, and that the south was empty in some areas. But we should naturally keep in mind that the base map Popper used to locate these place-names is the map from the *Description de l'Egypte*. The author therefore does not suggest that it represents the urbanized area, as Abu-Lughod does in her study *Cairo*.

3. See André Raymond, "La population du Caire de Maqrizi à la Description de l'Egypte," *BEO* 28 (1975); idem, "Cairo's Area and Population"; idem, "Le Caire sous les Ottomans," in B. Maury, A. Raymond, J. Revault, and M. Zakariya, *Palais et maisons du Caire*, vol. 2, *Epoque ottomane* (Paris, 1983), pp. 15–17. I take into account only the mosques dated and located by Maqrizi. The travelers are quoted in Wiet, *Cairo*, pp. 73–74.

4. Leonor Fernandes, "On Conducting the Affairs of State," *Annales Islamologiques* 24 (1988), 84–85.

5. Maqrizi, *Kitab al-suluk*, 3: 543 (1386), 574 (1388); 4: 869 (1432); Ibn Taghribirdi, *Al-nujum al-zahira fi muluk misr wa-al-qahira*, ed. William Popper, 7 vols. (Berkeley: University of California Press, 1926–1929), 6: 853; idem, *History of Egypt*, 4: 215; André Raymond and Gaston Wiet, *Les marchés du Caire. Traduction annotée du texte de Maqrizi* (Cairo: IFAO, 1979), pp. 195–196. On the *muhtasib*, see Ahmad Abd ar-Raziq, "La *hisba* et le *muhtasib* en Egypte au temps des mamluks," *Annales Islamologiques* 13 (1977), 13.

6. Maqrizi, *Kitab al-suluk*, 2: 54; 3: 446 (1381), 1016 (1400); Wiet, *Cairo*, p. 84; Raymond and Wiet, *Les marchés du Caire*, pp. 47, 65, 212.

7. See Raymond and Wiet, *Les marchés du Caire*, and the maps; Muhammad ibn Iyas, *Bada'i al-zuhur fi waqa'i al-duhur*, ed. Mohamed Mustafa, 5 vols. (Cairo and Wiesbaden, 1961–1983), 3: 375; 4: 17; 5: 139; idem, *Histoire des Mamlouks circassiens*, trans. Gaston Wiet (Cairo, 1945), p. 415; idem, *Journal d'un bourgeois du Caire*, trans. Gaston Wiet, 2 vols. (Paris, 1955, 1960), 1: 14; 2: 132. On the *rab*, see L. Ali Ibrahim, "Middle Class Living Units in Mamluk Cairo," *AARP* 14 (1978).

8. Maqrizi, *Khitat*, 2: 2. On the closing of the quarters, see Fernandes, "On Conducting the Affairs of State." See also Maqrizi, *Kitab al-suluk*, 2: 301 (1327); 3: 737 (1391); 4: 659 (1424), 717 (1426), 1120 (1439); idem, *Khitat*, 2: 149 (1323); Ibn Taghribirdi, *Al-nujum al-zahira*, 7: 526; idem, *History of Egypt*, 6: 90 (1460). On the *zu'ar*, see Maqrizi, *Kitab al-suluk*, 3: 650 (1389); Ibn Iyas, *Bada'i al-zuhur*, 4: 232; idem, *Journal d'un bourgeois*, 1: 219. See also I. M. Lapidus, *Muslim Cities in the Later Middle Ages* (Cambridge, Mass.: Harvard University Press, 1967), especially pp. 88–94, 153–157.

9. Carl F. Petry, *The Civilian Elite of Cairo in the Later Middle Ages* (Princeton: Princeton University Press, 1981); Raymond and Wiet, *Les marchés du Caire*, p. 152; Ibn Taghribirdi, *Al-nujum al-zahira*, 7: 499; idem, *History of Egypt*, 6: 75 (1458); Ibn Iyas, *Bada'i al-zuhur*, 3: 279; idem, *Histoire des Mamlouks*, p. 314 (1491); idem, *Bada'i al-zuhur*, 4: 41; idem, *Journal d'un bourgeois*, 1: 37 (1502).

10. See Donald Little, "Coptic Conversion to Islam under the Bahri Mamluks," *BSOAS* 21 (1976), 566 (quotation); also S. D. Goitein, *A Mediterranean Society: The Jerusalem Communities of the Arab World as Portrayed in the Documents of the Cairo Geniza*, 5 vols. (Berkeley: University of California Press, 1967–1988), 1: 19; D. Richards, "The Coptic Bureaucracy under the Mamluks," in *CIHC*; U. Vermeulen, "The Rescript of al-Malik al-Salih against the Dimmis," *Orientalia Lovaniensia* 9 (1978); Doris Behrens-Abouseif, "Locations of Non-Muslim Quarters in Medieval Cairo," *Annales Islamologiques* 22 (1986); Maqrizi, *Kitab al-suluk*, 2: 215–227 (1321), 922–923 (1354); Ibn Iyas, *Bada'i al-zuhur*, 3: 425; idem, *Histoire des Mamlouks*, p. 464.

11. Misr is well known to us thanks to Ibn Duqmaq (d. 1406) (*Kitab al-intisar*) and Maqrizi (*Khitat*), who described both the ancient and the recent city, and thanks also to the modern research of Paul Casanova (*Essai de reconstitution topographique*) and Sylvie Denoix (*La ville de Fustat*), who have interpreted the often unclear data of the two medieval authors.

12. See in particular A. R. Guest and E. T. Richmond, "Misr in the Fifteenth Century," *JRAS* 35 (1903); Paul Casanova, *Essai de reconstitution topographique de la ville d'al-Foustat ou Misr* (Cairo: IFAO, 1919); Sylvie Denoix, *Décrire le Caire. Fustat-Misr d'après Ibn Duqmaq et Maqrizi* (Cairo: IFAO, 1992); idem, "La ville de Fustat" (Diss., Université de Provence, 1984); also Ahmad Abd ar-Raziq, "Les muhtasibs de Fustat au temps des mamluks," *Annales Islamologiques* 14 (1978).

13. Maqrizi, *Histoire des sultans*, 3: 92 (1288); idem, *Kitab al-suluk*, 3: 536, 545; Gaston Wiet, "Les marchands d'épices," *Cahiers d'histoire egyptienne* (Cairo), 1955, pp. 117–118; Ahmad Darrag, *L'Egypte sous le règne de Barsbay: 825–841/ 1422–1438* (Damascus: Institut Français de Damas, 1961), pp. 66–67.

14. See Nelly Hanna, *An Urban History of Bulaq in the Mamluk and Ottoman Periods* (Cairo: IFAO, 1983); Maqrizi, *Kitab al-suluk*, 3: 894 (1398).

## 8. THE END OF AN ERA

1. On the evolution of the mamluk system and Cairo generally, see J.-C. Garcin, "Le système militaire mamelouk et le blocage de la société musulmane médiévale," *Annales Islamologiques* 24 (1988); idem, "Le Caire et l'évolution urbaine des pays musulmans," *Annales Islamologiques* 25 (1991).

2. Ibn Taghribirdi, *History of Egypt, 1382–1469*, trans. William Popper, 5 vols. (Berkeley: University of California Press, 1954–1960), 6: 11; Ahmad Darrag, *L'Egypte sous le règne de Barsbay, 825–841/1422–1438* (Damascus: Institut Français de Damas, 1961), pp. 26–27.

3. Ibn Taghribirdi, *Hawadith al-duhur fi mada al-ayyam wa-al-shuhur*, ed. William Popper, 4 vols. (Berkeley: University of California Press, 1930–1942), 3: 689 (1468); Darrag, *L'Egypte*, pp. 321–323; Muhammad ibn Iyas, *Bada'i al-zuhur fi waqa'i al-duhur*, ed. Mohamed Mustafa, 5 vols. (Cairo and Wiesbaden, 1961–1983), 5: 121, 134; translated by Gaston Wiet as *Histoire des Mamlouks circassiens* (Cairo, 1945), p. 425; idem, *Journal d'un bourgeois du Caire*, trans. Gaston Wiet, 2 vols. (Paris, 1955, 1960), 2: 113, 126. On the question of arms, see David Ayalon, *Gunpowder and Firearms in the Mameluk Kingdom: A Challenge to Mediaeval Society* (London: Vallentine, Mitchell, 1956).

4. Ibn Taghribirdi, *History of Egypt*, 4: 69–76 (1430); 5: 93–98 (1460); Ibn Iyas, *Bada'i al-zuhur*, 3: 278; 4: 15; idem, *Histoire des Mamlouks*, pp. 293 (1489), 303 (1490), 313 (1491), 326 (1492), 432 (1498); idem, *Journal d'un bourgeois*, 1: 13; Darrag, *L'Egypte*, pp. 59–60. On Egypt's economic crisis, see the many essays of Eliyahu Ashtor, gathered in a number of collections: *Studies on the Levantine Trade in the Middle Ages* (London: Variorum Reprints, 1978); *East-West Trade in the Medieval Mediterranean* (London: Variorum Reprints, 1986); *Technology, Industry, and Trade: The Levant versus Europe, 1250–1500* (Brookfield, Vt.: Variorum Reprints, 1992). On different aspects of this crisis and the importance of the technological lag, see idem: "Spice Prices in the Near East," *JRAS*, 1976; "Levantine Sugar Industry in the Later Middle Ages" *Israel Oriental Studies* 7 (1977); "L'apogée du commerce vénitien au Levant," *Venezia Centro di Mediazione* 1 (1977). On the monetary crisis: J. L. Bacharach, "Monetary Movements in Medieval Egypt," in *Precious Metals in the Later Medieval and Early Modern Worlds*, ed. J. F. Richards (Durham, N.C.: Carolina Academic Press, 1983).

5. Ibn Taghribirdi, *Al-nujum al-zahira fi muluk misr wa-al-qahira*, ed. William Popper, 7 vols. (Berkeley: University of California Press, 1929), 7: 417; idem, *History of Egypt*, 6: 26 (1453); idem, *Hawadith*, 3: 524; Ibn Iyas, *Histoire des Mamlouks*, p. 114 (1474); Gaston Wiet, *L'Egypte arabe*, vol. 4 of *Histoire de la nation égyptienne* (Paris, 1937), pp. 608 (1497), 614 (1501).

6. On the "Mediterraneanization" of Mamluk Egypt, see the studies of J.-C. Garcin: "La 'méditerranéisation' de l'empire mamluk sous les sultans Bahrides," *Rivista degli studi orientali*, 1974, p. 48; "Transport des épices et espace égyptien entre le XIe et le XVe siècle," *Annales de Bretagne* 85.2 (1978); "Pour un recours à l'histoire de l'espace vécu," *Annales* 35 (1980).

7. Ibn Taghribirdi, *Hawadith*, 1: 115 (1451); 2: 282–290 (1456); J.-C. Garcin, "Pour un recours," p. 448.

8. Joos van Ghistele, *Le voyage en Egypte 1482–83*, trans. Renée Bauwens-Préaux (Cairo: IFAO, 1979); Félix Fabri, *Le voyage en Egypte*, 3 vols. (Cairo, 1975), p. 400; Trevisano quoted in J. A. Williams, "Urbanization and Monument Construction in Mamluk Cairo," *Muqarnas* 2 (1984), 43.

9. Cleaning: Maqrizi, *Kitab al-suluk*, 4: 712 (1426); Ibn Iyas, *Bada'i al-zuhur*, 4: 59; 5: 14; idem, *Journal d'un bourgeois*, 1: 55 (1503); 2: 12 (1516). Lighting: Maqrizi,

*Kitab al-suluk,* 4: 875 (1432); Ibn Iyas, *Bada'i al-zuhur,* 3: 387; 4: 415; 5: 59; idem, *Histoire des Mamlouks,* p. 427 (1498); idem, *Journal d'un bourgeois,* 1: 384 (1514); 2: 48 (1516). Whitewashing: Ibn Iyas, *Bada'i al-zuhur,* 3: 399; idem, *Histoire des Mamlouks,* p. 441 (1498).

10. Ibn Taghribirdi, *Hawadith,* 2: 307 (1457); 4: 782 (1461); idem, *Al-nujum al-zahira,* 7: 499; idem, *History of Egypt,* 6: 75 (1458); Ibn Iyas, *Bada'i al-zuhur,* 3: 127, 138; idem, *Histoire des Mamlouks,* pp. 144, 154 (1477); *Kitab al-fawa'id . . . fi bayan hukm shawari al-Qahira,* Manuscript, Süleymaniye University Library, no. 1177.

11. On the city's revitalization, see J.-C. Garcin, "Habitat médiéval et histoire urbaine," in J.-C. Garcin, B. Maury, J. Revault, and M. Zakariya, *Palais et maisons du Caire,* vol. 1: *Epoque mamelouke (XIIIe au XVIe siècles)* (Paris, 1982), pp. 191–193; idem, "L'insertion sociale de Sha'rani," in *CIHC;* Maqrizi, *Kitab al-suluk,* 4: 672 (1424), 765 (1427), 1229 (1441); Ahmad Darrag, *L'acte de waqf de Barsbay* (Cairo, 1963); idem, *L'Egypte,* pp. 406–424.

12. Qaytbay's *waqf* has been published in L. A. Mayer, *The Buildings of Qaytbay as Described in His Endowment Deed* (London, 1938). On Ghuri's monuments, see Ibn Iyas, *Bada'i al-zuhur,* 4: 52–68, 230; 5: 94; idem, *Journal d'un bourgeois,* 1: 49–65, 216; 2: 90.

13. Jacques Revault, "L'architecture domestique au Caire à l'époque mamelouke (XIIIe–XVIe siècles)," in Garcin et al., *Palais et maisons du Caire,* vol. 1. These monuments have been assigned the numbers 9 and 75 (*wakalat* of Qaytbay) and 64 (*wakala* of Ghury).

14. Maqrizi, *Kitab al-suluk,* 4: 526 (1420); Ibn Taghribirdi, *History of Egypt,* 3: 76 (1420); idem, *Hawadith,* 2: 216 (1454); Ibn Iyas, *Histoire des Mamlouks,* pp. 176, 177 (1480); Doris Behrens-Abouseif, "A Circassian Mamluk Suburb North of Cairo," *AARP* 14 (1978); idem, "The North-Eastern Extensions of Cairo under the Mamluks," *Annales Islamologiques* 17 (1981), 157, 163, 165–171, 182–184; Williams, "Urbanization," p. 43.

15. Maqrizi, *Kitab al-suluk,* 4: 499 (1419), 1106 (1439), 1161 (1439), 1226 (1441).

16. Ibn Iyas, *Bada'i al-zuhur,* 4: 56, 102; 5: 94; idem, *Journal d'un bourgeois,* 1: 52 (1503), 99 (1507); 2: 91; Paul Casanova, "Histoire et description de la Citadelle du Caire." *MMAFC* 6 (1891–92), 705–706; Doris Behrens Abouseif, "The Citadel of Cairo," *Annales Islamologiques* 24 (1988); J.-C. Garcin, "Habitat médiéval," pp. 193–196.

17. K. A. C. Creswell, *The Muslim Architecture of Egypt: Ayyubids and Early Bahrite Mamluks, A.D. 1171–1326,* 2 vols. (Oxford: Clarendon Press, 1952, 1960), 1: 255–259; Ibn Iyas, *Bada'i al-zuhur,* 4: 110, 172; idem, *Journal d'un bourgeois,* 1: 107 (1507), 169–170 (1510).

18. Ibn Iyas, *Bada'i al-zuhur,* 4: 268–269; idem, *Journal d'un bourgeois,* 1: 251–252; Gaston Wiet, *Cairo: City of Art and Commerce,* trans. Seymour Feiler (Norman: University of Oklahoma Press, 1964), pp. 153–155 (Trevisano).

19. Doris Behrens-Abouseif has reconstructed the general organization of the site; see *Azbakiyya and Its Environs, from Azbak to Isma'il, 1476–1879* (Cairo: IFAO, 1985), pp. 22–33. See also Ibn Iyas, *Bada'i al-zuhur,* 3: 190, 292; idem, *Histoire des Mamelouks,* pp. 131–132; idem, *Journal d'un bourgeois,* 1: 134, 144.

20. I draw heavily on Nelly Hanna, *An Urban History of Bulaq in the Mamluk and Ottoman Periods* (Cairo: IFAO, 1983). See also Darrag, *L'Egypte,* pp. 244, 247, 255; Ibn Taghribirdi, *Al-nujum al-zahira,* 7: 499 (1458); idem, *Hawadith,* 1: 313–315; Ibn Iyas, *Bada'i al-zuhur,* 5: 94; idem, *Journal d'un bourgeois,* 2: 91.

21. E. N. Adler, *Jewish Travellers* (London, 1930), p. 167.

22. Leo Africanus, *Jean Léon, L'Africain, Description de l'Afrique,* French trans. A. Epaulard (Paris: Librairie d'Amérique et d'Orient, 1956), pp. 503–514; Eng. trans. J. Pory, *The History and Description of Africa* (London, 1896); Van Ghistele, *Le voyage en Egypte,* p. 57.

23. Ibn Iyas, *Bada'i al-zuhur,* 5: 38–42; idem, *Journal d'un bourgeois,* 2: 37–40.

## III. THE TRADITIONAL CITY

1. Ibn Iyas, *Journal d'un bourgeois du Caire,* trans. Gaston Wiet, 2 vols. (Paris, 1950, 1960), 2: 141.

2. Henry Laurens, *L'expédition d'Egypte* (Paris: Armand Colin, 1989), p. 90.

## 9. A NEW POLITICAL SYSTEM

1. On the organization of Egypt in the Ottoman period, see S. J. Shaw, *The Financial and Administrative Organization and Development of Ottoman Egypt, 1517–1798* (Princeton: Princeton University Press, 1962); P. M. Holt, *Egypt and the Fertile Crescent, 1516–1922* (Ithaca: Cornell University Press, 1966) and *Studies in the History of the Near East* (London: Cass, 1973); André Raymond, *Artisans et commerçants au Caire au XVIIIe siècle,* 2 vols. (Damascus: Institut Français de Damas, 1973, 1974); idem, "Les provinces arabes, XVI–XVIIIe siècles" in *Histoire de l'empire ottoman,* ed. R. Mantran (Paris, 1989).

2. The organization of the judiciary is described by Galal El-Nahal, *The Judicial Administration of Ottoman Egypt in the Seventeenth Century* (Minneapolis: Biblioteca Islamica, 1979). See also Nelly Hanna, *Habiter au Caire au XVIIe et XVIIIe siècles* (Cairo: IFAO, 1991).

3. On Egypt's finances, see Shaw, *Financial and Administrative Organization.*

4. Abd al-Rahman al-Jabarti (cited hereafter as Jabarti), *Aja'ib al-athhar fil-tarajim wal akhbar,* 4 vols. (Cairo: Bulaq Press, 1297/1879) (hereafter *Aja'ib al-athhar*), 4: 113; translation by Chefik Mansour et al., *Merveilles biographiques et historiques, ou Chroniques du cheikh Abd-el-Rahman el Djabarti,* 9 vols. (Cairo, 1888–1896) (hereafter *Merveilles bibliographiques*), 8: 253–254. This work is our primary source for the history of Ottoman Egypt. On Jabarti, see Gilbert Delanoue, "Abd al-Rahman al-Jabarti," *Les Africains* 12 (1978); idem, *Moralistes et politiques musulmans dans l'Egypte du XIXe siècle (1798–1882),* 2 vols. (Cairo: IFAO, 1982), 1: 3–83.

5. Jabarti, *Aja'ib al-athhar,* 1: 151; idem, *Merveilles biographiques,* 2:23.

6. Quoted in Raymond, *Artisans et commerçants,* 2: 574–576.

7. M. Winter, "A Seventeenth-Century Arabic Panegyric," *Asian and African*

*Studies* 13.2 (1979), 135; Jabarti, *Aja'ib al-athhar,* 2: 114; 3: 187; idem, *Merveilles biographiques,* 4: 205 (1786); 7: 31 (1801).

## 10. URBAN SOCIETY

1. André Raymond, *Artisans et commerçants au Caire au XVIIIe siècle,* 2 vols. (Damascus: Institut Français de Damas, 1973, 1974), 1: 2–6. I have examined these questions in "Le Caire. Economie et société urbaines à la fin du XVIIIe siècle," in *L'Egypte au XIXe siècle* (Paris, 1982); and "Le Caire sous les Ottomans," in B. Maury, A. Raymond, J. Revault, and M. Zakariya, *Palais et maisons du Caire,* vol. 2: *Epoque ottomane, XVIe–XVIIIe siècles* (Paris, 1983).

2. See P. M. Holt, "The Beylicate in Ottoman Egypt," in his *Studies in the History of the Near East* (London: Cass, 1973).

3. See H. A. R. Gibb and H. Bowen, *Islamic Society and the West,* 2 vols. (Oxford, 1950, 1957); Raymond, *Artisans et commerçants,* 2: 660 ff.; idem, "Le Caire sous les Ottomans," p. 37; idem, "Soldiers in Trade: The Case of Ottoman Cairo," *BJMES,* 1991, p. 18; Constantin François de Chasseboeuf, comte de Volney, *Voyage en Egypte et en Syrie* (Paris: J. Gaulmier, 1959), p. 101.

4. André Raymond, "Les constructions de l'émir Abd al-Rahman Katkhuda au Caire," *Annales Islamologiques* 11 (1972); Michel Tuchscherer, "Le pèlerinage de l'émir Sulayman Gawis al-Qazdugli . . . en 1739," *Annales Islamogiques* 24 (1988).

5. Ali al-Shadhili, "Dhikr ma waqa'a," ed. A. Tulaymat, *al-Majalla al-ta'rikhiyya* 14 (1968), 369, 389.

6. Jabarti, *Aja'ib al-athhar,* 2: 199 and 4: 237; idem, *Merveilles biographiques,* 5: 108 and 9: 156.

7. Raymond, *Artisans et commerçants,* 2: 373 ff.; idem, "Le Caire sous les Ottomans," p. 34.

8. M. de Chabrol, "Essai sur les moeurs des habitants modernes de l'Egypte," in *Description de l'Egypte, état moderne,* vol. 2.2 (Paris, 1822), pp. 516–517; and E. F. Jomard, "Description abrégée de la ville et de la citadelle du Caire," ibid., pp. 662, 696.

9. See Raymond, *Artisans et commerçants,* 2: 399–414; Jabarti, *Aja'ib al-athhar,* 1: 176; idem, *Merveilles biographiques,* 2: 81. To allow comparisons between different periods, the sums have been converted into constant values.

10. "Mémoire de la ville du Caire," Bibliothèque Nationale, Fonds Français, 15466, p. 174b; C. de la Jonquière, *L'Expédition d'Egypte (1798–1801),* 5 vols. (Paris, 1899–1907), 3: 490.

11. Raymond, "Le Caire sous les Ottomans," pp. 37–38.

12. Jabarti, *Aja'ib al-athhar,* 2: 110 and 3: 11; idem, *Merveilles bibliographiques* 4: 193 and 6: 23.

13. Raymond, "Le Caire sous les Ottomans," pp. 37–38.

14. André Raymond, "La fortune des Gabarti," in *Abd al-Rahman al-Gabarti,* ed. Izzat Abd al-Karim (Cairo, 1977); idem, *Artisans et commerçants,* 2: 686–688.

15. Henry Laurens, *L'expédition d'Egypte* (Paris: Armand Colin, 1989), pp. 76–77.

## 11. EXPANSION UNDER THE OTTOMANS

1. Marcel Clerget, *Le Caire. Etude de géographie urbaine et d'histoire économique*, 2 vols. (Cairo: Imprimerie Schindler, 1934), 1: 180, 187.
2. I do not think that the map by Matheo Pagano, published in Venice in 1549, can be considered an accurate representation of Cairo in the sixteenth century. See Viktoria Meinecke-Berg, "Eine Stadtansicht des mamlukischen Kairo," *Mitteilungen des Deutschen Archäologischen Instituts Kairo* 12 (1976); and B. Blanc, S. Denoix, J.-C. Garcin, and R. Gordiani, "A propos de la carte du Caire de Matheo Pagano," *Annales Islamologiques* 17 (1981). A remarkable document for its time, the map is inevitably approximate and, in certain respects, erroneous (for example, in the placement of the aqueduct), because of the difficulties that attended its making. It is interesting to compare it with the diagram drawn up by Pellegrino Brocardi in 1556, which is much more realistic even in its conception, since the map was made from the only place that provided an overall view of the city, the Muqattam Hills. See Ludovico Micara, "Il Cairo nella 'Chorographia' di Pellegrino Brocardi (1556)," *Storia della Citta* 46 (1989).
3. Pascal Coste, *Architecture arabe, ou Monuments du Kaire* (Paris, 1839), plate 27.
4. The document that gives the date and specific nature of the operation was discovered by Nelly Hanna in the Archives of the Tribunal of Bab al-Ali in Cairo (no. 73, art, 13, pp. 5–6, March 1600). I am very grateful to her for having shared this information with me. See André Raymond, "Le déplacement des tanneries à Alep, au Caire et à Tunis," *Revue d'histoire Maghrébine* 7–8 (1977); idem, "Essai de géographie des quartiers de résidence aristocratique," *JESHO*, 1963.
5. André Raymond, "Les grands waqfs et l'organisation de l'espace urbain à Alep et au Caire," *BEO* 31 (1979); idem, "L'activité architecturale au Caire à l'époque ottomane," *Annales Islamologiques* 25 (1990). On this topic see also Chapter 12.
6. André Raymond, *Artisans et commerçants au Caire au XVIIIe siècle*, 2 vols. (Damascus: Institut Français de Damas, 1973, 1974), 2: 787.
7. On the constructions at Azbakiyya, see Doris Behrens-Abouseif, *Azbakiyya and Its Environs, from Azbak to Isma'il, 1476–1879* (Cairo: IFAO, 1985), and her descripton of Uthman Katkhuda's complex, pp. 55–58.
8. Jabarti, *Aja'ib al-athhar*, 2: 7; André Raymond, "Les constructions de l'émir Abd al-Rahman Katkhuda au Caire," *Annales Islamologiques* 11 (1972).
9. André Raymond, "La population du Caire et de l'Egypte à l'époque ottomane," in *Mémorial Omer Lutfi Barkan* (Paris, 1980); idem, "Le Caire sous les Ottomans," in B. Maury, A. Raymond, J. Revault, and M. Zakariya, *Palais et maisons du Caire*, vol. 2: *Epoque ottomane, XVIe–XVIIIe siècles* (Paris, 1983).
10. This figure is challenged by Justin McCarthy, who criticizes the assumptions used by the scientists of the *Description de l'Egypte* in making their calculations. He proposes a lower estimate of 210,960; "Nineteenth-Century Egyptian Population," *Middle Eastern Studies* 12 (1976).
11. Leopoldo Torres Balbas, "Les villes musulmanes d'Espagne et leur urbanisation," *Annales* (Institut d'Etudes Orientales de l'Université d'Alger) 6 (1942–1947); idem, "Extension y demografía de las ciudades hispano-musulmanas," *Studia Islamica* 3 (1955); Alexander Lézine, *Deux villes d'Ifriqiya* (Paris, 1971).

12. André Raymond, "La conquête ottomane et le développement des grandes villes arabes," *ROMM* 27 (1979).

13. André Raymond, "Les grandes épidémies de peste au Caire aux XVIIe et XVIIIe siècles," *BEO* 25 (1972); Daniel Panzac, "Épidémies et démographie en Egypte au XIXe siècle," in *L'Egypte au XIXe siècle* (Paris, 1982); idem, *La peste dans l'empire ottoman* (Louvain, 1985).

## 12. CITY ADMINISTRATION AND DAILY LIFE

1. On Cairo's administration, see S. J. Shaw, *The Financial and Administrative Organization and Development of Ottoman Egypt, 1517–1798* (Princeton: Princeton University Press, 1962); Galal El-Nahal, *The Judicial Administration of Ottoman Egypt in the Seventeenth Century* (Minneapolis: Biblioteca Islamica, 1979); André Raymond, "Le Caire sous les Ottomans," in B. Maury, A. Raymond, J. Revault, and M. Zakariya, *Palais et maisons du Caire*, vol. 2: *Epoque ottomane, XVIe–XVIIIe siècles* (Paris, 1983), pp. 41–57; Layla Abd al-Latif, *al-idara fi misr* (Cairo, 1978); and Nelly Hanna, *Habiter au Caire aux XVIIe et XVIIIe siècles* (Cairo: IFAO, 1991).

2. This document (Top Kapi Library, ms. KK 888, fol. 324, order no. 1407, 1 sha'ban 959/23 July 1552) was brought to my notice by Gilles Veinstein (who also translated it). I owe him warm thanks for his friendly cooperation. The document from 1600 in the Cairo Archives is cited in Chapter 11, note 4.

3. André Raymond, "Problèmes urbains et urbanisme au Caire," in *CIHC*.

4. J. J. Marcel, *Contes du Cheykh el Mohdy*, 3 vols. (Paris, 1835), 3: 388; Jabarti, *Aja'ib al-athhar*, 1: 103–104; idem, *Merveilles biographiques*, 1: 239–240.

5. Jabarti, *Aja'ib al-athhar*, 1: 383; 2: 107; idem, *Merveilles biographiques*, 3: 162 (1770); 4: 184 (1786).

6. On these questions see Raymond, "Le Caire sous les Ottomans," pp. 41–44.

7. Ibid., pp. 44–45; El-Nahal, *Judicial Administration*.

8. On trade corporations, see G. Baer, *Egyptian Guilds in Modern Times* (Jerusalem, 1965); André Raymond, *Artisans et commerçants au Caire au XVIIIe siècle*, 2 vols. (Damascus: Institut Français de Damas, 1973, 1974), 2: 508–585.

9. On the residential quarters, see El-Nahal, *Judicial Administration*, pp. 54–55, for examples relating to daily life. See also André Raymond, "La géographie des 'hara' du Caire," *MIFAO* 104 (1980); idem, "Le Caire sous les Ottomans," p. 45; and Hanna, *Habiter au Caire*.

10. André Raymond, "Les grands waqfs et l'organisation de l'espace urbain à Alep et au Caire," *BEO* 31 (1979); idem, "Le Caire sous les Ottomans," pp. 45–46; idem, *Grandes villes arabes à l'époque ottomane* (Paris: Sindbad, 1985), pp. 221–226.

11. Gerd Winkelhane and Klaus Schwarz, *Des osmanische Statthalter Iskander Pasha* (Bamberg, 1985).

12. Jabarti, *Aja'ib al-athhar*, 1: 108; idem, *Merveilles biographiques*, 1: 250 (Hijazi). On the events of 1711, see André Raymond, "Une 'révolution' au Caire sous les Mamelouks," *Annales Islamologiques* 6 (1965).

13. See Raymond, *Artisans et commerçants*, 2: 689 (1786), 787 (1725), 795 (1786), 804–805 (1790).

14. Jean Coppin, *Les voyages en Egypte de Jean Coppin: 1638–1639, 1643–1646*

(Cairo: IFAO, 1971), pp. 127–128; Ibn Abi l-Surur, "Kitab al-kawakib," Manuscript, Bibliothèque Nationale, Paris, Arabic, 1852, pp. 75b, 169a; M. de Chabrol, "Essai sur les moeurs des habitants modernes de l'Egypte," in *Description de l'Egypte, état moderne,* vol. 2.2 (Paris, 1822), p. 424.

15. Jabarti, *Aja'ib al-athhar,* 1: 180; idem, *Merveilles biographiques,* 2: 91.
16. Ahmad Shalabi, *Awdah al-isharat* (Cairo: Abd al-Rahim, 1978), pp. 545–546.
17. Jabarti, *Aja'ib al-athhar,* 2: 17, 250, 263; idem, *Merveilles biographiques,* 3: 266; 5: 196, 219.
18. Jean de Thévenot, *Voyages . . . en Europe, Asie et Afrique* (Amsterdam, 1727), 2: 408; Jabarti, *Aja'ib al-athhar,* 4: 201–202; idem, *Merveilles biographiques,* 9: 72; J.-J. Ampère, *Voyage en Egypte et en Nubie* (Paris, 1881), p. 136.
19. Jabarti, *Aja'ib al-athhar,* 1: 79; 3: 7; idem, *Merveilles biographiques,* 1: 188 (Hijazi quote); 6: 14; Raymond, "Le Caire sous les Ottomans," p. 56.
20. Raymond, "Le Caire sous les Ottomans," pp. 56–57.
21. M. de Chabrol, "Essai sur les moeurs," pp. 365, 425.
22. André Raymond, "Les porteurs d'eau du Caire," *BIFAO* 57 (1958); idem, "Les fontaines publiques (sabil) du Caire," *Annales Islamologiques* 15 (1979); Waqfiyya of Abd al-Rahman Katkhuda, Ministry of Waqfs, Cairo, no. 941; Raymond, *Grandes villes arabes,* pp. 158–161.

## 13. SPHERES OF ACTIVITY

1. Such a structure has been described by Gideon Sjoberg, whose model seems to apply to traditional Arab cities; *The Pre-Industrial City, Past and Present* (New York, 1960). On Arab cities, see also André Raymond, *Grandes villes arabes à l'époque ottomane* (Paris: Sindbad, 1985), pp. 168–227. I addressed these topics in "Le Caire sous les Ottomans," in B. Maury, A. Raymond, J. Revault, and M. Zakariya, *Palais et maisons du Caire,* vol. 2: *Epoque ottomane, XVIe–XVIIIe siècles* (Paris, 1983), pp. 59–76.
2. See André Raymond and Gaston Wiet, *Les marchés du Caire. Traduction annotée du texte de Maqrizi* (Cairo: IFAO, 1979), including maps; André Raymond, *Artisans et commerçants au Caire au XVIIIe siècle,* 2 vols. (Damascus: Institut Français de Damas, 1973, 1974), 1: 366–368.
3. Registered as no. 460 and incorrectly dated to 1734 (it was mentioned as early as 1726): Raymond and Wiet, *Les marchés du Caire,* no. 313, p. 292.
4. Gabriel Brémond, *Voyage en Egypte* (Cairo, 1974), p. 47. For a detailed study of the Sagha, see M. Tuchscherer, "Evolution toponymique et topographique de la Sagha du Caire," *Annales Islamologiques* 25 (1990).
5. Edward Lane, *An Account of the Manners and Customs of the Modern Egyptians* (London, 1954), pp. 321–324; Jabarti, *Aja'ib al-athhar,* 3: 161.
6. Raymond, *Artisans et commerçants,* 1: 251–263. Of the Wakala Dhulfiqar, only the monumental door remains, but Pascal Coste made some fine diagrams of it in his *Architecture arabe ou Monuments du Kaire* (Paris, 1839), pp. 43 and 44. The deterioration of the Wakala Bazar'a has greatly accelerated in recent years. See Raymond, *Grandes villes arabes,* pp. 254–255.
7. There are many examples of such stereotypes in "Orientalist" literature and in the work of Arab scholars. See the characteristic discussion in Antoine Abdel

Nour, *Introduction à l'histoire urbaine de la Syrie ottomane* (Beirut, 1982). See Raymond, *Grandes villes arabes,* pp. 277–278.

8. Nelly Hanna, *Habiter au Caire aux XVIIe et XVIIIe siècles* (Cairo: IFAO, 1991). See also Maury et al., *Palais et maisons du Caire,* vol. 2, especially J. Revault, "L'architecture domestique au Caire à l'époque ottomane," pp. 91–295; André Raymond, "The Residential Districts of Cairo during the Ottoman Period," in *The Arab City: Its Character and Islamic Cultural Heritage,* ed. Ismail Serageldin and Samir El-Sadek (Arlington, Va., 1982).

9. Hanna, *Habiter au Caire,* pp. 183–208.

10. See the essays by B. Maury, J. Revault, and M. Zakariya in Maury et al., *Palais et maisons du Caire,* vol. 2; Hanna, *Habiter au Caire,* pp. 47–53.

11. M. Zakariya, "Le rab de Tabbana," *Annales Islamologiques* 16 (1980); André Raymond, "Le *rab,* un habitat collectif au Caire," *Mélanges de l'Université Saint-Joseph* 50 (1984) (map); Hanna, *Habiter au Caire,* pp. 59–64, 204–205 (map).

12. See Nelly Hanna, "Bayt al-Istambuli," *Annales Islamologiques* 16 (1980); idem, *Habiter au Caire,* pp. 54–58, 79–160. Comparable dwellings have been described for Medina: Saleh al-Hathloul, *Tradition, Continuity, and Change in the Physical Environment: The Arab-Muslim City* (Cambridge, Mass.: Harvard University Press. 1981), p. 119.

13. André Raymond, "Quartiers et mouvements populaires au Caire au XVIIIe siècle," in *Political and Social Change in Modern Egypt,* ed. P. M. Holt (London, 1968); idem, "La géographie des 'hara' du Caire au XVIIe siècle," *MIFAO* 104 (1980); Hanna, *Habiter au Caire,* pp. 160–166.

14. Lane, *Manners and Customs,* pp. 174–178; Galal El-Nahal, *The Judicial Administration of Ottoman Egypt in the Seventeenth Century* (Minneapolis: Biblioteca Islamica, 1979), p. 55; Nawal al-Messiri, "The Concept of the Hara," *Annales Islamologiques* 15 (1979), quotation p. 337; Raymond, *Grandes villes arabes,* pp. 295–305; Hanna, *Habiter au Caire,* pp. 162–164.

15. E. F. Jomard, "Description abrégée de la ville et de la citadelle du Caire," in *Description de l'Egypte, état moderne,* vol. 2.2 (Paris, 1822), pp. 662, 696; M. de Chabrol, "Essai sur les moeurs des habitants modernes de l'Egypte," ibid., pp. 516–517; Al-Hathloul, *Tradition, Continuity, and Change,* p. 100, fig. 25; Raymond, *Grandes villes arabes,* pp. 323–326; Hanna, *Habiter au Caire,* pp. 70–71.

16. André Raymond, "Essai de géographie des quartiers de résidence aristocratique au Caire," *JESHO,* 1963; Hanna, *Habiter au Caire,* pp. 217–219.

17. Fulgence, "Description de la situation de l'Egypte," Manuscript, Lille, no. 524, pp. 206–207.

18. Jabarti, *Aja'ib al-athhar,* 1: 204, 192; 3: 97; idem, *Merveilles biographiques,* 2: 145 (Sharaybi), 124; 6: 187 (Attar quotation); Claude Savary, *Lettres sur l'Egypte,* 3 vols. (Paris, 1786), 2: 183.

19. The inscription plays on the Arabic word *alaf* ("thousands") and the emir's name, "Alfi." Revault, "L'architecture domestique au Caire," pp. 106–113, 288–293; Hanna, *Habiter au Caire,* pp. 47–53; Jabarti, *Aja'ib al-athhar,* 1: 203; 3: 243; 4: 28; idem, *Merveilles biographiques,* 2: 142 (emirs' residences); 7: 168; 8: 60 (Alfi Bey).

20. Raymond, *Grandes villes arabes,* pp. 295–296; Doris Behrens-Abouseif, "Locations of Non-Muslim Quarters in Medieval Cairo," *Annales Islamologiques* 22 (1986); Hanna, *Habiter au Caire,* pp. 210–216.

21. André Raymond, "Une liste des corporations de métiers au Caire," *Arabica* 4 (1957); idem, *Artisans et commerçants*, 1: 247–248, 308–309, 515–517, 627–628, 656, 711; and especially Nelly Hanna, *An Urban History of Bulaq in the Mamluk and Ottoman Periods* (Cairo: IFAO, 1983), which has been my primary source.

22. Raymond, *Artisans et commerçants*, 1: 262; Savary, *Lettres*, 1: 82–83.

23. Savary, *Lettres*, 1: 72; Jean Coppin, *Les voyages en Egypte de Jean Coppin: 1638–1639, 1643–1646* (Cairo: IFAO, 1971), pp. 61, 163; Raymond, *Artisans et commerçants*, 1: 236, 248, 515–516.

24. On Imbaba, see R. Pockocke, *Voyages*, 3 vols. (Paris, 1772), 2: 43; Savary, *Lettres*, 1: 83; Raymond, *Artisans et commerçants*, 1: 230, 236. On Giza, see Savary, *Lettres*, 1: 134; Raymond, *Artisans et commerçants*, 1: 236.

25. Joseph Arthur de Gobineau, *Trois ans en Asie* (Paris: Pléiade, 1983), pp. 41–42.

## 14. A SLOW AWAKENING

1. See Justin McCarthy, "Nineteenth-Century Egyptian Population," *Middle Eastern Studies* 12 (1976), 31, proposing a population of 265,958 in 1849 and 305,297 in 1863. But McCarthy revises the 1800 figure downward to 210,960. The traditional estimate for 1846 is 256,679. Egypt's population grew from 4.5 million in 1800 to 5.4 million in 1846; see Daniel Panzac, "La population de l'Egypte à l'epoque contemporaine," in *L'Eypte d'aujourd'hui*, ed. R. Mantran (Paris, 1977); André Raymond, "La population du Caire et de l'Egypte à l'époque ottomane," in *Mémorial Omer Lûtfi Barkan* (Paris, 1980).

2. On the French Expedition, we now have Henry Laurens et al., *L'Expédition d'Egypte. Bonaparte et l'Islam: Le choc des cultures* (Paris: Armand Colin, 1989). Joseph Cuoq has translated into French Jabarti's volume on the history of Egypt during the French occupation: *Journal d'un notable du Caire durant l'expédition française* (Paris, 1979). Jabarti, *Aja'ib al-athhar*, 3: 19–139; idem, *Merveilles biographiques*, 6: 42–262; idem, *Journal d'un notable du Caire*, pp. 38–39, 87, 262–263, 267; C. de la Jonquière, *L'Expédition d'Egypte (1798–1801)* (Paris, 1899–1907), 5: 235–236; Laurens et al., *L'Expédition d'Egypte*, pp. 93, 117–118, 167, 289.

3. Poussielgue, 19 March 1799, Archives de la Guerre, Vincennes, Expédition d'Egypte, B 6 183; Jabarti, *Aja'ib al-athhar*, 3: 135, 142, 149; idem, *Merveilles biographiques*, 6: 254, 269, 282; idem, *Journal d'un notable du Caire*, pp. 260 (1800), 274 (1801), 292 (1801); André Raymond, "Une liste des corporations de métiers au Caire," *Arabica* 4 (1957).

4. Al-Qahira, which could logically have been divided into two districts along the axis of the Qasaba (as was done to the north with the Ghuri and Hamzawi areas, districts V and VII), was instead amputated of its southern portion. The Khalij formed a boundary only along its northern half, where it is the (approximate) line of demarcation for districts IV and VI, with district III drawn so as to straddle the Khalij.

5. André Raymond, "La géographie des 'hara' du Caire," *MIFAO* 104 (1980), 416; idem, "Problèmes urbains et urbanisme au Caire," in *CIHC*, p. 354.

6. Jabarti, *Journal d'un notable du Caire*, p. 57; "Expédition d'Egypte," Archives de la Guerre, Vincennes, B 6 135-2, Ordres de la place, no. 8, 10 Thermidor of Year

8; B 6, 193 and 194, Situation des prisons, no. 14, 27–28 December 1800, 21–22 January, 5–6 May 1801.

7. Detroye, journal, "Expédition d'Egypte, Mémoires historiques," Archives de la Guerre, pp. 526–527; Jabarti, *Journal d'un notable du Caire,* pp. 43, 54, 80 (doors), 72, 319–320 (benches).

8. Jabarti, *Journal d'un notable du Caire,* pp. 60, 61, 69, 129, 184, 285, 309.

9. Jabarti, *Aja'ib al-athhar,* 3: 25–28; idem, *Merveilles biographiques,* 6: 55 ff.; idem, *Journal d'un notable du Caire,* pp. 71–74, 205–231, 259, 316–319; Laurens et al., *L'Expédition d'Egypte,* pp. 149–150, 260–266. On Badr, see André Raymond, *Artisans et commerçants au Caire au XVIIIe siècle,* 2 vols. (Damascus: Institut Français de Damas, 1973, 1974), 2: 445–446; idem, "Urban Networks and Popular Movements in Cairo and Aleppo," in *Urbanism in Islam* (Tokyo, 1989), 2: 232 and n. 21.

10. Jabarti, *Journal d'un notable du Caire,* pp. 188, 316, 318–319, 322, 323; Doris Behrens-Abouseif, *Azbakiyya and Its Environs, from Azbak to Isma'il, 1476–1879* (Cairo: IFAO, 1985), pp. 71–79.

11. On the reign of Muhammad Ali, the most recent study is Afaf Lutfi Sayyid-Marsot, *Egypt in the Reign of Muhammad Ali* (Cambridge: Cambridge University Press, 1984). Although no recent studies of Cairo have displaced those of Marcel Clerget and Janet Abu-Lughod, which remain indispensable, Alexandria has been the subject of a thesis by Robert Ilbert, published as *Alexandrie, 1830–1930. Histoire d'une communauté citadine* (Cairo: IFAO, 1996).

12. Marcel Clerget, *Le Caire. Etude de géographie urbaine et d'histoire économique,* 2 vols. (Cairo: Imprimerie Schindler, 1934), 1: 189 ff.; Janet Abu-Lughod, *Cairo: 1001 Years of the City Victorious* (Princeton: Princeton University Press, 1971), pp. 87–88, 91n. (St. John), 95n. (Lane), 96 and n. 42; Ehud Toledano, *State and Society in Mid-Nineteenth-Century Egypt* (Cambridge: Cambridge University Press, 1990), pp. 222–224.

13. Clerget, *Le Caire,* 1: 191–193; Gaston Wiet, *Mohammed Ali et les beaux-arts* (Cairo, 1950), pp. 80, 85, 93, 97; Abu-Lughod, *Cairo,* pp. 92–97; Behrens-Abouseif, *Azbakiyya,* pp. 86–87; Jean-Luc Arnaud, "Des jardins à la ville, Le Caire au XIXe siècle," *Egypte/Monde arabe* 8 (1991), 91.

14. Arthur Rhoné, *L'Egypte à petites journées* (Paris, 1910), pp. 65, 67; Clerget, *Le Caire,* 1: 192; Edmond Pauty, *Les palais et les maisons d'époque musulmane au Caire* (Cairo, 1932), pp. 63–65; Wiet, *Mohammed Ali,* pp. 105 ff., 265 ff. The plan by Pascal Coste is preserved in his sketchbooks in the Bibliothèque Municipale de Marseille.

15. Wiet, *Mohammed Ali,* pp. 129–194 (Shubra), 219–242; Abu-Lughod, *Cairo,* pp. 90–91 (Bulaq).

16. Clerget, *Le Caire,* 1: 194, 197; Abu-Lughod, *Cairo,* pp. 99–100.

## 15. THE DREAM OF WESTERNIZATION

1. Robert Ilbert, "Note sur l'Egypte au XIXe siècle. Typologie architecturale et morphologie urbaine," *Annales Islamologiques* 17 (1981).

2. I have discussed these questions in "Le Caire," in *L'Eypte d'aujourd'hui,* ed. R. Mantran (Paris, 1977).

3. Marcel Clerget, *Le Caire. Etude de géographie urbaine et d'histoire économique*, 2 vols. (Cairo: Imprimerie Schindler, 1934), 2: 102; Janet Abu-Lughod, *Cairo: 1001 Years of the City Victorious* (Princeton: Princeton University Press, 1971), pp. 103–104.

4. On Ali Mubarak, see Gilbert Delanoue, *Moralistes et politiques musulmans dans l'Egypte du XIXe siècle* (Cairo, 1982), 2: 488–558 (quotation p. 504). On Cairo in the work of Ali Mubarak, see Jean-Pierre Theck, "Le Caire dans les Khitat al-Tawfiqiyya de Ali Pacha Mubarak," in *L'Egypte au XIXe siècle* (Paris, 1982). On Egypt's involvement with the Exposition of 1867 and the national festivities in 1869, see Zeynep Celik, *Displaying the Orient* (Berkeley: University of California Press, 1922), pp. 13, 32–39, 145–151.

5. Ghislaine Alleaume, "Une loi inédite de Ali Mubarak sur les corporations du bâtiment," *Annales Islamologiques* 21 (1985).

6. Abu-Lughod, *Cairo,* pp. 103–113; Mercédès Volait, "1850–1950. Un siècle d'aménagements urbains au Caire," *Cahiers de l'IAURI* 95 (1985), 75; idem, "Composition de la forme urbaine du Caire," *Peuples méditerranéens,* 1987–88, pp. 41–42.

7. Jean-Luc Arnaud, "Des jardins à la ville. Le Caire au XIXe siècle," *Egypte/Monde arabe* 8 (1991).

8. Doris Behrens-Abouseif, *Azbakiyya and Its Environs, from Azbak to Isma'il, 1476–1879* (Cairo: IFAO, 1985), pp. 92–96.

9. Jacques Berque, *L'Egypte. Impérialisme et révolution* (Paris, 1967), p. 85; translated by Jean Stewart as *Egypt: Imperialism and Revolution* (London: Faber & Faber, 1972).

10. Magdi Wahba, "Cairo Memories," in *Studies in Arab History,* ed. D. Hopwood (London, 1990).

11. Clerget, *Le Caire,* 1: 241–249; Abu-Lughod, *Cairo,* pp. 117–128; Gabriel Baer, "Social Change in Egypt, 1800–1914," in *Political and Social Change in Modern Egypt,* ed. P. M. Holt (Oxford: Oxford University Press, 1968), pp. 154–158; Daniel Panzac, "La population de l'Egypte à l'epoque contemporaine," in Mantran, *L'Egypte d'aujourd'hui,* p. 161.

12. The Mixed Tribunals were courts established in 1876 to adjudicate matters in which foreigners were concerned. Under the terms of the Convention of Montreux (1937), which abolished the Capitulations, the Mixed Tribunals were to be phased out after a transition period of twelve years.

13. Wahba, "Cairo Memories," pp. 105–111.

14. Roger Owen, "The Cairo Building Industry and the Building Boom of 1897 to 1907," in *CIHC,* pp. 337–338.

15. Pierre Marthelot, "Le Caire, nouvelle métropole," *Annales Islamologiques* 8 (1969), 189. See Clerget, *Le Caire,* 2: 107–113; Abu-Lughod, *Cairo,* pp. 132–138; 140–141.

16. Clerget, *Le Caire,* 2: 70, 102–104; Ghislaine Alleaume, "Hygiène publique et travaux publics," *Annales Islamologiques* 20 (1984); J. Coville, "L'évolution urbaine et les politiques de l'eau au Caire" (Diss., Université de Tours, 1991).

17. Clerget, *Le Caire,* 1: 256–261; Volait, "Composition de la forme urbaine," pp. 113–114; Abu-Lughod, *Cairo,* pp. 144–151.

18. The discussion that follows relies in large part on Robert Ilbert, *Héliopolis. Le Caire 1905–1922: Genèse d'une ville* (Paris: Centre National de la Recherche

Scientifique, 1981), quotations from pp. 45, 103, and 118. See also Clerget, *Le Caire*, 1: 205–206; Abu-Lughod, *Cairo*, pp. 138–139.

19. Ibrahim Farhi, Simonne Lacouture, and Eglal Zananiri, *L'Egypte que j'aime* (Paris, 1972), p. 131.

20. Jacques Berque and Mustafa Al-Shakaa, "La Gamaliyya depuis un siècle," in *CIHC*, pp. 78–79.

21. Wahba, "Cairo Memories," p. 104.

22. Ibid., p. 105.

23. Ilbert, "Note sur l'Egypte au XIXe siècle," p. 355; Robert Ilbert and Mercédès Volait, "Neo-Arabic Renaissance in Egypt, 1870–1930," *Mimar* 13 (1984). On the West's influence on Cairene architecture, see Mohamed Scharabi, *Kairo. Stadt und Architektur im Zeitalter des europäischen Kolonialismus* (Tübingen, 1989).

## 16. THE NIGHTMARES OF GROWTH

1. Pierre Marthelot, "Le Caire, nouvelle métropole," *Annales Islamologiques* 8 (1969). I have drawn largely on data from Daniel Panzac, "Espace et population en Egypte," *Méditerranée* 4 (1983); Galila El Kadi, *L'urbanisation spontanée au Caire* (Tours, 1987); Mercédès Volait, "Le Caire. Les problèmes de la croissance à la lumière du recensement de 1986," *Espaces, populations, sociétés* 2 (1988). The figures for Cairo's population vary according to whether they apply to the city of Cairo proper, Cairo and its suburbs, or the greater Cairo area, which is not always made clear; the three figures for 1986 are, respectively, 6,052,000, 8,634,000, and 9,754,000. Cairo's expansion and gradual absorption of areas lying within the three governmental entities of Cairo, Giza, and Qaliyubiyya have led to increasing recognition of a greater Cairo. Comparisons are consequently difficult: the figure for 1937 describes Cairo proper and therefore represents an underestimate with respect to the following census of Cairo and environs; the growth rate of 4.8 percent for the period 1937–1947 is therefore quite hypothetical.

2. Other than the sources already mentioned, see Frederic Shorter, *Cairo's Leap Forward: People, Households and Dwelling Space* (Cairo: American University of Cairo Press, 1989); Philippe Fargues, "La baisse de la fécondité arabe," *Population* 6 (1988).

3. See *Revue de la presse égyptienne*, 19.2 (1985), especially the article by Abd al-Baqi Ibrahim, "*al-Ahram al-iqtisadi*," 22 July 1985.

4. Volait, "Le Caire. Problèmes de la croissance," p. 219; G. Bianchi and R. Ilbert, "Les toits du Caire. La question des surélévations d'immeubles," *Maghreb-Machreq* 91 (1981), quotations pp. 66–67; Galila El Kadi, "La cité des morts au Caire. Un abri pour les sans abri," *Maghreb-Machreq* 127 (1990); idem, *L'urbanisation spontanée*, p. 26.

5. El Kadi, *L'urbanisation spontanée*; J. P. Lecoin, "L'aménagement du Grand-Caire," *Cahiers de l'IAURIF* 95 (1985); Marcel Belliot and Joseph Berthet, "Greater Cairo Region Master Scheme," May 1991 report; idem, "Le Grand-Caire dix ans après," 1991 report; Marcel Belliot, "Le Caire sort de son Nil," *Cahiers de l'IAURIF* 96 (1991); idem, "A propos de quelques tendances récentes d'évolution dans la région du Grand-Caire," *Lettre d'information de*

*l'Observatoire Urbain du Caire Contemporain* (hereafter *OUCC*) 24 (1991). I am greatly indebted to G. El Kadi and M. Belliot, not only for the published sources to which they directed my attention, but also for their efforts, during conversations and visits, to share with me their perfect knowledge of Cairo. I thank them warmly.

6. F. M. Musaylihi, *Tatawwur al-asima al-misriyya wa l-qahira l-kubra* (Cairo, 1988); Eckart Ehlers, "Cairo, Old and New: Land-use Conflicts," in *Eléments sur les centres villes dans le monde arabe, URBAMA* 19 (1988); Günter Meyer, *Kairo. Entwicklungsprobleme einer Metropole der Dritten Welt* (Cologne, 1989).

7. Galila El Kadi, "Trente ans de planification urbaine au Caire," *Revue Tiers-Monde* 121 (1990), 31; Belliot and Berthet, "Greater Cairo."

8. El Kadi, *L'urbanisation spontanée*. See also Galila El Kadi, "L'articulation de deux circuits de gestion foncière au Caire," *Peuples méditerranéens* 41–42 (1987–88); Philippe Panerai and Sawsan Noweir, "Du rural à l'urbain," *Egypte/Monde arabe* 1 (1990); Agnès Deboulet, "La diversification des filières de promotion foncière et immobilière au Caire," *Revue Tiers-Monde* 125 (1991), 32. On the Matarayya incident in 1987, see *Revue de la presse egyptienne* 29 (1987), 101–103.

9. "Les villes nouvelles en Egypte," CNRSC Colloquium, April 1986, CEDEJ, file 2, 1987; *Al-mudun al-jadida* (Cairo, 1989); N. Fahmi, *Madina al-ashir min ramadan* (Cairo, 1990); Günter Meyer, "New Desert Cities in Egypt," paper delivered at the conference "Urban Development in the Arab World," 1990.

10. See the above-cited studies by Belliot and Berthet; Lecoin, "L'aménagement du Grand-Caire"; CEDEJ press packet on the New Settlements, *Egypte/Monde arabe* 1 (1990); Sabine Jossifort, "Les New Settlements. Une tentative inachevée d'un habitat social au Caire," paper presented at the Institut d'Urbanisme de Paris, 1991.

11. "Les transports urbains au Caire," *Lettre d'information de l'OUCC* 17 (1989).

12. "Rod al-Farag," *Lettre d'information de l'OUCC* 11 (December 1987); "Réhabilitation des égouts du Caire," ibid., 14 (September 1988); J. Coville, "L'évolution urbaine et les politiques de l'eau au Caire" (Diss., Université de Tours, 1991); El Kadi, "Trente ans," p. 204; Belliot and Berthet, "Le Grand-Caire," p. 13.

13. Shorter, *Cairo's Leap Forward;* El Kadi, "Trente ans"; Deboulet, "La diversification."

14. Albert Labib and Tiziana Battain, "Le Caire-Mégapole perçue par ses habitants," *Egypte/Monde arabe* 5 (1991).

15. I resume here the line of argument followed by Galila El Khadi in his article "La division sociale de l'espace au Caire," *Maghreb-Machreq* 110 (1985).

16. Jacques Berque, *L'Egypte. Impérialisme et révolution* (Paris, 1967), p. 635; translated by Jean Stewart as *Egypt: Imperialism and Revolution* (London: Faber & Faber, 1972).

17. Günter Meyer, "Employment in Small-Scale Manufacturing in Cairo: A Socioeconomic Survey," *BSMES Bulletin* 14 (1988); Ehlers, "Cairo, Old and New."

# SELECT BIBLIOGRAPHY

Abu-Lughod, Janet. *Cairo: 1001 Years of the City Victorious.* Princeton: Princeton University Press, 1971.

Alleaume, Ghislaine. "Politiques urbaines et contrôle de l'entreprise. Une loi inédite de Ali Mubarak." *Annales Islamologiques* 21 (1985).

Anawati, Georges. "Factors and Effects of Arabization and Islamization in Medieval Egypt and Syria." In *Islam and Cultural Change in the Middle Ages,* ed. Speros Vryonis. Wiesbaden: Harrassowitz, 1975.

Ashtor, Eliyahu. "Levantine Sugar Industry in the Later Middle Ages." *Israel Oriental Studies* 7 (1977).

Ayalon, David. *Gunpowder and Firearms in the Mameluk Kingdom: A Challenge to Mediaeval Society.* London: Vallentine, Mitchell, 1956.

Baer, Gabriel. *Egyptian Guilds in Modern Times.* Jerusalem: Israel Oriental Society, 1965.

Bahgat, Ali, and Albert Gabriel. *Fouilles d'al-Foustat.* Cairo and Paris: Musée National de l'Art Arabe, 1921.

Behrens-Abouseif, Doris. *Azbakiyya and Its Environs, from Azbak to Isma'il, 1476–1879.* Cairo: IFAO, 1985.

——— *Islamic Architecture in Cairo: An Introduction.* Leiden: E. J. Brill, 1989.

Berque, Jacques. *Egypt: Imperialism and Revolution.* Trans. Jean Stewart. London: Faber & Faber, 1972.

Berthet, Joseph, and Marcel Belliot. "Greater Cairo Region Master Scheme." Cairo, May 1991.

Bianquis, Thierry. *Damas et la Syrie sous la domination fatimide.* 2 vols. Damascus: Institut Français de Damas, 1986, 1989.

Bourguet, Pierre du. *Les Coptes.* Paris: Presses Universitaires de France, 1988.

Canard, Marius. "Le cérémonial fatimide et le cérémonial byzantin." *Byzantion* 21 (1951).

Casanova, Paul. *Essai de reconstitution topographique de la ville d'al-Foustat ou Misr.* Cairo: IFAO, 1919.

——— "Histoire et description de la Citadelle du Caire." *MMAFC* 6 (1891–1892).

Chabrol, Volvic de. "Essai sur les moeurs des habitants modernes de l'Egypte." In *Etat moderne,* vol. 2.2 of *Description de l'Egypte.* Paris, 1822. Pp. 361–578.

Clerget, Marcel. *Le Caire. Etude de géographie urbaine et d'histoire économique.* 2 vols. Cairo: Imprimerie Schindler, 1934.

*Colloque international sur l'histoire du Caire.* Ed. André Raymond, Michael Rogers, and Magdi Wahba. Cairo: Ministry of Culture, 1969.

Creswell, K. A. C. "The Foundation of Cairo." *Bulletin of the Faculty of Arts* (University of Egypt) 1 (1933).

———— *The Muslim Architecture of Egypt: Ayyubids and Early Bahrite Mamluks, A.D. 1171–1326.* 2 vols. Oxford: Clarendon Press, 1959, 1960.

Darrag, Ahmad. *L'Egypte sous le règne de Barsbay: 825–841/1422–1438.* Damascus: Institut Français de Damas, 1961.

Denoix, Sylvie. *Décrire le Caire. Fustat-Misr d'après Ibn Duqmaq et Maqrizi.* Cairo: IFAO, 1992.

Dols, Michael W. *The Black Death in the Middle East.* Princeton: Princeton University Press, 1977.

Ehrenkreutz, Andrew. *Saladin.* Albany: State University of New York Press, 1972.

El Kadi, Galila. "La division sociale de l'espace au Caire." *Maghreb-Machreq* 110 (1985).

———— *L'urbanisation spontanée au Caire.* Tours, 1987.

Farhi, Ibrahim, Simonne Lacouture, and Eglal Zananiri. *L'Egypte que j'aime.* Paris, 1972.

Fernandes, Leonor. "On Conducting the Affairs of State: A Guideline of the Fourteenth Century." *Annales Islamologiques* 24 (1988).

Fu'ad Sayyid, Ayman. "La capitale de l'Egypte à l'époque fatimide. Al-Qahira et al-Fustat." Thesis, Université de Paris I, 1986.

Garcin, Jean-Claude. *Espaces, pouvoirs et idéologies de l'Egypte médiévale.* London: Variorum Reprints, 1987.

Garcin, Jean-Claude, B. Maury, J. Revault, and M. Zakariya. *Palais et maisons du Caire.* Vol. 1: *Epoque Mamelouke (XIIIe au XVIe siècles).* Paris, 1982.

Gayraud, Roland-Pierre. "Istabl-Antar (Fostat), 1987–1989. Rapport de fouilles." *Annales Islamologiques* 25 (1991).

Goitein, Shelomo Dov. *A Mediterranean Society: The Jerusalem Communities of the Arab World as Portrayed in the Documents of the Cairo Geniza.* 5 vols. Berkeley: University of California Press, 1967–1988.

Hanna, Nelly. *Habiter au Caire aux XVIIe et XVIIIe siècles.* Cairo: IFAO, 1991.

———— *An Urban History of Bulaq in the Mamluk and Ottoman Periods.* Cairo: IFAO, 1983.

Hautecoeur, Louis, and Gaston Wiet. *Les mosquées du Caire.* Paris, 1932.

Holt, Peter M. *Egypt and the Fertile Crescent, 1516–1922.* Ithaca: Cornell University Press, 1966.

———— *Studies in the History of the Near East.* London: Cass, 1973.

Hourani, Albert. *A History of the Arab Peoples.* Cambridge, Mass.: The Belknap Press of Harvard University Press, 1991.

Humphreys, Stephen. *From Saladin to the Mongols: The Ayyubids of Damascus, 1193–1260.* Albany: SUNY Press, 1977.

Ibn Iyas, Muhammad ibn Ahmad. *An Account of the Ottoman Conquest of Egypt in the Year A. H. 922 (A.D. 1516), Translated from the Third Volume of the*

*Arabic Chronicle of Muhammed ibn Ahmed Ibn Iyas, an Eyewitness of the Scenes he Describes.* Trans. W. H. Salmon. London: Royal Asiatic Society, 1921.

—— *Bada'i al-zuhur fi waqa'i al-duhur.* Ed. Mohamed Mustafa. 5 vols. Cairo and Wiesbaden, 1961–1983.

—— *Histoire des Mamlouks circassiens.* Trans. Gaston Wiet. Cairo, 1945.

—— *Journal d'un bourgeois du Caire.* Trans. Gaston Wiet. 2 vols. Paris, 1955, 1960.

Ibn Taghribirdi, Yusuf Abu al-Mahasin. *Hawadith al-duhur fi mada al-ayyam wa-al-shuhur.* Ed. William Popper. 4 vols. Berkeley: University of California Press, 1930–1942.

—— *History of Egypt, 1382–1469 A.D.* Trans. William Popper. 7 vols. Berkeley: University of California Press, 1954–1960.

—— *Al-nujum al-zahira fi muluk misr wa-al-qahira.* Ed. William Popper. 7 vols. Berkeley: University of California Press, 1926–1929.

Ibn Wasil, Jamal al-Din Muhammad. *Mufarrij al-kurub.* 5 vols. Ed. G. al-Shayyal (vol. 1) and H. M. Rabi (vols. 2–5). Cairo, 1957–1977.

Ilbert, Robert. *Heliopolis. Le Caire 1905–1922: Genèse d'une ville.* Paris: Centre National de la Recherche Scientifique, 1981.

*Index to Mohammedan Monuments in Cairo.* Giza: Survey of Egypt, 1951.

Jabarti, Abd al-Rahman al-. *Aja'ib al-athar fil-tarajim wal akhbar.* 4 vols. Cairo: Bulaq Press, 1297/1879.

—— *Chronicle of the First Seven Months of the French Occupation of Egypt.* Trans. S. Moreh. Leiden: E. J. Brill, 1975.

—— *Journal d'un notable du Caire durant l'Expédition française, 1798–1801.* Trans. J. Cuoq. Paris, 1979.

—— *Merveilles biographiques et historiques, ou Chroniques du cheikh Abd-el-Rahman el Djabarti.* Trans. Chefik Mansour et al. 9 vols. Cairo, 1888–1896.

Jomard, Edme-François. "Description abrégée de la ville et de la citadelle du Kaire." In *Etat moderne,* vol. 2.2 of *Description de l'Egypte.* Paris, 1822. Pp. 579–783.

Jomier, Jacques. "Kahira." In *Encyclopaedia of Islam.* 2d ed. 5 vols. to date. Leiden: E. J. Brill. 1960–.

Kubiak, Wladyslaw. "The Burning of Misr-al-Fustat in 1168." *Africana Bulletin* 25 (1976).

—— *Al-Fustat: Its Foundation and Early Urban Development.* Cairo: American University in Cairo Press, 1987.

Kubiak, Wladyslaw, and George T. Scanlon. *Fustat Expedition Final Report.* Vol. 2: *Fustat C.* Winona Lake, Ind.: Eisenbrauns, 1989.

Labib, Subhi Y. *Handelgeschichte Agyptens im Spätmittelalter (1171–1517).* Wiesbaden, 1965.

Lacouture, Jean, and Simonne Lacouture. *Egypt in Transition.* New York: Criterion, 1958.

Lane, Edward William. *An Account of the Manners and Customs of the Modern Egyptians.* London: 1836. Reprinted from the 1860 third edition as *The Manners and Customs of the Modern Egyptians.* London: J. M. Dent & Sons, 1908.

Lane-Poole, Stanley. *The Story of Cairo.* London: J. M. Dent & Sons, 1902.

Lapidus, Ira M. *Muslim Cities in the Later Middle Ages.* Cambridge, Mass.: Harvard University Press, 1967.

Laurens, Henry, et al. *L'Expédition d'Egypte. Bonaparte et l'Islam. Le choc des cultures.* Paris: Armand Colin, 1989.

*Lettre d'information de l'Observatoire Urbain du Caire Contemporain* (CEDEJ).

Lézine, Alexandre. "Persistance de traditions pré-islamiques dans l'architecture domestique de l'Egypte musulmane." *Annales Islamologiques* 11 (1972).

Mantran, Robert, ed. *L'Egypte d'aujourd'hui.* Paris, 1977.

Maqrizi, Taqi al-Din Ahmad ibn Ali. *Histoire d'Egypte de Makrizi.* Trans. E. Blochet. *Revue de l'Orient latin* 8–11 (1900–1908).

———— *Histoire des sultans mamlouks de l'Egypte.* Trans. M. Quatremère. 2 vols. Paris, 1845.

———— *A History of the Ayyubid Sultans of Egypt.* Trans. R. J. C. Broadhurst. Boston: G. K. Hall, 1980.

———— *Kitab al-suluk li ma'rifat duwal al-muluk.* Cairo: Lagnat al Ta'lif, 1936–1973.

———— *Al-mawa'iz wa al-I'tibar fi dhikr al-khitat wa al-athar.* 2 vols. Cairo: Bulaq Press, 1270/1853. Reprinted as *Kitab al-Khitat.* Cairo: Matba'at al-Nil, 1911.

Marthelot, Pierre. "Le Caire, nouvelle métropole." *Annales Islamologiques* 8 (1969).

Maury, B., A. Raymond, J. Revault, and M. Zakariya. *Palais et maisons du Caire.* Vol. 2: *Epoque ottomane, XVIe–XVIIIe siècles.* Paris, 1983.

Meinecke, Michael. "Mamluk Architecture: Regional Architectural Traditions: Evolution and Interrelations." *Damaszener Mitteilungen* 2 (1985).

Meinecke-Berg, Viktoria. "Quellen zu topographie und baugeschichte in Kairo unter Sultan an-Nasir." *ZDMG* (Wiesbaden) 3.1 (1977).

Meyer, Günter. *Kairo: Entwicklungsprobleme einer Metropole der Dritten Welt.* Cologne, 1989.

Musaylihi, Fathi. *Tatawwur al-asima al-misriyya wa l-qahira l-kubra.* Cairo, 1988.

Panzac, Daniel. *La Peste dans l'Empire ottoman, 1700–1750.* Louvain: Peeters, 1985.

Pauty, Edmond. "L'architecture au Caire depuis la période ottomane." *BIFAO* 35 (1936–37).

Petry, Carl F. *The Civilian Elite of Cairo in the Later Middle Ages.* Princeton: Princeton University Press, 1981.

Popper, William. *Egypt and Syria under the Circassian Sultans, 1382–1468 A.D.:*

*Systematic Notes to Ibn Taghri Birdi's Chronicles of Egypt.* 2 vols. Berkeley: University of California Press, 1955, 1957.

Ravaisse, Paul. "Essai sur l'histoire et sur la topographie du Caire à l'époque ottomane (1517–1798)." *MMAFC,* 1887–1890.

Raymond, André. "L'activité architecturale au Caire à l'époque ottomane (1517–1798)." *Annales Islamologiques* 25 (1990).

———— *Artisans et commerçants au Caire au XVIIIe siècle.* 2 vols. Damascus: Institut Français de Damas, 1973, 1974.

———— "Le Caire." In *L'Egypte aujourd'hui,* ed. R. Mantran. Paris, 1977.

———— "Le Caire sous les Ottomans." In Maury et al.

———— *Grandes villes arabes à l'époque ottomane.* Paris: Sindbad, 1985.

———— *The Great Arab Cities in the 16th to 18th Centuries: An Introduction.* New York: New York University Press, 1984.

———— "Les provinces arabes (XVIe–XVIIIe siècles)." In *Histoire de l'Empire ottoman,* ed. R. Mantran. Paris, 1989.

Raymond, André, and Gaston Wiet. *Les marchés du Caire. Traduction annotée du texte de Maqrizi.* Cairo: IFAO, 1979.

Revault, Jacques. "L'architecture domestique au Caire à l'époque mamelouke (XIIIe–XVIe siècles)." In Garcin et al.

———— "L'architecture domestique au Caire à l'époque ottomane (XVIe–XVIIIe siècles)." In Maury et al.

Rogers, Michael. "Kahira." In *Encyclopaedia of Islam.* 2d ed. 5 vols. to date. Leiden: E. J. Brill, 1960–.

Salmon, Georges. "Etudes sur la topographie du Caire: La Kal'at al-Kabch et la Birkat al-Fil." *MIFAO* 7 (1902).

Sayyid-Marsot, Afaf Lutfi. *Egypt in the Reign of Muhammad Ali.* Cambridge: Cambridge University Press, 1984.

Scanlon, George, and Wladyslaw Kubiak. "Preliminary Reports: Excavations at Fustat." *JARCE* 4–21 (1964–1978).

Shaw, Stanford J. *The Financial and Administrative Organization and Development of Ottoman Egypt, 1517–1798.* Princeton: Princeton University Press, 1962.

Shorter, Frederic. *Cairo's Leap Forward: People, Householders and Dwelling Space.* Cairo: American University in Cairo Press, 1989.

Staffa, Susan Jane. *Conquest and Fusion: The Social Evolution of Cairo, A.D. 642–1850.* Leiden: E. J. Brill, 1977.

Wahba, Magdi. "Cairo Memories." In *Studies in Arab History,* ed. D. Hopwood. London, 1990.

Wiet, Gaston. *Cairo: City of Art and Commerce.* Trans. Seymour Feiler. Norman: University of Oklahoma Press, 1964.

———— *L'Egypte arabe.* Vol. 4 of *Histoire de la nation égyptienne.* Paris, 1937.

Zakariya, Mona. "Le rab de Tabbana." *Annales Islamologiques* 16 (1980).

# INDEX